Contributions to Economics

The series *Contributions to Economics* provides an outlet for innovative research in all areas of economics. Books published in the series are primarily monographs and multiple author works that present new research results on a clearly defined topic, but contributed volumes and conference proceedings are also considered. All books are published in print and ebook and disseminated and promoted globally. The series and the volumes published in it are indexed by Scopus and ISI (selected volumes).

Hasan Dincer • Serhat Yüksel
Editors

Economic Development and the Environmental Ecosystem

The Role of Energy Policy in Economic Growth

Springer

Editors
Hasan Dincer
Business and Management
Istanbul Medipol University
Istanbul, Istanbul, Turkey

Serhat Yüksel
Istanbul Medipol University
Istanbul, Istanbul, Turkey

ISSN 1431-1933 ISSN 2197-7178 (electronic)
Contributions to Economics
ISBN 978-3-031-26595-2 ISBN 978-3-031-26596-9 (eBook)
https://doi.org/10.1007/978-3-031-26596-9

This Springer imprint is published by the registered company Springer Nature Switzerland AG
The registered company address is: Gewerbestrasse 11, 6330 Cham, Switzerland

Contents

Chapter 1
Evaluating Critical Points for the Improvement of Nuclear Energy Investments via Text Mining Methodology

Serkan Eti and Yaşar Gökalp

Keywords Nuclear energy · Energy investments · Text mining · Data mining · Energy economics

1.1 Introduction

The energy needed since the first day of human history is necessary for many things that are still used today to function. Energy is one of the main factors affecting the economies of all countries of the world (Martínez et al., 2022; Sun et al., 2022). With the increasing world population, the need for energy is also increasing (Kafka et al., 2022; Mukhtarov et al., 2022). Therefore, energy consumption tends to increase day by day. However, the energy supply is limited. This situation reveals the importance of the need for energy (Hong et al., 2020).

Energy has various forms. The history of humanity has started to use energy with muscle power. Subsequently, heat energy was discovered (Dong et al., 2022; Dinçer et al., 2022a, 2022b, 2022c). Later, energy types such as coal, oil, and natural gas, which are expressed as underground resources, were discovered. With the industrial revolution, energy use has been moved to a different dimension (Zhang et al., 2022; Yüksel & Dinçer, 2022). With the industrial revolution and the introduction of oil and electricity into human life, energy consumption has increased a lot (Gielen et al., 2019).

Energy is one of the most important elements that humanity needs. If the use of energy had not been developed at this level, many works would have to be done with manpower (Carayannis et al., 2022; Li et al., 2022a, 2022b; Yüksel et al., 2022a, 2022b). For this reason, every event related to energy has come to the fore among the

S. Eti (✉)
The IMU Vocational School, İstanbul Medipol University, Istanbul, Turkey
e-mail: seti@medipol.edu.tr

Y. Gökalp
The School of Health, İstanbul Medipol University, Istanbul, Turkey
e-mail: ygokalp@medipol.edu.tr

H. Dincer, S. Yüksel (eds.), *Economic Development and the Environmental Ecosystem*, Contributions to Economics,
https://doi.org/10.1007/978-3-031-26596-9_1

issues that concern humanity. The limited energy resources, the imbalance in the distribution of these resources, and the ever-increasing population cause major problems (Mikhaylov et al., 2022; Eti et al., 2023; Li et al., 2022a, 2022b). These problems pushed the states to produce alternative solutions. One of the alternative solutions is renewable investments (Poudyal et al., 2019).

Renewable energy sources are energy sources that can be used continuously without any depletion problems. Solar energy, wind energy, water, and geothermal energy are examples of renewable energy sources. Renewable energy sources are environmentally friendly sources. However, the initial investment costs are quite high (Haiyun et al., 2021; Yuan et al., 2021). On the other hand, non-renewable energy resources are resources that are limited in nature and whose amount decreases as they are used. Examples of non-renewable energy sources are coal, oil, and natural gas. Non-renewable energy sources are also called fossil fuels. Most of the energy consumption in the world is provided by fossil fuels. The fact that fossil fuels are exhaustible causes problems due to environmental damage and imbalances in the distribution of resources (Fang et al., 2021; Kayacık et al., 2022). For this reason, countries are aiming to abandon the use of fossil fuels and switch to renewable energy. Accordingly, incentive policies are implemented for the use of renewable energy (Cantarero, 2020).

1.2 The Types of Energy Generation

Energy is not something that can be created out of nothing or destroyed while it exists. Energy can only be converted from one form to another. To explain this situation with an example; For vehicle fuels, we can talk about the conversion of oil to gasoline or the conversion of electrical energy into heat energy when cooking in the oven. In transformations, the energy source is oil and electrical energy. Resources that help to produce energy by various methods are called energy resources. It is possible to classify the energy sources that we encounter with different formations according to the place where they are used, the way they are obtained, and the purpose of use (Nabat et al., 2020).

One of the classifications used in the literature is the classification made according to whether they have changed or not. Accordingly, energy is examined in two separate classes, primary and secondary. Resources that are used as energy without undergoing any change, such as oil, natural gas, and coal, are included in the scope of primary energy resources. Energy sources such as oil, natural gas, and coal, and energy forms that are more suitable for use such as electricity and heat energy with conversion methods are called secondary energy sources (Lapi et al., 2022). In addition, primary energy sources are also examined as renewable and non-renewable energy according to the way they are obtained.

Renewable energy resources are resources that can be used continuously without any depletion problems. Solar energy, wind energy, water, and geothermal energy are examples of renewable energy sources. Renewable energy sources are environmentally friendly. However, the initial investment costs are quite high. On the other hand, non-renewable energy resources are resources that are limited in nature and whose amount decreases as they are used. Coal, oil, and natural gas are examples of non-renewable energy sources (Olabi & Abdelkareem, 2022).

Most of the energy consumption in the world is carried out with fossil fuels. The exhaustion of these resources causes problems due to excessive damage to the environment and imbalances in their distribution (Eti et al., 2022; Dinçer et al., 2023). For this reason, countries are aiming to abandon the use of fossil fuels and switch to renewable energy. Accordingly, investments are made by the states, laws are enacted, and incentive policies are implemented for the use of renewable energy (Depren et al., 2022).

Non-renewable energy resources can be defined as resources that are completely dependent on natural processes. These resources, also called fossil fuels, are formed by the decay of plant and animal materials (Xu et al., 2022). However, the process of formation is quite long. It is foreseen that there will be no change in the reserves of non-renewable energy resources in the next few million years. Coal, uranium, oil, and natural gas are examples of fossil fuels (Mujtaba et al., 2022).

Since the industrialization process that started with the industrial revolution, fossil fuels have been widely used as a source of heat and motion. While wood and biomass resources were used in the first place, the use of coal, oil, and natural gas has become widespread due to the increasing need. When we look at today, it is seen that fossil fuel reserves are decreasing day by day (Bradu et al., 2022).

Oil is one of the non-renewable energy sources. Petroleum is made up of carbon and hydrogen. Fuels such as gasoline, LPG, diesel, diesel, aviation fuel can be obtained by passing petroleum through certain processes. Almost all transportation needs are met by petroleum and derivative products. This situation reveals the importance of oil for countries. However, the damage done by oil to nature is quite high, as is the case with other fossil fuels (Adekoya et al., 2022).

Natural gas is another non-renewable energy source. It is formed because of the exposure of organic wastes existing underground to various factors for millions of years. Natural gas is an energy source that can be used as it is extracted from the ground. Natural gas is transported to areas of use by pipelines or by being liquefied by tankers. The usage areas of natural gas vary widely. It is the main source of energy production in residential, commercial, and industrial areas. However, natural gas is an exhausting source of energy (Udeagha & Ngepah, 2022).

Coal is another non-renewable energy source. In the structure of coal, there are sulfur, oxygen, nitrogen, and hydrogen, mostly carbon. Coal undergoes many transformation processes in the formation process. It takes many years for coal to form as a fuel. The longer this formation time, the higher the quality of the coal. Coal mine detection and extraction are cost-effective. Therefore, the demand for coal is very high worldwide. However, the harmful gases that emerge after the burning of the coal mine cause global warming and harm the environment. Coal mine, in order according to the formation layer; is divided into varieties such as peat, lignite, hard coal, and anthracite (Solarz et al., 2022).

Renewable energy sources refer to energy sources that can be produced continuously and renewed themselves. It is foreseen that it will be the main energy that humanity will use in the future. Due to the damage caused by fossil fuels to the environment and the limited resources, the orientation towards renewable energy sources has increased. Considering today's conditions, it will not be possible to limit energy consumption. Therefore, it is quite clear that the energy demand will increase day by day. The most widely used renewable energy sources are solar energy, wind energy, hydroelectric energy, geothermal energy, and biomass energy (Li et al., 2020).

Solar energy is one of the largest energy sources. Thanks to the established system, the incoming sun rays are first converted into heat energy. Then electrical energy can be produced. One of the important features of solar energy is that it does not pollute the environment, as in all renewable energy sources (Bhuiyan et al., 2022; Kou et al., 2022). The important factor for a country to produce solar energy is the annual sunshine duration. Solar energy can be produced in two different ways. These are solar photovoltaics and solar thermals (Dinçer & Yüksel, 2019).

Solar energy is used in many areas of our lives. It is used in phones, recently produced hybrid cars, lighting, and many more. In the future, it is estimated that the usage areas will increase more. The use of solar energy and investments in it are increasing all over the world. When the change of solar energy installed power in the countries according to the years is examined, it can be said that it is an increasing trend (Schulte et al., 2022).

Wind energy, like other renewable energy sources, is a type of energy that does not harm the environment. Wind energy has an important place among renewable energy types. Air movement caused by the pressure and humidity difference in the air can be converted into energy by various methods. There are two important parameters for the conversion of wind into energy. These are the speed and direction of the wind. Wind turbines installed for wind energy generation convert the resulting air movement first into mechanical energy and then into electrical energy, making it usable. (Singh et al., 2022).

Two elements will provide the necessary air movement for countries to produce wind energy. These are climate and geographical location. However, the initial investment cost of wind turbine installation is quite high. Also, due to the weather, there is a variable energy generation capacity. Apart from these, the technology of wind turbines is simple. It does not harm the environment; it is nature friendly. Maintenance costs are also low (Kumar, 2022).

Hydroelectric energy is one of the renewable energy sources. Hydroelectric energy is formed by converting the movement of fluid water into energy. Similarly, the energy generated by wave and tidal movements is also considered within the scope of hydroelectric energy. In hydroelectric energy, the size of the energy to be produced is directly related to the flow of water and the rate of fall. Water pouring from a high place passes through turbines and provides energy production (Qu et al., 2022).

The operating and maintenance costs of hydroelectric energy are low. It does not harm the environment and does not create a greenhouse gas emission problem. The water stored in the electricity generation process can also be used as drinking water. Apart from these, it also provides regular irrigation for agricultural lands. Its biggest contribution is energy production (Aldawoud et al., 2022).

Another renewable energy source is geothermal energy. As with other renewable energy sources, geothermal energy is an energy source that does not harm the environment. Geothermal energy is a type of energy obtained by converting the heat formed because of the accumulation of heat and pressure underground. Geothermal energy sources are formed by feeding from the heat in the core. To produce electrical energy from geothermal resources, the source in question must be suitable for this generation. However, most of these resources are not suitable for electricity generation. Apart from electricity generation, geothermal resources are also used for health and tourism (Romanov & Leiss, 2022).

Biomass energy is one of the renewable energy sources. Biomass energy refers to the energy created using biological formations obtained from different organisms. Formations produced because of agricultural residues and solid organic wastes can be given as examples of biomass energy. If efficient biomass energy generation is aimed, long-term planning is required. The materials and wastes that can store solar energy in themselves may be used in the biomass energy generation process. Biomass energy has the potential to be converted into heat, electricity, and liquid fuels (Yana et al., 2022).

Biomass energy is the fourth largest energy source after coal, oil, and natural gas in terms of quantity. Among the renewable energy sources, it is the energy source with the greatest potential. It also has the potential to be used with other energy sources. It never harms nature; it is an environmentally friendly type of energy (Amjith & Bavanish, 2022).

1.3 General Information About Nuclear Energy Investments

Electricity is produced with nuclear energy by heating water in boilers using the energy released from the fission of atoms in a reactor. The rotation of the turbines caused by the created water vapor results in the production of electricity. In nuclear power plants, water vapor turns turbines, which transfer mechanical energy to the generators, which convert it to electrical power. Production of nuclear electricity consists of two distinct processes: fission and fusion. Nuclear fusion involves the combining of two light atoms to produce a heavy atom, whereas nuclear fission involves the splitting of an atom in half (Alwaeli & Mannheim, 2022).

Atoms with a high number of protons also have a high number of neutrons, whereas the opposite is true of atoms with a low number of neutrons. For a given number of protons, the amount of energy needed to keep them together grows proportionally, as each proton repels the others. Neutrinos can't be influenced by voltage. However, a powerful nuclear force holds all the atom's neutrons and protons together. This means that keeping protons within the atom may be achieved by increasing the number of neutrons, which in turn promotes atomic stability (Mathew, 2022).

Nuclear fission refers to the process of splitting the nucleus of an atom in two, whereas nuclear energy refers to the energy released during this process. Since radioactivity demonstrates that the nucleus of an atom is inherently unstable, fission opens the door to an infinite supply of energy. In fission, as opposed to radioactivity, the atomic nucleus divides in half. Massive amounts of energy are released during this fragmentation, leading to the dissolution of the tightly connected clusters of protons (Rehman et al., 2022).

The process of nuclear fusion involves the merger of two smaller atomic nuclei to create a larger and denser nucleus. The power of the sun and other stars comes from a process called nuclear fusion. This mechanism, through which the sun generates its energy, serves as the basis for all other energy generation methods, including nuclear fusion and renewable energy. Unlike nuclear fission, in which energy is lost in the splitting apart of heavy atoms, nuclear fusion releases energy in the form of light atoms (Majeed et al., 2022).

On our planet, nuclear fusion is most readily accomplished by joining together deuterium and tritium, two isotopes of hydrogen. Hydrogen, with only one proton and one electron, is the least dense element. Heavy water, or deuterium water, is created when one of the hydrogen atoms in regular water (H_2O) is replaced with deuterium, which contains an additional neutron in its nucleus. Since tritium contains two additional neutrons in addition to the one that makes up its atomic weight, it is three times as heavy as hydrogen. The combination of tritium and deuterium in a fusion cycle produces helium, the second-heaviest element in the periodic table, and a free neutron (Bandyopadhyay et al., 2022).

Nuclear power is quite useful. The health industry is perhaps the most important of these. It's a vital part of the diagnostic process, particularly for illness. In addition to conventional medicine, nuclear medicine is employed in certain cases. Nuclear energy has many applications and advantages, including the creation of nutritious food. For instance, nuclear energy is used to remove hazardous chemicals from food. It's also possible to use nuclear power in farming. Insects and other pests that cause damage to crops may be effectively removed. The use of radiation ensures that food is prepared without spoilage. In conclusion, nuclear energy is useful in many areas of science, including chemistry and biology, construction, the detection of oil tank leaks, and the development of certain types of aerospace technology, ships, and airplanes (Korkmaz & Önöz, 2022).

The use of fossil fuels in production is far more cost-effective. A similar level of output is achievable throughout the year. It is unaffected by changes in weather and other environmental factors. You can always give it your all and reach your full potential in the workplace. As a raw material, it has advantages over fossil fuels. When compared to similar power plants, it generates much more energy. It maximizes energy output while decreasing infrastructure footprint (Brown, 2022).

1.4 An Evaluation of Nuclear Energy Investments with Text Mining

The study aims to determine the developments in nuclear energy. In addition, it is aimed to determine strategies for future study and research areas. For this purpose, the studies in literature are included in the scope of analysis. In the literature, studies with the keyword "nuclear energy" in the web of science database have been taken into consideration. When the studies were examined, it was seen that there were 333 articles on nuclear energy between 1993 and 2022. In recent years, the interest of researchers on this subject has increased and text mining methods have been used to determine the subject or topics discussed. In this context, the KNIME (Konstanz Information Miner) program was used. The bag of Word and ngram nodules in the text mining add-in in the program in question and the texts in the abstract sections of the studies were analyzed. Bag of Word and (term frequency) TF nodules were used for word frequency in the abstract sections, while ngram nodules were used for double and triple word groups.

Text mining is a method of data mining that aims to reveal previously unknown hidden meanings in unstructured texts and to obtain regular data. Since the abstract texts considered in the analysis are not structural, they were analyzed by the text mining method for analysis. Many studies mine texts by considering the studies in the literature (Yüksel et al., 2022a, 2022b; Eti, 2019; Song & Chambers, 2014; Delen & Crossland, 2008).

In text mining, since the texts are not structural, pre-processing of the texts is required first. In this context, the data are made ready for analysis by performing operations such as turning letters into lower/uppercase letters, removing punctuation marks, deleting words that do not make sense (and, so, etc.), and separating the words into their roots. Case converter, punctuation erasure, stop word filter, and stemmer nodules in the KNIME program were used for these operations, respectively. As a result of these nodules, the tightness of the words in the regular and standardized texts was determined.

As a result of the analysis made for the frequency of the words in the abstracts of the articles containing the keyword nuclear energy, it is seen that words such as renewability, economy, emissions, development, and growth come to the forefront. The most common ten words from the words obtained with Bag of Word and TF nodules are given in Table 1.1.

Similarly, the double and triple word groups in the articles containing the keyword nuclear energy were analyzed by the Ngram method. As in single words, it has been seen that word groups such as renewable energy, economic growth, energy consumption, carbon emission, clean energy, and climate change come to the fore in binary word groups. In Table 1.2, ten most repeated binary word groups are summarized.

When the triple word groups are examined, the concepts of renewable and clean energy as well as carbon emission and causality testing attract attention. As a result, it is seen that academic studies on nuclear energy compare this energy source with

Table 1.1 The ten most frequently repeated words and their frequency

Term	f
Energy	1984
Renewable	648
Economy	626
Emission	612
Development	524
Growth	502
Hydrogen	502
Consumption	480
Effect	448
Carbon	384

Table 1.2 The most frequently repeated binary groups of words

2Grams	f
Renewable energy	526
Energy consumption	380
Economic growth	370
Hydrogen product	200
Carbon emission	162
Energy source	136
Nuclear energy	98
Climate change	80
Clean energy	78
Natural gas	70

renewable and clean energy. It was also concluded that they investigated the effects of nuclear energy on the country's economy and its reflections on economic growth. In addition, especially according to the 3Gram analysis, causality, and energy investments were seen to be among the research topics of academics.

1.5 Conclusion

In this chapter, it is aimed to determine the developments in nuclear energy. In addition, it is aimed to determine strategies for future study and research areas. For this purpose, the studies in literature are included in the scope of analysis. In the literature, studies with the keyword "nuclear energy" in the web of science database have been taken into consideration. When the studies were examined, it was seen that there were 333 articles on nuclear energy between 1993 and 2022. It is seen that the studies on nuclear energy have increased after 2015. In recent years, the interest of researchers on this subject has increased and text mining methods have been used to determine the subject or topics discussed. As a result of the analysis made for the frequency of the words in the abstracts of the articles containing the keyword nuclear energy, it is seen that words such as renewability, economy, emissions, development, and growth come to the forefront. It is seen that academic studies on nuclear energy compare this energy source with renewable and clean energy. It is also concluded that they investigated the effects of nuclear energy on the country's economy and its reflections on economic growth.

References

Adekoya, O. B., Oliyide, J. A., & Fasanya, I. O. (2022). Renewable and non-renewable energy consumption–ecological footprint nexus in net-oil exporting and net-oil importing countries: Policy implications for a sustainable environment. *Renewable Energy, 189*, 524–534.

Aldawoud, A., Aldawoud, A., & Assad, M. E. H. (2022, February). Life-cycle cost analysis for a hydroelectric energy system. In *2022 Advances in Science and Engineering Technology International Conferences (ASET)* (pp. 1–6). IEEE.

Alwaeli, M., & Mannheim, V. (2022). Investigation into the current state of nuclear energy and nuclear waste management–A state-of-the-art review. *Energies, 15*(12), 4275.

Amjith, L. R., & Bavanish, B. (2022). A review on biomass and wind as renewable energy for sustainable environment. *Chemosphere, 293*, 133579.

Bandyopadhyay, A., Rej, S., Villanthenkodath, M. A., & Mahalik, M. K. (2022). The role of nuclear energy consumption in abatement of ecological footprint: Novel insights from quantile-on-quantile regression. *Journal of Cleaner Production, 358*, 132052.

Bhuiyan, M. A., Dinçer, H., Yüksel, S., Mikhaylov, A., Danish, M. S. S., Pinter, G., et al. (2022). Economic indicators and bioenergy supply in developed economies: QROF-DEMATEL and random forest models. *Energy Reports, 8*, 561–570.

Bradu, P., Biswas, A., Nair, C., Sreevalsakumar, S., Patil, M., Kannampuzha, S., et al. (2022). Recent advances in green technology and industrial revolution 4.0 for a sustainable future. *Environmental Science and Pollution Research*, 1–32.

Brown, N. R. (2022). Engineering demonstration reactors: A stepping stone on the path to deployment of advanced nuclear energy in the United States. *Energy, 238*, 121750.

Cantarero, M. M. V. (2020). Of renewable energy, energy democracy, and sustainable development: A roadmap to accelerate the energy transition in developing countries. *Energy Research & Social Science, 70*, 101716.

Carayannis, E., Kostis, P., Dinçer, H., & Yüksel, S. (2022). Balanced-scorecard-based evaluation of knowledge-oriented competencies of distributed energy investments. *Energies, 15*(21), 8245.

Delen, D., & Crossland, M. D. (2008). Seeding the survey and analysis of research literature with text mining. *Expert Systems with Applications, 34*(3), 1707–1720.

Depren, S. K., Kartal, M. T., Çelikdemir, N. Ç., & Depren, Ö. (2022). Energy consumption and environmental degradation nexus: A systematic review and meta-analysis of fossil fuel and renewable energy consumption. *Ecological Informatics, 70*, 101747.

Dinçer, H., Aksoy, T., Yüksel, S., & Hacioglu, U. (2022b). Golden cut-oriented q-rung orthopair fuzzy decision-making approach to evaluation of renewable energy alternatives for microgeneration system investments. *Mathematical Problems in Engineering*.

Dinçer, H., & Yüksel, S. (2019). Multidimensional evaluation of global investments on the renewable energy with the integrated fuzzy decision-making model under the hesitancy. *International Journal of Energy Research, 43*(5), 1775–1784.

Dinçer, H., Yüksel, S., Çağlayan, Ç., Yavuz, D., & Kararoğlu, D. (2023). Can renewable energy investments be a solution to the energy-sourced high inflation problem?. In *Managing inflation and supply chain disruptions in the global economy* (pp. 220–238). IGI Global.

Dinçer, H., Yüksel, S., & Martínez, L. (2022c). Collaboration enhanced hybrid fuzzy decision-making approach to analyze the renewable energy investment projects. *Energy Reports, 8*, 377–389.

Dinçer, H., Yüksel, S., Mikhaylov, A., Pinter, G., & Shaikh, Z. A. (2022a). Analysis of renewable-friendly smart grid technologies for the distributed energy investment projects using a hybrid picture fuzzy rough decision-making approach. *Energy Reports, 8*, 11466–11477.

Dong, W., Zhao, G., Yüksel, S., Dinçer, H., & Ubay, G. G. (2022). A novel hybrid decision making approach for the strategic selection of wind energy projects. *Renewable Energy, 185*, 321–337.

Eti, S. (2019). Ulakbim İndeksinde Taranan Sosyal Bilimler Alanındaki Dergilerde Öne Çıkan Konu ve Yöntemlerin Metin Madenciliği Yaklaşımı ile Belirlenmesi. *Uluslararası Hukuk ve Sosyal Bilim Araştırmaları Dergisi, 1*(1), 61–66.

Eti, S., Dinçer, H., Gökalp, Y., Yüksel, S., & Kararoğlu, D. (2023). Identifying key issues to handle the inflation problem in the healthcare industry caused by energy prices: An evaluation with decision-making models. *In Managing Inflation and Supply Chain Disruptions in the Global Economy*, 162–178.

Eti, S., Dinçer, H., Yüksel, S., & Gökalp, Y. (2022). Analysis of the suitability of the solar panels for hospitals: A new fuzzy decision-making model proposal with the T-spherical TOP-DEMATEL method. *Journal of Intelligent & Fuzzy Systems (Preprint)*, 1–13.

Fang, S., Zhou, P., Dinçer, H., & Yüksel, S. (2021). Assessment of safety management system on energy investment risk using house of quality based on hybrid stochastic interval-valued intuitionistic fuzzy decision-making approach. *Safety Science, 141*, 105333.

Gielen, D., Boshell, F., Saygin, D., Bazilian, M. D., Wagner, N., & Gorini, R. (2019). The role of renewable energy in the global energy transformation. *Energy Strategy Reviews, 24*, 38–50.

Haiyun, C., Zhixiong, H., Yüksel, S., & Dinçer, H. (2021). Analysis of the innovation strategies for green supply chain management in the energy industry using the QFD-based hybrid interval valued intuitionistic fuzzy decision approach. *Renewable and Sustainable Energy Reviews, 143*, 110844.

Hong, T., Pinson, P., Wang, Y., Weron, R., Yang, D., & Zareipour, H. (2020). Energy forecasting: A review and outlook. *IEEE Open Access Journal of Power and Energy*, 7, 376–388. Accessed October 5, 2022, from https://worldpopulationreview.com/country-rankings/solar-power-by-country

Kafka, K. I., Dinçer, H., & Yüksel, S. (2022). Impact-relation map of innovative service development regarding the sustainable growth for emerging markets. *Journal of the Knowledge Economy*, 1–24.

Kayacık, M., Dinçer, H., & Yüksel, S. (2022). Using quantum spherical fuzzy decision support system as a novel sustainability index approach for analyzing industries listed in the stock exchange. *Borsa Istanbul Review, 22*(6), 1145–1157.

Korkmaz, O., & Önöz, B. (2022). Modelling the potential impacts of nuclear energy and renewables in the Turkish energy system. *Energies, 15*(4), 1392.

Kou, G., Yüksel, S., & Dinçer, H. (2022). Inventive problem-solving map of innovative carbon emission strategies for solar energy-based transportation investment projects. *Applied Energy, 311*, 118680.

Kumar, G. B. (2022). Optimal power point tracking of solar and wind energy in a hybrid wind solar energy system. *International Journal of Energy and Environmental Engineering, 13*(1), 77–103.

Lapi, T., Chatzimpiros, P., Raineau, L., & Prinzhofer, A. (2022). System approach to natural versus manufactured hydrogen: An interdisciplinary perspective on a new primary energy source. *International Journal of Hydrogen Energy, 47*(51), 21701–21712.

Li, W., Yüksel, S., & Dinçer, H. (2022b). Understanding the financial innovation priorities for renewable energy investors via QFD-based picture fuzzy and rough numbers. *Financial Innovation, 8*(1), 1–30.

Li, J., Yüksel, S., Dınçer, H., Mikhaylov, A., & Barykin, S. E. (2022a). Bipolar q-ROF hybrid decision making model with golden cut for analyzing the levelized cost of renewable energy alternatives. *IEEE Access, 10*, 42507–42517.

Li, X., Zhu, S., Yüksel, S., Dinçer, H., & Ubay, G. G. (2020). Kano-based mapping of innovation strategies for renewable energy alternatives using hybrid interval type-2 fuzzy decision-making approach. *Energy, 211*, 118679.

Majeed, M. T., Ozturk, I., Samreen, I., & Luni, T. (2022). Evaluating the asymmetric effects of nuclear energy on carbon emissions in Pakistan. *Nuclear Engineering and Technology, 54*(5), 1664–1673.

Martínez, L., Dinçer, H., & Yüksel, S. (2022). A hybrid decision making approach for new service development process of renewable energy investment. *Applied Soft Computing, 133*, 109897.

Mathew, M. D. (2022). Nuclear energy: A pathway towards mitigation of global warming. *Progress in Nuclear Energy, 143*, 104080.

Mikhaylov, A., Bhatti, I. M., Dinçer, H., & Yüksel, S. (2022). Integrated decision recommendation system using iteration-enhanced collaborative filtering, golden cut bipolar for analyzing the risk-based oil market spillovers. *Computational Economics*, 1–34.

Mujtaba, A., Jena, P. K., Bekun, F. V., & Sahu, P. K. (2022). Symmetric and asymmetric impact of economic growth, capital formation, renewable and non-renewable energy consumption on environment in OECD countries. *Renewable and Sustainable Energy Reviews, 160*, 112300.

Mukhtarov, S., Yüksel, S., & Dinçer, H. (2022). The impact of financial development on renewable energy consumption: Evidence from Turkey. *Renewable Energy, 187*, 169–176.

Nabat, M. H., Zeynalian, M., Razmi, A. R., Arabkoohsar, A., & Soltani, M. (2020). Energy, exergy, and economic analyses of an innovative energy storage system; liquid air energy storage (LAES) combined with high-temperature thermal energy storage (HTES). *Energy Conversion and Management, 226*, 113486.

Olabi, A. G., & Abdelkareem, M. A. (2022). Renewable energy and climate change. *Renewable and Sustainable Energy Reviews, 158*, 112111.

Poudyal, R., Loskot, P., Nepal, R., Parajuli, R., & Khadka, S. K. (2019). Mitigating the current energy crisis in Nepal with renewable energy sources. *Renewable and Sustainable Energy Reviews, 116*, 109388.

Qu, M., Wang, H., Zhang, R., Chen, Q., Zhao, Q., Liu, R., et al. (2022). Poly (phthalazinone ether ketone)–poly (3, 4-ethylenedioxythiophene) fiber for thermoelectric and hydroelectric energy harvesting. *Chemical Engineering Journal, 450*, 138093.

Rehman, A., Ma, H., Ozturk, I., & Radulescu, M. (2022). Revealing the dynamic effects of fossil fuel energy, nuclear energy, renewable energy, and carbon emissions on Pakistan's economic growth. *Environmental Science and Pollution Research*, 1–11.

Romanov, D., & Leiss, B. (2022). Geothermal energy at different depths for district heating and cooling of existing and future building stock. *Renewable and Sustainable Energy Reviews, 167*, 112727.

Schulte, E., Scheller, F., Sloot, D., & Bruckner, T. (2022). A meta-analysis of residential PV adoption: The important role of perceived benefits, intentions and antecedents in solar energy acceptance. *Energy Research & Social Science, 84*, 102339.

Singh, U., Rizwan, M., Malik, H., & García Márquez, F. P. (2022). Wind energy scenario, success and initiatives towards renewable energy in India–A review. *Energies, 15*(6), 2291.

Solarz, J., Gawlik-Kobylińska, M., Ostant, W., & Maciejewski, P. (2022). Trends in energy security education with a focus on renewable and nonrenewable sources. *Energies, 15*(4), 1351.

Song, M., & Chambers, T. (2014). Text mining with the Stanford CoreNLP. In *Measuring scholarly impact* (pp. 215–234). Springer.

Sun, L., Peng, J., Dinçer, H., & Yüksel, S. (2022). Coalition-oriented strategic selection of renewable energy system alternatives using q-ROF DEMATEL with golden cut. *Energy, 256*, 124606.

Udeagha, M. C., & Ngepah, N. (2022). Disaggregating the environmental effects of renewable and non-renewable energy consumption in South Africa: Fresh evidence from the novel dynamic ARDL simulations approach. *Economic Change and Restructuring, 55*(3), 1767–1814.

Xu, X., Yüksel, S., & Dinçer, H. (2022). An integrated decision-making approach with Golden cut and bipolar q-ROFSs to renewable energy storage investments. *International Journal of Fuzzy Systems*, 1–14.

Yana, S., Nizar, M., & Mulyati, D. (2022). Biomass waste as a renewable energy in developing bio-based economies in Indonesia: A review. *Renewable and Sustainable Energy Reviews, 160*, 112268.

Yuan, G., Xie, F., Dinçer, H., & Yüksel, S. (2021). The theory of inventive problem solving (TRIZ)-based strategic mapping of green nuclear energy investments with spherical fuzzy group decision-making approach. *International Journal of Energy Research, 45*(8), 12284–12300.

Yüksel, S., & Dinçer, H. (2022). Identifying the strategic priorities of nuclear energy investments using hesitant 2-tuple interval-valued Pythagorean fuzzy DEMATEL. *Progress in Nuclear Energy, 145*, 104103.

Yüksel, S., Dinçer, H., Eti, S., & Adalı, Z. (2022b). Strategy improvements to minimize the drawbacks of geothermal investments by using spherical fuzzy modelling. *International Journal of Energy Research, 46*, 10796–10807.

Yüksel, S., Dinçer, H., Mikhaylov, A., Adalı, Z., & Eti, S. (2022a). Key issues for the improvements of shallow geothermal investments. In H. Dinçer & S. Yüksel (Eds.), *Sustainability in energy business and finance: Contributions to finance and accounting*. Springer. https://doi.org/10.1007/978-3-030-94051-5_16

Zhang, Y., Zhang, Y., Gong, C., Dinçer, H., & Yüksel, S. (2022). An integrated hesitant 2-tuple Pythagorean fuzzy analysis of QFD-based innovation cost and duration for renewable energy projects. *Energy, 248*, 123561.

Chapter 2
The Critical Recommendations for Providing Energy Efficiency

Laura M. Baitenova, Lyailya M. Mutaliyeva, and Fi-John Chang

Keywords Development · Ecosystem · Economic growth · Energy technologies · Clean energy

2.1 Introduction

Despite the widespread introduction of the international standard in the field of energy management systems, which regulates the basic principles and aspects of systems operation, there is an urgent need to develop methods and approaches for its implementation in the context of continuous modernization of fixed assets of metallurgical enterprises and the transition from generally accepted business processes to management using digital transformation and digitalization technologies. The key problem, in my opinion, is that the majority of large metallurgical enterprises, when upgrading their main production equipment, ignore the issues of modernization of the energy system and insufficient involvement of personnel in the process of energy saving. This situation leads to a lack of consistency in the volumes of resources produced and consumed, a low level of energy consumption culture and, as a result, a decrease in energy efficiency in general.

The list of the most promising areas for improving management approaches, in addition to managing the infrastructure of energy farms, includes the development of

L. M. Baitenova (✉)
Almaty University of Power Engineering and Telecommunications (AUPET) named after G. Daukeev, Almaty, Kazakhstan

L. M. Mutaliyeva
L.N. Gumilyov Eurasian National University, Nur-Sultan, Kazakhstan

F.-J. Chang
Department of Bioenvironmental Systems Engineering, National Taiwan University, Taipei, Taiwan
e-mail: changfj@ntu.edu.tw

H. Dincer, S. Yüksel (eds.), *Economic Development and the Environmental Ecosystem*, Contributions to Economics,
https://doi.org/10.1007/978-3-031-26596-9_2

incentive tools for energy conservation and improving the quality of innovation activities of personnel.

The energy power and security of a country, the development of the economy and the standard of living of the population are determined by the amount of extraction, production and consumption of fuel and energy resources. Current trends in the development of modern industrial production, despite the relatively low prices for energy resources in Russia, in comparison with the prices of the world market, the value of fuel and energy costs in the cost of production ranges from 15 to 35%, depending on the type of growth. In total, industrial enterprises consume 125–130 million, which is more than a third of the country's fuel and energy resources and more than 50%7 of the electricity generated. According to the data of GDP growth dynamics, which reflect the main result of the functioning of industry, we can conclude that the Russian industry is lagging behind the industry of developed countries, such as the United States and China.

Energy efficiency is vital for the profitability of businesses to be sustainable (Eti et al., 2023; Li et al., 2022a, 2022b; Haiyun et al., 2021). In this context, it is necessary to determine the ways for businesses to carry out the same work with less energy (Li et al., 2022a, 2022b; Yüksel et al., 2022; Mikhaylov et al., 2022a, 2022b). In this way, it is possible to reduce energy costs. Thanks to the use of less energy in the production process, it will be possible to increase the profit margins of the enterprises. In this study, it is aimed to propose the necessary applications in order to ensure the energy efficiency of the enterprises.

2.2 Literature Review

In the context of existing trends for technological modernization of the country's economy and the introduction of innovations, the need to improve energy efficiency is becoming an important direction for the development of technologies and improving organizational processes for managing energy efficiency. The pace of development of information and telecommunications technologies leads to an increase in the growth of energy consumption in non-manufacturing industries, such as the development of information technologies, significantly outstripping the average growth rate of energy consumption. In these conditions, given the importance of the availability of electric energy as a limiting condition for infrastructure development, the current vector for digitalization of the economy leads to an increasing urgency of energy conservation and energy efficiency issues. In many developed countries, over the past decade, the energy intensity of the economy has decreased by 15–20%, while previously planned plans for improving energy efficiency have to be revised upwards (Nie et al., 2020; Bhuiyan et al., 2021; Dong et al., 2021; Mikhaylov, 2021a, 2021b; Barykin et al., 2022a; Liu et al., 2022a, 2022b; Bhuiyan, 2022b; Danish et al., 2022a, 2022b; Saqib et al., 2021; Mukhametov et al., 2021; Candila et al., 2021; Mikhaylov & Grilli, 2022; Li et al., 2022a,2022b, 2022c).

In the United States of America, it is planned to reduce the energy intensity of the economy by 25% by 2025 compared to 2005, in the European Union-by 20% compared to 2007, and in China, after 13 repeated revisions, the current goal is to reduce the energy intensity of the economy by 49% by 2025 compared to 2006. In the Russian Federation, the decline in the indicator in comparable prices was observed until the beginning of the 2008 crisis. Since then, no significant changes in real terms have been observed, and Russia has to catch up with its partners, whose energy intensity of the economy is 1.5–2 times lower (Khan et al., 2022; Dinçer et al., 2022a, 2022b; Badr et al., 2022; Barykin et al., 2022b; Mehta et al., 2022; Kalinina et al., 2022; Shaikh et al., 2022; Mikhaylov et al., 2022a, 2022b; Nyangarika et al., 2022).

In addition to the main task of reducing the energy intensity of GDP, targets were set for a number of industry indicators, such as the depth of oil refining, losses of electric energy in electric networks from the total volume of electric energy supply, and specific resource expenditures for the extraction of fuel and energy resources (Denisova et al., 2019; Nyangarika et al., 2019a, 2019b; Huang et al., 2021a, 2021b; Mikhaylov, 2018, 2022; Mikhaylov et al., 2019; Conteh et al., 2021; Sediqi et al., 2022; Khan et al., 2021; Bhuiyan et al., 2022a; Liu et al., 2021a, 2021b; Daniali et al., 2021; Moiseev et al., 2023).

The observed socio-economic situation significantly differs from the forecasts that formed the basis of the initial goal setting in the field of energy conservation and energy efficiency improvement (Zhang et al., 2022; Yüksel & Dinçer, 2022; Carayannis et al., 2022). Changes in the structure of the economy associated with the introduction of modern energy-saving technologies and the development of digital business transformation were supposed to reduce the energy intensity of GDP by 25% by 2020, but according to Rosstat research, the forecast was not confirmed and in fact it was possible to reduce the share of energy-intensive industries by only 2%, which indicates that energy consumption (Mikhaylov et al., 2023; Mikhaylov, 2021a; Varyash et al., 2020; Zhao et al., 2021; An & Mikhaylov, 2020; Alwaelya et al., 2021; Yumashev & Mikhaylov, 2020; Yumashev et al., 2020; Mutalimov et al., 2021; An & Mikhaylov, 2021).

In fact, when calculated at current prices, the energy intensity of Russia's GDP for the period 2012–2017 decreased by 34%. The significant lag in the actual values of indicators in the field of energy saving and energy efficiency from the target values was largely compounded in 2014–2017, when the Russian Federation was faced with foreign policy factors and economic instability. At the same time, the situation was characterized by a sharp decline in prices for oil and other export goods. Russian organizations were restricted access to international financial markets and access to modern technologies (An et al., 2019a, 2019b; An et al., 2020a, 2020b, 2020c; Moiseev et al., 2020, 2021; Gura et al., 2022; Dooyum et al., 2020; Mikhaylov et al., 2020; Mikhaylov & Tarakanov, 2020 Mikhaylov, 2020a, 2020b, 2020c).

That is why many researchers believe that the main impetus for the development of a systematic approach in the field of energy saving is various kinds of crises, as a result of which competition between enterprises in various industries becomes more acute (Yuan et al., 2021; Fang et al., 2021; Kayacık et al., 2022). Assessment of the potential for energy saving in industry, both in developed and developing countries, can become the basis for developing an effective organizational and economic mechanism for managing savings at the regional and individual enterprise levels. To assess the potential, it is necessary to analyze the directions and structure of energy consumption. In the coming years, the world's total energy consumption in industrial production is expected to grow by 75% from the level of 2012 (3115 million tons of conventional fuel) and amount to about 5300 million tons. Today, the most popular fuel and energy resource for metallurgical enterprises is electric energy. According to statistics, its consumption accounts for about 20% of the total global energy consumption, and in forecasts until the 50s, the share of electricity in the total structure of energy consumption is expected to grow to values of 25–27% in total consumption. This situation, according to scientists, will lead to a reduction in the consumption of petroleum products and coal relative to electric energy. In this regard, the list of priority tasks aimed at improving energy efficiency should include the development of renewable energy sources, as well as alternative energy resources, such as hydrogen. The target for the share of alternative energy sources is between 10 and 15% of all energy by 2050) (Dayong et al., 2020; Mikhaylov et al., 2018; Nyangarika et al., 2018; Danish et al., 2020, 2021; An et al., 2021, 2022; Uyeh et al., 2021; Tamashiro et al., 2021, 2023; Shaikh et al., 2021).

2.3 The Creation of Concept of Energy Efficiency

The metallurgical industry is one of the most conservative in terms of using alternative energy sources, since it is highly likely that changes in the technological processes of steel production are not expected in the near future, as well as fluctuations in the structure of steel production. The analysis and evaluation carried out showed that the share of energy consumption in the production cost of domestic industrial enterprises is too high even by Russian standards. In metallurgy, it reaches 20%, petrochemicals-more than 40%, and the copper industry-about 80%. It is possible to increase the energy efficiency of metallurgical enterprises primarily through large-scale modernization of production facilities and energy facilities (with the replacement or decommissioning of obsolete equipment), as well as the development of alternative energy (Martínez et al., 2022; Sun et al., 2022; Kafka et al., 2022).

In many industries (electric power, metallurgy, oil refining, and petrochemicals), enterprises continue to operate outdated, inefficient equipment and technologies, many of which have not been updated (at best) since the late 1980s. Despite the fact that modernization should take place every 15 years.

The results of the study show that in general, industrial production has a significant potential for energy saving. Based on experts' estimates, in modern conditions, about 40% of this potential is accounted for by ferrous and non-ferrous metallurgy.

To solve the problems of energy saving in the metallurgical industry, it is necessary to use the potential contained in the main technological processes, including through the use of recyclable materials and deep processing of waste (Mukhtarov et al., 2022; Dong et al., 2022; Dinçer et al., 2022a, 2022b, 2022d). So, for example, there is a four-fold reduction in energy consumption in steelmaking when processing scrap metal in electric steelmaking furnaces compared to outdated open-hearth and converter production (Bhuiyan et al., 2022a; Kou et al., 2022). In addition, deep processing of carbon-containing waste generated at the enterprise can not only meet the need of individual consumers for energy resources, but also reduce the impact of enterprises on the environment in the region of their presence (Eti et al., 2022; Dinçer et al., 2023; Xu et al., 2022).

The problems of management formation at Russian industrial enterprises are entirely related to the peculiarities of the current stage of socio-economic development, characterized by the formation of private ownership in the industrial sector and the transition to decentralized planning. Some authors believe that the emerging energy crisis negatively affected the formation of domestic approaches to energy conservation, opening up export channels for local energy carriers. A number of researchers note that the actualization of energy conservation problems in Russia is associated with the transition to a market economy in the early 1990s: energy prices in the conditions of competitive operation of private industrial enterprises, natural prices increased by an average of 15–20 percentage points, while maintaining the overall level of energy intensity of industrial products.

On the scale of the global economic system, the increase in prices for basic energy resources has a stimulating effect on the development of renewable and alternative energy sources, largely due to the investment attractiveness of these projects. However, for this reason, there is a deterioration in the socio-economic indicators of the state, associated with an increase in the specific cost of energy resources for the population, since the industrial group of consumers spends them most efficiently, with the least losses. Moreover, the increase in prices for energy resources is one of the most significant factors for increasing inflation, as practice shows, an increase in their cost by two times leads to an increase in the prices of consumer goods and services by 15–20%. It is obvious that the development of energy efficiency management systems at enterprises and the updating of energy saving issues are impossible without the participation of the state in the processes of tariff regulation.

2.4 Conclusion

The peculiarities of the national investment policy in the energy infrastructure during the 90s of the last millennium, aimed mainly at maintaining the technical condition, led to the moral and physical obsolescence of the vast majority of energy facilities by 2000. To a greater extent, the degradation affected information technology and monitoring support that supports the analysis of the current and future state of the elements of the energy sector. As a result, some manufacturers in the market operate with low efficiency, and their tariffs are not competitive in international comparison.

Based on the reviewed scientific works, it can be concluded that the management mechanism is a set of economic, social, legal, financial and managerial tools aimed at improving the efficiency of the enterprise's functioning. On the other hand, energy conservation is a set of implemented organizational, legal, technical, technological, and economic measures that are aimed at reducing the amount of energy resources used while maintaining the corresponding beneficial effect from their use. Obviously, energy conservation can be considered as a particular example of an energy efficiency management mechanism. This makes it possible to establish a clear link between the two concepts discussed in the first question.

References

Alwaelya, S. A., Yousif, N. B. A., & Mikhaylov, A. (2021). Emotional development in preschoolers and socialization. *Early Child Development and Care, 191*, 16.

An, J., & Mikhaylov, A. (2020). Russian energy projects in South Africa. *Journal of Energy in Southern Africa, 31*(3), 58–64.

An, J., & Mikhaylov, A. (2021). Analysis of energy projects financial efficiency and renewable energy generation in Russia. *Finance: Theory and Practice, 25*(5), 79–91.

An, J., Mikhaylov, A., Dinçer, H., & Yüksel, S. (2022). Economic modelling of electricity generation: Long short-term memory and Q-rung Orthopair fuzzy sets. *Heliyon, 8*, e10759.

An, J., Mikhaylov, A., & Jung, S.-U. (2020b). The strategy of South Korea in the global oil market. *Energies, 13*(10), 2491.

An, J., Mikhaylov, A., & Jung, S.-U. (2021). A linear programming approach for robust network revenue management in the airline industry. *Journal of Air Transport Management, 91*, 101979.

An, J., Mikhaylov, A., & Kim, K. (2020c). Machine learning approach in heterogeneous group of algorithms for transport safety-critical system. *Applied Sciences, 10*(8), 2670.

An, J., Mikhaylov, A., & Moiseev, N. (2019b). Oil price predictors: Machine learning approach. *International Journal of Energy Economics and Policy, 9*(5), 1–6.

An, J., Mikhaylov, A., & Richter, U. H. (2020a). Trade war effects: Evidence from sectors of energy and resources in Africa. *Heliyon, 6*, e05693. https://doi.org/10.1016/j.heliyon.2020.e05693

An, J., Mikhaylov, A., & Sokolinskaya, N. (2019a). Machine learning in economic planning: Ensembles of algorithms. *Journal of Physics: Conference Series, 1353*, 012126.

Badr, A. M. N. A. A., Mohamed, T. I., Osman, N. A. Q., & Mikhaylov, A. (2022). A review of social media website users' interaction paths with governmental accounts during the COVID-19 pandemic. *Informatics, 9*, 50. https://doi.org/10.3390/informatics9030050

Barykin, S. E., Kapustina, I. V., Sergeev, S. M., Daniali, S. M., Kopteva, L. A., Semenova, G. N., Pryadko, I. P., Mikhaylov, A., Baboshkin, P., Datsyuk, P., & Senjyu, T. (2022a). Financial logistics models based on systematic approach improving management solutions. *F1000Research, 11*, 570. https://doi.org/10.12688/f1000research.111252.1

Barykin, S., Mikheev, A., Kiseleva, E., Putikhin, Y., Alekseeva, N., & Mikhaylov, A. (2022b). An empirical analysis of Russian regions' debt sustainability. *Economies, 10*(4), 296.

Bhuiyan, M. A., An, J., Mikhaylov, A., Moiseev, N., & Danish, M. S. S. (2021). Renewable energy deployment and COVID-19 measures for sustainable development. *Sustainability, 13*, 4418.

Bhuiyan, M. A., Dinçer, H., Yüksel, S., Mikhaylov, A., Danish, M. S. S., Pinter, G., et al. (2022a). Economic indicators and bioenergy supply in developed economies: QROF-DEMATEL and random forest models. *Energy Reports, 8*, 561–570.

Bhuiyan, M. A., Zhang, Q., Khare, V., Mikhaylov, A., Pinter, G., & Huang, X. (2022b). Renewable energy consumption and economic growth nexus–A systematic literature review. *Frontiers in Environmental Science, 10*, 878394. https://doi.org/10.3389/fenvs.2022.878394

Candila, V., Maximov, D., Mikhaylov, A., Moiseev, N., Senjyu, T., & Tryndina, N. (2021). On the relationship between oil and exchange rates of oil-exporting and oil-importing countries: From the great recession period to the Covid-19 era. *Energies, 14*, 8065.

Carayannis, E., Kostis, P., Dinçer, H., & Yüksel, S. (2022). Balanced-scorecard-based evaluation of knowledge-oriented competencies of distributed energy investments. *Energies, 15*(21), 8245.

Conteh, F., Takahashi, H., Hemeida, A. M., Krishnan, N., Mikhaylov, A., & Senjyu, T. (2021). Hybrid grid-connected renewable power generation for sustainable electricity supply in Sierra Leone: Case study lungi town. *Sustainability, 13*(18), 11435.

Daniali, S. M., Barykin, S. E., Kapustina, I. V., Khortabi, F. M., Sergeev, S. M., Kalinina, O. V., Mikhaylov, A., Veynberg, R., Zasova, L., & Senjyu, T. (2021). Predicting volatility index according to technical index and economic indicators on the basis of deep learning algorithm. *Sustainability, 2021*(13), 14011.

Danish, M. S. S., Bhattacharya, A., Stepanova, D., Mikhaylov, A., Grilli, M. L., Khosravy, M., & Senjyu, T. (2020). A systematic review of metal oxide applications for energy and environmental sustainability. *Metals, 10*(12), 1604.

Danish, M. S. S., Senjyu, T., Sabory, N. R., Khosravy, M., Grilli, M. L., Mikhaylov, A., & Majidi, H. (2021). A forefront framework for sustainable aquaponics modeling and design. *Sustainability, 13*, 9313.

Danish, M. S., Senjyu, T. S., Sabory, N. R., & Mikhaylov, A. (2022a). Lessons from COVID-19 conferring environmental re-engineering opportunity. In M. Danish & T. Senjyu (Eds.), *Eco-friendly and agile energy strategies and policy development* (pp. 99–118). IGI Global. https://doi.org/10.4018/978-1-7998-9502-2.ch005

Danish, M. S., Senjyu, T. S., Sabory, N. R., & Mikhaylov, A. (2022b). Interplay consequences of COVID-19 on global environmental sustainability. In M. Danish & T. Senjyu (Eds.), *Eco-friendly and agile energy strategies and policy development*. IGI Global. https://doi.org/10.4018/978-1-7998-9502-2.ch003

Dayong, N., Mikhaylov, A., Bratanovsky, S., Shaikh, Z. A., & Stepanova, D. (2020). Mathematical modeling of the technological processes of catering products production. *Journal of Food Process Engineering, 43*(2), 1–9.

Denisova, V., Mikhaylov, A., & Lopatin, E. (2019). Blockchain infrastructure and growth of global power consumption. *International Journal of Energy Economics and Policy, 9*(4), 22–29.

Dinçer, H., Aksoy, T., Yüksel, S., & Hacioglu, U. (2022b). Golden cut-oriented q-rung orthopair fuzzy decision-making approach to evaluation of renewable energy alternatives for microgeneration system investments. *Mathematical Problems in Engineering*, 2022.

Dinçer, H., Yüksel, S., Çağlayan, Ç., Yavuz, D., & Kararoğlu, D. (2023). Can renewable energy investments be a solution to the energy-sourced high inflation problem?. In *Managing inflation and supply chain disruptions in the global economy* (pp. 220–238). IGI Global.

Dinçer, H., Yüksel, S., & Martínez, L. (2022c). Collaboration enhanced hybrid fuzzy decision-making approach to analyze the renewable energy investment projects. *Energy Reports, 8*, 377–389.

Dinçer, H., Yüksel, S., Mikhaylov, A., Barykin, S. E., Aksoy, T., & Hacioğlu, U. (2022d). Analysis of environmental priorities for green project investments using an integrated q-rung orthopair fuzzy modelling. *IEEE Access, 10*, 50996–51007. https://doi.org/10.1109/ACCESS.2022.3174058

Dinçer, H., Yüksel, S., Mikhaylov, A., Pinter, G., & Shaikh, Z. A. (2022a). Analysis of renewable-friendly smart grid technologies for the distributed energy investment projects using a hybrid picture fuzzy rough decision-making approach. *Energy Reports, 8*, 11466–11477. https://doi.org/10.1016/j.egyr.2022.08.275

Dong, B., Ikonnikova, I., Rogulin, R., Sakulyeva, T., & Mikhaylov, A. (2021). Environmentaleconomic approach to optimization of transport communication in megacities. *Journal of Environmental Science and Health, Part A, 56*(6), 660–666.
Dong, W., Zhao, G., Yüksel, S., Dinçer, H., & Ubay, G. G. (2022). A novel hybrid decision making approach for the strategic selection of wind energy projects. *Renewable Energy, 185*, 321–337.
Dooyum, U. D., Mikhaylov, A., & Varyash, I. (2020). Energy security concept in Russia and South Korea. *International Journal of Energy Economics and Policy, 10*(4), 102–107.
Eti, S., Dinçer, H., Gökalp, Y., Yüksel, S., & Kararoğlu, D. (2023). Identifying key issues to handle the inflation problem in the healthcare industry caused by energy prices: An evaluation with decision-making models. *Managing Inflation and Supply Chain Disruptions in the Global Economy*, 162–178.
Eti, S., Dinçer, H., Yüksel, S., & Gökalp, Y. (2022). Analysis of the suitability of the solar panels for hospitals: A new fuzzy decision-making model proposal with the T-spherical TOP-DEMATEL method. *Journal of Intelligent & Fuzzy Systems, Preprint*, 1–13.
Fang, S., Zhou, P., Dinçer, H., & Yüksel, S. (2021). Assessment of safety management system on energy investment risk using house of quality based on hybrid stochastic interval-valued intuitionistic fuzzy decision-making approach. *Safety Science, 141*, 105333.
Gura, D., Mikhaylov, A., Glushkov, S., Zaikov, M., & Shaikh, Z. A. (2022). Model for estimating power dissipation along the interconnect length in single on-chip topology. *Evolutionary Intelligence, 15*, 2369–2373. https://doi.org/10.1007/s12065-020-00407-7
Haiyun, C., Zhixiong, H., Yüksel, S., & Dinçer, H. (2021). Analysis of the innovation strategies for green supply chain management in the energy industry using the QFD-based hybrid interval valued intuitionistic fuzzy decision approach. *Renewable and Sustainable Energy Reviews, 143*, 110844.
Huang, Y., Masrur, H., Shigenobu, R., Hemeida, A. M., Mikhaylov, A., & Senjyu, T. (2021a). A comparative design of a campus microgrid considering a multi-scenario and multi-objective approach. *Energies, 14*, 2853.
Huang, Y., Yona, A., Takahashi, H., Hemeida, A. M., Mandal, P., Mikhaylov, A., Senjyu, T., & Lotfy, M. E. (2021b). Energy management system optimization of drug store operate electric vehicles charging station. *Sustainability, 14*, 1217836.
Kafka, K. I., Dinçer, H., & Yüksel, S. (2022). Impact-relation map of innovative service development regarding the sustainable growth for emerging markets. *Journal of the Knowledge Economy*, 1–24.
Kalinina, O. V., Barykin, S. E., Sergeev, S. M., Semenova, G. N., Fatkullina, A., Mikhaylov, A., & De La Poza, E. (2022). Smart city perspectives in post-pandemic governance: Externalities reduction policy. *F1000 Research, 11*, 1032. https://doi.org/10.12688/f1000research.123195.1
Kayacık, M., Dinçer, H., & Yüksel, S. (2022). Using quantum spherical fuzzy decision support system as a novel sustainability index approach for analyzing industries listed in the stock exchange. *Borsa Istanbul Review, 22*(6), 1145–1157.
Khan, A. A., Laghari, A. A., Gadekallu, T. R., Shaikh, Z. A., Javed, A. R., Rashid, M., Estrela, V. V., & Mikhaylov, A. (2022). A drone-based data management and optimization using metaheuristic algorithms and blockchain smart contracts in a secure fog environment. *Computers and Electrical Engineering, 102*, 108234. https://doi.org/10.1016/j.compeleceng.2022.108234
Khan, A. A., Shaikh, Z. A., Baitenova, L., Mutaliyeva, L., Moiseev, N., Mikhaylov, A., Laghari, A. A., Idris, S. A., & Alshazly, H. (2021). QoS-ledger: Smart contracts and metaheuristic for secure quality-of-service and cost-efficient scheduling of medical-data processing. *Electronics, 10*, 3083.
Kou, G., Yüksel, S., & Dinçer, H. (2022). Inventive problem-solving map of innovative carbon emission strategies for solar energy-based transportation investment projects. *Applied Energy, 311*, 118680.

Li, J., Dinçer, H., Yüksel, S., Mikhaylov, A., & Barykin, S. E. (2022a). Bipolar q-ROF hybrid decision making model with golden cut for analyzing the levelized cost of renewable energy alternatives. *IEEE Access, 10*, 35900–35900. https://doi.org/10.1109/ACCESS.2022.3168315

Li, W., Yüksel, S., & Dinçer, H. (2022c). Understanding the financial innovation priorities for renewable energy investors via QFD-based picture fuzzy and rough numbers. *Financial Innovation, 8*(1), 1–30.

Li, J., Yüksel, S., Dınçer, H., Mikhaylov, A., & Barykin, S. E. (2022b). Bipolar q-ROF hybrid decision making model with golden cut for analyzing the levelized cost of renewable energy alternatives. *IEEE Access, 10*, 42507–42517.

Liu, L., Kato, T., Mandal, P., Mikhaylov, A., Hemeida, A. M., & Senjyu, T. (2021a). Multi-area power system load frequency control by using model predictive control by introducing renewable energy sources. *International Conference on Science & Contemporary Technologies (ICSCT), 2021*, 1–6. https://doi.org/10.1109/ICSCT53883.2021.9642521

Liu, L., Kato, T., Mandal, P., Mikhaylov, A., Hemeida, A. M., Takahashi, H., & Tomonobu, S. (2021b). Two cases studies of model predictive control approach for hybrid renewable energy systems. *AIMS Energy, 9*(6), 1241–1259.

Liu, Z., Panfilova, E., Mikhaylov, A., & Kurilova, A. (2022a). Assessing stability in the relationship between parties in crowdfunding and crowdsourcing projects during the COVID-19 crisis. *Journal of Global Information Management (JGIM), 30*(4), 1–18. https://doi.org/10.4018/JGIM.297905

Liu, Z.-J., Panfilova, E., Mikhaylov, A., & Kurilova, A. (2022b). COVID-19 crisis impact on the stability between parties in crowdfunding and crowdsourcing. *Wireless Personal Communications, 122*, 915–930.

Martínez, L., Dinçer, H., & Yüksel, S. (2022). A hybrid decision making approach for new service development process of renewable energy investment. *Applied Soft Computing, 133*, 109897.

Mehta, R., Verghese, J., Mahajan, S., Barykin, S., Bozhuk, S., Kozlova, N., Kapustina, I., Mikhaylov, A., Naumova, E., & Dedyukhina, N. (2022). Consumers' behavior in conversational commerce marketing based on messenger chatbots. *F1000Research, 11*(647), 647. https://doi.org/10.12688/f1000research.122037.1

Mikhaylov, A. (2018). The yield of the carry trade strategy. *Finance: Theory and Practice, 22*(3), 52–63. https://doi.org/10.26794/2587-5671-2018-22-3-52-63

Mikhaylov, A. (2020a). Cryptocurrency market analysis from the open innovation perspective. *Journal of Open Innovation: Technology, Market, and Complexity, 6*(4), 197.

Mikhaylov, A. (2020b). Geothermal energy development in Iceland. *International Journal of Energy Economics and Policy, 10*(4), 31–35.

Mikhaylov, A. (2020c). Cryptocurrency market development: Hurst method. *Finance: Theory and Practice, 24*(3), 81–91.

Mikhaylov, A. (2021a). Development of Friedrich von Hayek's theory of private money and economic implications for digital currencies. *Terra Economicus, 19*(1), 53–62.

Mikhaylov, A. (2021b). Lichens as indicators of atmospheric pollution in urban ecosystems. *Israel Journal of Ecology & Evolution, 67*(1–2), 60–68. https://doi.org/10.1163/22244662-bja10016

Mikhaylov, A. (2022). Sustainable development and renewable energy: A new view to a global problem. *Energies, 15*, 1397. https://doi.org/10.3390/en15041397

Mikhaylov, A., Bhatti, I. M., Dinçer, H., & Yüksel, S. (2022a). Integrated decision recommendation system using iteration-enhanced collaborative filtering, golden cut bipolar for analyzing the risk-based oil market spillovers. *Computational Economics*, 1–34. https://doi.org/10.1007/s10614-022-10341-8

Mikhaylov, A., Burakov, D., & Didenko, V. (2019). Relationship between oil price and macroeconomic indicators in Russia. *Finance: Theory and Practice, 23*(2), 105–116. https://doi.org/10.26794/2587-5671-2019-23-2-105-116

Mikhaylov, A., Dinçer, H., & Yüksel, S. (2023). Analysis of financial development and open innovation oriented fintech potential for emerging economies using an integrated decision-making approach of MF-X-DMA and golden cut bipolar q-ROFSs. *Financ Innov, 9*, 10. https://doi.org/10.1186/s40854-022-00234-w

Mikhaylov, A., & Grilli, M. L. (2022). Machine learning methods and sustainable development: Metal oxides and multilayer metal-oxides. *Metals, 12*(4), 836.

Mikhaylov, A., Moiseev, N., Aleshin, K., & Burkhardt, T. (2020). Global climate change and greenhouse effect. *Entrepreneurship and Sustainability Issues, 7*(4), 2897–2913. https://doi.org/10.9770/jesi.2020.7.4(21)

Mikhaylov, A., Sokolinskaya, N., & Nyangarika, A. (2018). Optimal carry trade strategy based on currencies of energy and developed economies. *Journal of Reviews on Global Economics, 7*, 582–592.

Mikhaylov, A., & Tarakanov, S. (2020). Development of Levenberg-Marquardt theoretical approach for electric network. *Journal of Physics: Conference Series, 1515*, 052006.

Mikhaylov, A., Yumashev, A., & Kolpak, E. (2022b). Quality of life, anxiety and depressive disorders in patients with extrasystolic arrhythmia. *Archives of Medical Science, 18*(2), 328. https://doi.org/10.5114/aoms.2020.101359

Moiseev, N., Mikhaylov, A., Dinçer, H., & Yüksel, S. (2023). Effects of market capitalization shocks for open innovation models in e-commerce industry: Golden cut QROF MCDM analysis. *Financ Innov, 9*, 32.

Moiseev, N., Mikhaylov, A., Varyash, I., & Saqib, A. (2020). Investigating the relation of GDP per capita and corruption index. *Entrepreneurship and Sustainability Issues, 8*(1), 780–794.

Moiseev, N., Sorokin, A., Zvezdina, N., Mikhaylov, A., Khomyakova, L., & Danish, M. S. S. (2021). Credit risk theoretical model on the base of DCC-GARCH in time-varying parameters framework. *Mathematics, 9*, 2423. https://doi.org/10.3390/math9192423

Mukhametov, A., Bekhorashvili, A., Avdeenko, A., & Mikhaylov, A. (2021). The impact of growing legume plants under conditions of Biologization and soil cultivation on Chernozem fertility and productivity of rotation crops. *Legume Research, 44*, 12.

Mukhtarov, S., Yüksel, S., & Dinçer, H. (2022). The impact of financial development on renewable energy consumption: Evidence from Turkey. *Renewable Energy, 187*, 169–176.

Mutalimov, V., Kovaleva, I., Mikhaylov, A., & Stepanova, D. (2021). Assessing regional growth of small business in Russia. *Entrepreneurial Business and Economics Review, 9*(3), 119–133. https://doi.org/10.15678/EBER.2021.090308

Nie, D., Panfilova, E., Samusenkov, V., & Mikhaylov, A. (2020). E-learning financing models in Russia for sustainable development. *Sustainability, 12*(11), 4412.

Nyangarika, A., Mikhaylov, A., Muyeen, S. M., Yadykin, V., Mottaeva, A., Pryadko, I., Barykin, S., Fomenko, N., Rykov, G., & Shvandar, K. (2022). Energy stability and decarbonization in developing countries: Random Forest approach for forecasting of crude oil trade flows and macro indicators. *Frontiers in Environmental Science, 10*, 1031343. https://doi.org/10.3389/fenvs.2022.1031343

Nyangarika, A., Mikhaylov, A., & Richter, U. (2019a). Influence oil price towards economic indicators in Russia. *International Journal of Energy Economics and Policy, 9*(1), 123–129.

Nyangarika, A., Mikhaylov, A., & Richter, U. (2019b). Oil price factors: Forecasting on the base of modified auto-regressive integrated moving average model. *International Journal of Energy Economics and Policy, 9*(1), 149–159.

Nyangarika, A., Mikhaylov, A., & Tang, B.-J. (2018). Correlation of oil prices and gross domestic product in oil producing countries. *International Journal of Energy Economics and Policy, 8*(5), 42–48.

Saqib, A., Chan, T.-H., Mikhaylov, A., & Lean, H. H. (2021). Are the responses of sectoral energy imports asymmetric to exchange rate volatilities in Pakistan? Evidence from recent foreign exchange regime. *Frontiers in Energy Research, 9*, 614463. https://doi.org/10.3389/fenrg.2021.614463

Sediqi, M. M., Nakadomari, A., Mikhaylov, A., Krishnan, N., Lotfy, M. E., Yona, A., & Senjyu, T. (2022). Impact of time-of-use demand response program on optimal operation of Afghanistan real power system. *Energies, 15*, 296.

Shaikh, Z. A., Kraikin, A., Mikhaylov, A., & Pinter, G. (2022). Forecasting stock prices of companies producing solar panels using machine learning methods. *Complexity, 2022*, 9186265. https://doi.org/10.1155/2022/9186265

Shaikh, Z. A., Moiseev, N., Mikhaylov, A., & Yüksel, S. (2021). Facile synthesis of copper oxide-cobalt oxide/nitrogen-doped carbon (Cu2O-Co3O4/CN) composite for efficient water splitting. *Applied Sciences., 11*, 9974. https://doi.org/10.3390/app11219974

Sun, L., Peng, J., Dinçer, H., & Yüksel, S. (2022). Coalition-oriented strategic selection of renewable energy system alternatives using q-ROF DEMATEL with golden cut. *Energy, 256*, 124606.

Tamashiro, K., Alharbi, T., Mikhaylov, A., Hemeida, A. M., Krishnan, N., Lotfy, M. E., & Senjyu, T. (2021). Investigation of home energy management with advanced direct load control and optimal scheduling of controllable loads. *Energies, 14*, 7314. https://doi.org/10.3390/en14217314

Tamashiro, K., Omine, E., Krishnan, N., Mikhaylov, A., Hemeida, A. M., & Senjyu, T. (2023). Optimal components capacity based multi-objective optimization and optimal scheduling based MPC-optimization algorithm in smart apartment buildings. *Energy & Buildings, 278*, 112616. https://doi.org/10.1016/j.enbuild.2022.112616

Uyeh, D. D., Asem-Hiablie, S., Park, T., Kim, K.-M., Mikhaylov, A., Woo, S., & Ha, Y. (2021). Could japonica rice be an alternative variety for increased global food security and climate change mitigation? *Food, 10*, 1869. https://doi.org/10.3390/foods10081869

Varyash, I., Mikhaylov, A., Moiseev, N., & Aleshin, K. (2020). Triple bottom line and corporate social responsibility performance indicators for Russian companies. *Entrepreneurship and Sustainability Issues, 8*(1), 313–331.

Xu, X., Yüksel, S., & Dinçer, H. (2022). An integrated decision-making approach with Golden cut and bipolar q-ROFSs to renewable energy storage investments. *International Journal of Fuzzy Systems*, 1–14.

Yuan, G., Xie, F., Dinçer, H., & Yüksel, S. (2021). The theory of inventive problem solving (TRIZ)-based strategic mapping of green nuclear energy investments with spherical fuzzy group decision-making approach. *International Journal of Energy Research, 45*(8), 12284–12300.

Yüksel, S., & Dinçer, H. (2022). Identifying the strategic priorities of nuclear energy investments using hesitant 2-tuple interval-valued Pythagorean fuzzy DEMATEL. *Progress in Nuclear Energy, 145*, 104103.

Yüksel, S., Dinçer, H., Eti, S., & Adalı, Z. (2022). Strategy improvements to minimize the drawbacks of geothermal investments by using spherical fuzzy modelling. *International Journal of Energy Research, 46*(8), 10796–10807.

Yumashev, A., & Mikhaylov, A. (2020). Development of polymer film coatings with high adhesion to steel alloys and high wear resistance. *Polymer Composites, 41*(7), 2875–2880.

Yumashev, A., Ślusarczyk, B., Kondrashev, S., & Mikhaylov, A. (2020). Global indicators of sustainable development: Evaluation of the influence of the human development index on consumption and quality of energy. *Energies, 13*, 2768.

Zhang, Y., Zhang, Y., Gong, C., Dinçer, H., & Yüksel, S. (2022). An integrated hesitant 2-tuple Pythagorean fuzzy analysis of QFD-based innovation cost and duration for renewable energy projects. *Energy, 248*, 123561.

Zhao, Q., Cherkasov, S., Avdeenko, A., Kondratenko, L., & Mikhaylov, A. (2021). Integral estimate of the added value of agricultural crops in the synergetic agriculture on the example of Vicia faba (Vicia faba L.). *Polish Journal of Environmental Studies, 30*(5), 1–9. https://doi.org/10.15244/pjoes/131949

Chapter 3
The Importance of Having Nuclear Power Technologies for Sustainable Energy Development

Serhat Yüksel, Çağatay Çağlayan, and Alexey Mikhaylov

Keywords Nuclear energy · Energy investments · DEMATEL · Energy economics · Sustainable energy

3.1 Introduction

After the industrial revolution, the concept of energy has spread to all areas of life and has increased its importance day by day. With intensified production, consumption and urbanization, the need for energy has become a common problem in all people and countries (Kim & Barles, 2012). Because industrialization and urbanization have increased the human population and increased the energy demand considerably. Therefore, the energy issue will be the most important issue of the twenty first century and perhaps the next centuries. The fact that energy resources are limited, unevenly distributed and some of them have negative effects on the environment and human health show that intensive studies on energy should be done. Energy resources are divided into non-renewable and renewable resources. In this context, various fuels are used as an energy source. Fossil fuels can be listed simply as coal, natural gas and oil. Renewable energy sources are solar, wind, geothermal, hydrogen, wave, biomass and hydraulic. In addition to all these, nuclear energy sources are thorium and uranium (Ulutaş, 2005).

Fossil fuels meet most of the increasing energy demand in the world. Fuels formed by the decay of plants and animals over millions of years are carbon-based. Since the rate of formation of these carbon-based fuels is much lower than the rate of consumption, fossil fuels are included in the class of non-renewable energy sources. Although various energy crises and environmental reasons question

S. Yüksel (✉) · Ç. Çağlayan
The School of Business, Istanbul Medipol University, Istanbul, Turkey
e-mail: serhatyuksel@medipol.edu.tr; cagatay.caglayan@std.medipol.edu.tr

A. Mikhaylov
Financial University under the Government of the Russian Federation, Moscow, Russia

H. Dincer, S. Yüksel (eds.), *Economic Development and the Environmental Ecosystem*, Contributions to Economics,
https://doi.org/10.1007/978-3-031-26596-9_3

the dominance of fossil fuels over energy production, fossil fuels remain important because they are cheap and easily accessible. However, the environmental damage caused by carbon-based fuels shows that carbon emissions should be reduced in the long run. In this context, it is necessary to reduce the use of fossil fuels (Sheng & Guo, 2016). One of the environmental damage caused by fossil fuels is air pollution. Air pollution not only reduces people's quality of life, but also brings health problems in the long run. Therefore, it creates fragility in the economy by increasing health expenditures (Yuksel et al., 2022a, 2022b). Besides, high carbon emission is one of the main causes of global warming and directly or indirectly causes climate change. Under these circumstances, renewable energy sources have become an important alternative to fossil fuels. Because renewable energy sources do not create carbon-based pollution to the environment during the energy production process, so they have a reducing effect on carbon emissions (Dinçer et al., 2021). Although they are quite environmentally friendly and have high potential energy types, renewable energies also have disadvantages (Dincer et al., 2023). The high cost of renewable energy investments and the fact that energy production cannot provide uninterrupted energy due to weather conditions are among the most obvious disadvantages. Considering all these disadvantages, it is clear that the importance of nuclear energy is quite high (Çağlayan et al., 2022).

Uranium, the element with the most protons and neutrons, is enriched and used as fuel in nuclear power plants. The method used to produce energy from uranium is the fission reaction. Neutrons formed as a result of the fission reaction react with uranium atoms and this reaction continues until the neutrons are removed from the environment. The energy produced during the fission reaction is quite high, so it needs to be controlled. The uncontrolled fission reaction creates huge explosions and causes serious losses. Therefore, neutron controllers are used to control the fission reaction. The high-temperature water that emerges from the uranium, which is decomposed in a controlled way, evaporates and turns the turbines connected to the generator and the necessary energy is produced. The biggest environmental advantage of this energy production process is that it does not contain any carbon emissions (Hassan et al., 2022). In addition to this feature, it is an important advantage that the thorium and uranium reserves that can be used as fuel in nuclear power plants are relatively high. In addition, the energy obtained through nuclear power plants is uninterrupted, unlike renewable energies. It is not affected by weather conditions. In this way, since nuclear energy provides efficient energy flow to investor countries, it reduces energy imports of countries, prevents foreign dependency in energy and reduces energy-based current account deficit. The existence of more than one nuclear power plant in many countries and the fact that the world has gained experience in the field of nuclear energy is the most important driving force in the development of nuclear energy (Carayannis et al., 2022; Li et al., 2022a, 2022b; Yükel et al., 2022a, 2022b; Mikhaylov et al., 2022). Despite this, nuclear energy still has not proven itself against society and people have some concerns. Among these concerns, safety, waste management and installation cost are the main factors (Yüksel et al., 2021). Scientific studies and researches instill hope that they will solve problems such as safety concerns about nuclear energy, environmental concerns related to waste management, in the short or long term. Therefore, nuclear energy will continue to be one of the most effective types of energy that can meet the energy needs of countries in the future.

3.2 Generations of Nuclear Reactors

After the nuclear power plant accidents in Chernobyl and Fukushima, the future of nuclear energy and the status of existing reactors were questioned (Kim et al., 2013). There is a need for the development of the nuclear energy field on various issues, especially security problems, for existing power plants and future nuclear power plant investments. Because knowing the pros and cons of nuclear energy will increase the acceptance of nuclear energy by the public and will positively affect the future of nuclear energy (Xie et al., 2020). One of the most important concepts in the development of nuclear energy is sustainability. Because, with the protection of natural resources and the environment, the ability of future generations to easily meet their needs will be preserved. Existing nuclear power plants and newly designed nuclear power plants seem to help sustainability with their carbon zero characteristics (Fiore, 2006). Reducing carbon emissions with electricity generation through nuclear energy will both slow down the rate of increase in global warming and reduce long-term health costs based on air pollution. In this sense, nuclear power plants are known as a very environmentally friendly energy source.

Although the carbon zero feature of nuclear power plants is an important advantage, the radioactive wastes generated by nuclear power plants are one of the biggest obstacles to sustainability by threatening the environment and future generations. Therefore, it is clear that waste management in line with sustainability goals is a weakness for nuclear power plants (Prăvălie & Bandoc, 2018). Despite this, studies are continuing intensively for the development of nuclear technology in terms of increasing the advantages and eliminating the weaknesses of the said power plants. As stated before, the issue of safety is one of the factors that necessitate the development of nuclear energy systems such as waste management. The process of generating electricity from the nuclear power plant, which dates back to the 1940s, has experienced very few nuclear power plant accidents until today. Therefore, the fact that nuclear power plants are operated with intense security measures and that there are very few accidents shows that nuclear energy gives a good test in terms of safety. However, when compared to other energy systems, the danger of nuclear energy causes greater losses. Therefore, although nuclear power plants have performed well in terms of safety, it is clear that there is still a long way to go. Thus, it can be said that the future of nuclear power plants depends on the developments to be followed in the field of safety as well as waste management.

Considering all this, it should be said that the establishment and development of existing and future nuclear power plants is influenced by more than one factor. Factors such as cost factor, security and compatibility with existing electricity grid are some of them. Based on cost effectiveness, the price per kilowatt hour of nuclear energy is expected to be competitive compared to other energy systems such as renewable energy and fossil fuels. Additionally, the safety factor can be said to be one of the most compelling determinants in this context. There are multiple risk factors in terms of safety, such as the explosion risk of the nuclear reactor, the risks posed by radioactive waste, and natural disasters (Basu, 2019). In this context, existing and planned nuclear power plants must meet the expectations in terms of safety. Other important considerations when it comes to the principle of security are non-proliferation and terrorism prevention. It is expected that existing and newly established power plants will be prepared against the risks of nuclear theft and terrorism and will minimize these risks. The suitability of nuclear power plants to the existing grid is another important factor. The capacities of the local or national electricity networks must be able to meet the power of the electricity to be produced by the reactor planned to be established. Therefore, nuclear power plant investments bring with it an additional investment requirement on existing grids. Various designs of nuclear reactors, which are prepared by considering various factors such as cost, safety and network compatibility, are divided into categories as "generations". Gen I, II, III, III+ and IV characterize the basic features of the power plants that have been or will be built and make the differences between the nuclear power plants in question clear.

Gen I

The first reactors established between the 1940s and 1960s, which can be assumed as prototypes, can be given as examples of Gen I nuclear reactors. One of the said power plants is the Magnox reactor. The reactor takes its name from the composition of the rods in which the fuel is located. This compound is known as magnesium non-oxidizing. The Magnox reactor is one of the first commercial nuclear reactor types used in the world. The cooling gas of the Magnox reactor, which belongs to the gas-cooled reactor class, is carbon dioxide. The fuel of the reactor, in which graphite is used as the moderator, is natural uranium coated with Magnox. It is known that the reactor was exported to other countries, although it was mostly built in Great Britain since 1950. Currently, there is no Magnox reactor known to be operating. The last reactor was shut down in 2015.26 Magnox Reactors in the UK have been shut down since 1989. Another example of a Gen I nuclear power plant is the Shippingport Atomic Energy Plant. Shippingport is known as the first commercial centralized power generation station in the United States to use nuclear power. It is stated by various sources that Shippingport is a pressurized water reactor (PWR) in which the reactor core is cooled with high pressure water (Cummins & Matzie, 2018). The activities of the mentioned nuclear power plant were stopped in 1982. Another important Gen I nuclear power plant is the Dresden-1 nuclear power plant. The power plant is the first privately financed nuclear power plant established in the USA. The Dresden-1 became operational in 1960 and was discontinued in 1978. Units 2 and 3 of Dresden have been operational since 1970.

Gen II

Gen II nuclear power plants are one of the design classifications for a nuclear reactor, such as Gen I nuclear power plants, and generally refer to reactors built until the late 1990s. Gen II nuclear power plant is a class of commercial reactor designed to be economical and reliable. Older models of reactor types such as pressurized water reactors (PWR), boiling water reactors (BWR), advanced gas-cooled reactors (AGR) are among Gen II reactors. In addition, the number four reactor that caused the accident in Chernobyl and the three damaged reactors of Fukushima are Gen II reactors. Known examples of Gen II reactors include CANDU. The CANDU reactor is a Canadian pressurized water-powered nuclear reactor. It was designed in the 1960s. CANDU is an acronym formed from the initials of the words CANada Deuterium Uranium. The first CANDU reactor started operation in 1962 as Canada's first nuclear power plant and operated until 1987. These types of reactors are used in Canada, China, Pakistan, India, South Korea and many more countries. In this context, another important reactor type is the water-water energetic reactor, abbreviated as WWER or VVER. This type of reactor is a kind of pressurized water reactor. Although VVER was developed before 1970, it is a type of reactor that has been continuously improved. Thus, it would not be wrong to associate VVERs with multiple types of reactor designs, from Gen I reactors to Gen III+ reactor designs. VVER power plants were used in the former Soviet Union and Russia. In addition, this type of reactor is seen in many countries such as Ukraine, Germany and India. Turkey, on the other hand, is one of the countries that is preparing to put the VVER reactor into operation.

Gen III

Gen III nuclear power plants refer to a class of reactors with improvements in their design to replace Gen II reactors. Therefore, the Gen III reactor is actually a Gen II reactor with state-of-the-art equipment. Advanced safety systems, including passive nuclear safety systems, designs aimed at thermal efficiency and cost reduction are the focus of Gen III reactors. As an example, the first Gen III nuclear power plants installed in 1996 and 1997, Kashiwazaki six and Kashiwazaki seven, were ABWRs with advanced boiling water reactors. Both reactors were shut down as a result of various safety concerns. ABWR turns the turbine connected to the generator and provides power by evaporating the water after the high temperature released as a result of the fission reactions. Although most ABWR construction projects have been cancelled, it is licensed to operate in the US and Japan. Lastly, the AP600 is a type of reactor designed by Westinghouse Electric Company, which is in the Gen III reactor class with its passive safety system features.

Gen III+

Gen III+ reactors can be called the advanced version of the Gen III reactors. In this context, various reactor designs can be mentioned. For example, the Advanced CANDU Reactor, ACR-1000, is an example of such designs. The design was developed by Atomic Energy of Canada Limited (AECL) to be a Gen III+ nuclear reactor. The system combined the features of existing CANDU pressurized heavy water reactors (PHWR) with those of light water-cooled pressurized water reactors (PWR). The ACR-1000 was introduced as a lower-priced option compared to the CANDU 9, a larger version of the base CANDU being designed. The ACR was slightly larger but cheaper to build and operate. Another design is the Economic Simplified Boiling Water Reactor (ESBWR). The system is a passively safe Gen III+ reactor design derived from the Simplified Boiling Water Reactor (SBWR) and the Advanced Boiling Water Reactor (ABWR). The biggest difference between the Gen III+ designs and the designs that can be evaluated under this generation from the Gen II designs is that they have passive safety system designs that do not require active controls or various interventions.

Gen IV

Gen IV nuclear reactors are one of the reactor designs aimed at improved safety, sustainability, efficiency and cost. One of the most advanced Gen IV nuclear reactors is the sodium-cooled fast reactor. The reactor represents a fast neutron reactor cooled by liquid sodium. Various sodium-cooled fast reactors have been built over time, and there are operating reactors in Russia. In addition to Russia, Japan, India, China, France and the USA are among the countries investing in technology. Another important IV. Another important Gen IV technology is the molten salt reactor (Buckthorpe, 2017). The molten salt reactor (MSR) uses molten salt for higher thermodynamic efficiency. The heat efficiency of the reactor, which can operate at high temperatures thanks to molten salt, is quite high compared to today's reactors. Because the molten salt is responsible for both the movement of the fuel in the nuclear reactor and the transfer of heat energy (Marsden et al., 2017). In the next few decades, fourth generation reactors can be expected to start commercial operations and become widespread (Locatelli et al., 2013; Horvath & Rachlew, 2016). The majority of operating reactors today are Gen II reactors, since nearly all Gen I systems have been decommissioned. In addition, several Gen III reactors are in operation today. Gen V reactors, on the other hand, are purely theoretical and not yet feasible.

3.3 An Evaluation for the Critical Issues in Nuclear Energy Technology Investments

Having nuclear energy technologies is vital for countries' energy policies to be sustainable. In this context, countries need to pay attention to some issues to have these technologies (Martínez et al., 2022; Sun et al., 2022; Kafka et al., 2022; Mukhtarov et al., 2022). In this context, the necessary budget should be allocated for research and development studies. Secondly, qualified personnel must also be employed. Thanks to these personnel, it will be possible to operate nuclear power plants with complex processes in a safer way (Dong et al., 2022; Dinçer et al., 2022b, 2022c, 2022a; Zhang et al., 2022; Yüksel & Dinçer, 2022). Third, government incentives are also important for the development of these technologies. Finally, the economic growth of countries is another important issue in this context. In other words, to have up-to-date technologies related to nuclear energy, countries must first be economically developed (Xu et al., 2022; Bhuiyan et al., 2022; Kou et al., 2022). Priority analysis of these four different factors will be made under this heading. In this process, the DEMATEL method will be considered. DEMATEL technique is used to find the most important ones among different criteria (Eti et al., 2023; Li et al., 2022a, 2022b; Haiyun et al., 2021; Yuan et al., 2021). On the other hand, it is possible to determine the causal relationship between the specified criteria with this method (Fang et al., 2021; Kayacık et al., 2022; Eti et al., 2022; Dinçer et al., 2023). The analysis results obtained are presented in Table 3.1.

It is determined that economic development is the key factor for the purpose of improving nuclear energy technologies. Research and development studies also have a significant role in this respect. Qualified personnel and government incentives are in the last ranks.

3.4 Conclusion

Nuclear energy is very important for the sustainability of energy policies of countries. In this context, countries focus on nuclear energy investments. On the other hand, some countries are worried about nuclear energy due to risks such as radioactive waste and explosion. In this context, it is possible to minimize these problems thanks to new generation nuclear energy technologies. In this study, it is aimed to determine the priority issues for the development of nuclear energy technologies. To

Table 3.1 Weighting Results

Criteria	Weights
Research and Development studies	0.2412
Qualified personnel	0.2117
Government incentives	0.2386
Economic development	0.3085

achieve this aim, an analysis was carried out with the DEMATEL method. It is determined that economic development is the key factor for the purpose of improving nuclear energy technologies. Research and development studies also have a significant role in this respect. Qualified personnel and government incentives are in the last ranks.

It is obvious that the establishment and development of existing and future nuclear power plants is influenced by more than one factor. Factors such as cost factor, security and compatibility with existing electricity grid are some of them. Based on cost effectiveness, the price per kilowatt hour of nuclear energy is expected to be competitive compared to other energy systems such as renewable energy and fossil fuels. Additionally, the safety factor can be said to be one of the most compelling determinants in this context. There are multiple risk factors in terms of safety, such as the explosion risk of the nuclear reactor, the risks posed by radioactive waste, and natural disasters.

The results obtained from this study show us that for the development of nuclear energy technologies, countries must first grow their economies. In other words, countries with underdeveloped economies will not be able to find the necessary budget for nuclear energy technologies. In this case, the necessary research and development studies for these current technologies will not be able to be carried out. This will create an important barrier to the development of nuclear energy technologies. On the other hand, there will be a problem of qualified personnel in countries whose economy is not developed enough. Therefore, stabilizing the economies of the countries is very necessary for the development of nuclear energy technologies. In this context, it is important for countries to implement policies that will develop their economies first.

References

Basu, P. C. (2019). Site evaluation for nuclear power plants–the practices. *Nuclear Engineering and Design, 352*, 110140.

Bhuiyan, M. A., Dinçer, H., Yüksel, S., Mikhaylov, A., Danish, M. S. S., Pinter, G., et al. (2022). Economic indicators and bioenergy supply in developed economies: QROF-DEMATEL and random forest models. *Energy Reports, 8*, 561–570.

Buckthorpe, D. (2017). Introduction to generation IV nuclear reactors. In *Structural materials for generation IV nuclear reactors* (pp. 1–22). Woodhead Publishing.

Çağlayan, Ç., Kararoğlu, D., & Yavuz, D. (2022). Determining the right location for Turkey's nuclear energy investment projects based on zero-carbon emission purposes. In *Clean energy investments for zero emission projects* (pp. 77–88). Springer.

Carayannis, E., Kostis, P., Dinçer, H., & Yüksel, S. (2022). Balanced-scorecard-based evaluation of knowledge-oriented competencies of distributed energy investments. *Energies, 15*(21), 8245.

Cummins, W. E., & Matzie, R. (2018). Design evolution of PWRs: Shippingport to generation III+. *Progress in Nuclear Energy, 102*, 9–37.

Dinçer, H., Aksoy, T., Yüksel, S., & Hacioglu, U. (2022b). Golden cut-oriented q-rung orthopair fuzzy decision-making approach to evaluation of renewable energy alternatives for microgeneration system investments. *Mathematical Problems in Engineering*.

Dinçer, H., Lisin, A., Ubay, G. G., & Çağlayan, Ç. (2021). Identifying the best financing sources for renewable energy companies in Latin American countries. In *Strategic approaches to energy management* (pp. 1–12). Springer.

Dinçer, H., Yüksel, S., Çağlayan, Ç., Yavuz, D., & Kararoğlu, D. (2023). Can renewable energy investments be a solution to the energy-sourced high inflation problem?. In *Managing inflation and supply chain disruptions in the global economy* (pp. 220–238). IGI Global.

Dinçer, H., Yüksel, S., & Martínez, L. (2022c). Collaboration enhanced hybrid fuzzy decision-making approach to analyze the renewable energy investment projects. *Energy Reports, 8*, 377–389.

Dinçer, H., Yüksel, S., Mikhaylov, A., Pinter, G., & Shaikh, Z. A. (2022a). Analysis of renewable-friendly smart grid technologies for the distributed energy investment projects using a hybrid picture fuzzy rough decision-making approach. *Energy Reports, 8*, 11466–11477.

Dong, W., Zhao, G., Yüksel, S., Dinçer, H., & Ubay, G. G. (2022). A novel hybrid decision making approach for the strategic selection of wind energy projects. *Renewable Energy, 185*, 321–337.

Eti, S., Dinçer, H., Gökalp, Y., Yüksel, S., & Kararoğlu, D. (2023). Identifying key issues to handle the inflation problem in the healthcare industry caused by energy prices: An evaluation with decision-making models. *Managing Inflation and Supply Chain Disruptions in the Global Economy*, 162–178.

Eti, S., Dinçer, H., Yüksel, S., & Gökalp, Y. (2022). Analysis of the suitability of the solar panels for hospitals: A new fuzzy decision-making model proposal with the T-spherical TOP-DEMATEL method. *Journal of Intelligent & Fuzzy Systems (Preprint)*, 1–13.

Fang, S., Zhou, P., Dinçer, H., & Yüksel, S. (2021). Assessment of safety management system on energy investment risk using house of quality based on hybrid stochastic interval-valued intuitionistic fuzzy decision-making approach. *Safety Science, 141*, 105333.

Fiore, K. (2006). Nuclear energy and sustainability: Understanding ITER. *Energy Policy, 34*(17), 3334–3341.

Haiyun, C., Zhixiong, H., Yüksel, S., & Dinçer, H. (2021). Analysis of the innovation strategies for green supply chain management in the energy industry using the QFD-based hybrid interval valued intuitionistic fuzzy decision approach. *Renewable and Sustainable Energy Reviews, 143*, 110844.

Hassan, S. T., Khan, D., Zhu, B., & Batool, B. (2022). Is public service transportation increase environmental contamination in China? The role of nuclear energy consumption and technological change. *Energy, 238*, 121890.

Horvath, A., & Rachlew, E. (2016). Nuclear power in the 21st century: Challenges and possibilities. *Ambio, 45*(1), 38–49.

Kafka, K. I., Dinçer, H., & Yüksel, S. (2022). Impact-relation map of innovative service development regarding the sustainable growth for emerging markets. *Journal of the Knowledge Economy*, 1–24.

Kayacık, M., Dinçer, H., & Yüksel, S. (2022). Using quantum spherical fuzzy decision support system as a novel sustainability index approach for analyzing industries listed in the stock exchange. *Borsa Istanbul Review, 22*(6), 1145–1157.

Kim, E., & Barles, S. (2012). The energy consumption of Paris and its supply areas from the eighteenth century to the present. *Regional Environmental Change, 12*(2), 295–310.

Kim, Y., Kim, M., & Kim, W. (2013). Effect of the Fukushima nuclear disaster on global public acceptance of nuclear energy. *Energy Policy, 61*, 822–828.

Kou, G., Yüksel, S., & Dinçer, H. (2022). Inventive problem-solving map of innovative carbon emission strategies for solar energy-based transportation investment projects. *Applied Energy, 311*, 118680.

Li, W., Yüksel, S., & Dinçer, H. (2022b). Understanding the financial innovation priorities for renewable energy investors via QFD-based picture fuzzy and rough numbers. *Financial Innovation, 8*(1), 1–30.

Li, J., Yüksel, S., Dınçer, H., Mikhaylov, A., & Barykin, S. E. (2022a). Bipolar q-ROF hybrid decision making model with golden cut for analyzing the levelized cost of renewable energy alternatives. *IEEE Access, 10*, 42507–42517.

Locatelli, G., Mancini, M., & Todeschini, N. (2013). Generation IV nuclear reactors: Current status and future prospects. *Energy Policy, 61*, 1503–1520.

Marsden, B. J., Jones, A. N., Hall, G. N., Treifi, M., & Mummery, P. M. (2017). Graphite as a core material for generation IV nuclear reactors. In *Structural materials for generation IV nuclear reactors* (pp. 495–532). Woodhead Publishing.

Martínez, L., Dinçer, H., & Yüksel, S. (2022). A hybrid decision making approach for new service development process of renewable energy investment. *Applied Soft Computing, 133*, 109897.

Mikhaylov, A., Bhatti, I. M., Dinçer, H., & Yüksel, S. (2022). Integrated decision recommendation system using iteration-enhanced collaborative filtering, golden cut bipolar for analyzing the risk-based oil market spillovers. *Computational Economics*, 1–34.

Mukhtarov, S., Yüksel, S., & Dinçer, H. (2022). The impact of financial development on renewable energy consumption: Evidence from Turkey. *Renewable Energy, 187*, 169–176.

Prăvălie, R., & Bandoc, G. (2018). Nuclear energy: Between global electricity demand, worldwide decarbonisation imperativeness, and planetary environmental implications. *Journal of Environmental Management, 209*, 81–92.

Sheng, P., & Guo, X. (2016). The long-run and short-run impacts of urbanization on carbon dioxide emissions. *Economic Modelling, 53*, 208–215.

Sun, L., Peng, J., Dinçer, H., & Yüksel, S. (2022). Coalition-oriented strategic selection of renewable energy system alternatives using q-ROF DEMATEL with golden cut. *Energy, 256*, 124606.

Ulutaş, B. H. (2005). Determination of the appropriate energy policy for Turkey. *Energy, 30*(7), 1146–1161.

Xie, Y., Peng, Y., Yüksel, S., Dınçer, H., Uluer, G. S., Çağlayan, Ç., & Li, Y. (2020). Consensus-based public acceptance and mapping of nuclear energy investments using spherical and pythagorean fuzzy group decision making approaches. *IEEE Access, 8*, 206248–206263.

Xu, X., Yüksel, S., & Dinçer, H. (2022). An integrated decision-making approach with Golden cut and bipolar q-ROFSs to renewable energy storage investments. *International Journal of Fuzzy Systems*, 1–14.

Yuan, G., Xie, F., Dinçer, H., & Yüksel, S. (2021). The theory of inventive problem solving (TRIZ)-based strategic mapping of green nuclear energy investments with spherical fuzzy group decision-making approach. *International Journal of Energy Research, 45*(8), 12284–12300.

Yüksel, S., & Dinçer, H. (2022). Identifying the strategic priorities of nuclear energy investments using hesitant 2-tuple interval-valued Pythagorean fuzzy DEMATEL. *Progress in Nuclear Energy, 145*, 104103.

Yüksel, S., Dinçer, H., Çağlayan, Ç., & Uluer, G. S. (2021). Determining the optimal financial strategies for nuclear energy companies. In *Financial strategies in competitive markets* (pp. 1–16). Springer.

Yüksel, S., Dinçer, H., Çağlayan, Ç., Uluer, G. S., & Lisin, A. (2022a). Bitcoin mining with nuclear energy. In *Multidimensional strategic outlook on global competitive energy economics and finance*. Emerald Publishing Limited.

Yüksel, S., Dinçer, H., Eti, S., & Adalı, Z. (2022b). Strategy improvements to minimize the drawbacks of geothermal investments by using spherical fuzzy modelling. *International Journal of Energy Research., 46*, 10796–10807.

Zhang, Y., Zhang, Y., Gong, C., Dinçer, H., & Yüksel, S. (2022). An integrated hesitant 2-tuple Pythagorean fuzzy analysis of QFD-based innovation cost and duration for renewable energy projects. *Energy, 248*, 123561.

Chapter 4
Framing Effects on Renewable Energy News

Merve Yazici and Duygu Güner Gültekin

Keywords Energy news · Renewable energy · Framing effects · Energy economics · Sustainable energy

4.1 Introduction

In times when worries regarding climate change, scarcity of energy supplies, and the security and cost of energy are getting more critical on both national and global levels, the way the media frames the pros and cons of all energy sources poses greater conspicuity (Delshad & Raymond, 2013). The different presentations of the same reality can reveal some desired aspects while concealing the undesired facets to shape public opinion. Hence, framing effects were heavily employed in both conventional and contemporary media. Different scholars defined the framing in various concepts; however, the main idea prevails. Frames are the different presentations which cause agents to deduce diverse contexts of the same phenomenon. Entman (1993) summarises framing as making a selected piece of information more noticeable to the audience with the help of selection and salience. The famous Asian disease experiment was the most widely cited example of the power of framing and how it operates (Entman, 1993; Kahneman & Tversky, 1984; Tversky & Kahneman, 1981). This experiment exposed that decisions and preferences can shift drastically per the representations of the same truth. This simple notion brings forward the potential power of framing in shaping or changing public opinion.

As one of the most debated topics, renewable energy caused accelerated studies on its public acceptance and general public knowledge (Haber et al., 2021). The

M. Yazici (✉)
The School of Communication, Istanbul Medipol University, Istanbul, Turkey
e-mail: myazici@medipol.edu.tr

D. G. Gültekin
The School of Business, Istanbul Medipol University, Istanbul, Turkey
e-mail: dgultekin@medipol.edu.tr

H. Dincer, S. Yüksel (eds.), *Economic Development and the Environmental Ecosystem*, Contributions to Economics,
https://doi.org/10.1007/978-3-031-26596-9_4

media is an intermediary in informing the public about the energy sector, as in all other sectors. Moreover, the representations employed by the media have influenced public opinion on policies (Dehler-Holland et al., 2021). Hence frames are embedded in all types and sources of media. As Wolsink (2020) underlined, framing is fundamental to political processes, including decision-making on renewables since the research regarding the social acceptance of energy innovation illustrated that energy is one of the most political domains ever (Martínez et al., 2022; Sun et al., 2022; Kafka et al., 2022; Mukhtarov et al., 2022). For example, with the effect of both national and international energy agencies, internet resources and global energy organisations' efforts to inform and promote individuals, solar energy, which very few people knew and benefited from until a decade ago, has become an important alternative energy source used by a significant part of the society (Özkul et al., 2010).

4.2 Frames and Framing Effects

The rational choice theory dictates that the choices should not be altered in response to different frames of the same stimuli. However, Kahneman and Tversky (1984); Tversky and Kahneman (1981) stated that people's preferences deviate from the rational course of action when the decision problems are formulated differently. Since then, framing effects have yielded many fruits in various disciplines. The framing effects cause the violation of the assumption of well-ordered preferences, hence depicting a departure from the rational choice theory (LeBoeuf & Shafir, 2003). As Tversky and Kahneman (1981) put it, the decision frames are the decision-makers' conceptions and the contingencies of the outcomes associated with particular decisions. Kühberger (1995) defined framing as the decision situations in that different presentations caused agents to deduce different contexts of the same phenomenon. Wolsink (2020) classified frames as biased problem definitions and mental shortcuts created to affect decision-making processes.

So, whenever the alternative depiction of the same reality is given, the predictability of the shifted decisions leads to the studies of framing effects (LeBoeuf & Shafir, 2003). Since the publication of Kahneman and Tversky's seminal paper, dozens of studies have documented framing effects. The framing effects have been applied widely in psychology, political science, decision-making rubrics, and communications studies (Nelson et al., 1997). Studies on manipulating decisions by employing framing effects are vast in medicine, voting, gambling, shaping public opinion, consumer judgment, and persuasion (LeBoeuf & Shafir, 2003).

Frames function to define problems, diagnose potential causes, assert moral judgments, and offer remedies (Entman, 1993). Tversky and Kahneman (1981) argue that formulating the concepts, agents' norms, habits, and personal characteristics have created the frames. According to Entman (1993), framing encompasses selection and salience so that some selected piece of information becomes more noticeable and memorable and makes more sense to the audience. For mass communication, literature identified framing as constructing and defining a social or political issue for its targeted audience by a communication source (Nelson et al., 1997). Framing is about selecting specific aspects of any reality and making them more salient to promote a particular idea, definition, interpretation, evaluation, or recommendation (Entman, 1993). Leeper and Slothuus (2020) also agree with Entman (1993) and define framing as selectively presenting and interpreting issues and events.

Kahneman and Tversky offered the most widely cited example of the power of framing and the way it operates (Entman, 1993; Kahneman & Tversky, 1984; Tversky & Kahneman, 1981). The case is well known as the Asian disease experiment. According to the scenario, an Asian disease was expected to kill 600 people, and two different programs were proposed to combat it. The authors asked the participants the same question: select the best-fitting program to fight the disease. However, there was a manipulation, so the proposed program details were framed differently (positive/negative) for the two experimental groups. In the positive framing, subjects were informed that if program A were to be adopted, 200 hundred people would be saved. Whereas if program B was to be implemented, there is a 1/3 probability that 600 people would be saved and a 2/3 probability that no one would be saved. In the negative frame setting, subjects were informed that if program C were to be adopted, 400 hundred people would die. Whereas if program D was to be implemented, there is a 1/3 probability that nobody would die and a 2/3 probability that 600 people would die. Programs A–C and B–D were identical regarding consequences, with different frames. In programs A and B, the outcomes were described by the saved lives, while in C and D, the description was done by the lost lives. In the first setting, 72% of the subjects chose program A, while the twin option, program C, was elected only by 22% of the participants (LeBoeuf & Shafir, 2003; Entman, 1993; Kahneman & Tversky, 1984; Tversky & Kahneman, 1981). Even though the positive and negative frames suggested equivalent contingencies, the choices differed dramatically (LeBoeuf & Shafir, 2003). This simple example is a strong demonstration of the effects of framing on the cognition, reminiscence, evaluation, action, and choice of people. LeBoeuf and Shafir (2003) replicated Kahneman and Tversky's (1984) experiments with additional manipulations; they asked participants their intentions regarding the Asian disease scenario and others concerning health, monetary and voting preferences. Despite asking subjects to propose a justification for their decisions for each problem, the framing effect was found to be robust and statistically reliable (LeBoeuf & Shafir, 2003). So, the authors concluded that effortful thinking was not a remedy for framing effects. Controversially Kühberger (1995) replicated the Asian disease experiment with more explicitly described program options. For example, program A was described in more detail: 200 hundred people will be saved, and 400 hundred people will not be saved. However, he still reported prevailing framing effects with more moderate levels. Since plenty of studies presented robust framing effects, they became a danger for all decision-makers in different contexts. Simply because even when aware of multiple frames, people are prone to be pulled back and forth between the alternate depictions of the same decision problem (Kahneman & Tversky, 1984).

Hence, it became well-known that frames are subjective interpretations or emphases of objective reality (Carter, 2013). In different settings, frames serve the exact purpose; prime and emphasise specific elements to construct an argument and provide causation, evaluation, and solution (Entman, 1993). The power of frames comes from how they help the processor select and highlight some aspects of reality while omitting others. Carter (2013) agrees with Entman and states that frames make some aspects of stories more salient and influence individual and public opinion. On the other hand, Tversky and Kahneman (1981) argue that the frames are created by the formulation of the concepts and the agents' norms, habits, and personal characteristics. Carter (2013) describes frames as the socially shared organising principles which structure the social world. In the political communications field, framing was identified as defining a specific problem by underlying some particular social or political issues while outlining other (relevant) issues (Nelson et al., 1997). Then again, Leeper and Slothuus (2020) described the phenomenon as selecting some aspects of reality and making them more salient to promote a particular stance on any matter. According to Delshad and Raymond (2013), framing acts to influence public opinion by emphasising specific aspects of an issue. This process has been mainly carried out by news stories in newspapers or on TV Gamson and Modigliani (1989) claimed that formal production patterns, including media packages, are chosen by reporters or columnists according to political and cultural implications and prejudices. Despite the variation in definitions, the scholars generally agree on the general principles of framing to boost a selected facet of the issues.

Entman (1993) primarily draws attention to a good understanding of the framing concept since it probes the attention to the details of how communication tools (such as news, texts, surveys, and speeches) utilise the power of framing. Kahneman and Tversky (1984) also hints that human reasoning (especially system I) is unsuitable for uniting differently framed pieces of information into abstract forms. Hence it is almost impossible to avoid the traps of framing while making decisions. Carter (2013) emphasizes the role of frames as constructive tools because they can blur the objective reality and influence public opinion.

4.3 Framing Effects in Mass Communication on Renewable Energy

The media is an intermediary in informing the public about the energy sector, as in all other sectors. In addition, media reports are essential in policymaking, interrelating politicians and the public (Dehler-Holland et al., 2021). Also, frames are embedded in all media types, like print or broadcast. Moreover, they convey meaning through the interaction between the audience and the message. Therefore, framing studies concern how meanings are transmitted across media because media reconstructs the social world by stating it in various ways (Carter, 2013). This reconstruction can be done by distorting the meaning of events by avoiding the historical context, phrasing the reality differently, and placing the news in a specified paper column.

Furthermore, frames are critical determinants of public opinion since communication sources such as the news media frequently reckon on framing to structure the representations of information (Nelson et al., 1997). Delshad and Raymond (2013) suggested that since media is the primary source of information, it has a significant potential impact on public attitudes regarding political issues. Recent cases reported by Rochyadi-Reetz et al. (2019) also support the hypothesis that media can profoundly influence citizens' thinking and opinions towards social and political issues. Hence, framing becomes a valuable tool for potential persuaders to influence public or individual opinion and political behaviour. Bayulgen and Benegal (2019) also found that in the US, framing renewable energy policies in terms of costs has more influenced the attitudes than framing it in terms of economic benefits (Dong et al., 2022; Dinçer et al., 2022a, 2022b, 2022c; Zhang et al., 2022; Yüksel & Dinçer, 2022; Carayannis et al., 2022). However, positive frames in which renewable energy is linked to job creation and economic development seemed less effective. The researchers related this asymmetrical framing effect to the individual evaluation of the direct financial costs to themselves as more important than societal, economic benefits.

With the rise of the concerns aroused by climate change and global warming, many developed countries intensified their policies regarding green and renewable energy supplies (Li et al., 2022a, 2022b; Yüksel et al., 2022; Mikhaylov et al., 2022; Eti et al., 2023). The legislative and scientific efforts and media framing have focused on promoting green energy sources. These escalated and contested renewable energy policies also increased the importance of public stance in matters. Hence recently, most of the research on the media coverage of renewable energy heavily depends on framing the concept in favour of some specific perspective (Rochyadi-Reetz et al., 2019).

Previous research has established that the dominant frames in media on renewable energy bear traces of two main factors; national context and recent events (Rochyadi-Reetz et al., 2019; Djerf-Pierre et al., 2016). The national context is the structural condition of the country, including actual and historical matters such as the structure of the energy system, institutional settings, environmental politics, national ideologies, elite opinions, and societal stance. Whereas recently faced events such as natural disasters, wars, political unrest, and climate change consequences, nuclear accidents may serve as paradigm shifters for energy framings.

The existing literature suggests that national structural conditions have a considerable impact on the framing context of the issue; for instance, in the oil-extracting states of the USA, regional media proposed more opposition to biofuels. At the same time, Australian and Swedish newspapers were more concerned with natural energy resources like solar and wind power (Rochyadi-Reetz et al., 2019). Wright and Reid (2010) stated three media frames in the US press: economic development, environment, and national security. The authors claimed that using these three frames, the US media claim-makers try to link the benefits of green energy to the citizens' long-standing concerns. Rochyadi-Reetz et al. (2019) added one more aspect—economic, technological, environmental, and societal—in existing US media concerning renewable energy news. Finally, Zukas (2015) analysed the online news sources in the US and claimed that stories had common frames for governmental, environmental, and societal issues.

Delshad and Raymond (2013) analysed 600 articles from US newspapers from 1999 to 2008. Likewise, they classified the news's general frames into seven categories: national security, environmental costs/benefits, unfair/fair, and economic costs/benefits. This framing resulted in a relatively negative public opinion on the issue in a national survey conducted in 2010. These findings fortified the potency of the framing effect employed by media in shaping public attitudes. Likewise, Djerf-Pierre et al. (2016) identified the common frames in articles in two major newspapers in Australia and Sweden between 2010 and 2011. The typical framing categories they classified were economic, environmental, science and technological, political, and civil society. The authors deduced that the frames combined the limited growth worries with economic and technological progress in Sweden, hence remaining vague.

Johansen et al. (2020) investigated 309 news articles and tried to explain the objectification of energy efficiency and its connections in Norwegian media. According to their findings, the positive overtones surrounded the energy efficiency phenomenon and were used flexibly to include different meanings and effects. Furthermore, the authors stated that energy efficiency provided interpretive flexibility and linked incommensurable perspectives on the need to influence energy consumption. Finally, Lyytimäki (2018) studied the long-term coverage of biogas in two Finnish national newspapers. He claimed that the newspaper debates illustrate overly optimistic impressions of the current significance of biogas, and locally focused framings underestimate the future transformative potential of biogas. These finds are in support of the European concerns for environmental issues.

On the contrary, in Austria, frames seemed to be shaped by the conflicting forces of climate controversy, denialism, and the coal lobby. On the other hand, Delshad and Raymond (2013) documented an increase in the negative frames regarding biofuels in the USA, emphasising the potential adverse economic effects, especially between 2004–2008. The media's framing of green energy sources in the US tends to reflect the recent social and economic changes (Wright & Reid, 2010). Those findings supported the hypothesis that the dominant frames of the news were contingent on the ongoing discussions of renewable energy in those countries.

Dehler-Holland et al. (2021) collected approximately 6500 articles from five national newspapers in Germany between 2000–2017 to understand the changes in media framing of a renewable energy support act, the German Renewable Energy Act. The authors discovered that this shift occurred in 2011. Their findings indicated that media coverage has shifted from positive accounts of renewable energy toward the costs that the new act imposes on society. Stauffacher et al. (2015) analysed how different actors framed deep geothermal energy in Swiss media and discovered that the industry predominantly uses an energy transition frame while scientists emphasise a risk frame. Furthermore, the researchers underlined that the Swiss media frames were similar to German media frames but with less emphasis on morality, ethics, and public accountability concerns. Finally, Mercado-Sáez et al. (2019) reviewed the Spanish newspapers from 2008 to 2012 and exposed that the environmental problems were less apparent while eco-efficiency was highlighted. In addition, they discovered that the Spanish press emphasised the views of interest groups and politicians rather than those of scientists and other experts, ecologists, or citizens.

Pan et al. (2019) examined the media coverage of COP21 from the US, the UK and China on the climate negotiations, reporting COP21 and declaring differing frames for countries. For instance, the Chinese mainly underlined that China contributed to the success of COP21 and played a proactive role in climate control. Furthermore, the researchers discovered that British and American news media shared more similarities; they both implied that COP21 was to present a rules-based order to solve climate problems.

Ersoy and İşeri (2021) examined three mainstream and one online media outlet to identify Turkey's nuclear program frames between 2011 and 2019. Their findings showed that one of the mainstream national newspaper's coverages remained pro-nuclear even after the Fukushima disaster despite the intense hostile coverage elsewhere, highlighting potential social progress and economic competitiveness. Contrarily one of the opponent newspapers kept an anti-nuclear stance emphasising the environmental risks and the debatable public accountability of the current government. On the other hand, Becerikli et al. (2017) tried to reveal how energy efficiency is handled in Turkish media's news and advertisement content. It is discovered that, instead of making more macro and social determinations about the energy problem, the media focuses on more micro frameworks. For example, it focuses on energy efficiency in homes and ignores national and international energy policy discussions. Media texts in Turkey seemed unable to expand their dimension and constantly repeated the narrative cycle of advising energy saving in houses, buildings or individually. The researchers stated that there is a need for diversification and democratisation of expert opinion (NGO representative, scientist, researcher, etc.) on the news to reach diversified views.

Another significant aspect of framing context has been affected by recent occurrences such as war, political disturbance, and natural disasters. For instance, after the catastrophes like Chornobyl, nuclear energy plants were framed as dangerous. Afterwards, they were reframed as the technological solution to climate change because of the intensified concerns about global warming (Rochyadi-Reetz et al., 2019). Then again, after the 9/11 attacks, biofuels were elevated to alleviate USA's reliance on Middle Eastern oil (Delshad & Raymond, 2013). Rochyadi-Reetz et al. (2019) studied the framing of renewable energy before and after the Fukushima incident in two daily newspapers of Australia, New Zealand, the USA, Canada, Ireland, Great Britain, Austria, Germany, South Africa, Indonesia, and India. They found that in all 11 countries, the positive frames which emphasise the economic, social, environmental, and technological benefits dominated the articles. However, a controversial finding is that after the Fukushima incident, the technical and financial benefits frames increased in countries, which authors relate to the activities of lobbyists and other powerful interest groups.

Additionally, Park et al. (2016)'s results claim differences in coverage of energy issues in the US and German press post-Fukushima incident. The US portrayed the Fukushima incident as a natural disaster and partly blamed the Japanese government for the lack of regulations. Conversely, the German press was more focused on discussing non-nuclear energy sources.

Gamson and Modigliani (1989) investigated the relationship between the media discourse and public opinion regarding nuclear energy by analysing the four media sources in the US: TV news, news magazines, editorial cartoons, and syndicated opinion columns. Gamson and Modigliani (1989) draw attention to various frameworks in their studies of nuclear energy's media discourse worldwide. The first and the most dominant framework is the "progress package", in which nuclear power was related to society's commitment to technological and economic development. Hence this package was pro-nuclear; it was cultivated to deal with the accidents like Three Mile Island (TMI) or Chornobyl. This pro-nuclear package reigned the US media during the 50s and 70s; even after the Fermi accident in 1966, were not any critics in Times (Gamson & Modigliani, 1989). Nevertheless, an anti-nuclear discourse has risen with the energy crisis in the 70s. Especially after the TMI incident, the media displayed a somewhat anti-nuclear frame emphasising the non-cost-effectiveness and the lack of public accountability. Authors also claimed that after Chornobyl, the anti-nuclear frames in media have become more pervasive.

In their investigation on Swiss media framing, Stauffacher et al. (2015) reported that after the Basel earthquake in 2006, con arguments outnumbered pro arguments regarding renewable energy technologies. Furthermore, their study explored that Swiss newspapers were prone to be driven by contemporary events such as public votes, seismic events, and catastrophes like the Fukushima accident.

Du and Han (2020) analysed the media frames of nuclear energy between 2000–2016 by assessing the 1790 reports in national and local newspapers in China and enclosed a negative shift in the media's positive stance after the Fukushima incident. According to the researchers, the Chinese press supported nuclear energy until the Fukushima incident. Then, the accident increased the frames, focusing on the risks while decreasing the ones focused on the benefits. They also remarked that the national newspapers openly supported nuclear power while the locals tended to abstain.

Interestingly, natural disasters or catastrophic accidents are not the only frame shifters in media. Mišić and Obydenkova (2022) analysed the Serbian mass media's environmental framing of small hydropower plants (SHPs) by covering 359 articles published by major national online newspapers and news portals between 2000–2020. Their findings disclosed two opposite views, which engaged confronting frames regarding the SHP publicity. The pro arguments accentuated the various advantages, such as new job opportunities, taxes for local municipalities, national energy security, and potential EU membership were dominant during 2000–2014. On the contrary, the opponents stressed the disadvantageous aspects, such as the risks of diminishing water supply and the legality of the current projects, which were dominant between 2015–2020. The authors offered the protests and movements led by local communities and environmental organisations as the source of this drastic framing shift. Bayram (2020) studied the representations of Turkey on social media in the Eastern Mediterranean energy competition and tried to cover energy competition and socially constructed realities. The study aimed to reveal the constructed representations of Turkey on social media, which plays a vital role in the international energy competition with the Eastern Mediterranean region. The tweets made with the Eastern Mediterranean Hashtag (#Eastern Mediterranean) are analysed on Twitter, covering the dates between January first and December 31st, and collected 566 tweets about #EastMediterranean. The findings illustrated three different representations of Turkey in the Eastern Mediterranean energy competition, which depicted Turkey as the owner, the right holder, and the rising power (Bayram, 2020). This study showed that those frames aligned with the country's contemporary economic plans.

4.4 Conclusion

As Tversky and Kahneman (1981) put it, the decision frames are the decision-makers' conceptions and the contingencies of the outcomes associated with particular decisions. Kühberger (1995) defined framing as the decision situations in that different presentations caused agents to deduce different contexts of the same phenomenon. However, with the various definitions scholars offered on framing, the primary purpose of the phenomenon remains the same across all fields: changing opinions, attitudes or behaviours by presenting an alternative depiction of the same reality. Therefore, frames and framing are applied broadly in various disciplines, such as marketing, psychology, sociology, political science, medicine, decision-making rubrics, consumer judgment, and communications studies (LeBoeuf & Shafir, 2003; Nelson et al., 1997). Eventually, framing becomes a valuable tool for potential persuaders to influence public or individual opinion and attitudes and even political behaviour. Hence they are essential for policymakers to shape public opinion on specific issues. Moreover, the people must support any policy to be successfully implemented. So the media and press offer the necessary tools and methods for communicating with the masses.

The US press seems mainly concerned with national security, economic development and environmental costs (Delshad & Raymond, 2013; Rochyadi-Reetz et al., 2019; Wright & Reid, 2010; Zukas, 2015). On the other hand, European media pointed out the long-term achievements of societal benefits and energy efficiency (Dehler-Holland et al., 2021; Djerf-Pierre et al., 2016; Johansen et al., 2020; Lyytimäki, 2018; Mercado-Sáez et al., 2019; Stauffacher et al., 2015). The optimistic view is another typical frame in European media regarding renewable energy. Then, the Chinese press seems to approach the issue from an international contribution view, focusing on promoting the Chinese contribution to the solutions to the climate crisis (Pan et al., 2019).

Apart from the current political or economic agenda, natural disasters, nuclear accidents, political unrest or wars drastically influence the presentations of renewable energy in media. For example, in the USA, issues such as Three Mile Island Accident (1979), Chornobyl (1986), and the Fukushima incident (2011) had limited influence on the way the press framed renewable energies. However, the global energy crisis (the 70s) and the 9/11 attacks had immediate shifts in framing (Delshad & Raymond, 2013). On the other hand, countries Australia, New Zealand, Canada, Ireland, the UK, Austria, Germany, South Africa, Indonesia, and India promoted nuclear energy's potential economic and technological benefits even more after the Fukushima event (Rochyadi-Reetz et al., 2019). Contrarily in China Fukushima accident had a reversal effect; it increased the frames, focusing on the risks while decreasing the ones focused on the benefits (Du & Han, 2020).

In sum, the literature on energy and media revealed the deficiencies, mistakes and orientations of news and reporting practices by indicating the dominant stance. Furthermore, the findings proved that the communication tools employed by national presses are framed to serve a pre-determined cause regarding renewable energy technologies and sources (Li et al., 2022a, 2022b; Haiyun et al., 2021; Yuan et al., 2021; Fang et al., 2021).

References

Bayram, P. (2020). Doğu Akdeniz Enerji Rekabetinde Türkiye Temsilleri: Sosyal Medya Üzerinden Bir Analiz. In S. Özer (Ed.), *Doğu Akdeniz; Jeopolitik ve Ekonomik Dinamiklerin Dünü ve Bugünü*. Paradigma.

Bayulgen, O., & Benegal, S. (2019). Green priorities: How economic frames affect perceptions of renewable energy in the United States. *Energy Research & Social Science, 47*, 28–36. https://doi.org/10.1016/j.erss.2018.08.017

Becerikli, S., Altun, A., & Yüksel Özmen, Ş. (2017). Medya ve Enerji: Medyada Enerji Verimliliğini İçeren Metinlerin Analizi. *İletişim Kuram ve Araştırma Dergisi, 44*, 193–214.

Carayannis, E., Kostis, P., Dinçer, H., & Yüksel, S. (2022). Balanced-scorecard-based evaluation of knowledge-oriented competencies of distributed energy investments. *Energies, 15*(21), 8245.

Carter, M. J. (2013). The hermeneutics of frames and framing: An examination of the media's construction of reality. *SAGE Open, 3*(2), 1–12. https://doi.org/10.1177/2158244013487915

Dehler-Holland, J., Schumacher, K., & Fichtner, W. (2021). Topic modeling uncovers shifts in media framing of the German renewable energy act. *Patterns, 2*(1), 1–14. https://doi.org/10.1016/j.patter.2020.100169

Delshad, A., & Raymond, L. (2013). Media framing and public attitudes toward biofuels. *Review of Policy Research, 30*(2), 190–210. https://doi.org/10.1111/ropr.12009

Dinçer, H., Aksoy, T., Yüksel, S., & Hacioglu, U. (2022b). Golden cut-oriented q-rung orthopair fuzzy decision-making approach to evaluation of renewable energy alternatives for microgeneration system investments. *Mathematical Problems in Engineering*.

Dinçer, H., Yüksel, S., & Martínez, L. (2022c). Collaboration enhanced hybrid fuzzy decision-making approach to analyze the renewable energy investment projects. *Energy Reports, 8*, 377–389.

Dinçer, H., Yüksel, S., Mikhaylov, A., Pinter, G., & Shaikh, Z. A. (2022a). Analysis of renewable-friendly smart grid technologies for the distributed energy investment projects using a hybrid picture fuzzy rough decision-making approach. *Energy Reports, 8*, 11466–11477.

Djerf-Pierre, M., Cokley, J., & Kuchel, L. J. (2016). Framing renewable energy: A comparative study of newspapers in Australia and Sweden. *Environmental Communication, 10*(5), 634–655. https://doi.org/10.1080/17524032.2015.1056542

Dong, W., Zhao, G., Yüksel, S., Dinçer, H., & Ubay, G. G. (2022). A novel hybrid decision making approach for the strategic selection of wind energy projects. *Renewable Energy, 185*, 321–337.

Du, Q., & Han, Z. (2020). The framing of nuclear energy in Chinese media discourse: A comparison between national and local newspapers. *Journal of Cleaner Production, 245*, 118695. https://doi.org/10.1016/j.jclepro.2019.118695

Entman, R. M. (1993). Framing: Towards clarification of a fractured paradigm. *Journal of Communication, 43*(4), 51–58. https://doi.org/10.1111/j.1460-2466.1993.tb01304.x

Eti, S., Dinçer, H., Gökalp, Y., Yüksel, S., & Kararoğlu, D. (2023). Identifying key issues to handle the inflation problem in the healthcare industry caused by energy prices: An evaluation with decision-making models. *Managing Inflation and Supply Chain Disruptions in the Global Economy*, 162–178.

Fang, S., Zhou, P., Dinçer, H., & Yüksel, S. (2021). Assessment of safety management system on energy investment risk using house of quality based on hybrid stochastic interval-valued intuitionistic fuzzy decision-making approach. *Safety Science, 141*, 105333.

Gamson, W. A., & Modigliani, A. (1989). Media discourse and public opinion on nuclear power: A constructionist approach. *American Journal of Sociology, 95*(1), 1–37. Retrieved from https://www.jstor.org/stable/2780405

Haber, I. E., Toth, M., Hajdu, R., Haber, K., & Pinter, G. (2021). Exploring public opinions on renewable energy by using conventional methods and social media analysis. *Energies, 11*, 1–13. https://doi.org/10.3390/en14113089

Haiyun, C., Zhixiong, H., Yüksel, S., & Dinçer, H. (2021). Analysis of the innovation strategies for green supply chain management in the energy industry using the QFD-based hybrid interval valued intuitionistic fuzzy decision approach. *Renewable and Sustainable Energy Reviews, 143*, 110844.

Johansen, J. P., Røyrvik, J., & Fyhn, H. (2020). Energy efficiency in norwegian news media: A glitch in the discourse-as-usual. *Nordic Journal of Science and Technology Studies, 8*(2), 18–32. https://doi.org/10.5324/njsts.v8i2.3393

Kafka, K. I., Dinçer, H., & Yüksel, S. (2022). Impact-relation map of innovative service development regarding the sustainable growth for emerging markets. *Journal of the Knowledge Economy*, 1–24.

Kahneman, D., & Tversky, A. (1984). Choice, values, and frames. *American Psychologist, 39*, 341–350.

Kühberger, A. (1995). The framing of decisions: A new look at old problems. *Organisational Behavior and Human Decision Processes, 62*(2), 230–240. https://doi.org/10.1006/obhd.1995.1046

LeBoeuf, R. A., & Shafir, E. (2003). Deep thoughts and shallow frames: On the susceptibility to framing effects. *Journal of Behavioral Decision Making, 16*, 77–92. https://doi.org/10.1002/bdm.433

Leeper, T. J., & Slothuus, R. (2020). How the news media persuades: Framing effects and beyond. In B. Grofman, E. Suhay, & A. Trechsel (Eds.), *Oxford handbook of electoral persuasion* (pp. 151–168). Oxford University Press.

Li, W., Yüksel, S., & Dinçer, H. (2022b). Understanding the financial innovation priorities for renewable energy investors via QFD-based picture fuzzy and rough numbers. *Financial Innovation, 8*(1), 1–30.

Li, J., Yüksel, S., Dınçer, H., Mikhaylov, A., & Barykin, S. E. (2022a). Bipolar q-ROF hybrid decision making model with golden cut for analyzing the levelized cost of renewable energy alternatives. *IEEE Access, 10*, 42507–42517.

Lyytimäki, J. (2018). Renewable energy in the news: Environmental, economic, policy and technology discussion of biogas. *Sustainable Production and Consumption, 15*, 65–73. https://doi.org/10.1016/j.spc.2018.04.004

Martínez, L., Dinçer, H., & Yüksel, S. (2022). A hybrid decision making approach for new service development process of renewable energy investment. *Applied Soft Computing, 133*, 109897.

Mercado-Sáez, M. T., Marco-Crespo, E., & Álvarez-Villa, À. (2019). Exploring news frames, sources and editorial lines on newspaper coverage of nuclear energy in Spain. *Environmental Communication, 13*(4), 546–559. https://doi.org/10.1080/17524032.2018.1435558

Mikhaylov, A., Bhatti, I. M., Dinçer, H., & Yüksel, S. (2022). Integrated decision recommendation system using iteration-enhanced collaborative filtering, golden cut bipolar for analyzing the risk-based oil market spillovers. *Computational Economics*, 1–34.

Mišić, M., & Obydenkova, A. (2022). Environmental conflict, renewable energy, or both? Public opinion on small hydropower plants in Serbia. *Post-Communist Economies, 34*(5), 684–713. https://doi.org/10.1080/14631377.2021.1943928

Mukhtarov, S., Yüksel, S., & Dinçer, H. (2022). The impact of financial development on renewable energy consumption: Evidence from Turkey. *Renewable Energy, 187*, 169–176.

Nelson, T. E., Oxley, Z. M., & Clawson, R. A. (1997). Toward a psychology of framing effects. *Political Behavior, 19*(3), 221–246. https://www.jstor.org/stable/586517

Özkul, E., Bilgin, Y., & Çifçi, S. (2010). Enerji Sektörü Kümelenmelerinde Medyanın Rolü ve Önemi. In H. Eraslan (Ed.), *Sürdürülebilir Rekabet Avantajı Elde Etmede Enerji Sektörü Sektörel Stratejiler ve Uygulamalar* (pp. 1099–1115). URAK.

Pan, Y., Opgenhaffen, M., & Van Gorp, B. (2019). Negotiating climate change: A frame analysis of COP21 in British, American, and Chinese news media. *Public Understanding of Science.* https://doi.org/10.1177/0963662518823969

Park, D. J., Wang, W., & Pinto, J. (2016). Beyond disaster and risk: Post-Fukushima nuclear news in US and German press. *Communication, Culture & Critique, 9*, 417–437. https://doi.org/10.1111/cccr.12119

Rochyadi-Reetz, M., Arlt, D., Wolling, J., & Bräuer, M. (2019). Explaining the Media's framing of renewable energies: An international comparison. *Frontiers in Environmental Science, 7*(119), 1–12. https://doi.org/10.3389/fenvs.2019.00119

Stauffacher, M., Muggli, N., Scolobig, A., & Moser, C. (2015). Framing deep geothermal energy in mass media: The case of Switzerland. *Technological Forecasting and Social Change, 98*, 60–70. https://doi.org/10.1016/j.techfore.2015.05.018

Sun, L., Peng, J., Dinçer, H., & Yüksel, S. (2022). Coalition-oriented strategic selection of renewable energy system alternatives using q-ROF DEMATEL with golden cut. *Energy, 256*, 124606.

Tversky, A., & Kahneman, D. (1981). The framing of decisions and the psychology of choice. *Science, 211*(4481), 453–458.

Wolsink, M. (2020). Framing in renewable energy policies: A glossary. *Energies, 13*(11), 1–32. https://doi.org/10.3390/en13112871

Wright, W., & Reid, T. (2010). Green dreams or pipe dreams?: Media framing of the US biofuels movement. *Biomass and Bioenergy, 35*(4), 1390–1399. https://doi.org/10.1016/j.biombioe.2010.07.020

Yuan, G., Xie, F., Dinçer, H., & Yüksel, S. (2021). The theory of inventive problem solving (TRIZ)-based strategic mapping of green nuclear energy investments with spherical fuzzy group decision-making approach. *International Journal of Energy Research, 45*(8), 12284–12300.

Yüksel, S., & Dinçer, H. (2022). Identifying the strategic priorities of nuclear energy investments using hesitant 2-tuple interval-valued Pythagorean fuzzy DEMATEL. *Progress in Nuclear Energy, 145*, 104103.

Yüksel, S., Dinçer, H., Eti, S., & Adalı, Z. (2022). Strategy improvements to minimize the drawbacks of geothermal investments by using spherical fuzzy modelling. *International Journal of Energy Research, 46*(8), 10796–10807.

Zhang, Y., Zhang, Y., Gong, C., Dinçer, H., & Yüksel, S. (2022). An integrated hesitant 2-tuple Pythagorean fuzzy analysis of QFD-based innovation cost and duration for renewable energy projects. *Energy, 248*, 123561.

Zukas, K. J. (2015). New media, new structures: How digital journalists frame renewable energy stories. *GSTF Journal on Media & Communications (JMC), 2*(2), 1–8. https://doi.org/10.7603/s40874-014-0012-7

Chapter 5
Modern Approaches to Energy Efficiency Management

Yulia Budaeva, David Philippov, and Tsangyao Chang

Keywords Energy technologies · Clean energy · Development · Efficiency · Economic growth

5.1 Introduction

Considering the insufficient pace of modernization of the energy infrastructure of metallurgical enterprises and the acute shortage of their own investment funds, the search for sources of financing for projects outside the organization becomes an urgent issue (Kafka et al., 2022; Martínez et al., 2022; Mukhtarov et al., 2022; Sun et al., 2022). The procedure for such relations between an investor and an enterprise is regulated by the Federal Law on Energy Saving since its entry into force in 2009. Considering the existing demand for borrowed capital for the modernization of the energy sector, a large number of energy service companies, as well as energy management companies, have appeared in the markets of developed and developing countries. The role of these companies is not limited only to investing in energy efficiency projects, but also includes a comprehensive approach to their implementation—from preparing a justification for the need for improvements to implementing the measures and solutions themselves (Dinçer, Aksoy, et al., 2022; Dinçer, Yüksel, & Martínez, 2022; Dinçer, Yüksel, Mikhaylov, Barykin, et al., 2022; Dinçer, Yüksel, Mikhaylov, Pinter, et al., 2022; Dong et al., 2022).

As a result, enterprises can use their own capital in the areas of core production development, development of new products and development of new markets. In

Y. Budaeva (✉)
State University of Management, Moscow, Russia

D. Philippov
Higher School of Finance, Plekhanov Russian University of Economics, Moscow, Russia

T. Chang
Feng Chia University, Taichung City, Taiwan
e-mail: tychang@fcu.edu.tw

H. Dincer, S. Yüksel (eds.), *Economic Development and the Environmental Ecosystem*, Contributions to Economics,
https://doi.org/10.1007/978-3-031-26596-9_5

this regard, both enterprises and investors seek to reduce the amount of funds required for their implementation when developing projects (Carayannis et al., 2022; Li, Yüksel and Dinçer, 2022; Yüksel & Dinçer, 2022; Zhang et al., 2022).

Our macroeconomic analysis emphasized the relevance of the research topic, showing that energy resources are of strategic importance not only at the level of national economies, but also in the management system of an industrial enterprise. The total energy saving potential that can be achieved in the next few years in the world is approaching 40 %. Significant progress can be achieved by attracting private investment, and the State only needs to provide appropriate organizational support and infrastructure construction.

5.2 Literature Review

The development of technologies for the use of alternative energy sources is now becoming one of the most studied topics in the economy of energy consumption due to the aggravation of global environmental problems. Studies show that alternative energy should become an important object of macroeconomic regulation (Eti et al., 2023; Li, Yüksel and Dinçer, 2022; Mikhaylov, Bhatti, et al., 2022; Yüksel et al., 2022): a one-percent increase in consumption of alternative energy sources leads to an overall GDP growth of 0.105 %, and GDP per capita by 0.1% (Alwaelya et al., 2021; An & Mikhaylov, 2020, 2021; Mikhaylov, 2021a; Mikhaylov et al., 2023; Mutalimov et al., 2021; Nie et al., 2020; Varyash et al., 2020; Yumashev et al., 2020; Yumashev & Mikhaylov, 2020; Zhao et al., 2021).

Developing countries that are dominated by industrialization processes are adapting their legislation to introduce alternative sources of energy into the production and infrastructure of urbanized areas. Even in countries that cultivate energy-intensive industrial technologies of a medium level of development, such as metallurgy and the production of petroleum products, solar, wind, water and biomass energy occupy a prominent place in the overall structure of consumption (Badr et al., 2022; Barykin, Kapustina, et al., 2022; Dinçer, Aksoy, et al., 2022; Dinçer, Yüksel, & Martínez, 2022; Dinçer, Yüksel, Mikhaylov, Barykin, et al., 2022; Dinçer, Yüksel, Mikhaylov, Pinter, et al., 2022; Kalinina et al., 2022; Khan et al., 2022; Mehta et al., 2022; Mikhaylov, Bhatti, et al., 2022; Mikhaylov, Yumashev, et al., 2022; Nyangarika et al., 2022; Shaikh et al., 2022).

A necessary step in implementing alternative sources is to adapt technologies to local conditions, as well as train and motivate employees at enterprises that are the main consumers of energy resources. A number of projects in developing countries are sometimes carried out in the form of pilot production, which aims to demonstrate the advantages and disadvantages of alternative sources. The main goal of developing such projects is to achieve supply sustainability and commercial efficiency, along with increasing the specific productivity of each new unit of production capacity introduced. Cooperation and organization of technological transfers between developed and developing countries is a promising direction in the use of alternative resources (Barykin, Mikheev, et al., 2022; Bhuiyan et al., 2021; Bhuiyan, Zhang, et al., 2022; Candila et al., 2021; Danish et al., 2022a, 2022b; Dong et al., 2021; Li, Yüksel and Dinçer, 2022; Liu et al., 2022a, 2022b; Mikhaylov, 2021b; Mikhaylov & Grilli, 2022; Mukhametov et al., 2021; Saqib et al., 2021).

The next area of research is the interdisciplinary nature of energy saving projects and the continuous improvement of technologies. Modern energy saving projects are always interdisciplinary in nature, that is, they consider technological, environmental, social and financial aspects (Fang et al., 2021; Haiyun et al., 2021; Kayacık et al., 2022; Yuan et al., 2021). A significant part of the innovative solutions implemented in industry around the world involve optimizing energy costs (Bhuiyan, Dinçer, et al., 2022; Conteh et al., 2021; Daniali et al., 2021; Denisova et al., 2019; Huang, Masrur, et al., 2021; Huang, Yona, et al., 2021; Khan et al., 2021; Liu, Kato, Mandal, Mikhaylov, Hemeida, & Senjyu, 2021; Liu, Kato, Mandal, Mikhaylov, Hemeida, Takahashi, et al., 2021; Mikhaylov, 2018, 2022; Mikhaylov et al., 2019; Moiseev et al., 2023; Nyangarika et al., 2019a, 2019b; Sediqi et al., 2022).

The technological component, as a rule, provides a reduction in energy consumption by reducing the irretrievable loss of resources or a fundamentally different solution to any production task. For example, low-carbon production technologies are widely promoted and adapted in industry in developing countries (An et al., 2022; An, Mikhaylov, & Jung, 2020; An, Mikhaylov, & Kim, 2020; An, Mikhaylov, & Moiseev, 2019; An, Mikhaylov, & Richter, 2020; An, Mikhaylov, & Sokolinskaya, 2019; Dooyum et al., 2020; Gura et al., 2022; Mikhaylov, 2020a, 2020b, 2020c; Mikhaylov et al., 2020; Mikhaylov & Tarakanov, 2020; Moiseev et al., 2020, 2021).

Of course, these technologies are linked to the environmental indicators of industrial modernization projects and the level of social responsibility of enterprises, and they also focus on innovative financing methods. Some works on management are related to the parallel study of organizational aspects and the principal structure of the main technological solutions that have a great prospect of implementation. Thus, a modern manager should also have the basics of engineering education to understand the principles of energy-saving technologies (An et al., 2021; Danish et al., 2020, 2021; Dayong et al., 2020; Mikhaylov et al., 2018; Nyangarika et al., 2018; Shaikh et al., 2021; Tamashiro et al., 2021, 2023; Uyeh et al., 2021).

5.3 Results

The interdisciplinary nature of projects gives technological solutions a qualitatively new level of economic efficiency, allowing us to consider the long-term impact of technologies on sustainable development and the dynamics of implementing internal improvements. The principle of continuous improvement (continuous improvement) is laid down in the international management standard, it is aimed at adjusting the energy policy of enterprises after analyzing the internal and external environment of energy consumption and checking the results of energy saving programs (Bhuiyan,

Dinçer et al.. 2022; Dinçer et al., 2023; Eti et al., 2022; Kou et al., 2022; Xu et al., 2022). A change in the price of one ton of carbon dioxide emissions (for example, an increase in the emission tax), along with the expected increase in energy prices, has a significant impact on the diffusion of energy-efficient low-carbon technologies in industrial enterprises.

Another direction is the development of financial instruments. Globally, there is a tendency to increase the efficiency of investments in energy conservation in industry, which is also due to the aggravation of environmental problems and the increased dependence of industry on fossil fuels. In the last decade, new instruments for financing energy efficiency projects have been developed. Of particular interest is the experience of large developing countries that are significant players in the markets, such as India and China, since the internal environment is characterized by complex institutional conditions, lack of methodological tools and imperfect infrastructure. It shows that stakeholders providing funding need to use a number of tools. First, these are tools for collecting information about the current level of energy efficiency, the specifics of the functioning of energy markets, institutions for the development of energy technologies, and key development barriers. Transaction costs for finding information about sources of funding and organizing projects remain a serious limiting factor. Many banks, for example, overestimate the amount of risks due to ignorance of the specifics of energy saving projects. In this regard, the government organizes targeted bank financing for energy efficiency projects, in which a number of specialized banks participate, including providing consulting services. Secondly, these are methods for assessing the compliance of the investment climate with the nature and objectives of the project, the impact of socio-economic and political factors on the investment attractiveness of energy-saving technologies. Third, these are practical approaches to clearly defining responsibility centers that would monitor and adjust each stage of the investment project implementation.

Over the past 20 years, the practice of concluding energy efficiency contracts, which is a mechanism for distributing responsibility for energy conservation between an enterprise and an investor, has become widely used. Due to the implementation of such a financing scheme, the enterprise receives from the company not only a ready-made project aimed at improving energy efficiency, but also personnel training services. At the same time, the responsibility of the enterprise will be to pay the difference between the initial costs of providing energy resources and the costs of operating energy-efficient equipment at the expense of the capital costs of the service company. The company's responsibilities include installation and adjustment of energy-efficient equipment, monitoring resource consumption and calculating savings. The spread of such mechanisms is noted in European countries,

In the United States and developed Asian countries, and this is largely due to support at the level of government organizations. The concept of a contract is also reflected in Russian legislation within the framework of the federal law on Energy Saving. However, due to the fact that the company is obliged to ensure the operation of power equipment throughout the entire term of the contract, there is a risk of non-return of investment funds.

And the last direction of improving energy efficiency in the studies considered is the updating of intellectual resources. The need to improve the competitiveness of energy systems encourages companies to use the full range of resources available to them, the key among which is the intellectual potential of personnel. A number of innovative solutions in the intellectualization of technical systems are proposed by domestic authors. Modern approaches to energy resource management are also widely covered by the authors, including through planning methods using digital tools, investment project portfolio management methods, and the formation of information systems for analyzing energy systems at the regional and federal levels.

The most important source of knowledge and experience needed to implement energy saving programs at all levels of government is higher education institutions, which are the mainstay of engineering and research competencies. This is due to the fact that in developed countries, when developing training programs for engineering specialties, the principles of energy efficiency management are included in the scope of training. Russia is also updating its internal educational technologies for developing competencies in the field of energy conservation. The main direction of improving approaches to the educational process is considered to be the implementation of the principle of lifelong learning, which involves the involvement of employees of enterprises in the learning process in parallel with the work process. Also, the participation of higher education institutions in the ongoing programs on energy efficiency research has a huge impact on the formation of advanced competence bases based on theoretical research and industrial experience. Russian universities, along with international ones, are the drivers of promoting innovative developments related to energy saving technologies in the real industrial sector and the ordinary life of mankind. In the future research, we will focus in more detail on the problems of managing intellectual resources in energy management, trace their role at each stage of planning, organizing and controlling energy saving projects at industrial enterprises.

In comparison with external educational institutions, the participation of internal managers in this process is also important in terms of activating creative potential. Moreover, a well-chosen and formulated long-term strategy for staff training and incentives for energy conservation is the key to successful implementation of energy efficiency management approaches. The manager should be involved in the process of creating an energy-efficient production, starting from the development of policies and ending with the implementation of energy-saving measures in the structural division of the enterprise. The list of competencies of managers implementing strategic energy efficiency management should primarily include the ability to carry out long-term planning in the field of energy consumption, knowledge in the field of personnel management and a high level of technical training necessary for the development of technical measures.

Considering the specifics, functional features and high energy intensity of metallurgical production processes, the impact of energy efficiency indicators on the competitiveness of the enterprise as a whole is significantly noticeable. That is why there is a huge potential for improving the efficiency of energy farms in all areas of the enterprise's activity, without exception, and its successful implementation depends on a clearly formulated management strategy.

According to Russian studies, the promotion of the management strategy is limited by the presence of unfavorable environmental factors, which in turn are caused by problems in the national energy sector. The list of main shortcomings in the operation of power systems includes a low degree of information support, morally and physically outdated technical means, inefficient methods, lack of the necessary level of professional training of personnel, etc. Due to the lag in the efficiency of the existing infrastructure from current trends, there is a slowdown in the implementation of monitoring systems and digitalization of energy processes.

Nevertheless, despite the presence of negative factors, we can note positive trends in improving energy efficiency, namely: increasing requirements for the reliability of energy systems, developing healthy competition in energy markets and dialogue between energy producers, which ultimately leads to the formation of information flows. There is also a trend towards universal integration of international standards into existing management systems at enterprises. Based on the available data and the desire of business owners to improve the efficiency of production processes, it can be assumed that in the long term, a clear trend will be established aimed at developing energy efficiency management mechanisms.

Based on the results of the study of foreign and domestic literature, we were able to focus on the main directions of development of the energy saving sector, so that in subsequent chapters it will be possible to identify promising areas for improving organizational and technical mechanisms for managing energy efficiency. The key drivers of the development of management systems at the present time include the need for continuous improvement of the result, which is caused by the desire of enterprise owners to satisfy their own interests and not lose out in the face of tougher competition. In addition, significant potential lies in improving the efficiency of using human resources and directing the intellectual capabilities of personnel to solve energy saving problems.

Summing up the theoretical research, it is possible to identify the following recommendations for improving management at a metallurgical enterprise:

When developing the energy policy of a metallurgical enterprise, it should be formed as a balanced strategy based on technocratic, innovative and systematic approaches. Determining the share values of a particular approach depends on the current financial performance of the company and the business processes that require attracting investment, whether it is technical solutions or investments in employee development. The list of priority goals of the management policy may include reducing the absolute values of fuel and energy consumption or achieving energy efficiency indicators.

5.4 Conclusion

The key to successful implementation of the energy efficiency management mechanism is primarily the quality of managers' work. That is why one of the factors of management efficiency is considered to be the presence of fundamental knowledge of technological and organizational and economic features of the energy saving process among managers. Managers should also have the ability to create teams that can effectively implement policy principles.

The key direction in forming an energy saving strategy at a metallurgical enterprise is to work with personnel, as it allows increasing the loyalty of employees at all levels to energy policy and maximally involving their innovative potential in solving energy saving problems. The main tasks of managers in realizing the potential of employees include increasing knowledge in the field of energy efficiency, informing about the commitment of management to the principles of economy and improving the energy consumption culture.

The formation and implementation of an energy efficiency management strategy is one of the most important factors for improving the competitiveness of a metallurgical enterprise, ensuring savings in fuel and energy resources, improving environmental performance of production, systematic planning of the enterprise's production systems, and creating a positive image of the company as a leader in energy conservation.

A large potential for energy saving at a metallurgical enterprise lies in the field of personnel management: the effectiveness of its disclosure directly depends on the quality of the techniques and practices used to train and motivate personnel using industry benchmarking. Therefore, along with attracting investments for the modernization of fixed assets, it is worth paying attention to financing personnel development issues.

References

Alwaelya, S. A., Yousif, N. B. A., & Mikhaylov, A. (2021). Emotional development in preschoolers and socialization. *Early Child Development and Care, 191*, 16.

An, J., & Mikhaylov, A. (2020). Russian energy projects in South Africa. *Journal of Energy in Southern Africa, 31*(3).

An, J., & Mikhaylov, A. (2021). Analysis of energy projects financial efficiency and renewable energy generation in Russia. *Finance: Theory and Practice, 25*(5), 79–91.

An, J., Mikhaylov, A., Dinçer, H., & Yüksel, S. (2022). Economic modelling of electricity generation: Long short-term memory and Q-Rung Orthopair fuzzy sets. *Heliyon, 8*, e10759.

An, J., Mikhaylov, A., & Jung, S.-U. (2020). The strategy of South Korea in the global oil market. *Energies, 13*(10), 2491.

An, J., Mikhaylov, A., & Jung, S.-U. (2021). A linear programming approach for Robust network revenue management in the airline industry. *Journal of Air Transport Management, 91*, 101979.

An, J., Mikhaylov, A., & Kim, K. (2020). Machine learning approach in heterogeneous group of algorithms for transport safety-critical system. *Applied Sciences, 10*(8), 2670.

An, J., Mikhaylov, A., & Moiseev, N. (2019). Oil price predictors: Machine learning approach. *International Journal of Energy Economics and Policy, 9*(5), 1–6.
An, J., Mikhaylov, A., & Richter, U. H. (2020). Trade war effects: Evidence from sectors of energy and resources in Africa. *Heliyon, 6*, e05693. https://doi.org/10.1016/j.heliyon.2020.e05693
An, J., Mikhaylov, A., & Sokolinskaya, N. (2019). Machine learning in economic planning: Ensembles of algorithms. *Journal of Physics: Conference Series, 1353*, 012126.
Badr, A. M. N. A. A., Mohamed, T. I., Osman, N. A. Q., & Mikhaylov, A. (2022). A review of social media website users' interaction paths with governmental accounts during the COVID-19 pandemic. *Informatics, 9*, 50. https://doi.org/10.3390/informatics9030050
Barykin, S. E., Kapustina, I. V., Sergeev, S. M., Daniali, S. M., Kopteva, L. A., Semenova, G. N., Pryadko, I. P., Mikhaylov, A., Baboshkin, P., Datsyuk, P., & Senjyu, T. (2022). Financial logistics models based on systematic approach improving management solutions. *F1000Research, 11*, 570. https://doi.org/10.12688/f1000research.111252.1
Barykin, S., Mikheev, A., Kiseleva, E., Putikhin, Y., Alekseeva, N., & Mikhaylov, A. (2022). An empirical analysis of Russian regions' debt sustainability. *Economies, 10*(4), 296.
Bhuiyan, M. A., An, J., Mikhaylov, A., Moiseev, N., & Danish, M. S. S. (2021). Renewable energy deployment and COVID-19 measures for sustainable development. *Sustainability, 13*, 4418.
Bhuiyan, M. A., Dinçer, H., Yüksel, S., Mikhaylov, A., Danish, M. S. S., Pinter, G., Uyeh, D. D., & Stepanova, D. (2022). Economic indicators and bioenergy supply in developed economies: QROF-DEMATEL and random forest models. *Energy Reports, 8*(2022), 561–570.
Bhuiyan, M. A., Zhang, Q., Khare, V., Mikhaylov, A., Pinter, G., & Huang, X. (2022). Renewable energy consumption and economic growth nexus—A systematic literature review. *Frontiers in Environmental Science, 10*, 878394. https://doi.org/10.3389/fenvs.2022.878394
Candila, V., Maximov, D., Mikhaylov, A., Moiseev, N., Senjyu, T., & Tryndina, N. (2021). On the relationship between oil and exchange rates of oil-exporting and oil-importing countries: from the great recession period to the Covid-19 era. *Energies, 14*, 8065.
Carayannis, E., Kostis, P., Dinçer, H., & Yüksel, S. (2022). Balanced-scorecard-based evaluation of knowledge-oriented competencies of distributed energy investments. *Energies, 15*(21), 8245.
Conteh, F., Takahashi, H., Hemeida, A. M., Krishnan, N., Mikhaylov, A., & Senjyu, T. (2021). Hybrid grid-connected renewable power generation for sustainable electricity supply in Sierra Leone: Case study Lungi Town. *Sustainability, 13*(18).
Daniali, S. M., Barykin, S. E., Kapustina, I. V., Khortabi, F. M., Sergeev, S. M., Kalinina, O. V., Mikhaylov, A., Veynberg, R., Zasova, L., & Senjyu, T. (2021). Predicting volatility index according to technical index and economic indicators on the basis of deep learning algorithm. *Sustainability, 2021*(13), 14011.
Danish, M. S. S., Bhattacharya, A., Stepanova, D., Mikhaylov, A., Grilli, M. L., Khosravy, M., & Senjyu, T. (2020). A systematic review of metal oxide applications for energy and environmental sustainability. *Metals, 10*(12), 1604.
Danish, M. S. S., Senjyu, T., Sabory, N. R., Khosravy, M., Grilli, M. L., Mikhaylov, A., & Majidi, H. (2021). A forefront framework for sustainable aquaponics modeling and design. *Sustainability, 13*, 9313.
Danish, M. S., Senjyu, T. S., Sabory, N. R., & Mikhaylov, A. (2022a). Lessons from COVID-19 conferring environmental re-engineering opportunity. In M. Danish & T. Senjyu (Eds.), *Eco-friendly and agile energy strategies and policy development* (pp. 99–118). IGI Global). https://doi.org/10.4018/978-1-7998-9502-2.ch005
Danish, M. S., Senjyu, T. S., Sabory, N. R., & Mikhaylov, A. (2022b). Interplay consequences of COVID-19 on global environmental sustainability. In M. Danish & T. Senjyu (Eds.), *Eco-friendly and agile energy strategies and policy development*. IGI Global. https://doi.org/10.4018/978-1-7998-9502-2.ch003
Dayong, N., Mikhaylov, A., Bratanovsky, S., Shaikh, Z. A., & Stepanova, D. (2020). Mathematical modeling of the technological processes of catering products production. *Journal of Food Process Engineering, 43*(2), 1–9.

Denisova, V., Mikhaylov, A., & Lopatin, E. (2019). Blockchain infrastructure and growth of global power consumption. *International Journal of Energy Economics and Policy, 9*(4), 22–29.

Dinçer, H., Aksoy, T., Yüksel, S., & Hacioglu, U. (2022). Golden cut-oriented q-rung orthopair fuzzy decision-making approach to evaluation of renewable energy alternatives for microgeneration system investments. *Mathematical Problems in Engineering*. https://doi.org/10.1155/2022/2261166

Dinçer, H., Yüksel, S., Çağlayan, Ç., Yavuz, D., & Kararoğlu, D. (2023). Can renewable energy investments be a solution to the energy-sourced high inflation problem?. In *Managing inflation and supply chain disruptions in the global economy* (pp. 220–238). IGI Global.

Dinçer, H., Yüksel, S., & Martínez, L. (2022). Collaboration enhanced hybrid fuzzy decision-making approach to analyze the renewable energy investment projects. *Energy Reports, 8*, 377–389.

Dinçer, H., Yüksel, S., Mikhaylov, A., Barykin, S. E., Aksoy, T., & Hacioğlu, U. (2022). Analysis of environmental priorities for green project investments using an integrated q-rung orthopair fuzzy modelling. *IEEE Access, 10*. https://doi.org/10.1109/ACCESS.2022.3174058

Dinçer, H., Yüksel, S., Mikhaylov, A., Pinter, G., & Shaikh, Z. A. (2022). Analysis of renewable-friendly smart grid technologies for the distributed energy investment projects using a hybrid picture fuzzy rough decision-making approach. *Energy Reports, 8*, 11466–11477. https://doi.org/10.1016/j.egyr.2022.08.275

Dong, B., Ikonnikova, I., Rogulin, R., Sakulyeva, T., & Mikhaylov, A. (2021). Environmental economic approach to optimization of transport communication in megacities. *Journal of Environmental Science and Health, Part A, 56*(6), 660–666.

Dong, W., Zhao, G., Yüksel, S., Dinçer, H., & Ubay, G. G. (2022). A novel hybrid decision making approach for the strategic selection of wind energy projects. *Renewable Energy, 185*, 321–337.

Dooyum, U. D., Mikhaylov, A., & Varyash, I. (2020). Energy security concept in Russia and South Korea. *International Journal of Energy Economics and Policy, 10*(4), 102–107.

Eti, S., Dinçer, H., Gökalp, Y., Yüksel, S., & Kararoğlu, D. (2023). Identifying key issues to handle the inflation problem in the healthcare industry caused by energy prices: An evaluation with decision-making models. *Managing Inflation and Supply Chain Disruptions in the Global Economy*, 162–178.

Eti, S., Dinçer, H., Yüksel, S., & Gökalp, Y. (2022). Analysis of the suitability of the solar panels for hospitals: A new fuzzy decision-making model proposal with the T-Spherical TOP-DEMATEL method. *Journal of Intelligent & Fuzzy Systems*, (Preprint), 1–13.

Fang, S., Zhou, P., Dinçer, H., & Yüksel, S. (2021). Assessment of safety management system on energy investment risk using house of quality based on hybrid stochastic interval-valued intuitionistic fuzzy decision-making approach. *Safety Science, 141*, 105333.

Gura, D., Mikhaylov, A., Glushkov, S., Zaikov, M., & Shaikh, Z. A. (2022). Model for estimating power dissipation along the interconnect length in single on-chip topology. *Evolutionary Intelligence, 15*, 2369–2373. https://doi.org/10.1007/s12065-020-00407-7

Haiyun, C., Zhixiong, H., Yüksel, S., & Dinçer, H. (2021). Analysis of the innovation strategies for green supply chain management in the energy industry using the QFD-based hybrid interval valued intuitionistic fuzzy decision approach. *Renewable and Sustainable Energy Reviews, 143*, 110844.

Huang, Y., Masrur, H., Shigenobu, R., Hemeida, A. M., Mikhaylov, A., & Senjyu, T. (2021). A comparative design of a campus microgrid considering a multi-scenario and multi-objective approach. *Energies, 14*, 2853.

Huang, Y., Yona, A., Takahashi, H., Hemeida, A. M., Mandal, P., Mikhaylov, A., Senjyu, T., & Lotfy, M. E. (2021). Energy management system optimization of drug store operate electric vehicles charging station. *Sustainability, 14*, 1217836.

Kafka, K. I., Dinçer, H., & Yüksel, S. (2022). Impact-relation map of innovative service development regarding the sustainable growth for emerging markets. *Journal of the Knowledge Economy*, 1–24.

Kalinina, O. V., Barykin, S. E., Sergeev, S. M., Semenova, G. N., Fatkullina, A., Mikhaylov, A., & De La Poza, E. (2022). Smart city perspectives in post-pandemic governance: Externalities reduction policy. *F1000Research, 11*, 1032. https://doi.org/10.12688/f1000research.123195.1

Kayacık, M., Dinçer, H., & Yüksel, S. (2022). Using quantum spherical fuzzy decision support system as a novel sustainability index approach for analyzing industries listed in the stock exchange. *Borsa Istanbul Review, 22*(6), 1145–1157.

Khan, A. A., Laghari, A. A., Gadekallu, T. R., Shaikh, Z. A., Javed, A. R., Rashid, M., Estrela, V. V., & Mikhaylov, A. (2022). A drone-based data management and optimization using metaheuristic algorithms and blockchain smart contracts in a secure fog environment. *Computers and Electrical Engineering, 102*, 108234. https://doi.org/10.1016/j.compeleceng.2022.108234

Khan, A. A., Shaikh, Z. A., Baitenova, L., Mutaliyeva, L., Moiseev, N., Mikhaylov, A., Laghari, A. A., Idris, S. A., & Alshazly, H. (2021). QoS-Ledger: Smart contracts and metaheuristic for secure quality-of-service and cost-efficient scheduling of medical-data processing. *Electronics, 10*, 3083.

Kou, G., Yüksel, S., & Dinçer, H. (2022). Inventive problem-solving map of innovative carbon emission strategies for solar energy-based transportation investment projects. *Applied Energy, 311*, 118680.

Li, W., Yüksel, S., & Dinçer, H. (2022). Understanding the financial innovation priorities for renewable energy investors via QFD-based picture fuzzy and rough numbers. *Financial Innovation, 8*(1), 1–30.

Li, J., Yüksel, S., Dınçer, H., Mikhaylov, A., & Barykin, S. E. (2022). Bipolar q-ROF hybrid decision making model with golden cut for analyzing the levelized cost of renewable energy alternatives. *IEEE Access, 10*, 42507–42517. https://doi.org/10.1109/ACCESS.2022.3168315

Liu, L., Kato, T, Mandal, P., Mikhaylov, A, Hemeida, A. M., & Senjyu T. (2021). Multi-area power system load frequency control by using model predictive control by introducing renewable energy sources. In *2021 International conference on science & contemporary technologies (ICSCT)* (pp. 1–6). https://doi.org/10.1109/ICSCT53883.2021.9642521

Liu, L., Kato, T., Mandal, P., Mikhaylov, A., Hemeida, A. M., Takahashi, H., & Tomonobu, S. (2021). Two cases studies of model predictive control approach for hybrid renewable energy systems. *AIMS Energy, 9*(6), 1241–1259.

Liu, Z., Panfilova, E., Mikhaylov, A., & Kurilova, A. (2022a). Assessing stability in the relationship between parties in crowdfunding and crowdsourcing projects during the COVID-19 crisis. *Journal of Global Information Management (JGIM), 30*(4), 1–18. https://doi.org/10.4018/JGIM.297905

Liu, Z.-J., Panfilova, E., Mikhaylov, A., & Kurilova, A. (2022b). COVID-19 crisis impact on the stability between parties in crowdfunding and crowdsourcing. *Wireless Personal Communications, 122*, 915–930.

Martínez, L., Dinçer, H., & Yüksel, S. (2022). A hybrid decision making approach for new service development process of renewable energy investment. *Applied Soft Computing, 133*, 109897.

Mehta, R., Verghese, J., Mahajan, S., Barykin, S., Bozhuk, S., Kozlova, N., Kapustina, I., Mikhaylov, A., Naumova, E., & Dedyukhina, N. (2022). Consumers' behavior in conversational commerce marketing based on messenger chatbots. *F1000Research, 11*(647). https://doi.org/10.12688/f1000research.122037.1

Mikhaylov, A. (2018). The yield of the carry trade strategy. *Finance: Theory and Practice, 22*(3), 52–63. https://doi.org/10.26794/2587-5671-2018-22-3-52-63

Mikhaylov, A. (2020a). Cryptocurrency market analysis from the open innovation perspective. *Journal of Open Innovation: Technology, Market, and Complexity, 6*(4), 197.

Mikhaylov, A. (2020b). Geothermal energy development in Iceland. *International Journal of Energy Economics and Policy, 10*(4), 31–35.

Mikhaylov, A. (2020c). Cryptocurrency market development: hurst method. *Finance: Theory and Practice, 24*(3), 81–91.

Mikhaylov, A. (2021a). Development of Friedrich von Hayek's theory of private money and economic implications for digital currencies. *Terra Economicus, 19*(1).

Mikhaylov, A. (2021b). Lichens as indicators of atmospheric pollution in urban ecosystems. *Israel Journal of Ecology & Evolution, 67*(1–2), 60–68. https://doi.org/10.1163/22244662-bja10016

Mikhaylov, A. (2022). Sustainable development and renewable energy: A new view to a global problem. *Energies, 15*, 1397. https://doi.org/10.3390/en15041397

Mikhaylov, A., Bhatti, I. M., Dinçer, H., & Yüksel, S. (2022). Integrated decision recommendation system using iteration-enhanced collaborative filtering, golden cut bipolar for analyzing the risk-based oil market spillovers. *Computational Economics*. https://doi.org/10.1007/s10614-022-10341-8

Mikhaylov, A., Burakov, D., & Didenko, V. (2019). Relationship between oil price and macroeconomic indicators in Russia. *Finance: Theory and Practice, 23*(2), 105–116. https://doi.org/10.26794/2587-5671-2019-23-2-105-116

Mikhaylov, A., Dinçer, H., & Yüksel, S. (2023). Analysis of financial development and open innovation oriented fintech potential for emerging economies using an integrated decision-making approach of MF-X-DMA and golden cut bipolar q-ROFSs. *Financial Innovation, 9*, 10. https://doi.org/10.1186/s40854-022-00234-w

Mikhaylov, A., & Grilli, M. L. (2022). Machine learning methods and sustainable development: Metal oxides and multilayer metal-oxides. *Metals, 12*(4).

Mikhaylov, A., Moiseev, N., Aleshin, K., & Burkhardt, T. (2020). Global climate change and greenhouse effect. *Entrepreneurship and Sustainability Issues, 7*(4), 2897–2913. https://doi.org/10.9770/jesi.2020.7.4(21)

Mikhaylov, A., Sokolinskaya, N., & Nyangarika, A. (2018). Optimal carry trade strategy based on currencies of energy and developed economies. *Journal of Reviews on Global Economics, 7*, 582–592.

Mikhaylov, A., & Tarakanov, S. (2020). Development of Levenberg-Marquardt theoretical approach for electric network. *Journal of Physics: Conference Series, 1515*, 052006.

Mikhaylov, A., Yumashev, A., & Kolpak, E. (2022). Quality of life, anxiety and depressive disorders in patients with extrasystolic arrhythmia. *Archives of Medical Science, 18*(2). https://doi.org/10.5114/aoms.2020.101359

Moiseev, N., Mikhaylov, A., Dinçer, H., & Yüksel, S. (2023). Effects of market capitalization shocks for open innovation models in e-commerce industry: Golden cut QROF MCDM analysis. *Financial Innovation, 9*, 32.

Moiseev, N., Mikhaylov, A., Varyash, I., & Saqib, A. (2020). Investigating the relation of GDP per capita and corruption index. *Entrepreneurship and Sustainability Issues, 8*(1), 780–794.

Moiseev, N., Sorokin, A., Zvezdina, N., Mikhaylov, A., Khomyakova, L., & Danish, M. S. S. (2021). Credit risk theoretical model on the base of DCC-GARCH in time-varying parameters framework. *Mathematics, 9*, 2423. https://doi.org/10.3390/math9192423

Mukhametov, A., Bekhorashvili, A., Avdeenko, A., & Mikhaylov, A. (2021). The impact of growing legume plants under conditions of Biologization and Soil Cultivation on Chernozem fertility and productivity of rotation crops. *Legume Research, 44*, 12.

Mukhtarov, S., Yüksel, S., & Dinçer, H. (2022). The impact of financial development on renewable energy consumption: Evidence from Turkey. *Renewable Energy, 187*, 169–176.

Mutalimov, V., Kovaleva, I., Mikhaylov, A., & Stepanova, D. (2021). Assessing regional growth of small business in Russia. *Entrepreneurial Business and Economics Review, 9*(3), 119–133. https://doi.org/10.15678/EBER.2021.090308

Nie, D., Panfilova, E., Samusenkov, V., & Mikhaylov, A. (2020). E-Learning financing models in Russia for sustainable development. *Sustainability, 12*(11), 4412.

Nyangarika, A., Mikhaylov, A., Muyeen, S. M., Yadykin, V., Mottaeva, A., Pryadko, I., Barykin, S., Fomenko, N., Rykov, G., & Shvandar, K. (2022). Energy stability and decarbonization in developing countries: Random Forest approach for forecasting of crude oil trade flows and macro indicators. *Frontiers in Environmental Science, 10*, 1031343. https://doi.org/10.3389/fenvs.2022.1031343

Nyangarika, A., Mikhaylov, A., & Richter, U. (2019a). Influence oil price towards economic indicators in Russia. *International Journal of Energy Economics and Policy, 9*(1), 123–129.

Nyangarika, A., Mikhaylov, A., & Richter, U. (2019b). Oil price factors: Forecasting on the base of modified auto-regressive integrated moving average model. *International Journal of Energy Economics and Policy, 9*(1), 149–159.

Nyangarika, A., Mikhaylov, A., & Tang, B.-J. (2018). Correlation of oil prices and gross domestic product in oil producing countries. *International Journal of Energy Economics and Policy, 8*(5), 42–48.

Saqib, A., Chan, T.-H., Mikhaylov, A., & Lean, H. H. (2021). Are the responses of sectoral energy imports asymmetric to exchange rate volatilities in Pakistan? Evidence from recent foreign exchange regime. *Frontiers in Energy Research, 9*, 614463. https://doi.org/10.3389/fenrg.2021.614463

Sediqi, M. M., Nakadomari, A., Mikhaylov, A., Krishnan, N., Lotfy, M. E., Yona, A., & Senjyu, T. (2022). Impact of time-of-use demand response program on optimal operation of Afghanistan real power system. *Energies, 15*, 296.

Shaikh, Z. A., Kraikin, A., Mikhaylov, A., & Pinter, G. (2022). Forecasting stock prices of companies producing solar panels using machine learning methods. *Complexity, 2022*, 9186265. https://doi.org/10.1155/2022/9186265

Shaikh, Z. A., Moiseev, N., Mikhaylov, A., & Yüksel, S. (2021). Facile synthesis of copper oxide-cobalt oxide/nitrogen-doped carbon (Cu2O-Co3O4/CN) composite for efficient water splitting. *Applied Sciences., 11*, 9974. https://doi.org/10.3390/app11219974

Sun, L., Peng, J., Dinçer, H., & Yüksel, S. (2022). Coalition-oriented strategic selection of renewable energy system alternatives using q-ROF DEMATEL with golden cut. *Energy, 256*, 124606.

Tamashiro, K., Alharbi, T., Mikhaylov, A., Hemeida, A. M., Krishnan, N., Lotfy, M. E., & Senjyu, T. (2021). Investigation of home energy management with advanced direct load control and optimal scheduling of controllable loads. *Energies, 14*, 7314. https://doi.org/10.3390/en14217314

Tamashiro, K., Omine, E., Krishnan, N., Mikhaylov, A., Hemeida, A. M., & Senjyu, T. (2023). Optimal components capacity based multi-objective optimization and optimal scheduling based MPC-optimization algorithm in smart apartment buildings. *Energy & Buildings, 278*, 112616. https://doi.org/10.1016/j.enbuild.2022.112616

Uyeh, D. D., Asem-Hiablie, S., Park, T., Kim, K.-M., Mikhaylov, A., Woo, S., & Ha, Y. (2021). Could Japonica rice be an Alternative variety for increased global food security and climate change mitigation? *Food, 10*, 1869. https://doi.org/10.3390/foods10081869

Varyash, I., Mikhaylov, A., Moiseev, N., & Aleshin, K. (2020). Triple bottom line and corporate social responsibility performance indicators for Russian companies. *Entrepreneurship and Sustainability Issues, 8*(1), 313–331.

Xu, X., Yüksel, S., & Dinçer, H. (2022). An integrated decision-making approach with golden cut and bipolar q-ROFSs to renewable energy storage investments. *International Journal of Fuzzy Systems*, 1–14.

Yuan, G., Xie, F., Dinçer, H., & Yüksel, S. (2021). The theory of inventive problem solving (TRIZ)-based strategic mapping of green nuclear energy investments with spherical fuzzy group decision-making approach. *International Journal of Energy Research, 45*(8), 12284–12300.

Yüksel, S., & Dinçer, H. (2022). Identifying the strategic priorities of nuclear energy investments using hesitant 2-tuple interval-valued Pythagorean fuzzy DEMATEL. *Progress in Nuclear Energy, 145*, 104103.

Yüksel, S., Dinçer, H., Eti, S., & Adalı, Z. (2022). Strategy improvements to minimize the drawbacks of geothermal investments by using spherical fuzzy modelling. *International Journal of Energy Research.*

Yumashev, A., & Mikhaylov, A. (2020). Development of polymer film coatings with high adhesion to steel alloys and high wear resistance. *Polymer Composites, 41*(7), 2875–2880.

Yumashev, A., Ślusarczyk, B., Kondrashev, S., & Mikhaylov, A. (2020). Global indicators of sustainable development: Evaluation of the influence of the human development index on consumption and quality of energy. *Energies, 13*, 2768.

Zhang, Y., Zhang, Y., Gong, C., Dinçer, H., & Yüksel, S. (2022). An integrated hesitant 2-tuple Pythagorean fuzzy analysis of QFD-based innovation cost and duration for renewable energy projects. *Energy, 248*, 123561.

Zhao, Q., Cherkasov, S., Avdeenko, A., Kondratenko, L., & Mikhaylov, A. (2021). Integral estimate of the added value of agricultural crops in the synergetic agriculture on the example of Vicia faba (Vicia faba L.). *Polish Journal of Environmental Studies, 30*(5), 1–9. https://doi.org/10.15244/pjoes/131949

Chapter 6
How to Increase the Efficiency of Biomass Energy Investments

Hasan Dinçer, Duygu Yavuz, and Natalia Sokolinskaya

Keywords Biomass energy · Energy investments · DEMATEL · Energy economics · Sustainable energy

6.1 Introduction

Renewable energy usage has a positive contribution to both social and economic improvements of the countries (Dong et al., 2022; Kafka et al., 2022; Martínez et al., 2022; Mukhtarov et al., 2022; Sun et al., 2022). The main superiority of these projects is that carbon emission problem can be minimized (Carayannis et al., 2022; Dinçer, Aksoy, et al., 2022; Dinçer, Yüksel, & Martínez, 2022; Dinçer, Yüksel, Mikhaylov, et al. 2022; Li, Yüksel, & Dinçer, 2022; Yüksel & Dinçer, 2022; Zhang et al., 2022). This situation has a powerful influence on the decrease of environmental pollution. Additionally, energy independence can be provided with the help of renewable energy projects (Eti et al., 2023; Haiyun et al., 2021; Li, Yüksel, & Dinçer, 2022; Mikhaylov et al., 2022; Yüksel et al., 2022). Hence, the countries current account balance is affected in a very positive manner from this situation. There are different types of renewable energy projects that are solar, wind, geothermal, hydropower and biomass (Eti et al., 2022; Fang et al., 2021; Kayacık et al., 2022; Yuan et al., 2021).

Today, the most widely used materials as biomass fuel are corn grain (ethanol) and soybean (biodiesel). The raw material of biomass consists of biological materials and wastes that absorb solar energy, and the energy obtained from these materials is called biomass energy. When we look at renewable energy sources, biomass energy is an energy source that can be stored continuously and uninterruptedly. In addition,

H. Dinçer (✉) · D. Yavuz
The School of Business, İstanbul Medipol University, Istanbul, Turkey
e-mail: hdincer@medipol.edu.tr; duygu.yavuz@std.medipol.edu.tr

N. Sokolinskaya
Financial University under the Government of the Russian Federation, Moscow, Russia

H. Dincer, S. Yüksel (eds.), *Economic Development and the Environmental Ecosystem*, Contributions to Economics,
https://doi.org/10.1007/978-3-031-26596-9_6

biomass energy is a type of energy that is environmentally friendly and contributes to the region economically with its employment-increasing effect (Yuan et al., 2008). Electricity generation using biomass as an energy source is based on two basic ideas. The first type of change is thermochemical transformation, and the second type is biochemical change. Combustion, pyrolysis, gasification and liquefaction are a few stages that make up the thermochemical conversion process. The metabolic exchange process can be staged at various points as digestion and fermentation. Both of these processes use waste and other biological resources as fuel sources (Angenent et al., 2004). Basic properties of energy obtained from biomass;

- It is the second most common energy consumption source in the world after fossil fuels.
- The option of using renewable energy sources is the best choice in terms of the amount of raw materials that can be used.
- It is advantageous in that it can be used with other types of energy sources and converted into other forms of energy.
- Compared to other types of renewable energy, it is superior in terms of both consistency and storage capacity.
- It can be found in all conditions and at any time.
- It is a type of energy that has been used for a very long time, so the technology for its production and conversion has also been around for a very long time.

Biofuel applications represent the most promising energy source when compared to other energy sources. The number of contexts in which biofuels produced from biomass can be used is constantly increasing. The three biofuel categories are as follows:

- Solid Biofuels (Biochar, Biobriquette)
- Liquid Biofuels (Biogas, Biosynthesis Gas, Biohydrogen)
- Gas Biofuels (Biodiesel, Bioethanol, Bio methanol, Bio-oil)

In terms of raw materials used in the production process, biofuels are divided into one of two categories, depending on whether they are also used for food. The first category is biofuels, which are obtained as a by-product of agricultural production and serve as a source of raw materials for the manufacture of plant products suitable for consumption as food (Banowetz et al., 2008). The vast majority of biofuels produced fall into this category and are therefore referred to as “first generation biofuels”. “Second generation biofuels” are so-called because they are made from lignocellulosic biomass that was not originally intended for use. Banowetz, However, the cost of the equipment used in the conversion process is quite high. Therefore, the production of second generation biofuels is not economically feasible (Cook & Beyea, 2000).

6.2 Energy Production from Biomass

Today, there are both contemporary and traditional approaches to biomass energy. It is the traditional form of energy derived from biomass from forests. Traditional biomass includes animal and plant wastes used as fuel, in addition to wood that is burned as fuel. The use of direct combustion techniques and various means of combustion during the conversion of biomass material to increasingly higher levels of energy is the primary distinguishing feature of the traditional use of biomass for energy production. Modern sources of biomass include poplar, eucalyptus, willow, forest and wood industry waste, plant and animal waste from the agricultural sector, agro-industrial waste, and waste from urban areas (Demirbas & Demirbas, 2007).

The processing of biomass-by-biomass conversion techniques results in the conversion of biomass products into gaseous, solid and liquid fuels. At the end of the cycle, primary products such as biodiesel, biogas, pyrolytic gas-like fuel and bioethanol and by-products such as hydrogen and fertilizer are collected. Biomass energy is obtained through the use of anaerobic decomposers producing methanol, biodiesel, ethanol and the production of biofuels containing their derivatives (Jåstad & Bolkesjø, 2022). This allows the production of starch, sugar and oil containing plants as well as the use of biogas for cellulose, combustible solid waste, electricity and heat. Both the physical and chemical structures of fossil fuels and the structures of biomass consisting of biomass are different from each other. Biomass conversion methods currently in use are analyzed according to three main categories;

- Physical processes
- Chemical processes
- Biological processes

6.3 Bioenergy Resources

Biomass, a collective term for all organic compounds produced by plants directly through photosynthesis and indirectly through animal wastes formed by the digestion of these organic materials, is well known. Photosynthesis is the process by which plants take carbon dioxide (CO2) from the air and convert it into structural components of the plant, including cellulose, hemicellulose, lignin, and carbohydrates. In the light of these explanations, it is clear that plants are the primary source of bioenergy (Gan, 2007). As an added advantage, it can be used as a source of bioenergy in the form of domestic, industrial and commercial organic and inorganic waste (Scarlat et al., 2011). Due to the prevalence and breadth of the idea of plants and litter, it is difficult to classify bioenergy sources; In the light of these definitions, they are categorized under the following headings;

Forest Origin Resources: Both natural and man-made forests cover about 30% of the planet. Any garbage left in these forests can be used to generate bioenergy. Bioenergy can be produced from anywhere in a forest, including leaves, branches and even dead trees. A practice known as energy forestry, which uses different types of forest and wood waste, has contributed to an increase in bioenergy production in recent years (Junginger et al., 2008).

Agricultural Resources: Energy from agricultural sources, including agricultural waste, animal waste, and by-products and resources from agricultural production. There has been a worldwide increase in agricultural production for energy needs. It has become quite common in this field, especially in America and some Far East countries. Sunflower, rapeseed, soybean, cotton, corn and beet are just a few of the oily plants that can be produced within the scope of energy-oriented agricultural production activities to produce bioenergy. As the need for bioenergy grows, more and more land is being farmed and farmers are increasingly turning to this type of crop. Bioenergy is produced from agricultural by-products such as animal carcasses and manure. Animal manure, which is used as fertilizer after drying in the sun, is also an important source of bioenergy in our country. It can be converted into biogas, which is used as a source of bioenergy, and the by-products can be used well as fertilizer for crops (Ferreira et al., 2009).

Industrial and Municipal Wastes: The industrialization that has increased in recent years throughout the world and all kinds of industrial waste brought by this industrialization and all kinds of waste generated in urban life have the potential to be considered as a bioenergy source. To put it more clearly, all kinds of organic and inorganic wastes generated in our homes and all kinds of junkyard, park and garden wastes, fruit and vegetable market and market wastes, purification and sorting wastes and pet wastes generated as a result of municipal services can be evaluated in bioenergy production. In addition, wastes produced or released by hospitals and industrial establishments in the city can also be considered as a source of bioenergy. Considering the negative effects of industrial wastes on the environment, the evaluation of these wastes in bioenergy production gains a special importance (Domac et al., 2005).

6.4 Bioenergy Products

The idea of developing bioenergy in the modern sense started in the 1970s in the world. Liquid fertilizer and animal feed obtained from the last wastes released as final products are not meant here. It refers to energy supply, which is the main target of bioenergy production. For this reason, in this chapter of the study, the types of bioenergy products obtained in bioenergy production will be emphasized. These products are biogas, biodiesel and bioethanol.

Biogas: It is obtained as a result of fermentation of plant and animal wastes and urban wastes whose organic part is decomposed in an airless environment. As a result of this process, methane, CO2 and H2 are produced as products. Methane from these resulting products is used as a renewable energy source for heating, by converting it into electrical energy as biogas or directly. Biogas production around the world is mostly provided by anaerobic production methods from one type of animal manure. With this method, it has become an important source in meeting the energy needs of large animal farms and rural population, especially in rural areas. Such a strategy; It is applied in countries such as Brazil and Argentina where large farms from European countries and especially Denmark, USA, China and South American countries are common. In recent years, the use of urban household waste as biogas, especially in metropolitan cities, has become widespread in many countries.

Biodiesel: Biodiesel can be defined as an alternative diesel fuel obtained by processing resources such as vegetable and animal oils by chemical or thermal methods. Its production is carried out by two methods as thermal and chemical; chemical method is preferred. Chemical method; thinning (dilution), micro-emulsification, pyrolysis and transestrification are examined in sections. Oily agricultural products such as rapeseed, safflower, soybean, coconut, hemp and sunflower can be used as a source, as well as biodiesel production from frozen oils and fish oil. It can also be produced from seaweed and waste cooking oil. The use of biodiesel is encouraged in many countries. The increasing use of vehicles and the fight against environmental pollution caused by this situation constitute the main reason for these incentives. Especially in European Union countries, governments have been forced to create policies with various goals. For this reason, biodiesel production and consumption has increased significantly in recent years in all European countries, especially in Germany, Italy and Austria. Production and consumption have increased in the USA and other American continent countries, especially in Brazil and Argentina, as well as in Asian countries such as China, Indonesia, Malaysia and Japan. In addition, 2% biodiesel use became mandatory with the Kyoto Protocol and 10% after 2010 (Schröder et al., 2008).

Bioethanol: Bioethanol; cereals, molasses, fruits, sugar cane pulp, cellulose and other plant sources are produced biologically by the fermentation of sugars by microorganisms and can then be obtained by distillation. Production is not a new type of energy. The first cars produced by Henry Ford and Nikola Otto and their internal combustion engines were powered by ethanol. The use of bioethanol produced from cereals in the transport sector is theoretically considered to be a carbon neutral process and beneficial for the environment. However, considering the carbon emission in the production processes of its source grains, although it is not a completely neutral process, it is a process with lower carbon emissions than gasoline. Bioethanol constitutes 85% of the biofuel market and its production has increased even more after 2000 years. The United States and Brazil are leaders in this field, producing together approximately 86% of bioethanol worldwide. The majority of the remaining production is made by the European Union countries and China (Fischer & Schrattenholzer, 2001).

6.5 The Effects of Bioenergy Policies on Different Sectors

As a type of renewable energy, bioenergy is an energy source that has a direct relationship with many different fields in its production and has an impact capacity with its consumption. It has a share in the positive or negative effects of energy consumption. Similarly, due to its agricultural, animal and forest origin, it sometimes has a direct and sometimes indirect relationship with these sectors. Therefore, these two sectors have the capacity to affect all sectors and fields that are in contact. In this section, the relationship between bioenergy production and different fields and the positive and negative aspects of this relationship will be discussed. Possible problems that may be encountered in case of widespread production will be tried to be determined theoretically.

The Impact of Bioenergy on Rural Development: Mostly plant, animal and forest products are used as a source of bioenergy around the world. Therefore, the supply of bioenergy has a direct impact on the agricultural sector. The need for raw materials will cause a deficit in agricultural production. This will lead to an increase in production and will allow an increase in employment in this field. Meeting the need for bioenergy resources will lead to increases in production, as well as the use of products produced for food purposes as a resource and the increase in demand in this area will increase price levels and subsequently increase the income of farmers. In addition, planning errors, low-productivity and low-yield products cause fertile land areas to decrease day by day. The idle state of productive agricultural lands constitutes a negative situation in terms of national wealth and rural development (Rose et al., 2014).

Developing policies that will ensure the most efficient use of these areas will be encouraging for farmers to utilize productive agricultural areas. In addition, the use of agricultural wastes as a source of bioenergy will become a new type of income for producers. For this purpose, bioenergy appears to be an important alternative that encourages investments. Since the bioenergy resource is rural and many investments avoid the cost of resource transportation, it establishes facilities in these areas where access to resources is easier and meets the need for labor in these areas (Giampietro, 2008).

The Effect of Bioenergy on Food Security: Global food crises and hunger problem in different parts of the world; demonstrates the importance of the food security problem. In particular, international organizations working in this field and local governments carry out various policies. Ensuring food safety, which is an indispensable element for the continuation of life, struggles to control the factors that negatively affect food supply, access to food and access to food, and struggles to eliminate or minimize the negative effects of these factors on food safety. Bioenergy has the potential to affect food security in two different ways. First of all, with the spread of energy-oriented agriculture, the competition between energy-oriented agriculture and food-oriented agricultural production has emerged (Smeets & Faaij, 2007). The transition of agricultural areas, which are produced for food purposes, to agricultural production for energy purposes, adversely affects the dimension of food supply. Secondly, bioenergy affects food security in terms of food prices. It has been stated that if the agricultural lands used for food purposes turn to agricultural production for energy purposes, it will cause a contraction in the food supply. This will cause food prices to rise. It has been observed that the use of food for energy purposes adversely affects food supply security and causes a contraction in food supply. It is seen that there is an inverse relationship between bioenergy and food security depending on resource use, and each increase in bioenergy use globally has a suppressive effect on food security.

Impact of Bioenergy on Energy Security: Energy is very important in terms of being effective in all production activities of a country and directly affecting growth and development. Economic stability is among the leading causes of foreign trade deficit and budget deficits. Gathering the global distribution of common energy resources to certain regions has become one of the most important topics for many countries to ensure energy supply security (Gonzalez et al., 2012). The vital importance of energy security, R&D studies on domestic production and alternative energy sources have gained importance. When all energy security definitions and indices are examined, it is seen that domestic production has a positive effect on ensuring energy security. For this reason, bioenergy is an important factor in terms of energy security in terms of being renewable and being produced from domestic sources. The increase in bioenergy supply will increase the rate of domestic production in energy supply. The increase in domestic energy supply will also have a positive effect on food security (Roos et al., 1999).

6.6 Conclusion

Bioenergy investments have crucial advantages. It improves the socio-economic structure of the rural area and provides local job opportunities. It prevents migration. It provides new job opportunities. It provides strategic and economic contribution to countries by reducing foreign dependency in oil. It benefits public health as combustion products are cleaner. It ensures the protection of the environment and our natural energy resources. It supports the sustainability of energy. The development of oilseed agriculture is an alternative to exhaustible and limited energy resources. It reduces the emission of harmful greenhouse gases in the use of biodiesel and reduces CO emissions by 50%. There is a decrease in air pollution. It has an anti-toxic effect and does not contain sulfur.

On the other side, the use of bioenergy stimulates the agricultural sector and supports rural development. Although it is thought to reduce poverty, if it is not done in a sustainable way, it poses a significant threat to food security (Mutran et al., 2020). When Bio-Fuel is produced in an uncontrolled and unbalanced way, more farmland is needed, farmland required for food production is used for the production of fuel raw materials, local agricultural people lose their land, which leads to unemployment, economic problems and the food problems that may result from them, deforestation and erosion, will have negative consequences such as increased global warming (Bhuiyan et al., 2022; Dinçer et al., 2023; Eti et al., 2022; Kou et al., 2022; Xu et al., 2022).

References

Angenent, L. T., Karim, K., Al-Dahhan, M. H., Wrenn, B. A., & Domíguez-Espinosa, R. (2004). Production of bioenergy and biochemicals from industrial and agricultural wastewater. *TRENDS in Biotechnology, 22*(9), 477–485.

Banowetz, G. M., Boateng, A., Steiner, J. J., Griffith, S. M., Sethi, V., & El-Nashaar, H. (2008). Assessment of straw biomass feedstock resources in the Pacific Northwest. *Biomass and Bioenergy, 32*(7), 629–634.

Bhuiyan, M. A., Dinçer, H., Yüksel, S., Mikhaylov, A., Danish, M. S. S., Pinter, G., Uyeh, D. D., & Stepanova, D. (2022). Economic indicators and bioenergy supply in developed economies: QROF-DEMATEL and random forest models. *Energy Reports, 8*, 561–570.

Carayannis, E., Kostis, P., Dinçer, H., & Yüksel, S. (2022). Balanced-scorecard-based evaluation of knowledge-oriented competencies of distributed energy investments. *Energies, 15*(21), 8245.

Cook, J., & Beyea, J. (2000). Bioenergy in the United States: progress and possibilities. *Biomass and Bioenergy, 18*(6), 441–455.

Demirbas, A. H., & Demirbas, I. (2007). Importance of rural bioenergy for developing countries. *Energy Conversion and Management, 48*(8), 2386–2398.

Dinçer, H., Aksoy, T., Yüksel, S., & Hacioglu, U. (2022). Golden cut-oriented q-rung orthopair fuzzy decision-making approach to evaluation of renewable energy alternatives for microgeneration system investments. *Mathematical Problems in Engineering*. https://doi.org/10.1155/2022/2261166

Dinçer, H., Yüksel, S., Çağlayan, Ç., Yavuz, D., & Kararoğlu, D. (2023). Can renewable energy investments be a solution to the energy-sourced high inflation problem?. In *Managing inflation and supply chain disruptions in the global economy* (pp. 220–238). IGI Global.

Dinçer, H., Yüksel, S., & Martínez, L. (2022). Collaboration enhanced hybrid fuzzy decision-making approach to analyze the renewable energy investment projects. *Energy Reports, 8*, 377–389.

Dinçer, H., Yüksel, S., Mikhaylov, A., Pinter, G., & Shaikh, Z. A. (2022). Analysis of renewable-friendly smart grid technologies for the distributed energy investment projects using a hybrid picture fuzzy rough decision-making approach. *Energy Reports, 8*, 11466–11477.

Domac, J., Richards, K., & Risovic, S. (2005). Socio-economic drivers in implementing bioenergy projects. *Biomass and Bioenergy, 28*(2), 97–106.

Dong, W., Zhao, G., Yüksel, S., Dinçer, H., & Ubay, G. G. (2022). A novel hybrid decision making approach for the strategic selection of wind energy projects. *Renewable Energy, 185*, 321–337.

Eti, S., Dinçer, H., Gökalp, Y., Yüksel, S., & Kararoğlu, D. (2023). Identifying key issues to handle the inflation problem in the healthcare industry caused by energy prices: An evaluation with decision-making models. *Managing Inflation and Supply Chain Disruptions in the Global Economy,* 162–178.

Eti, S., Dinçer, H., Yüksel, S., & Gökalp, Y. (2022). Analysis of the suitability of the solar panels for hospitals: A new fuzzy decision-making model proposal with the T-Spherical TOP-DEMATEL method. *Journal of Intelligent & Fuzzy Systems*, (Preprint), 1–13.

Fang, S., Zhou, P., Dinçer, H., & Yüksel, S. (2021). Assessment of safety management system on energy investment risk using house of quality based on hybrid stochastic interval-valued intuitionistic fuzzy decision-making approach. *Safety Science, 141*, 105333.

Ferreira, S., Moreira, N. A., & Monteiro, E. (2009). Bioenergy overview for Portugal. *Biomass and Bioenergy, 33*(11), 1567–1576.

Fischer, G., & Schrattenholzer, L. (2001). Global bioenergy potentials through 2050. *Biomass and Bioenergy, 20*(3), 151–159.

Gan, J. (2007). Supply of biomass, bioenergy, and carbon mitigation: Method and application. *Energy Policy, 35*(12), 6003–6009.

Giampietro, M. (2008). Studying the "addiction to oil" of developed societies using the multi-scale integrated analysis of societal metabolism (MSIASM). In *Sustainable energy production and consumption* (pp. 87–138). Springer.

Gonzalez, A. O., Karali, B., & Wetzstein, M. E. (2012). A public policy aid for bioenergy investment: Case study of failed plants. *Energy Policy, 51*, 465–473.

Haiyun, C., Zhixiong, H., Yüksel, S., & Dinçer, H. (2021). Analysis of the innovation strategies for green supply chain management in the energy industry using the QFD-based hybrid interval valued intuitionistic fuzzy decision approach. *Renewable and Sustainable Energy Reviews, 143*, 110844.

Jåstad, E. O., & Bolkesjø, T. F. (2022). Modelling emission and land-use impacts of altered bioenergy use in the future energy system. *Energy, 265*, 126349.

Junginger, M., Bolkesjø, T., Bradley, D., Dolzan, P., Faaij, A., Heinimö, J., Hektor, B., Leistad, Ø., Ling, E., Perry, M., Piacente, E., Rosillo-Calle, F., Ryckmans, Y., Schouwenberg, P. P., Solberg, B., Trømborg, E., Walter, A. D. S., & de Wit, M. (2008). Developments in international bioenergy trade. *Biomass and Bioenergy, 32*(8), 717–729.

Kafka, K. I., Dinçer, H., & Yüksel, S. (2022). Impact-relation map of innovative service development regarding the sustainable growth for emerging markets. *Journal of the Knowledge Economy*, 1–24.

Kayacık, M., Dinçer, H., & Yüksel, S. (2022). Using quantum spherical fuzzy decision support system as a novel sustainability index approach for analyzing industries listed in the stock exchange. *Borsa Istanbul Review, 22*(6), 1145–1157.

Kou, G., Yüksel, S., & Dinçer, H. (2022). Inventive problem-solving map of innovative carbon emission strategies for solar energy-based transportation investment projects. *Applied Energy, 311*, 118680.

Li, W., Yüksel, S., & Dinçer, H. (2022). Understanding the financial innovation priorities for renewable energy investors via QFD-based picture fuzzy and rough numbers. *Financial Innovation, 8*(1), 1–30.

Li, J., Yüksel, S., Dınçer, H., Mikhaylov, A., & Barykin, S. E. (2022). Bipolar q-ROF hybrid decision making model with golden cut for analyzing the levelized cost of renewable energy alternatives. *IEEE Access, 10*, 42507–42517.

Martínez, L., Dinçer, H., & Yüksel, S. (2022). A hybrid decision making approach for new service development process of renewable energy investment. *Applied Soft Computing, 133*, 109897.

Mikhaylov, A., Bhatti, I. M., Dinçer, H., & Yüksel, S. (2022). Integrated decision recommendation system using iteration-enhanced collaborative filtering, golden cut bipolar for analyzing the risk-based oil market spillovers. *Computational Economics,* 1–34.

Mukhtarov, S., Yüksel, S., & Dinçer, H. (2022). The impact of financial development on renewable energy consumption: Evidence from Turkey. *Renewable Energy, 187*, 169–176.

Mutran, V. M., Ribeiro, C. O., Nascimento, C. A., & Chachuat, B. (2020). Risk-conscious optimization model to support bioenergy investments in the Brazilian sugarcane industry. *Applied Energy, 258*, 113978.

Roos, A., Graham, R. L., Hektor, B., & Rakos, C. (1999). Critical factors to bioenergy implementation. *Biomass and Bioenergy, 17*(2), 113–126.

Rose, S. K., Kriegler, E., Bibas, R., Calvin, K., Popp, A., van Vuuren, D. P., & Weyant, J. (2014). Bioenergy in energy transformation and climate management. *Climatic Change, 123*(3), 477–493.

Scarlat, N., Dallemand, J. F., Skjelhaugen, O. J., Asplund, D., & Nesheim, L. (2011). An overview of the biomass resource potential of Norway for bioenergy use. *Renewable and Sustainable Energy Reviews, 15*(7), 3388–3398.

Schröder, P., Herzig, R., Bojinov, B., Ruttens, A., Nehnevajova, E., Stamatiadis, S., Memon, A., Vassilev, A., Caviezel, M., & Vangronsveld, J. (2008). Bioenergy to save the world. *Environmental Science and Pollution Research, 15*(3), 196–204.

Smeets, E. M., & Faaij, A. P. (2007). Bioenergy potentials from forestry in 2050. *Climatic Change, 81*(3), 353–390.

Sun, L., Peng, J., Dinçer, H., & Yüksel, S. (2022). Coalition-oriented strategic selection of renewable energy system alternatives using q-ROF DEMATEL with golden cut. *Energy, 256*, 124606.

Xu, X., Yüksel, S., & Dinçer, H. (2022). An integrated decision-making approach with golden cut and bipolar q-ROFSs to renewable energy storage investments. *International Journal of Fuzzy Systems*, 1–14.

Yuan, J. S., Tiller, K. H., Al-Ahmad, H., Stewart, N. R., & Stewart, C. N., Jr. (2008). Plants to power: bioenergy to fuel the future. *Trends in Plant Science, 13*(8), 421–429.

Yuan, G., Xie, F., Dinçer, H., & Yüksel, S. (2021). The theory of inventive problem solving (TRIZ)-based strategic mapping of green nuclear energy investments with spherical fuzzy group decision-making approach. *International Journal of Energy Research, 45*(8), 12284–12300.

Yüksel, S., & Dinçer, H. (2022). Identifying the strategic priorities of nuclear energy investments using hesitant 2-tuple interval-valued Pythagorean fuzzy DEMATEL. *Progress in Nuclear Energy, 145*, 104103.

Yüksel, S., Dinçer, H., Eti, S., & Adalı, Z. (2022). Strategy improvements to minimize the drawbacks of geothermal investments by using spherical fuzzy modelling. *International Journal of Energy Research*. https://doi.org/10.1002/er.7880

Zhang, Y., Zhang, Y., Gong, C., Dinçer, H., & Yüksel, S. (2022). An integrated hesitant 2-tuple Pythagorean fuzzy analysis of QFD-based innovation cost and duration for renewable energy projects. *Energy, 248*, 123561.

Chapter 7
Evaluation of Green Employment Policies of G7 Countries for Reducing Carbon Emissions

İrfan Ersin and Halim Baş

Keywords Carbon emission reduction · Green employment policies · G7 countries · Sustainability

7.1 Introduction

Green employment policies play an essential role in overcoming the recession while helping the transition to a low-carbon and resource-efficient economy. Reducing carbon emissions is among the critical agenda items of the world. All countries have duties to reduce carbon emissions. Countries must take the necessary measures with their monetary and fiscal policies (Kafka et al., 2022; Martínez et al., 2022; Sun et al., 2022). Because the United Nations Framework Convention on Climate Change was signed at the UN meeting held in Paris in 2015 for sustainable development, and this contract entered the literature as the Paris Agreement. Within the framework of this agreement, the world needs to reduce emissions by 45% by 2030 and reach net zero by 2050 in order not to keep global warming above 1.5 °C as envisaged in the Paris Agreement. Policies are essential to comply with these targets.

Carbon emissions in the world are seen as an important problem for the future. In this context, environmental policies aimed at reducing carbon emissions have been among the priority agendas of countries. In this regard, especially developed countries have taken various actions. At the beginning of these actions, symposiums, conferences and agreements where countries came together were held. While developed countries implemented a series of policies to reduce carbon emissions, they aimed to shift employment to green sectors. This study aims to reveal the green

İ. Ersin (✉)
Vocational School of Social Sciences, Istanbul Medipol University, Istanbul, Turkey
e-mail: iersin@medipol.edu.tr

H. Baş
Faculty of Economics, Marmara University, Istanbul, Turkey
e-mail: halim.bas@marmara.edu.tr

H. Dincer, S. Yüksel (eds.), *Economic Development and the Environmental Ecosystem*, Contributions to Economics,
https://doi.org/10.1007/978-3-031-26596-9_7

employment policies on the G7 countries, representing developed countries, based on the literature review. In this context, in the second part of our study, environmental policy practices at the global level are included. In other sections, country-based employment policies are mentioned. In the conclusion part, employment policies were evaluated and suggestions were presented.

7.2 Policies and Practices for Reducing Carbon Emissions in the World

Sustainable development comes to the fore in today's world with factors such as population concentration, economic crises and environmental pollution. Since 1970, the world economy has taken decisions at both the global and national levels and set political targets in order to create an environmentally friendly production. For sustainable development and a clean environment, countries have come together many times in the past and made conferences, symposiums, and agreements. These are, respectively Stockholm Environment Conference (1972), United Nations Framework Convention on Climate Change (UNFCCC-1992), Rio Conference (1992), Kyoto Protocol (1997), Cancun Conference (2010), Doha Climate Summit (2012), Paris Climate Change Meeting (2015), Glasgow Climate Pact (2021) and Sharm El-Sheikh Climate Change Conference (2022). As a result of these meetings and agreements, the concept of a green economy developed and gained new content in the reports published by the United Nations Environment Program (UNEP) in 2009 and 2011. According to the UNEP report published in 2011, the green economy is defined as one that results in improved human well-being and social equity and significantly reduces environmental risks and ecological scarcities. Thus, in such a socially inclusive system that uses low-carbon resources effectively, public and private sector investments will be provided to increase income and employment, reduce carbon emissions and pollution, increase energy and resource efficiency, and prevent bio-diversity and ecosystem service losses. It is attached special importance to the state and fiscal policies in the green economic model (UNEP, 2011).

According to the study "Climate Change 2021: The Physical Science Foundation" prepared by the Intergovernmental Panel on Climate Change (IPCC), global warming has increased at an unprecedented rate in the last 2000 years due to the impact of human activities. The intensity of carbon emissions in the atmosphere reached its highest level in 2 million years in 2019. Concentrations of important greenhouse gases, methane and nitrous oxide, were at their highest level in 800,000 years in 2019. Since 1850, the United States has released 509 billion tons of carbon dioxide into the atmosphere, according to the Carbon Brief website, which performs research on climate change. This represents 20% of the global carbon dioxide emission rate. China is the second most polluting country in the world, after the United States, at 11%. Russia comes in second with 7%, followed by Brazil with 5% and Indonesia with 4%.

The carbon tax is one of the policies implemented to reduce carbon emissions. The carbon tax is the tax levied on the amount of carbon dioxide emissions resulting from the combustion of fossil fuels (Dinçer, Aksoy, et al., 2022; Dinçer, Yüksel, & Martínez, 2022; Dinçer, Yüksel, Mikhaylov, et al., 2022; Dong et al., 2022; Mukhtarov et al., 2022). Carbon dioxide emissions occur, especially as a result of burning fossil fuels. Producers are subject to tax per carbon dioxide emission amount due to the damage they cause to the environment as a result of burning fossil fuels (Organ & Çiftçi, 2013). When we look at the carbon tax in the world, it is difficult to come across a common carbon tax application in the global sense. Today, in 24 countries and some local regions, the carbon tax is implemented or planned in various ways according to the development level of the countries.

Another type of tax similar to the carbon tax is the pollution tax. The taxes used to ensure environmental efficiency and the transition to the green economy concept are generally known as "pollution taxes" and draw attention as compensatory taxes taken from economic actors who pollute the environment as a result of their economic activities. This taxation method is generally realized by taxing the ones that cause more harm to the environment at a higher level and those that do less harm to the environment at a lower level (Pal & Saha, 2015).

While motor vehicle tax is essentially a type of wealth tax, it is potentially one of the types of tax best suited to the green economy concept. Because, in terms of sectors, the transportation sector has a share of 24% in global carbon emissions. The share of the road transport sub-sector within the transport sector is 88%. As such, paying more attention to environmental priorities in the taxation of vehicles in the road transport sector, which has the highest contribution to global carbon emissions and uses fossil fuels at a high level, will be a very effective financial tool in the transition to the green economy (Yalçin, 2016). Today, 20 European countries have started to tax motor vehicles, taking into account the carbon dioxide emission of the vehicle (Odabaş & Hayrullahoğlu, 2017). Another potential tax that can be applied during the transition to a green economy is the value-added and special consumption taxes, among the indirect taxes. The value-added tax and the special consumption tax are vital financial instruments in changing the consumption patterns of individuals (Yalçin, 2016).

In addition to taxation, important initiatives exist to limit carbon emissions (Carayannis et al., 2022; Yüksel & Dinçer, 2022; Zhang et al., 2022). In several U.S. states, for instance, there are political practices regarding the energy sector. A portfolio standard is one of the most prevalent government laws, requiring electric utilities to provide a set amount of electricity from renewable or clean energy sources (C2ES, 2022). Additionally, the European Union has made steps to limit carbon emissions. These policies include incentives to increase renewable energy (wind, solar, biomass) and combined heat and power installations, enable the use of improved energy efficiency in buildings, industry, and household appliances, reduce CO2 emissions from new passenger cars, and reduce emissions from landfills and manufacturing.

7.3 Green Employment Policies in the USA

The initiatives and action plans of the USA to reduce carbon emissions have made substantial contributions to the employment sector. Particularly as a result of the increase in renewable energy production, new employment sectors have emerged, as has green employment. According to the US Energy and Employment Report, solar power was the fastest-growing electricity generation technology in 2021, creating 17,212 jobs and expanding by 5.4%. Despite the economic slowdown caused by COVID-19, electric and hybrid vehicles have continued to create jobs. According to the report, renewable energy jobs comprised approximately 40% of all energy jobs in 2021. In addition, it has been determined that investments in solar energy generate 1.5 times as many jobs as investments in fossil fuels (Department of Energy, 2022).

There have also been times when the USA did not implement employment policies meant to cut carbon emissions. Republican presidents and the Republican Party have generally avoided engaging in American efforts to combat global warming. Ronald Reagan, George H. W. Bush Jr., George H. W. Bush Sr., and more recently, as evidenced by President Trump's actions, have all opposed adopting practices and changes to environmental and climate laws. The primary cause of this is the Republican Party's worry that neo-liberal policies and environmental action will have a detrimental impact on economic indicators, decrease earnings, and eliminate jobs. Obama, one of the US presidents, has green economic initiatives that help lower carbon emissions. The announcement of the coal moratorium is the most significant of these. Although those employed in the coal industry and several other sectors responded negatively to this circumstance, it increased employment in the USA's renewable energy sector (Kansu et al., 2021).

One of the essential policies of the USA to reduce carbon emissions to increase green employment is the Green New Deal (GND) legislation package. The GND is a text that emerged in 2019 by Senator Alexandria Ocasio-Cortez and Senator Ed Markey and was adopted with expansion in 2020 and 2021. The Green New Deal harnesses the full power of the federal government to build an inclusive, renewable energy economy, helping to survive multiple crises simultaneously. This decision sets goals to build infrastructures, modernize cities, and overhaul energy, transportation, industry and agriculture systems to achieve 100% renewable energy as soon as possible. Besides production for a clean environment, GND's most crucial contribution is a roadmap for creating high-quality jobs in the green economy with workers' wage regulations, fringe benefits, worker protections and the right to form unions. Their main goals are to radically decarbonize the US economy and regulate workers' rights while significantly reducing economic inequality (Cha et al., 2022; Galvin & Healy, 2020).

7.4 Green Employment Policies in Germany

Germany has developed environmental policies to reduce carbon emissions both within its own country and within the EU. By supporting the transformation to a green economy with the eco-innovation policy within the EU, it has been possible to increase environmentally friendly investments and create new green business opportunities. Eco-innovation is defined as a powerful tool that combines a reduced negative impact on the environment with a positive impact on the economy and society. Eco-innovation in companies leads to lower costs, improves their capacity to seize new growth opportunities and increases their reputation among customers. Eco-innovation is vital to support the transition to a circular economy and to achieve the goals of the European Green Deal (EU Commission, 2022).

The creation of green jobs is part of the European Union's overall strategy in tackling the crisis to transform economies to promote sustainable and inclusive growth. The European Commission has created four action plans to promote green employment policies and the creation of green jobs (Pociovălişteanu et al., 2015):

- Incorporating green employment policies into national strategies
- Educational skills needed in a green economy
- Use of financial instruments for smart green investments
- The creation of partnerships between labor market actors

With climate change finally coming to the fore in politics, Germany ranks first in the international arena (rank 6) in the field of environmental policies. Its score in this measure increased by 0.4 points compared to 2014. The country's CO2 intensity has decreased but remains high by international standards due to the intensity of industrial production. The energy sector is still heavily dependent on fossil fuels. Nuclear power is planned to be phased out by 2022. A carbon tax was introduced in 2021. Beginning in 2021, heating oil, natural gas, gasoline, and diesel producers will be required to pay a CO2 charge for these goods. While CO2 emissions are priced via the European Emissions Trading System, these national regulations now establish a CO2 price for the heating and transportation sectors. Starting at 25 € in 2021, this tax on CO2 emissions will climb to 55 € by 2025. The new government has reaffirmed its commitment to continue along this course (Koalitionsvertrag, 2021, p. 63).

Policies to reduce carbon emissions in Germany are not made directly through employment. In the increase of green employment, Germany's renewable energy policies have led to an increase in employment in this sector and employment has been shaped as a result of green economy policies. The solar and wind technology sectors have become important job providers in the German economy. Although there is no data on the net number of jobs created, there are reliable data on gross employment created both directly through capacity investment and indirectly through maintenance, operation and other support activities (Aşkın & Aşkın, 2019; Lütkenhorst & Pegels, 2014). Between 2000 and 2021, the number of jobs in the renewable energy sector nearly tripled. In 2021, this figure was around

344,100 people. Biomass and wind power now have the largest share (Federal Ministry of Economy and Climate Protection, 2022).

7.5 Green Employment Policies in Canada

Canada, which includes reducing carbon emissions among its priority policies, has important environmental policies for this. It has important policy implications at both the federal and state levels. Green economic policies in Canada are policies that contribute to transforming the Canadian economy into an environmentally more sustainable one. Instead of direct employment policies, Canada makes carbon pricing, which is among the environmental policies, increasing investments in the green economy, limiting the greenhouse gas emissions of enterprises, credit incentives for companies investing in the green economy, and legal regulations to prevent greenhouse gas emissions (Loiseau et al., 2016).

Canada is among the important policies to provide concessional financing to initiatives to reduce carbon emissions. This type of financing, which includes low-interest or long-term loans, will help mobilize significant and additional private and public investment in climate initiatives and will result in a shift of employment to these areas. It supports women's skills development and job opportunities in science and environmental fields to ensure that the social and economic benefits of development are shared equally. Canada attaches great importance to women's employment and provides incentives for such initiatives. It provides significant financial support, especially for this private employment (Government of Canada, 2022).

7.6 Green Employment Policies in UK

In the last two decades, developed countries that tend to reduce emissions have attempted to construct a legal basis for climate change readiness. In this situation, The 2008 Climate Change Act is the United Kingdom's strategy for decreasing emissions and preparing for climate change (Government Property Agency, 2022). It was created with a legal aim to reduce Greenhouse Gas (GHG) Emissions in the United Kingdom by at least 80% by 2050 (relative to 1990 levels). Then, in June 2019, supplementary legislation was enacted that increased the aim to "at least 100%." Over time, with the sanctions of international agreements and the acceleration of climate change in the world, revised the targets in law, and in June of 2019, additional legislation was enacted that increased the aim to "at least one hundred percent." (Climate Change Act 2008; Climate Change Act 2008 Order, 2019). It is expected that the transition plan to zero emissions and its implications on a legal basis are not homogenous. Therefore, it is predicted that this will mostly depend on the sectoral composition of regional employment and will vary across the United

Kingdom (Green Jobs Taskforce, 2021; House of Commons Environmental Audit Committee, 2022). According to current data, over 400 thousand individuals are employed in the low-carbon economy.To raise this target, published policy documents supporting the green economy after the law update in 2019.

The first is the ten-point plan for the green industrial revolution, which came to the fore in 2020, and the Net Zero Strategy, which the government put forward in 2021. In this framework, The ten-point plan consists of the following phases: (1) Advancing Offshore Wind, (2) Driving the Growth of Low Carbon Hydrogen, (3) Delivering New and Advanced Nuclear Power, (4) Accelerating the Shift to Zero-Emission Vehicles, (5) Green Public Transport, Cycling and Walking, (6) Jet Zero and Green Ships, (7) Greener Buildings, (8) Investing in Carbon Capture, Usage, and Storage, (9) Protecting Our Natural Environment, (10) Green Finance and Innovation

To raise this target, published policy documents supporting the green economy after the law update in 2019. The first is the ten-point plan for the green industrial revolution, which came to the fore in 2020, and the Net Zero Strategy, which the government put forward in 2021. Additionally, the green jobs task force was an essential part of the implementation phase of the ten-point plan. This structure was created with the participation of the main actors and other stakeholders, such as government, industry, and education, to seize the opportunities for the green industrial revolution. The structure, established in 2020 and designed as a transition phase, has completed its mission in 2021, transitioning to green jobs and determining the direction in the production of jobs that require high skills (Green Jobs Taskforce, 2021). Another supporting structure was the Green Jobs Delivery Group, which the government established to contribute to creating green job opportunities. The purpose of this group is to support the green business goals outlined in the net zero and energy security strategies (Prospect, 2022). A significant result was that it generated 68,000 green jobs after implementing the ten-point plan (British Energy Security Strategy, 2022).

In addition to this situation, the net zero strategies provide a framework that supports policies, expenditures, and employment. The nature of this support is two-dimensional. The first is the creation of high-quality jobs for the government's strategic goals set by its ten-point plan. The other is the continuous improvement in the intrinsic quality of jobs. In addition, the Draft Employment Law envisages regulations supporting the said objectives. In this way, it is aimed to create 190,000 jobs by 2025 and 440,000 jobs by 2030 with the policies and budget specified in the strategy (Net Zero Strategy, 2021).

7.7 Green Employment Policies in Japan

Law No. 117 on the Promotion of Measures Against Global Warming, which came into effect in 1998 and has undergone multiple amendments since then, established the legal basis for lowering carbon emissions in Japan roughly 25 years ago. In addition to this situation, measures have been taken to change the energy policies significantly and, thus, the employment structure. For example, a carbon tax introduced in 2012 demonstrated commitment to the goals of the Paris Climate Agreement. In this new era, the guiding principles of Japan's energy policy have been energy security, environmental concerns, economic efficiency, and security (3E + S). These principles are designed to accomplish the goals of the Paris Climate Agreement until 2030, particularly the national contribution outlined in the prepared framework agreements, government plans that consider the most crucial employment sectors, and all strategy documents based on green growth.

In this direction, significant progress has been made in the last 7 years. The framework agreement submitted to the UN in 2015 set the target of reducing greenhouse gas emissions by 26% by 2030 compared to 2013. Then, in 2016, the measures against global warming and the government action plan, prepared based on the 1998 law, were approved by the cabinet. In 2018, the new strategic energy plan was approved, the first document in which renewable energy is positioned as the primary power source for the economy and all sectors. It has been announced that there has been a decrease in greenhouse gas emissions since the implementation of the said documents began, and Japan is progressing with great determination to become a 2050-neutral carbon society by 2050. The "Green Growth Strategy Through Achieving Carbon Neutrality in 2050", which aims to be a neutral society and envisages structural reforms and innovation investments, was prepared in coordination with other ministries under the Ministry of Economy, Industry leadership, and Trade and announced in October 2020 (D'Ambrogio, 2021). The strategy draws attention to 14 key sectors and assigns a key role for growth. This positive expectation underlines the importance of sectors that grow with supportive policies and create employment opportunities from the employment point of view (METI, 2022).

According to the International Renewable Energy Agency (IRENA), renewable jobs decreased from 241,000 in 2019 to 220,000 in 2020. Recently, Japan adopted IRENA's 1.5-degree scenario, which prioritizes a technological path and investments. Although there is a decrease in the number of jobs, it is expected that the number of jobs will increase after adopting a roadmap with this new policy understanding. According to the Planned Energy Scenario (PES), it is expected to be 290,000 in 2030 and 340,000 in 2050, with a more modest increase. On the other hand, the IRENA scenario estimates 800,000 in 2050. Therefore, the policy followed has significant potential in terms of creating employment (IRENA, 2021, 2022).

7.8 Green Employment Policies in Italy

In Italy, awareness and importance of the potential benefits of increased renewable energy sources and energy efficiency, including reducing polluting and climate-changing emissions, improving energy security, and economic and employment opportunities for families and the production system is increasing markedly

(Bhuiyan et al., 2022; Kou et al., 2022; Xu et al., 2022). For this purpose, policies and planning prepared at the national level is a citizen-oriented strategy, including producers, consumers and businesses (Ministry of Economic Development, 2019).

Within the Green New Deal framework, each member country's National Energy and Climate Plan (NECP) to reduce carbon emissions by 2030 is one of the most up-to-date and essential steps in this regard. At the same time, this approach is a requirement of the EU legislation and directives of which it is a member. In this context, at the end of 2019, Italy enacted Law No. 160, encouraging new initiatives to transpose EU directives into domestic law (European Commission, 2019). Additionally, like Germany, Italy also attaches importance to eco-innovation in the creation of green business opportunities within the framework of the European Green Consensus (Fabrizi et al., 2022).

Nearly half of Italy's emissions come from transport and "other emissions", including buildings. Between 2005 and 2019, energy industry emissions fell by 42%, placing the industry in third place in overall emissions. Italy has reduced its emissions by 13% by 2020 compared to 2005. It carries out strategies to reach its target of 33% by 2030. In 2019, Italy had 18% Renewable Energy Source (RES). The country's 30% target for 2030 is focused on wind and solar energy. However, while energy efficiency initiatives focus on buildings and transportation, businesses and households are supported (European Parliament, 2021). According to a 2018 report by a consortium of stakeholders in the Italian mobility and energy sector (1), the transition from a fossil fuel-fueled system to one based on locally produced renewable energy is expected to generate 19,225 additional jobs in 2030 and more than 50,000 jobs in 2050 (European Climate Foundation, 2018). In the report published by the IMF on Italy's labor productivity, it is predicted in the model study that the carbon tax will contribute positively to employment and revive labor-intensive sectors in the transition to renewable energy. Based on the model study, the employment-supporting aspect of tax policy regulations in the energy transition process becomes more visible (IMF, 2022).

Since 2000, 18 policies have been developed and put into practice on a legal basis in Italy. Most of the policies are in the role of supporting and setting national targets in sectoral terms. Italy's other policies are generally based on climate change and national strategies. The 2007 Climate Change Action Plan, 2013 National Energy Strategy, 2015 Climate Adaptation Strategy, and 2019 Italy's Integrated National and Energy Climate Plan are prominent policies. These policies support reducing carbon emissions by specifying targets such as energy security and energy efficiency, and as a result, incentives that contribute positively to employment are vital (Grantham Research Institute, 2022).

7.9 Green Employment Policies in France

There are many policies in the fight against climate change in France. Some of these offer national and directly inclusive content. The National Low Carbon Strategy (Stratégie Nationale Bas-Carbone SNBC), published in 2015, is one of them. It concerns all sectors of activity in scope and has binding provisions for citizens, communities, and businesses. It also provides guidelines to ensure the transition to a low-carbon economy in all business sectors (Dinçer et al., 2023; Eti et al., 2022; Kayacık et al., 2022). It sets carbon budgets and caps that will not exceed every 5 years until 2033. This strategy paper has two objectives:

- Achieve carbon neutrality by 2050
- Reducing the carbon footprint of the French people

On the path to the strategy's 2050 carbon neutral aim, it is a desirable objective that the low carbon transition will gradually improve the quality of life, including environment and health, and positively impact employment. The document emphasizes sector-based governance and seeks to cut emissions by promoting sectoral energy efficiency. In this context, governance's correct and systematic operation can be viewed as a form of indirect employment support for a carbon-neutral economy (Ministere De La Transition Ecologıque et Solidaire, 2015).

Another policy of France regarding climate change is the National Climate Change Plan. The National Low Carbon Strategy was revised in 2017 and had a role in accelerating the implementation of the provisions of the Paris Agreement with the energy and climate law that came into force in 2019 (one of the first European countries to pass a carbon-neutral law) and current legislation aims to reduce emissions by 40% by 2030 relative to 1990 levels. (Ministere De La Transition Ecologıque et Solidaire, 2020; Tapolsky, 2021).

Between 2015 and 2035, an estimated 100,000–350,000 additional jobs are projected to be created yearly. In the strategy document prepared by the Ministry of Ecology, Sustainable Development, and Energy for decision-makers, it is suggested to promote the National Low Carbon Strategy policies for the creation of regional approaches to managing jobs and skills, with an emphasis on the development of qualifications in the construction industry. In addition, it is emphasized that the policies established for the agricultural sector (food security guarantee, approaches that protect public health, natural resources, rural and social dynamics, and the environment) provide opportunities for green growth and job creation while preserving competitiveness (Ministere De L'Ecologie, du Developpement Durable et de L'Energie, 2015).

France places a premium on educational materials that promote the transition to a sustainable lifestyle. For this reason, key industries in France (industrial sectors associated with digitalization, environmental change, economic dominance, and production relocation) are bolstered for "strategic professions of the future" in education (García Vaquero et al., 2021).

7.10 Conclusion

As a result of the environmental policy practices of developed countries, green business opportunities come to the fore. In general, when the employment policies of the G7 countries are examined in the literature, it is difficult to say that there are direct employment policies aimed at reducing carbon emissions. G7 countries include green employment on their agenda as an indirect result of their environmental policies. This result is also emphasized in some studies in the literature.

In recent years, transformations related to economic, social and political risk factors have been accelerating worldwide. This transformation strengthens the precautionary and implementation tendencies towards both risk and new opportunities for countries with strong industrial infrastructures and developing depending on industrial production (Eti et al., 2023; Li, Yüksel and Dinçer, 2022; Mikhaylov et al., 2022; Yüksel et al., 2022). For this reason, developed countries have given priority to renewable energy investments to achieve sustainable-centered economic transformation and as a result, they have focused on policies to integrate employment into green sectors. At this point, they have implemented important policies such as improving educational skills for green sectors, financial incentives for increasing green investments, eco-innovation, tax measures to reduce fossil fuel-based jobs, and sector-based greenhouse gas emission limits.

Developed countries should attach importance to the implementation of a just transition for employment to shift to green sectors in reducing carbon emissions. In this framework, it is considered important for developed countries to diversify active employment policy tools to increase the quality of employment while ensuring a fair transition (Fang et al., 2021; Haiyun et al., 2021; Li, Yüksel and Dinçer, 2022; Yuan et al., 2021). For this, it is recommended to make separate programming for green employment or just transition in active employment policy programs. Because adapting the low-skilled workforce of these countries to the green sector faster will contribute to the development of employment policies.

References

Aşkın, E., & Aşkın, U. (2019). Yeşil İşler: Yenilenebilir enerji sektörünün istihdam yaratma potansiyeli. In *International congress of energy economy and security*.

Bhuiyan, M. A., Dinçer, H., Yüksel, S., Mikhaylov, A., Danish, M. S. S., Pinter, G., Uyeh, D. D., & Stepanova, D. (2022). Economic indicators and bioenergy supply in developed economies: QROF-DEMATEL and random forest models. *Energy Reports, 8*, 561–570.

British Energy Security Strategy. (2022). British energy security strategy secure, clean and affordable British energy for the long term. https://assets.publishing.service.gov.uk/government/uploads/system/uploads/attachment_data/file/1069969/british-energy-security-strategy-web-accessible.pdf. Date accessed 26.11.2022.

C2ES. (2022). State climate policy maps. https://www.c2es.org/content/state-climate-policy/. Date accessed 26.11.2022.

Carayannis, E., Kostis, P., Dinçer, H., & Yüksel, S. (2022). Balanced-scorecard-based evaluation of knowledge-oriented competencies of distributed energy investments. *Energies, 15*(21), 8245.
Cha, J. M., Stevis, D., Vachon, T. E., Price, V., & Brescia-Weiler, M. (2022). A green new deal for all: The centrality of a worker and community-led just transition in the US. *Political Geography, 95*, 102594.
Climate Change Act. 2008. (2008). https://www.legislation.gov.uk/ukpga/2008/27/contents
D'Ambrogio, E. (2021). *Japan's 2050 goal: A carbon-neutral society*. European Parliament.
Department of Energy. (2022). The U.S. Energy and Employment Report. https://www.energy.gov/sites/default/files/2022-06/USEER%202022%20National%20Report_1.pdf. Date accessed 26.11.2022.
Dinçer, H., Aksoy, T., Yüksel, S., & Hacioglu, U. (2022). Golden cut-oriented q-rung orthopair fuzzy decision-making approach to evaluation of renewable energy alternatives for microgeneration system investments. *Mathematical Problems in Engineering*.
Dinçer, H., Yüksel, S., Çağlayan, Ç., Yavuz, D., & Kararoğlu, D. (2023). Can renewable energy investments be a solution to the energy-sourced high inflation problem?. In *Managing inflation and supply chain disruptions in the global economy* (pp. 220–238). IGI Global.
Dinçer, H., Yüksel, S., & Martínez, L. (2022). Collaboration enhanced hybrid fuzzy decision-making approach to analyze the renewable energy investment projects. *Energy Reports, 8*, 377–389.
Dinçer, H., Yüksel, S., Mikhaylov, A., Pinter, G., & Shaikh, Z. A. (2022). Analysis of renewable-friendly smart grid technologies for the distributed energy investment projects using a hybrid picture fuzzy rough decision-making approach. *Energy Reports, 8*, 11466–11477.
Dong, W., Zhao, G., Yüksel, S., Dinçer, H., & Ubay, G. G. (2022). A novel hybrid decision making approach for the strategic selection of wind energy projects. *Renewable Energy, 185*, 321–337.
Eti, S., Dinçer, H., Gökalp, Y., Yüksel, S., & Kararoğlu, D. (2023). Identifying key issues to handle the inflation problem in the healthcare industry caused by energy prices: An evaluation with decision-making models. *Managing Inflation and Supply Chain Disruptions in the Global Economy*, 162–178.
Eti, S., Dinçer, H., Yüksel, S., & Gökalp, Y. (2022). Analysis of the suitability of the solar panels for hospitals: A new fuzzy decision-making model proposal with the T-Spherical TOP-DEMATEL method. *Journal of Intelligent & Fuzzy Systems*, (Preprint), 1–13.
EU Commission. (2022). Eco-innovation. https://green-business.ec.europa.eu/eco-innovation_en. Date accessed 27.11.2022.
European Climate Foundation. (2018). Fuelling Italy's future: How the transition to low-carbon mobility strengthens the economy. https://europeanclimate.org/resources/fuelling-italys-future-how-the-transition-to-low-carbon-mobility-strengthens-the-economy/. Date accessed 26.11.2022.
European Commission. (2019). Summary of the commission assessment of the draft National Energy Climate Plan 2021-2030 Italy. https://energy.ec.europa.eu/system/files/2019-06/necp_factsheet_it_final_0.pdf. Date accessed 22.11.2022.
European Parliament. (2021). Climate action in Italy latest state of play. https://www.europarl.europa.eu/RegData/etudes/BRIE/2021/690663/EPRS_BRI(2021)690663_EN.pdf. Date accessed 26.11.2022.
Fabrizi, A., Guarini, G., & Meliciani, V. (2022). Environmental networks and employment creation: Evidence from Italy. *Journal of Cleaner Production, 359*, 132056. Date accessed 29.11.2022.
Fang, S., Zhou, P., Dinçer, H., & Yüksel, S. (2021). Assessment of safety management system on energy investment risk using house of quality based on hybrid stochastic interval-valued intuitionistic fuzzy decision-making approach. *Safety Science, 141*, 105333.
Federal Ministry of Economy and Climate Protection. (2022). Gross employment from renewable energies 2000 to 2021. https://www.erneuerbare-energien.de/EE/Redaktion/DE/Downloads/zeitreihe-der-beschaeftigungszahlen-seit-2000.html. Date accessed 27.11.2022.

Galvin, R., & Healy, N. (2020). The green new deal in the United States: What it is and how to pay for it. *Energy Research & Social Science, 67*, 101529.

García Vaquero, M., Sánchez-Bayón, A., & Lominchar, J. (2021). European green deal and recovery plan: Green jobs, skills and wellbeing economics in Spain. *Energies, 14*(14), 4145.

Government of Canada. (2022). Action area policy: Environment and climate action. https://www.international.gc.ca/world-monde/issues_development-enjeux_developpement/priorities-priorites/fiap_environment-paif_environnement.aspx?lang=eng#a2. Date accessed 27.11.2022.

Government Property Agency. (2022). Net zero programme: Looking beyond carbon emissions. https://www.gov.uk/government/case-studies/net-zero-programme-looking-beyond-carbon-emissions. Date accessed 20.11.2022.

Grantham Research Institute. (2022). Climate change laws of the world. https://climate-laws.org/geographies/italy. Date accessed 10.11.2022.

Green Jobs Taskforce. (2021). Department for Business, Energy & Industrial Strategy. https://assets.publishing.service.gov.uk/government/uploads/system/uploads/attachment_data/file/1003570/gjtf-report.pdf. Date accessed 26.10.2022.

Haiyun, C., Zhixiong, H., Yüksel, S., & Dinçer, H. (2021). Analysis of the innovation strategies for green supply chain management in the energy industry using the QFD-based hybrid interval valued intuitionistic fuzzy decision approach. *Renewable and Sustainable Energy Reviews, 143*, 110844.

House of Commons Environmental Audit Committee. (2022). Green jobs: Government response to the committee's third report fourth special report of session 2021-22. https://committees.parliament.uk/publications/8559/documents/86458/default/. Date accessed 26.11.2022.

International Monetary Fund (IMF). (2022). *Selected issues Italy*. IMF Country Report No. 22/256.

IRENA. (2021). *World energy transition outlook: 1.5°C pathway*. International Renewable Energy Agency.

IRENA. (2022). *Socio-economic footprint of the energy transition: Japan*. International Renewable Energy Agency.

Kafka, K. I., Dinçer, H., & Yüksel, S. (2022). Impact-relation map of innovative service development regarding the sustainable growth for emerging markets. *Journal of the Knowledge Economy*, 1–24.

Kansu, Z. N., Turanli, M., & Turanlı, R. (2021). Amerika Birleşik Devletleri'nin Barack Obama Dönemi İklim ve Çevre Politikalarının Analizi. *Sosyal Bilimler Araştırma Dergisi, 10*(1), 205–213.

Kayacık, M., Dinçer, H., & Yüksel, S. (2022). Using quantum spherical fuzzy decision support system as a novel sustainability index approach for analyzing industries listed in the stock exchange. *Borsa Istanbul Review, 22*(6), 1145–1157.

Koalitionsvertrag. (2021). Mehr Fortschritt wagen, Bündnis für Freiheit, Gerechtigkeit und Nachhaltigkeit, Koalitionsvertrag zwischen SPD, Bündnis 90/Die Grünen und FDP.

Kou, G., Yüksel, S., & Dinçer, H. (2022). Inventive problem-solving map of innovative carbon emission strategies for solar energy-based transportation investment projects. *Applied Energy, 311*, 118680.

Li, W., Yüksel, S., & Dinçer, H. (2022). Understanding the financial innovation priorities for renewable energy investors via QFD-based picture fuzzy and rough numbers. *Financial Innovation, 8*(1), 1–30.

Li, J., Yüksel, S., Dınçer, H., Mikhaylov, A., & Barykin, S. E. (2022). Bipolar q-ROF hybrid decision making model with golden cut for analyzing the levelized cost of renewable energy alternatives. *IEEE Access, 10*, 42507–42517.

Loiseau, E., Saikku, L., Antikainen, R., Droste, N., Hansjürgens, B., Pitkänen, K., Leskinen, P., Kuikman, P., & Thomsen, M. (2016). Green economy and related concepts: An overview. *Journal of cleaner production, 139*, 361–371.

Lütkenhorst, W., & Pegels, A. (2014, January). *Stable policies—turbulent markets. Germany's green industrial policy: The costs and benefits of promoting solar PV and wind energy*. International Institute for Sustainable Development Research Report. IISD.

Martínez, L., Dinçer, H., & Yüksel, S. (2022). A hybrid decision making approach for new service development process of renewable energy investment. *Applied Soft Computing, 133*, 109897.

METI. (2022). Green growth strategy through achieving carbon neutrality in 2050. https://www.meti.go.jp/english/policy/energy_environment/global_warming/ggs2050/index.html. Date accessed 13.12.2022.

Mikhaylov, A., Bhatti, I. M., Dinçer, H., & Yüksel, S. (2022). Integrated decision recommendation system using iteration-enhanced collaborative filtering, golden cut bipolar for analyzing the risk-based oil market spillovers. *Computational Economics,* 1–34.

Ministere De La Transition Ecologıque et Solidaire. (2015). National low carbon strategy. https://unfccc.int/sites/default/files/resource/en_SNBC-2_summary_4-pages.pdf. Date accessed 20.11.2022.

Ministere De La Transition Ecologıque et Solidaire. (2020). The ecological and inclusive transition towards carbon neutrality. https://unfccc.int/sites/default/files/resource/en_SNBC-2_summary_compl.pdf. Date accessed 15.11.2022.

Ministere De L'Ecologie, du Developpement Durable et de L'Energie. (2015). Strategie Nationale Bas-Carbone. https://www.ecologie.gouv.fr/sites/default/files/SNBC_SPM_Eng_Final.pdf. Date accessed 14.11.2022.

Ministry of Economic Development. (2019). Integrated National Energy and Climate Plan Italy. https://energy.ec.europa.eu/system/files/2020-02/it_final_necp_main_en_0.pdf. Date accessed 16.11.2022.

Mukhtarov, S., Yüksel, S., & Dinçer, H. (2022). The impact of financial development on renewable energy consumption: Evidence from Turkey. *Renewable Energy, 187*, 169–176.

Net Zero Strategy. (2021). Net zero strategy: Build back Grener. https://assets.publishing.service.gov.uk/government/uploads/system/uploads/attachment_data/file/1033990/net-zero-strategy-beis.pdf. Date accessed 16.11.2022.

Odabaş, H., & Hayrullahoğlu, B. (2017). Çevresel sorunların çözümünde motorlu taşıtlar vergisine bakış: AB üyesi ülke örnekleri. *Kastamonu Üniversitesi İktisadi ve İdari Bilimler Fakültesi Dergisi, 17*(3), 54–70.

Organ, İ., & Çiftçi, T. E. (2013). Karbon vergisi. *Niğde Üniversitesi İktisadi ve İdari Bilimler Fakültesi Dergisi, 6*(1), 81–95.

Pal, R., & Saha, B. (2015). Pollution tax, partial privatization and environment. *Resource and Energy Economics, 40*, 19–35.

Pociovălişteanu, D. M., Novo-Corti, I., Aceleanu, M. I., Şerban, A. C., & Grecu, E. (2015). Employment policies for a green economy at the European Union level. *Sustainability, 7*(7), 9231–9250.

Prospect. (2022). Green Jobs Delivery Group takes first steps to delivering green jobs promise. https://prospect.org.uk/news/green-jobs-delivery-group-takes-first-steps-to-delivering-green-jobs-promise. Date accessed 26.11.2022.

Sun, L., Peng, J., Dinçer, H., & Yüksel, S. (2022). Coalition-oriented strategic selection of renewable energy system alternatives using q-ROF DEMATEL with golden cut. *Energy, 256*, 124606.

Tapolsky, S. (2021). France's current law targets decrease emissions by 40% by 2030 compared to 1990 levels. https://www.climatescorecard.org/2021/07/frances-current-law-targets-decrease-emissions-by-40-by-2030-compared-to-1990-levels/. Date accessed 26.11.2022.

The Climate Change Act 2008 (2050 Target Amendment) Order 2019. (2019). https://www.legislation.gov.uk/ukdsi/2019/9780111187654. Date accessed 26.11.2022.

UNEP. (2011). Towards a green economy: Pathways to sustainable development and poverty eradication. https://sustainabledevelopment.un.org/content/documents/126GER_synthesis_en.pdf. Date accessed 25.11.2022.

Xu, X., Yüksel, S., & Dinçer, H. (2022). An integrated decision-making approach with golden cut and bipolar q-ROFSs to renewable energy storage investments. *International Journal of Fuzzy Systems,* 1–14.

Yalçin, A. Z. (2016). Sürdürülebilir kalkınma için yeşil ekonomi düşüncesi ve mali politikalar. *Çankırı Karatekin Üniversitesi İktisadi ve İdari Bilimler Fakültesi Dergisi, 6*(1), 749–775.

Yuan, G., Xie, F., Dinçer, H., & Yüksel, S. (2021). The theory of inventive problem solving (TRIZ)-based strategic mapping of green nuclear energy investments with spherical fuzzy group decision-making approach. *International Journal of Energy Research, 45*(8), 12284–12300.

Yüksel, S., & Dinçer, H. (2022). Identifying the strategic priorities of nuclear energy investments using hesitant 2-tuple interval-valued Pythagorean fuzzy DEMATEL. *Progress in Nuclear Energy, 145*, 104103.

Yüksel, S., Dinçer, H., Eti, S., & Adalı, Z. (2022). Strategy improvements to minimize the drawbacks of geothermal investments by using spherical fuzzy modelling. *International Journal of Energy Research.*

Zhang, Y., Zhang, Y., Gong, C., Dinçer, H., & Yüksel, S. (2022). An integrated hesitant 2-tuple Pythagorean fuzzy analysis of QFD-based innovation cost and duration for renewable energy projects. *Energy, 248*, 123561.

Chapter 8
Analysis of the Efficiency of Energy Management at the Metallurgical Enterprise

Tomonobu Sengyu and Vikas Khare

Keywords Efficiency · Ecosystem · Economic growth · Energy technologies · Clean energy

8.1 Introduction

The classification of energy intensity by the object being characterized is also important. So, for example, the object of determining energy intensity at a metallurgical enterprise can be a technological process, a production operation and cycle, as well as finished products. Therefore, based on this classification, a division is proposed for the energy intensity of the technological process, production operation, cycle or finished product (Kafka et al., 2022; Martínez et al., 2022; Sun et al., 2022). This classification allows you to identify the most energy-intensive objects and develop energy-saving measures for specific objects.

Also, the enterprises set standard consumption values: for products considering the specifics of their manufacture (seamless or welded pipes), for operations performed (steel smelting) and work (for generating steam boiler heat). For these cases, it is advisable to distinguish such a classification feature as "attitude to the standard", according to which the energy intensity can be within the standard and above the norm (Dinçer, Aksoy, et al., 2022; Dinçer, Yüksel, & Martínez, 2022; Dinçer, Yüksel, Mikhaylov, & Barykin, et al., 2022; Dinçer, Yüksel, Mikhaylov, & Pinter, et al., 2022; Dong et al., 2022; Mukhtarov et al., 2022).

Modern metallurgical enterprises produce a fairly large range of finished products, and each of them can significantly differ in the energy intensity of

T. Sengyu (✉)
University of the Ryukyus, Nishihara, Okinawa, Japan
e-mail: b985542@tec.u-ryukyu.ac.jp

V. Khare
School of Technology, Management and Engineering, NMIMS, Indore, Madhya Pradesh, India
e-mail: vikas.khare@nmims.edu

H. Dincer, S. Yüksel (eds.), *Economic Development and the Environmental Ecosystem*, Contributions to Economics,
https://doi.org/10.1007/978-3-031-26596-9_8

manufacturing. That is why, in order to identify the least energy-intensive types of products and increase the efficiency of use at enterprises, the energy intensity of various types of products is calculated (Carayannis et al., 2022; Yüksel & Dinçer, 2022; Zhang et al., 2022). Accordingly, according to the product range, the energy intensity of the i-th type of product is distinguished.

It should be noted that during the production of products, they are consumed, which in turn relate to the cost items for technological, shop, repair and general factory needs. Fuel and energy costs attributed directly to the cost of manufacturing a particular product are the costs of fuel and energy for technological needs, on the basis of which the technological energy intensity is calculated (Li, Yüksel, & Dinçer, 2022; Mikhaylov, Bhatti, et al., 2022; Yüksel et al., 2022). General shop expenses include expenses incurred by a certain structural division in the production of finished products for the maintenance of fixed assets, repair, maintenance and production management. The aggregate of fuel and energy costs used in performing capital and other repairs can be attributed to the item of the repair fund and in order to determine the energy efficiency of this process, the energy intensity of repair work is calculated (Eti et al., 2023; Haiyun et al., 2021; Li, Yüksel, Dınçer, Mikhaylov, & Barykin, 2022). Factory-wide expenses are fuel and energy costs that do not relate to a specific division or product, but occurred during the maintenance of the enterprise, for example, the cost of maintaining the factory territory in proper condition, watering lawn grass and trees (factory-wide energy intensity) (Ermiş & Güven, 2022).

The following type of classification, by time period, allows you to calculate the energy intensity of a unit of production for any time period: month, quarter, half-year, year. Detailed information by time period allows you to analyze the dynamics of energy intensity in comparison with previous periods and make timely management decisions aimed at optimizing this indicator.

For the purposes of planning and analyzing energy intensity in a given time interval, the concepts of planned and actual energy intensity are used. Comparing these values of energy intensity helps to draw conclusions about the dynamics of the indicator, understand the reasons for possible deviations from the plan, and develop corrective measures.

8.2 Literature Review

The company's production facilities include an electric steelmaking shop, a pipe rolling shop, and a pipe welding shop. The structure of the plant's energy service includes two auxiliary workshops—power and electric, as well as the department of the chief power engineer, which provides general management of the service and performs the function of analysis, planning and monitoring of use. Professional training of technical specialists and service personnel is carried out on the site of our own training center, which has good technical equipment with various information and production support systems (Bhuiyan, Dinçer, et al., 2022; Conteh et al., 2021; Daniali et al., 2021; Denisova et al., 2019; Huang, Masrur, et al., 2021; Huang,

Yona, et al., 2021; Khan et al., 2021; Liu, Kato, Mandal, Mikhaylov, Hemeida, & Senjyu, 2021; Liu, Kato, Mandal, Mikhaylov, Hemeida, Takahashi, et al., 2021; Mikhaylov, 2018, 2022; Mikhaylov et al., 2019; Moiseev et al., 2023; Nie et al. 2020; Nyangarika et al., 2019a, 2019b; Sediqi et al., 2022).

The primary task of the analysis is to identify the fuel and energy resources used in the enterprise. At the surveyed enterprise, there is a significant shortage of energy metering systems, which significantly complicates control over their use and does not allow for an adequate assessment of the actual efficiency and energy intensity (Barykin, Mikheev, et al., 2022; Bhuiyan et al., 2021; Bhuiyan, Zhang, et al., 2022; Candila et al., 2021; Danish et al., 2022a, 2022b; Dong et al., 2021; Li, Yüksel, Dınçer, Mikhaylov, et al., 2022; Liu et al., 2022a, 2022b; Mikhaylov, 2021b; Mikhaylov & Grilli, 2022; Mukhametov et al., 2021; Saqib et al., 2021).

Analysis of indicators indicates the presence of the main consumer of energy resources, which is a pipe rolling shop. However, due to the specific nature of electric steel production, more than 50% of the electricity consumed is consumed by the electric steelmaking shop, making it the undisputed leader in this category. If you perform a comparative analysis of consumption relative to the previous year, you can see a decrease in most indicators, which is due to a decrease in production volumes due to the introduction of anti-covid restrictions around the world. At the same time, there is an increase in natural gas consumption in the pipe welding shop, which is explained by the stabilization of demand in the market of welded pipes and, as a result, a large load, relative to 2019, of this division (An et al., 2022; Badr et al., 2022; Barykin, Kapustina, et al., 2022; Dinçer, Aksoy, et al., 2022; Dinçer, Yüksel, & Martínez, 2022; Dinçer, Yüksel, Mikhaylov, & Barykin, et al., 2022; Dinçer, Yüksel, Mikhaylov, & Pinter, et al., 2022; Kalinina et al. 2022; Khan et al., 2022; Mehta et al., 2022; Mikhaylov, Bhatti, et al., 2022; Mikhaylov, Yumashev, et al., 2022; Nyangarika et al., 2022; Shaikh et al., 2022).

A more detailed analysis of energy consumption by main consumers indicates that the specific consumption depends on the stage of conversion. So, for example, the highest indicators are typical for the main processing areas, namely, steel smelting and hot rolled pipe billets, and a significant decrease in specific consumption at the finishing and delivery of finished products. This fact is explained by the high energy intensity of the process of primary processing of steel and its reduction as it passes through the technological chain (Alwaelya et al., 2021; An & Mikhaylov, 2020, 2021; Mikhaylov, 2021a; Mikhaylov et al., 2023; Mutalimov et al., 2021; Varyash et al., 2020; Yumashev et al., 2020; Yumashev & Mikhaylov, 2020; Zhao et al., 2021).

When analyzing the main technical measures for energy saving carried out at the enterprise from 2019 to 2020, the average annual effect of these measures is 90 million rubles. The main directions in the implementation of measures are organizational actions of personnel aimed at seasonal reduction of consumption due to decommissioning of electricity consumers, as well as replacement of electric drives with less powerful ones (An, Mikhaylov, & Jung, 2020; An, Mikhaylov, & Kim, 2020; An, Mikhaylov, & Moiseev, 2019; An, Mikhaylov, & Richter, 2020; An, Mikhaylov, & Sokolinskaya 2019; Dooyum et al., 2020; Gura et al., 2022;

Mikhaylov, 2020a, 2020b, 2020c; Mikhaylov & Tarakanov, 2020; Moiseev et al., 2020, 2021).

A comparative analysis shows a decrease in savings for all resources in 2020 and a complete lack of implementation of projects to save thermal energy. The explanation for this is the exhaustion of the potential of previously proposed organizational and technical measures and the reduction of funding for energy-saving measures in 2020 (An et al., 2021; Danish et al., 2020, 2021; Dayong et al., 2020; Nyangarika et al., 2018; Shaikh et al., 2021; Tamashiro et al., 2021, 2023; Uyeh et al., 2021).

8.3 Assessment of the Internal and External Energy Consumption Environment

The analysis of the internal and external environment will be carried out on the basis of qualitative analysis using expert assessments. Managers and technical specialists who are more or less involved in the management development process will be involved as experts. Audit reports are considered as documentary materials confirming the compliance of the company's management system with international standards.

The assessment of the internal and external environment in this section is based on the opinions of experts participating in the study. The main task of this section of the dissertation is to determine the dependence of economic indicators obtained as a result of the introduction of energy-saving measures on the efficiency of managing the processes of planning, distribution, consumption and savings (Fang et al., 2021; Kayacık et al., 2022; Yuan et al., 2021).

The main business processes that characterize the internal environment of energy management are planning of energy resources, organization of energy supply to consumers, control of energy consumption efficiency and motivation of employees to implement the principles of energy conservation. In order to analyze the internal environment, the method of constructing organizational and managerial profiles that reflect the development of various management subsystems is widely used. The benefits of this method are the ability to generalize qualitative assessments of energy efficiency, the ability to determine the maturity of the company's energy policy, and this method allows you to see a complete picture of the level of management development (Dinçer et al., 2023; Eti et al., 2022). However, this tool has a number of drawbacks, namely, it shows only a generalized view of energy efficiency problems and relies only on the opinions of the experts involved.

In one of the studies, a fairly effective method for building a management profile is proposed. The principle of building a profile is based on filling in the fields of the energy management matrix, which reflect on the one hand—the management directions, on the other—the level of development of each of the directions on a scale from zero to four points. The main directions include energy policy, organization and motivation, development of information systems, marketing and investment activity of the company. The energy profile makes it possible to identify acute problems in the field of management and the degree of balanced development of elements of the internal environment. The study notes that achieving energy efficiency is possible only if there is a balance of all criteria and a uniform development of the energy management system.

The degree of development of the management system is ranked on a five-point scale: for example, the management system is at zero level and there is no idea about it at all. At this stage, there is also no monitoring of energy consumption and energy efficiency, there are no staff motivation programs, etc. At the next stage of development, individual specialists in the field of management appear, but due to the lack of personal responsibility, key performance indicators are not regularly recorded. All implemented measures relate to private energy facilities, do not have a strategic focus and operate in the short term.

The second level of development is characterized by senior managers' acceptance of the importance of energy efficiency management principles. At the same time, in the style of management and decision-making, a technocratic approach is mainly applied to the development and implementation of energy saving measures, which is expressed in the predominance of technical solutions over organizational ones. The basis of motivation is the enthusiasm of the team members involved in management issues.

At the third level of development, the organizational structures that are assigned for the organization and functioning of the management system become clearly distinguishable, and they provide technical and methodological support for managerial decision-making. The information system is at the initial stage of development and monitors basic energy efficiency indicators (Bhuiyan, Dinçer, et al., 2022; Kou et al., 2022; Xu et al., 2022). However, a big step towards implementing the energy saving policy at this stage is the developed and coordinated program of management activities.

At the same time, management is not yet perceived as a full-fledged direction in management, but is considered as a technical mechanism. At the fourth level of development, the procedure for delegating responsibility in the field of management at various levels of management is fully functioning. A clearly formulated energy policy appears at the enterprise, as well as the strategic direction of development of the management system is traced. When planning investment costs, all possible effects from the implementation of energy saving projects (economic, environmental) are considered. Comprehensive support for the effective integration of energy management into the company's management system is provided by the processes of personnel training, informing employees about their role in achieving the goal, as well as all possible assistance from top management. The fourth level of development is characterized by the probability of risks associated with the phenomena of formalism and bureaucracy of energy efficiency management processes. In addition, attracting long-term investments can have an impact on reducing the performance indicators of some technical projects and solutions.

Building an organizational profile, in itself, is a rather complex process that requires compliance with a certain sequence of actions. The initial profile design is based on an expert assessment conducted by a specific manager or a group of them. After that, the same procedure for developing the profile is repeated the required number of times, considering the opinions of other experts of the enterprise. After each iteration, explanatory work is required in case of discrepancies in the ratings for individual criteria, which allows you to objectively evaluate a particular direction and identify strengths and weaknesses.

Identification of priorities and critical factors that can affect the energy efficiency of the enterprise under consideration is very important when building an organizational profile. In addition, critical points are subjected to comparative analysis, followed by decomposition and offering the most rational justification. The in-depth analysis carried out during the brainstorming discussion also involves identifying responsibility centers for each area and performance indicators that allow for subsequent monitoring of changes in this area.

Significant contradictions in the obtained estimates are noted in the areas of marketing and organization of management, in this regard, to determine the root causes of such differences, it is necessary to continue studying these areas. The high value of the assessment in the direction of energy policy indicates that there is an understanding of its importance for the development of the system, at this stage it is an element of the company's strategy. This is confirmed by the majority of managers surveyed. At the same time, it is noted that management is not sufficiently integrated into the management structure, and there is no clear delegation of responsibility in the use of energy resources. Information systems in the management structure also received a fairly high rating, which indicates the adoption of a new business model based on digital transformation and awareness of the importance of this area in strategic development. However, the most important task for the long-term development of the enterprise, along with the integration of digital transformation processes, is to create a system for continuous monitoring and analysis of energy consumption data.

Internal system marketing reflects the promotion of ideas in the field of energy saving among the company's personnel, as well as the organization of a developed benchmarking system (comparison of specific energy consumption in the production of products and services). The current state is characterized by insufficient awareness of employees on the main management tasks and methods of energy-efficient work. To improve this direction, it is necessary to organize a process for covering energy saving issues at all levels of the enterprise, including using internal information resources (mass media, information tools, social networks, etc.).

Investments in energy infrastructure received the lowest rating when building an enterprise profile. The main reason for this situation is the lack of funding for global energy sector modernization projects aimed at improving energy efficiency. Currently, the company implements activities with a relatively short payback period at the expense of the budget for current repairs and maintenance of fixed assets. Analysis of the organizational profile shows that the company is currently trying to ensure competitiveness by maximizing profits, while implementing minor energy-saving measures. However, in the long run, it seeks to make a transition to the implementation of large investment projects.

It is equally important to establish communication with the external environment for information exchange. At the enterprise under consideration, such communication is provided by the external relations department through the media, as well as through round tables, open dialogues, and participation of management representatives in regional and national conferences and exhibitions.

8.4 Conclusion

The analysis of consumption shows that there is a significant potential for savings in the pipe rolling shop for most resources, except for electricity. The leader in consumption and, as a result, the greatest potential for saving electricity has an electric steelmaking shop. The realization of potential is mainly related to the organization of production process planning and monitoring of resource consumption using digital systems.

The data obtained as a result of audits is of great importance in the analysis of energy efficiency. As a rule, the purpose of the audit is to establish the compliance of the management documentation developed at the enterprise with the requirements of the standard. If necessary, an in-depth audit can be performed with the study of energy flows and the proposal of economically justified measures, depending on the tasks of a particular enterprise. The cost of conducting an audit in different countries can reach 2% of the total energy costs of the facility, and the duration of the audit is from 20 to 50 days and depends on the volume of the management system. After implementing the recommendations received during the audit, in most cases it is possible to reduce energy costs by up to 20%. At the same time, the cost of conducting an audit is recouped in the next 2–3 years. During the audit, data from existing energy consumption devices and portable devices (if there are no standard ones) can be used. During the first stage, a flow chart is developed from raw materials to finished products with a description of the main energy consumers (boilers, furnaces, pumps, compressors, etc.). For each consumer, a flow balance is performed and the reasons for exceeding the planned indicators are analyzed.

During the audit, a number of shortcomings were identified that limit the implementation of strategic management principles. This included a low level of analysis at the enterprise, as auditors were not provided with confirmation of the achieved level of energy efficiency and an assessment of the degree of achievement of management goals. Due to the lack of the necessary principles for reporting on qualitative changes in energy efficiency, there is a possibility of incorrect interpretation of the analysis output. Energy efficiency indicators can include both production and organizational indicators, which include making managerial decisions.

References

Alwaelya, S. A., Yousif, N. B. A., & Mikhaylov, A. (2021). Emotional development in preschoolers and socialization. *Early Child Development and Care, 191*, 16.

An, J., & Mikhaylov, A. (2020). Russian energy projects in South Africa. *Journal of Energy in Southern Africa, 31*(3).

An, J., & Mikhaylov, A. (2021). Analysis of energy projects financial efficiency and renewable energy generation in Russia. *Finance: Theory and Practice, 25*(5), 79–91.

An, J., Mikhaylov, A., Dinçer, H., & Yüksel, S. (2022). Economic modelling of electricity generation: long short-term memory and Q-Rung orthopair fuzzy sets. *Heliyon, 8*, e10759.

An, J., Mikhaylov, A., & Jung, S.-U. (2020). The strategy of South Korea in the global oil market. *Energies, 13*(10), 2491.

An, J., Mikhaylov, A., & Jung, S.-U. (2021). A linear programming approach for Robust network revenue management in the airline industry. *Journal of Air Transport Management, 91*, 101979.

An, J., Mikhaylov, A., & Kim, K. (2020). Machine learning approach in heterogeneous group of algorithms for transport safety-critical system. *Applied Sciences, 10*(8), 2670.

An, J., Mikhaylov, A., & Moiseev, N. (2019). Oil price predictors: Machine learning approach. *International Journal of Energy Economics and Policy, 9*(5), 1–6.

An, J., Mikhaylov, A., & Richter, U. H. (2020). Trade war effects: Evidence from sectors of energy and resources in Africa. *Heliyon, 6*, e05693. https://doi.org/10.1016/j.heliyon.2020.e05693

An, J., Mikhaylov, A., & Sokolinskaya, N. (2019). Machine learning in economic planning: Ensembles of algorithms. *Journal of Physics: Conference Series, 1353*, 012126.

Badr, A. M. N. A. A., Mohamed, T. I., Osman, N. A. Q., & Mikhaylov, A. (2022). A review of social media website users' interaction paths with governmental accounts during the COVID-19 pandemic. *Informatics, 9*, 50. https://doi.org/10.3390/informatics9030050

Barykin, S. E., Kapustina, I. V., Sergeev, S. M., Daniali, S. M., Kopteva, L. A., Semenova, G. N., Pryadko, I. P., Mikhaylov, A., Baboshkin, P., Datsyuk, P., & Senjyu, T. (2022). Financial logistics models based on systematic approach improving management solutions. *F1000Research, 11*, 570. https://doi.org/10.12688/f1000research.111252.1

Barykin, S., Mikheev, A., Kiseleva, E., Putikhin, Y., Alekseeva, N., & Mikhaylov, A. (2022). An empirical analysis of Russian regions' debt sustainability. *Economies, 10*(4), 296.

Bhuiyan, M. A., An, J., Mikhaylov, A., Moiseev, N., & Danish, M. S. S. (2021). Renewable energy deployment and COVID-19 measures for sustainable development. *Sustainability, 13*, 4418.

Bhuiyan, M. A., Dinçer, H., Yüksel, S., Mikhaylov, A., Danish, M. S. S., Pinter, G., Uyeh, D. D., & Stepanova, D. (2022). Economic indicators and bioenergy supply in developed economies: QROF-DEMATEL and random forest models. *Energy Reports, 8*(2022), 561–570.

Bhuiyan, M. A., Zhang, Q., Khare, V., Mikhaylov, A., Pinter, G., & Huang, X. (2022). Renewable energy consumption and economic growth nexus—a systematic literature review. *Frontiers in Environmental Science, 10*, 878394. https://doi.org/10.3389/fenvs.2022.878394

Candila, V., Maximov, D., Mikhaylov, A., Moiseev, N., Senjyu, T., & Tryndina, N. (2021). On the relationship between oil and exchange rates of oil-exporting and oil-importing countries: from the great recession period to the Covid-19 era. *Energies, 14*, 8065.

Carayannis, E., Kostis, P., Dinçer, H., & Yüksel, S. (2022). Balanced-scorecard-based evaluation of knowledge-oriented competencies of distributed energy investments. *Energies, 15*(21), 8245.

Conteh, F., Takahashi, H., Hemeida, A. M., Krishnan, N., Mikhaylov, A., & Senjyu, T. (2021). Hybrid grid-connected renewable power generation for sustainable electricity supply in Sierra Leone: Case study Lungi Town. *Sustainability, 13*(18).

Daniali, S. M., Barykin, S. E., Kapustina, I. V., Khortabi, F. M., Sergeev, S. M., Kalinina, O. V., Mikhaylov, A., Veynberg, R., Zasova, L., & Senjyu, T. (2021). Predicting volatility index according to technical index and economic indicators on the basis of deep learning algorithm. *Sustainability, 13*, 14011.

Danish, M. S. S., Bhattacharya, A., Stepanova, D., Mikhaylov, A., Grilli, M. L., Khosravy, M., & Senjyu, T. (2020). A systematic review of metal oxide applications for energy and environmental sustainability. *Metals, 10*(12), 1604.

Danish, M. S. S., Senjyu, T., Sabory, N. R., Khosravy, M., Grilli, M. L., Mikhaylov, A., & Majidi, H. (2021). A forefront framework for sustainable aquaponics modeling and design. *Sustainability, 13*, 9313.

Danish, M. S., Senjyu, T. S., Sabory, N. R., & Mikhaylov, A. (2022a). Lessons from COVID-19 conferring environmental re-engineering opportunity. In M. Danish & T. Senjyu (Eds.), *Eco-friendly and agile energy strategies and policy development* (pp. 99–118). IGI Global). https://doi.org/10.4018/978-1-7998-9502-2.ch005

Danish, M. S., Senjyu, T. S., Sabory, N. R., & Mikhaylov, A. (2022b). Interplay consequences of COVID-19 on global environmental sustainability. In M. Danish & T. Senjyu (Eds.), *Eco-friendly and agile energy strategies and policy development.* IGI Global. https://doi.org/10.4018/978-1-7998-9502-2.ch003

Dayong, N., Mikhaylov, A., Bratanovsky, S., Shaikh, Z. A., & Stepanova, D. (2020). Mathematical modeling of the technological processes of catering products production. *Journal of Food Process Engineering, 43*(2), 1–9.

Denisova, V., Mikhaylov, A., & Lopatin, E. (2019). Blockchain infrastructure and growth of global power consumption. *International Journal of Energy Economics and Policy, 9*(4), 22–29.

Dinçer, H., Aksoy, T., Yüksel, S., & Hacioglu, U. (2022). Golden cut-oriented q-rung orthopair fuzzy decision-making approach to evaluation of renewable energy alternatives for microgeneration system investments. *Mathematical Problems in Engineering*.

Dinçer, H., Yüksel, S., Çağlayan, Ç., Yavuz, D., & Kararoğlu, D. (2023). Can renewable energy investments be a solution to the energy-sourced high inflation problem?. In *Managing inflation and supply chain disruptions in the global economy* (pp. 220–238). IGI Global.

Dinçer, H., Yüksel, S., & Martínez, L. (2022). Collaboration enhanced hybrid fuzzy decision-making approach to analyze the renewable energy investment projects. *Energy Reports, 8*, 377–389.

Dinçer, H., Yüksel, S., Mikhaylov, A., Barykin, S. E., Aksoy, T., & Hacioğlu, U. (2022). Analysis of environmental priorities for green project investments using an integrated q-rung orthopair fuzzy modelling. *IEEE Access, 10*. https://doi.org/10.1109/ACCESS.2022.3174058

Dinçer, H., Yüksel, S., Mikhaylov, A., Pinter, G., & Shaikh, Z. A. (2022). Analysis of renewable-friendly smart grid technologies for the distributed energy investment projects using a hybrid picture fuzzy rough decision-making approach. *Energy Reports, 8*, 11466–11477. https://doi.org/10.1016/j.egyr.2022.08.275

Dong, B., Ikonnikova, I., Rogulin, R., Sakulyeva, T., & Mikhaylov, A. (2021). Environmental economic approach to optimization of transport communication in megacities. *Journal of Environmental Science and Health, Part A, 56*(6), 660–666.

Dong, W., Zhao, G., Yüksel, S., Dinçer, H., & Ubay, G. G. (2022). A novel hybrid decision making approach for the strategic selection of wind energy projects. *Renewable Energy, 185*, 321–337.

Dooyum, U. D., Mikhaylov, A., & Varyash, I. (2020). Energy security concept in Russia and South Korea. *International Journal of Energy Economics and Policy, 10*(4), 102–107.

Ermiş, A. M., & Güven, M. E. (2022). The role of green energy investments in energy supply security. In *Circular economy and the energy market* (pp. 67–77). Springer.

Eti, S., Dinçer, H., Gökalp, Y., Yüksel, S., & Kararoğlu, D. (2023). Identifying key issues to handle the inflation problem in the healthcare industry caused by energy prices: An evaluation with decision-making models. *Managing Inflation and Supply Chain Disruptions in the Global Economy,* 162–178.

Eti, S., Dinçer, H., Yüksel, S., & Gökalp, Y. (2022). Analysis of the suitability of the solar panels for hospitals: A new fuzzy decision-making model proposal with the T-Spherical TOP-DEMATEL method. *Journal of Intelligent & Fuzzy Systems*, (Preprint), 1–13.

Fang, S., Zhou, P., Dinçer, H., & Yüksel, S. (2021). Assessment of safety management system on energy investment risk using house of quality based on hybrid stochastic interval-valued intuitionistic fuzzy decision-making approach. *Safety Science, 141*, 105333.

Gura, D., Mikhaylov, A., Glushkov, S., Zaikov, M., & Shaikh, Z. A. (2022). Model for estimating power dissipation along the interconnect length in single on-chip topology. *Evolutionary Intelligence, 15*, 2369–2373. https://doi.org/10.1007/s12065-020-00407-7

Haiyun, C., Zhixiong, H., Yüksel, S., & Dinçer, H. (2021). Analysis of the innovation strategies for green supply chain management in the energy industry using the QFD-based hybrid interval valued intuitionistic fuzzy decision approach. *Renewable and Sustainable Energy Reviews, 143*, 110844.

Huang, Y., Masrur, H., Shigenobu, R., Hemeida, A. M., Mikhaylov, A., & Senjyu, T. (2021). A comparative design of a campus microgrid considering a multi-scenario and multi-objective approach. *Energies, 14*, 2853.

Huang, Y., Yona, A., Takahashi, H., Hemeida, A. M., Mandal, P., Mikhaylov, A., Senjyu, T., & Lotfy, M. E. (2021). Energy management system optimization of drug store operate electric vehicles charging station. *Sustainability, 14*, 1217836.

Kafka, K. I., Dinçer, H., & Yüksel, S. (2022). Impact-relation map of innovative service development regarding the sustainable growth for emerging markets. *Journal of the Knowledge Economy*, 1–24.

Kalinina, O. V., Barykin, S. E., Sergeev, S. M., Semenova, G. N., Fatkullina, A., Mikhaylov, A., & De La Poza, E. (2022). Smart city perspectives in post-pandemic governance: Externalities reduction policy. *F1000Research, 11*, 1032. https://doi.org/10.12688/f1000research.123195.1

Kayacık, M., Dinçer, H., & Yüksel, S. (2022). Using quantum spherical fuzzy decision support system as a novel sustainability index approach for analyzing industries listed in the stock exchange. *Borsa Istanbul Review, 22*(6), 1145–1157.

Khan, A. A., Laghari, A. A., Gadekallu, T. R., Shaikh, Z. A., Javed, A. R., Rashid, M., Estrela, V. V., & Mikhaylov, A. (2022). A drone-based data management and optimization using metaheuristic algorithms and blockchain smart contracts in a secure fog environment. *Computers and Electrical Engineering, 102*, 108234. https://doi.org/10.1016/j.compeleceng.2022.108234

Khan, A. A., Shaikh, Z. A., Baitenova, L., Mutaliyeva, L., Moiseev, N., Mikhaylov, A., Laghari, A. A., Idris, S. A., & Alshazly, H. (2021). QoS-ledger: Smart contracts and metaheuristic for secure quality-of-service and cost-efficient scheduling of medical-data processing. *Electronics, 10*, 3083.

Kou, G., Yüksel, S., & Dinçer, H. (2022). Inventive problem-solving map of innovative carbon emission strategies for solar energy-based transportation investment projects. *Applied Energy, 311*, 118680.

Li, W., Yüksel, S., & Dinçer, H. (2022). Understanding the financial innovation priorities for renewable energy investors via QFD-based picture fuzzy and rough numbers. *Financial Innovation, 8*(1), 1–30.

Li, J., Yüksel, S., Dınçer, H., Mikhaylov, A., & Barykin, S. E. (2022). Bipolar q-ROF hybrid decision making model with golden cut for analyzing the levelized cost of renewable energy alternatives. *IEEE Access, 10*, 42507–42517, 35900. https://doi.org/10.1109/ACCESS.2022.3168315

Liu, L., Kato, T, Mandal, P., Mikhaylov, A, Hemeida, A. M., & Senjyu T. (2021). Multi-area power system load frequency control by using model predictive control by introducing renewable energy sources. In *2021 international conference on science & contemporary technologies (ICSCT)* (pp. 1–6). https://doi.org/10.1109/ICSCT53883.2021.9642521

Liu, L., Kato, T., Mandal, P., Mikhaylov, A., Hemeida, A. M., Takahashi, H., & Tomonobu, S. (2021). Two cases studies of model predictive control approach for hybrid renewable energy systems. *AIMS Energy, 9*(6), 1241–1259.

Liu, Z., Panfilova, E., Mikhaylov, A., & Kurilova, A. (2022a). Assessing stability in the relationship between parties in crowdfunding and crowdsourcing projects during the COVID-19 crisis.

Journal of Global Information Management (JGIM), 30(4), 1–18. https://doi.org/10.4018/JGIM.297905

Liu, Z.-J., Panfilova, E., Mikhaylov, A., & Kurilova, A. (2022b). COVID-19 crisis impact on the stability between parties in crowdfunding and crowdsourcing. *Wireless Personal Communications, 122*, 915–930.

Martínez, L., Dinçer, H., & Yüksel, S. (2022). A hybrid decision making approach for new service development process of renewable energy investment. *Applied Soft Computing, 133*, 109897.

Mehta, R., Verghese, J., Mahajan, S., Barykin, S., Bozhuk, S., Kozlova, N., Kapustina, I., Mikhaylov, A., Naumova, E., & Dedyukhina, N. (2022). Consumers' behavior in conversational commerce marketing based on messenger chatbots. *F1000Research, 11*(647). https://doi.org/10.12688/f1000research.122037.1

Mikhaylov, A. (2018). The yield of the carry trade strategy. *Finance: Theory and Practice, 22*(3), 52–63. https://doi.org/10.26794/2587-5671-2018-22-3-52-63

Mikhaylov, A. (2020a). Cryptocurrency market analysis from the open innovation perspective. *Journal of Open Innovation: Technology, Market, and Complexity, 6*(4), 197.

Mikhaylov, A. (2020b). Geothermal energy development in Iceland. *International Journal of Energy Economics and Policy, 10*(4), 31–35.

Mikhaylov, A. (2020c). Cryptocurrency market development: hurst method. *Finance: Theory and Practice, 24*(3), 81–91.

Mikhaylov, A. (2021a). Development of Friedrich von Hayek's theory of private money and economic implications for digital currencies. *Terra Economicus, 19*(1).

Mikhaylov, A. (2021b). Lichens as indicators of atmospheric pollution in urban ecosystems. *Israel Journal of Ecology & Evolution, 67*(1–2), 60–68. https://doi.org/10.1163/22244662-bja10016

Mikhaylov, A. (2022). Efficiency of renewable energy generation in Russia. *Anais da Academia Brasileira de Ciências, 94*(4), e20191226. https://doi.org/10.1590/0001-3765202220191226

Mikhaylov, A., Bhatti, I.M., Dinçer, H., & Yüksel, S. (2022). Integrated decision recommendation system using iteration-enhanced collaborative filtering, golden cut bipolar for analyzing the risk-based oil market spillovers. *Computational Economics*, 1–34. https://doi.org/10.1007/s10614-022-10341-8

Mikhaylov, A., Burakov, D., & Didenko, V. (2019). Relationship between oil price and macroeconomic indicators in Russia. *Finance: Theory and Practice, 23*(2), 105–116. https://doi.org/10.26794/2587-5671-2019-23-2-105-116

Mikhaylov, A., Dinçer, H., & Yüksel, S. (2023). Analysis of financial development and open innovation oriented fintech potential for emerging economies using an integrated decision-making approach of MF-X-DMA and golden cut bipolar q-ROFSs. *Financial Innovation, 9*, 10. https://doi.org/10.1186/s40854-022-00234-w

Mikhaylov, A., & Grilli, M. L. (2022). Machine learning methods and sustainable development: Metal oxides and multilayer metal-oxides. *Metals, 12*(4).

Mikhaylov, A., & Tarakanov, S. (2020). Development of Levenberg-Marquardt theoretical approach for electric network. *Journal of Physics: Conference Series, 1515*, 052006.

Mikhaylov, A., Yumashev, A., & Kolpak, E. (2022). Quality of life, anxiety and depressive disorders in patients with extrasystolic arrhythmia. *Archives of Medical Science, 18*(2). https://doi.org/10.5114/aoms.2020.101359

Moiseev, N., Mikhaylov, A., Dinçer, H., & Yüksel, S. (2023). Effects of market capitalization shocks for open innovation models in e-commerce industry: Golden cut QROF MCDM analysis. *Financial Innovation, 9*, 32.

Moiseev, N., Mikhaylov, A., Varyash, I., & Saqib, A. (2020). Investigating the relation of GDP per capita and corruption index. *Entrepreneurship and Sustainability Issues, 8*(1), 780–794.

Moiseev, N., Sorokin, A., Zvezdina, N., Mikhaylov, A., Khomyakova, L., & Danish, M. S. S. (2021). Credit risk theoretical model on the base of DCC-GARCH in time-varying parameters framework. *Mathematics, 9*, 2423. https://doi.org/10.3390/math9192423

Mukhametov, A., Bekhorashvili, A., Avdeenko, A., & Mikhaylov, A. (2021). The impact of growing legume plants under conditions of biologization and soil cultivation on chernozem fertility and productivity of rotation crops. *Legume Research, 44*, 12.
Mukhtarov, S., Yüksel, S., & Dinçer, H. (2022). The impact of financial development on renewable energy consumption: Evidence from Turkey. *Renewable Energy, 187*, 169–176.
Mutalimov, V., Kovaleva, I., Mikhaylov, A., & Stepanova, D. (2021). Assessing regional growth of small business in Russia. *Entrepreneurial Business and Economics Review, 9*(3), 119–133. https://doi.org/10.15678/EBER.2021.090308
Nie, D., Panfilova, E., Samusenkov, V., & Mikhaylov, A. (2020). E-Learning financing models in Russia for sustainable development. *Sustainability, 12*(11), 4412.
Nyangarika, A., Mikhaylov, A., Muyeen, S. M., Yadykin, V., Mottaeva, A., Pryadko, I., Barykin, S., Fomenko, N., Rykov, G., & Shvandar, K. (2022). Energy stability and decarbonization in developing countries: Random Forest approach for forecasting of crude oil trade flows and macro indicators. *Frontiers in Environmental Science, 10*, 1031343. https://doi.org/10.3389/fenvs.2022.1031343
Nyangarika, A., Mikhaylov, A., & Richter, U. (2019a). Influence oil price towards economic indicators in Russia. *International Journal of Energy Economics and Policy, 9*(1), 123–129.
Nyangarika, A., Mikhaylov, A., & Richter, U. (2019b). Oil price factors: Forecasting on the base of modified auto-regressive integrated moving average model. *International Journal of Energy Economics and Policy, 9*(1), 149–159.
Nyangarika, A., Mikhaylov, A., & Tang, B.-J. (2018). Correlation of oil prices and gross domestic product in oil producing countries. *International Journal of Energy Economics and Policy, 8*(5), 42–48.
Saqib, A., Chan, T.-H., Mikhaylov, A., & Lean, H. H. (2021). Are the responses of sectoral energy imports asymmetric to exchange rate volatilities in Pakistan? Evidence from recent foreign exchange regime. *Frontiers in Energy Research, 9*, 614463. https://doi.org/10.3389/fenrg.2021.614463
Sediqi, M. M., Nakadomari, A., Mikhaylov, A., Krishnan, N., Lotfy, M. E., Yona, A., & Senjyu, T. (2022). Impact of time-of-use demand response program on optimal operation of afghanistan real power system. *Energies, 15*, 296.
Shaikh, Z. A., Kraikin, A., Mikhaylov, A., & Pinter, G. (2022). Forecasting stock prices of companies producing solar panels using machine learning methods. *Complexity*. https://doi.org/10.1155/2022/9186265
Shaikh, Z. A., Moiseev, N., Mikhaylov, A., & Yüksel, S. (2021). Facile synthesis of copper oxide-cobalt oxide/nitrogen-doped carbon (Cu2O-Co3O4/CN) composite for efficient water splitting. *Applied Sciences, 11*, 9974. https://doi.org/10.3390/app11219974
Sun, L., Peng, J., Dinçer, H., & Yüksel, S. (2022). Coalition-oriented strategic selection of renewable energy system alternatives using q-ROF DEMATEL with golden cut. *Energy, 256*, 124606.
Tamashiro, K., Alharbi, T., Mikhaylov, A., Hemeida, A. M., Krishnan, N., Lotfy, M. E., & Senjyu, T. (2021). Investigation of home energy management with advanced direct load control and optimal scheduling of controllable loads. *Energies, 14*, 7314. https://doi.org/10.3390/en14217314
Tamashiro, K., Omine, E., Krishnan, N., Mikhaylov, A., Hemeida, A. M., & Senjyu, T. (2023). Optimal components capacity based multi-objective optimization and optimal scheduling based MPC-optimization algorithm in smart apartment buildings. *Energy & Buildings, 278*, 112616. https://doi.org/10.1016/j.enbuild.2022.112616
Uyeh, D. D., Asem-Hiablie, S., Park, T., Kim, K.-M., Mikhaylov, A., Woo, S., & Ha, Y. (2021). Could Japonica rice be an Alternative variety for increased global food security and climate change mitigation? *Food, 10*, 1869. https://doi.org/10.3390/foods10081869
Varyash, I., Mikhaylov, A., Moiseev, N., & Aleshin, K. (2020). Triple bottom line and corporate social responsibility performance indicators for Russian companies. *Entrepreneurship and Sustainability Issues, 8*(1), 313–331.

Xu, X., Yüksel, S., & Dinçer, H. (2022). An integrated decision-making approach with golden cut and bipolar q-ROFSs to renewable energy storage investments. *International Journal of Fuzzy Systems*, 1–14.

Yuan, G., Xie, F., Dinçer, H., & Yüksel, S. (2021). The theory of inventive problem solving (TRIZ)-based strategic mapping of green nuclear energy investments with spherical fuzzy group decision-making approach. *International Journal of Energy Research, 45*(8), 12284–12300.

Yüksel, S., & Dinçer, H. (2022). Identifying the strategic priorities of nuclear energy investments using hesitant 2-tuple interval-valued Pythagorean fuzzy DEMATEL. *Progress in Nuclear Energy, 145*, 104103.

Yüksel, S., Dinçer, H., Eti, S., & Adalı, Z. (2022). Strategy improvements to minimize the drawbacks of geothermal investments by using spherical fuzzy modelling. *International Journal of Energy Research.*

Yumashev, A., & Mikhaylov, A. (2020). Development of polymer film coatings with high adhesion to steel alloys and high wear resistance. *Polymer Composites, 41*(7), 2875–2880.

Yumashev, A., Ślusarczyk, B., Kondrashev, S., & Mikhaylov, A. (2020). Global indicators of sustainable development: Evaluation of the influence of the human development index on consumption and quality of energy. *Energies, 13*, 2768.

Zhang, Y., Zhang, Y., Gong, C., Dinçer, H., & Yüksel, S. (2022). An integrated hesitant 2-tuple Pythagorean fuzzy analysis of QFD-based innovation cost and duration for renewable energy projects. *Energy, 248*, 123561.

Zhao, Q., Cherkasov, S., Avdeenko, A., Kondratenko, L., & Mikhaylov, A. (2021). Integral estimate of the added value of agricultural crops in the synergetic agriculture on the example of Vicia faba (Vicia faba L.). *Polish Journal of Environmental Studies, 30*(5), 1–9. https://doi.org/10.15244/pjoes/131949

Chapter 9
The Impacts of Energy Transparency for the Improvements of Health Tourism

Hasan Dinçer, Qiang Wang, Rongrong Li, Serhat Yüksel, Büşra Çelebi, and Esma Vatandaş

Keywords Energy transparency · Health tourism · Energy investments · Energy efficiency

9.1 Introduction

For centuries, secrecy was accepted as one of the basic principles in government. It is also a fact that the dominant legal structure of the past provides a facilitating and supportive ground for the maintenance of this confidentiality principle. Later on, the principle of confidentiality became questionable due to the replacement of democracy. The right to information, which was granted to individuals with the constitutional arrangement made in Sweden in 1766, has become one of the common regulation and supervision principles in all developed democratic countries since the end of the twentieth century. With the spread of democracy and the right to full information, there has been a break from the traditional management approach. The widely accepted meaning in the period when the idea of transparency started to become widespread was the recognition of the right of access to the requested information and documents. Accordingly, it can be said that the transparency process in management is closely related to the recognition of the right to information, especially by the governed. As a result of all these developments, over time, the

H. Dinçer (✉) · S. Yüksel · B. Çelebi
The School of Business, İstanbul Medipol University, Istanbul, Turkey
e-mail: hdincer@medipol.edu.tr; serhatyuksel@medipol.edu.tr; busra.celebi@std.medipol.edu.tr

Q. Wang · R. Li
China University of Petroleum (East China), Qingdao, China
e-mail: wangqiang7@upc.edu.cn; lirr@upc.edu.cn

E. Vatandaş
The School of Business, İstanbul University, Istanbul, Turkey

H. Dincer, S. Yüksel (eds.), *Economic Development and the Environmental Ecosystem*, Contributions to Economics,
https://doi.org/10.1007/978-3-031-26596-9_9

principles of transparency and accountability have begun to be adopted by moving away from the principle of confidentiality.

Transparency is also a result of globalization. Globalization has made the actions of important actors all over the world very closely related to each other. At the same time, it has begun to be seen as a structural element of the democracy ideology in modern times. On the other hand, it is accepted as one of the basic criteria for the healthy execution of all functions and activities of the states. Today, the concept of transparency in national modern law dates back to the last 30 years. Transparency in the legal language is a tool used in the disclosure of financial matters, in the policy proposals and organizations or laws of institutions. In interstate relations, it is accepted as "a good governance tool that shows the reliability of the parties" and "institutional accountability mechanism".

9.2 The Concept of Energy Transparency

Energy transparency is explained in dictionaries with the meanings of transparency, openness, clarity, active disclosure, reliable information for the energy companies. As a matter of fact, openness, which is one of the meanings corresponding to the concept of transparency, is one of the four conditions required for the existence of a perfectly competitive market in economics books. Accordingly, openness means that all actors performing production activities have full and unhindered access to all kinds of information in the decision-making processes regarding profit maximization and all actors in consumption in decision-making processes. In terms of terminology, transparency in institutions means regular information sharing, good governance, accountability, and information acquisition (Dinçer, Aksoy, et al., 2022; Dinçer, Yüksel, & Martínez, 2022; Dinçer, Yüksel, Mikhaylov, et al., 2022; Dong et al., 2022; Yüksel & Dinçer, 2022; Zhang et al., 2022).

In its most succinct terms, transparency for the markets can be expressed as providing information to stakeholders on issues such as companies themselves, their activities, performance, and financial status. Although this concept is only one of the contents within the framework of corporate governance, it is considered as one of the leading indicators of successful corporate governance practices as it is the measure of how and how openly the financial information about the company and other corporate governance practices are presented to the public. In particular, the importance of transparency in capital markets has been increasing in recent years (Dai et al., 2022).

When we look at the studies in the literature, transparency is handled in three groups in terms of the areas it is applied: transparency in the public sector, transparency in the private sector and transparency in voluntary non-governmental organizations. Transparency in the public sector is considered as one of the tools that is based on the concept of democracy and ensures both citizens' trust in the state and states' trust in each other in terms of international relations. Transparency in the private sector is substituted as one of the tools based on corporate governance and good governance and ensuring that companies are open to their stakeholders and can give confidence. Finally, in non-governmental organizations, which are the third sector based on volunteerism, transparency is important in terms of providing openness and reliability regarding activities that create a critical social benefit (Bistline et al., 2021).

On the other hand, there are different levels of transparency. These can be expressed as corporate transparency, operational transparency, financial transparency and general transparency. At this point, the least sensitive level of transparency is financial transparency. The grievances that have occurred as a result of the scandals in the accounting reports and audits, especially in recent years, prove this situation. For example, one of the most important factors causing the 2008 global economic crisis is the lack of transparency regarding financial instruments.

Transparency is closely related to many concepts such as accountability, legitimacy, participation, good governance, democracy and independence. However, when we look at the literature, it is seen that transparency is mostly discussed in relation to the concept of accountability. Accordingly, transparency is put forward as a principle that has been revealed in order to ensure or increase accountability. The second concept most associated with the concept of transparency is the concept of governance. Today, in most countries and sectors, transparency is considered as one of the fundamental principles of good governance, in line with the excessive development of tools such as information technologies and the internet. Corporate governance, which can be defined as the management of senior management in institutions, corresponds to the area or system in which institutions are managed and audited. The main purpose of corporate governance is to prevent the formation of a dominant or privileged stakeholder group within the enterprise and to keep the interests of this stakeholder group first.

Transparency is the most important tool used in the supervision and surveillance of companies in the market economy. Transparency is important to companies, organizations, governments and communities. As a result of the increase in the general welfare and education level in the society, the expectations of individuals from good management have changed. One of these new expectations is the transition from a closed and hierarchical order to a structure in which participatory and transparency is ensured. Another important aspect of transparency is that it helps to easily see which actions were taken and in what ways. Transparency enables all the above mentioned stakeholders to focus on real, accurate and reliable data (Zhi et al., 2021).

On the other hand, it prevents or ensures that corruptions such as bribery and nepotism are noticed in a short time in all kinds of activities. It is also very important as it allows the implementation of business ethics principles, the expansion of the area of accountability from the management and the strengthening of non-governmental institutions. At the same time, it avoids wasting time or cost against any wrong, unreliable or useless data. Because transparency allows the actors in the market related to each other to fully understand each other's perspectives, needs, demands and goals. Especially when it is considered from a commercial and economic point of view, it allows making decisions with reasonable, functional and conscious choices in a way that prevents all kinds of negativities that may cause injustice.

Another importance of transparency is that it helps to ensure an efficient resource allocation and efficiency. Because deficiencies such as the absence of consolidated balance sheets and poor accounting practices prevent the efficient allocation of resources. However, lack of information in the market can lead to increased transaction costs and market imbalances. It is necessary to provide full, timely and accurate information regarding the financial statements and financial positions of national companies or international institutions. When this cannot be achieved, difficulties may arise in comparative analyzes to be made in the markets and may lead to wrong investment decisions. All these situations cause instability in the market, may lead to undesirable perceptions in the global communication network and unfairly change the direction of the market. Therefore, transparency enables financial markets to function regularly, to increase the confidence of domestic and foreign investors, to stimulate growth, to detect and correct mistakes or wrong choices in a short time (Xia et al., 2021).

Small businesses that can successfully maintain transparency will grow faster and higher than other non-transparent small businesses. Finland, for example, is a country that demonstrates that small businesses with higher transparency are more financially successful. Thus, it is possible to say that transparency is a very important part of adaptation to globalization and modern service delivery.

Transparency not only changes the way actors work and do business in markets, but also allows for greater collaboration. In this way, it provides the opportunity for the actors in the market to be involved in the policy-making processes and to make suggestions that can compensate for mistakes based on past experiences. It supports markets both financially and as a trust building by mobilizing civic participation. To be able to benefit from new technologies in order to realize advanced ideals that can affect the world; It lays the groundwork for following innovations in the world. Therefore, the right to know as one of the meanings of transparency in an entrepreneurial age has turned into a compulsory need to know. Therefore, the principle of transparency is not a choice or an advantage for institutions; is a must.

There are some necessary conditions for the systematic and effective implementation of the transparency principle. These; It can be listed as determining the tools that will provide transparency suitable for each business's own dynamics, developing accounting practices that will ensure the reliability of information and increasing its quality, establishing a control mechanism in order to eliminate the negativities that may cause violations of business ethics, and establishing institutions and policies where problems related to sectors or markets or suggestions that will contribute can be conveyed.

Looking at the literature, it is understood that energy transparency is expected to have qualities such as accessibility, relevance, intelligibility, reliability and timeliness (Kafka et al., 2022; Martínez et al., 2023; Mukhtarov et al., 2022; Sun et al., 2022). These qualifications, on the other hand, must be regulated by laws and followed through audits. Above all, transparency needs to be accessible. Because if the data is not available in a complete and accessible form, it cannot create an added value and cannot fully reveal its potential. Information obtained only on request or by paying a fee for access cannot be said to be publicly available in a meaningful and useful way. On the other hand, all data should be published as it is in the source without any changes. In order to preserve the value and functionality of the data, it should be disclosed to the relevant stakeholders as soon as possible.

However, there is a point that should not be overlooked when applying the principle of transparency: For today's free competition markets, the protection of commercial confidentiality is as critical as the problem of transparency. Because the public disclosures about the markets or companies should not lead to the public disclosure of trade secrets about not harming the interests of the institutions in question. Maintaining the delicate balance between ensuring transparency in the markets and protecting commercial confidentiality is a must for a sustainable market.

It is also important to establish functional feedback mechanisms or transparency portals for the spread of transparency. Participating digital platforms and applications can be used to achieve this. Of course, for this, it is necessary to have a good command of technological developments and new digital tools and services. In particular, new generations need to implement successful strategies that can empower the skills and tools they need to process information with the goal of ensuring that quality data can be passed on to the next generation of institutions. Therefore, it is important for market actors to constantly monitor and participate in innovations in order to increase the potential and functionality of new technologies.

In fact, it is necessary to change the mentality and establish institutional structures for transparency. For this, it is necessary to create a culture of full transparency within institutions or markets. The ways to achieve this can be listed as follows: to replace justice and honesty, to determine moral principles that facilitate compliance with the law, to ensure an efficient organizational structure, qualified distribution of duties and authorities, open communication with stakeholders with auto-control and reporting mechanisms, and a healthy internal audit activity. On the other hand, in order to ensure transparency, it is necessary to make strategic plans to adapt to globalization and to survive as companies in an increasingly competitive environment (Liang et al., 2022). It is necessary to correctly understand and interpret all the developments in the market and all the decisions taken, to make comparative analyzes, and to evaluate the experiences of companies that have failed financially, together with all their advantages and disadvantages.

In order to increase the transparency level of companies in the markets, tools such as independent auditing, accounting and financial reporting standards, internal control and risk management, and mandatory public disclosure obligation are used. Accordingly, in order to ensure that markets and companies implement the principle of transparency, it is necessary to ensure that there is no negative situation that they will fear or want to hide. Therefore, it is important that they establish strong information disclosure and openness policies. Because they can be moderate about transparency only if there are no consequences to fear and hide. For this, first of all, they must fulfill all their activities in a legal way, the companies must perform their risk management in a functional way, make good balance sheet analyzes, set up feedback tools and give regular feedback, regularly fulfill their accounting and financial reporting, have reliable human resources, regularly informing the public/ stakeholders and organizing press releases can be encouraged (Yi et al., 2021).

Unlike other markets, in the case of a merger or acquisition in the energy markets, in addition to the permission of the Competition Board, from the establishment of the company subject to the merger and acquisition to the day of the transaction and even to the continuation of this process, as well as the Energy Market Regulatory Authority. It has been accepted that it is subject to control and permission. Transparency in energy markets, as one of the areas where information security is most critical, is seen as one of the necessary conditions for ensuring free competition. In most energy markets such as electricity, natural gas, petroleum or liquefied petroleum gases, it is stated that almost all laws aim to maintain the energy market activities in a transparent, equitable and stable manner. Transparency of the market, which is one of the aims of the laws on the energy market, is based on the principle that companies operating in these markets do not keep information about their activities confidential and share them. Transparency of the energy market is only possible if all market participants share statistical information on the market within the framework of relevant regulations or voluntarily.

There have been economic and political developments, climate crises, environmental problems and security problems in the field of energy in the global energy markets. These have brought about some important structural changes and more frequent use of international law in solving problems in this field. Accordingly, transition to low-carbon markets was aimed primarily. These important structural change and transformation processes in the energy markets have started to make transparency and accountability mandatory. It is anticipated that accountability and transparency will provide more effective and permanent solutions to the problems in both global and national energy markets. It has been understood that transparency is also of critical importance for the establishment and functioning of the free competition market (Kim et al., 2021).

As a case study showing the importance of transparency; The bankruptcy of Enron, one of the largest energy companies in the United States, had consequences that shook the country as much as the post-9/11 financial crisis. Considering the related studies in the literature, one of the important reasons for Enron's bankruptcy is suggested as the problem of transparency. Accordingly, the business management and the accounting system, taking advantage of the gaps in the legal regulations, to change the information in the financial statements for their own benefit; The fact that the independent audit company ignored this just to protect its own interests brought Enron's bankruptcy. By the way, the fact that the financial statements are not reflecting the real financial situation of the business and, worse, the audit company's ignoring this is naturally caused by the gaps in the legal regulations and legal deficiencies. Therefore, first of all, legal regulations and audits should be healthy and reliable.

9.3 The Role of Energy Transparency on Health Tourism

Greenhouse gases represent chemical gases in the atmosphere that create a greenhouse effect. Greenhouse gases can occur from human and natural causes. The job of greenhouse gases is to absorb and re-emit infrared gases in the atmosphere. In fact, at a certain balance in the atmosphere, the greenhouse effect is useful for balancing the air temperature. However, if this balance is disturbed, it will become harmful. Greenhouse gases are divided into natural and indirect types. Natural greenhouse gases are classified as water vapor (H_2O), carbon dioxide (CO_2), methane (CH_4), nitrous oxide (N_2O) and ozone (O_3). Indirect greenhouse gases consist of fluorinated compounds such as hydrofluorocarbons (HFCs), perfluorocarbons (PFCs) and sulfur hexafluoride (SF_6) gases. Most of these gases are CO_2 emissions because carbon dioxide can live longer compared to other gases. Carbon dioxide emission is called the polluted gas formed as a result of the emission of carbon-containing sources into the atmosphere. If explained in more detail, carbon dioxide emission occurs when the carbon in the content of primary fossil fuels such as coal, oil and natural gas is burned and then combined with oxygen. The amount of carbon dioxide emission is measured by the carbon footprint. The carbon footprint defines the amount of CO_2 emissions emitted by an energy-consuming source (Carayannis et al., 2022; Li, Yüksel and Dinçer, 2022; Mikhaylov et al., 2022; Yüksel et al., 2022).

In other words, it is the amount of measurement of the negative effects of products and processes and human activities on the environment in terms of unit carbon. It is possible to classify the carbon footprint in two subgroups. The first subgroup consists of domestic energy consumption and the amount of carbon dioxide emitted from transportation activities. The second is the amount of carbon dioxide that comes out indirectly from the manufacture of a product and its final conversion to scrap. In the world, energy was first obtained with the help of humans and animals. In later times, it began to be obtained from various sources. In this sense, today's industrial activities, technology and population growth have led to an increase in energy demand. Fossil fuels have been used to meet this energy demand. The use of fossil fuels causes CO_2 emissions and can cause many problems. These problems have increased global warming by causing climate change in the first place. When the effect of the greenhouse effect on climate change is examined, it is said that it is related to the density of greenhouse gases remaining in the atmosphere for many years. Because these accumulated greenhouse gases cover the earth and reflect them back again by holding long wavelengths. This causes the earth to overheat, causing global warming. In short, global warming causes climate change.

It is necessary both to prevent the increase of problems and to realize sustainable development. For this reason, renewable energy sources, which are alternative sources, are recommended. Renewable energy resources are basically obtained with the help of natural resources such as solar, wind, geothermal energy resources. When evaluated from an economic point of view, there are five basic factors that affect carbon emissions. These are economic growth, energy consumption, deforestation, population growth and per capita income. The relationship between these elements defines the relationship between carbon emissions and economic growth. If this relationship is explained, first the population size affects the economic output and then the economic output and energy consumption. Then, energy consumption determines the amount of carbon emissions by affecting the use of fossil fuels. Forest areas based on economic growth are being destroyed. Forests have two positive tasks: absorbing carbon emissions and emitting oxygen. Therefore, there is a direct relationship between carbon emissions and deforestation. In this direction, forest areas are destroyed due to population growth, increase in the number of vehicles, industrial development and increase in energy consumption. A country has two main objectives as increasing the scarce resources it has and improving the quality of these resources (Eti et al., 2023; Haiyun et al., 2021; Li et al., 2022; Yuan et al., 2021).

These goals are achieved by increasing the production possibilities and technology, resulting in higher production. In this context, the economic cycle that has taken place is gradually affecting the environment negatively. The aim of maintaining this economic cycle is evaluated from different perspectives for developed and developing countries. In general, developing countries attach importance to physical capital accumulation such as development financing, while developed countries focus on human capital in order to maintain welfare. In addition, developed countries adversely affect the environment due to production, energy and raw material consumption. On the contrary, developing countries affect the environment in terms of water use, waste generation and transportation. Population growth increases carbon emissions by consuming energy as a result of food, beverage, shelter and clothing needs. If only economic growth is given importance without evaluating the effects on the environment, irreversible problems will occur. Environmental destructions affect human health, agricultural production and natural life. For this reason, it causes significant damage to the country and the global economy. If the per capita income of an individual in a country increase, the amount of consumption will also increase. In this context, the increase in the amount of consumption causes an increase in carbon emissions.

A country tends to show continuous growth. The main reason behind this is to realize economic development. Economic development increases energy consumption. Because the increase in economic development will increase per capita income. In this context, increasing income per person will lead to an increase in energy consumption. If the energy demand is obtained from dirty energy sources instead of clean energy sources, it will cause an increase in carbon emissions, which have a negative impact on the environment. The level of development of a country and the amount of energy it consumes have a direct proportion. In this sense, developed countries have a responsibility. Owing to air pollution, melting glaciers, disappearing animal species and the reduction of forests are gradually causing global warming (Dinçer et al., 2023; Eti et al., 2022; Fang et al., 2021; Kayacık et al., 2022). In addition, increasing economic growth will harm the nature and increase the cost of financial development. Inasmuch as a business will not continue its activities because fossil fuels are not sustainable. For this reason, it will increase the financial cost while transitioning to sustainable resources. In particular, it has been discussed that businesses in all countries in the Kyoto Protocol should use renewable energy sources and that governments should impose sanctions on this issue.

This protocol advocates that each country should keep the amount of carbon dioxide emitted at an equal level. In this way, countries that emit less carbon will not be affected economically. In fact, there are cascading effects. In this direction, if industrialization is established irregularly, it will adversely affect the environment. These negative effects will gradually pollute the air and cause problems that will affect human health. There will be a need for treatment to fulfill human health. Therefore, input costs will increase. In addition, the individual who takes time for treatment will affect the economy by disrupting school and work duties. Although the developed countries have a great role in the spread of carbon emissions, it is the less developed and poor countries that are most affected. Because the inadequacy of public and health services will reduce the human power and prevent the development of their economy. The reason for this obstacle is the decrease in manpower, the decrease in income levels and the increase in patient-death rates. Due to their capacity to fight climate change is insufficient. For these reasons, the competitive advantage of countries is affected by carbon emission emissions through indirect and direct effects.

When it comes to competition, medical tourism has a great importance for countries. Because tourists coming from another country to improve their health contribute to the country's economy in addition to developing health enterprises. These contributions also address other sectors such as accommodation, nutrition and entertainment. In short, health tourism is the movement of individuals to get treatment from their own countries to other countries in order to regain their health. Health tourists are called international patients. These patients are being treated in different countries for three purposes. The first is the classical medical tourist visiting another country from his own country in order to receive treatment. The second occurs when a tourist traveling to another country for vacation needs urgent treatment. Finally, according to the agreements of the countries, people who come for treatment benefit from health services in another country. Health tourism is not active according to a certain season, but operates in all seasons. Therefore, the development of health tourism is important. Thanks to health tourism, a person's health is very valuable, so he can benefit from potentials that are not available in his own country. In addition, it keeps the global economy active by stimulating the country's domestic and foreign tourism.

Public health is being affected day by day with the damages caused by industrialization in the world. A nation without health will see a reduction in the potential for work and production. For this reason, a country's health opportunities will support both domestic and foreign tourism. A foreign tourist supports the income of that country by using the health resources of another country. Unlike the export activity of health tourism, it is provided by the tourist's entry into the country rather than the transfer of a good and service to another country. In this context, a tourist tends to choose the country or city where he/she will receive health services in the best criteria. This choice is made according to better service, more affordable price and more qualified health personnel. Today, the health tourism sector tends to develop further. For example, in addition to treatment services, interest in beauty activities is increasing. In addition, the marketing activity in the health sector is also different. While this difference is that the normal product marketing strategy is aimed at selling more products, the strategy of selling more drugs in health tourism is not pleasant. In this sense, the country that makes health tourism should be sent off from the country by satisfying the tourist. Because, thanks to the recommendation strategy, the country will increase its competitiveness by increasing the development of health tourism.

When evaluated from the perspective of the country's economy, the development of health tourism will improve the country's economy. This will also be beneficial by contributing to the income of the country. In addition, it will increase competition by contributing to the development of the state and private sector. In addition, it will increase employment opportunities, which is an economic indicator. On the other hand, from a socio-economic perspective, it aims to bring income to the country, increase per capita income, help the development of regions and provide employment. Recently, awareness in the development of health tourism has increased. Therefore, rehabilitation services and services for the elderly have increased. In particular, people from different countries attach great importance to quality in the health service they receive because they have different cultures. This quality and the service provided must be sustainable. In order for a health institution to be of high quality, it is necessary to have a developed infrastructure network, organize it in accordance with standards, determine the suitability of accommodation and ensure the development of transportation networks. In addition to these, it is necessary to provide services that will benefit tourists and to apply advanced technological systems. Thus, the country engaged in health tourism will create a sustainable and quality health tourism profile.

Considering the demographic structure of developed countries, it has an elderly population. For this reason, their needs for health services have increased day by day. These healthcare costs often vary from country to country. Other reasons, it is said that the effects of globalization, problems in the infrastructure, the length of treatment periods, increasing costs, poor quality of services, increase in health literacy and protection of current health. For these reasons, citizens in developed countries with high welfare travel to other countries for treatment purposes. On the other hand, the reason for the increase in health tourism is the increasing industrialization in developed countries. Because with industrialization, air pollution and deterioration of ecological balance have increased. When evaluated within this framework, health services have been started to be received from different countries in order to protect the health of individuals and not to reduce the workforce. In fact, the relationship between health tourism and economy defines the relationship of CO2 emissions. If this relationship is explained, there are two approaches. The first approach is health tourism, which increases the economic growth of the developed country and raises the per capita income level. However, as mentioned before, increasing per capita income increases energy consumption and causes CO2 emissions.

The second approach, on the other hand, increases the health tourism activity by increasing industrialization activities by negatively affecting human health and directing them to receive health services. There are indirect effects between health tourism and CO2 emissions. For example, an individual who leaves his/her home country and visits another country in order to receive health care travels by a long way. This transportation is usually done by plane. For this reason, transportation by plane causes an increase in CO2 emissions, leading to an increase in air pollution. There are chain effects that cause an increase in the environmental crisis in the world. Therefore, local health services need to be increased. In addition, tourists who come to the country engaged in health tourism stay for at least 3 weeks. While benefiting from different activities in these 3 weeks, it causes an increase in the carbon footprint. Generally, health facilities or other places that provide health tourism are places with a large population. In addition to the activities of this crowded population, the activities of health tourists are added, and the amount of CO2 emissions intensifies and pollutes the environment. The amount of energy consumed and the amount of waste produced by health facilities have the highest share in the country's share. For this reason, the increasing number of patients due to health tourism also indirectly increases the carbon footprint by increasing the amount of energy and the amount of waste produced.

As a result, economic growth causes CO2 emissions. Economic growth has positive effects in terms of raising the welfare level of countries. However, economic growth also has a negative effect by increasing CO2 emissions. Because the industrialization activities of especially developed countries have increased. These increasing industrialization activities have led to an increase in CO2 emissions by consuming too much energy and using fossil fuels, which are dirty energy sources. In addition, the increasing population caused the destruction of forest areas and increased energy consumption. In addition, with the economic growth, the per capita income of individuals has increased, which has increased energy consumption with more comfortable needs, unlike their basic needs. In this context, air pollution due to increased CO2 emissions has increased and adversely affected human health (Bhuiyan et al., 2022; Ermiş & Güven, 2022; Kou et al., 2022; Xu et al., 2022). Therefore, the negative impact of human health has increased the need for health services. In this direction, service exports, called health tourism, have been created in order for individuals who cannot receive adequate health services in their own country to benefit from other countries. Health tourism, on the other hand, has an important share for countries to gain competitive advantage. Because the share of health tourism increases economic growth by providing income to the country's economy or by providing employment opportunities.

9.4 Conclusion

As a result, the evolution of the use and meaning of transparency is more relevant to transnational organizations and non-governmental organizations. Therefore, it can be said that the phenomenon of transparency, whether invented by a particular person or not, has become more popular as a result of the interconnectedness and networking of supranational organizations. However, despite all its contributions and benefits, transparency is still a controversial concept. Given the novelty of the concept, the confusion over its many meanings, and the conflict between privacy and confidentiality, some elected officials, executives, and analysts may overlook transparency. For this reason, it is necessary to monitor the implementation of the transparency principle with a good control.

References

Bhuiyan, M. A., Dinçer, H., Yüksel, S., Mikhaylov, A., Danish, M. S. S., Pinter, G., Uyeh, D. D., & Stepanova, D. (2022). Economic indicators and bioenergy supply in developed economies: QROF-DEMATEL and random forest models. *Energy Reports, 8*, 561–570.

Bistline, J., Budolfson, M., & Francis, B. (2021). Deepening transparency about value-laden assumptions in energy and environmental modelling: improving best practices for both modellers and non-modellers. *Climate Policy, 21*(1), 1–15.

Carayannis, E., Kostis, P., Dinçer, H., & Yüksel, S. (2022). Balanced-scorecard-based evaluation of knowledge-oriented competencies of distributed energy investments. *Energies, 15*(21), 8245.

Dai, Z., Li, D., Zhou, Z., Zhou, S., Liu, W., Liu, J., Wang, X., & Ren, X. (2022). A strategy for high performance of energy storage and transparency in KNN-based ferroelectric ceramics. *Chemical Engineering Journal, 427*, 131959.

Dinçer, H., Aksoy, T., Yüksel, S., & Hacioglu, U. (2022). Golden cut-oriented q-rung orthopair fuzzy decision-making approach to evaluation of renewable energy alternatives for microgeneration system investments. *Mathematical Problems in Engineering*.

Dinçer, H., Yüksel, S., Çağlayan, Ç., Yavuz, D., & Kararoğlu, D. (2023). Can renewable energy investments be a solution to the energy-sourced high inflation problem?. In *Managing inflation and supply chain disruptions in the global economy* (pp. 220–238). IGI Global.

Dinçer, H., Yüksel, S., & Martínez, L. (2022). Collaboration enhanced hybrid fuzzy decision-making approach to analyze the renewable energy investment projects. *Energy Reports, 8*, 377–389.

Dinçer, H., Yüksel, S., Mikhaylov, A., Pinter, G., & Shaikh, Z. A. (2022). Analysis of renewable-friendly smart grid technologies for the distributed energy investment projects using a hybrid picture fuzzy rough decision-making approach. *Energy Reports, 8*, 11466–11477.

Dong, W., Zhao, G., Yüksel, S., Dinçer, H., & Ubay, G. G. (2022). A novel hybrid decision making approach for the strategic selection of wind energy projects. *Renewable Energy, 185*, 321–337.

Ermiş, A. M., & Güven, M. E. (2022). The role of green energy investments in energy supply security. In *Circular economy and the energy market* (pp. 67–77). Springer.

Eti, S., Dinçer, H., Gökalp, Y., Yüksel, S., & Kararoğlu, D. (2023). Identifying key issues to handle the inflation problem in the healthcare industry caused by energy prices: An evaluation with decision-making models. *Managing Inflation and Supply Chain Disruptions in the Global Economy*, 162–178.

Eti, S., Dinçer, H., Yüksel, S., & Gökalp, Y. (2022). Analysis of the suitability of the solar panels for hospitals: A new fuzzy decision-making model proposal with the T-Spherical TOP-DEMATEL method. *Journal of Intelligent & Fuzzy Systems*, (Preprint), 1–13.

Fang, S., Zhou, P., Dinçer, H., & Yüksel, S. (2021). Assessment of safety management system on energy investment risk using house of quality based on hybrid stochastic interval-valued intuitionistic fuzzy decision-making approach. *Safety Science, 141*, 105333.

Haiyun, C., Zhixiong, H., Yüksel, S., & Dinçer, H. (2021). Analysis of the innovation strategies for green supply chain management in the energy industry using the QFD-based hybrid interval valued intuitionistic fuzzy decision approach. *Renewable and Sustainable Energy Reviews, 143*, 110844.

Kafka, K. I., Dinçer, H., & Yüksel, S. (2022). Impact-relation map of innovative service development regarding the sustainable growth for emerging markets. *Journal of the Knowledge Economy*, 1–24.

Kayacık, M., Dinçer, H., & Yüksel, S. (2022). Using quantum spherical fuzzy decision support system as a novel sustainability index approach for analyzing industries listed in the stock exchange. *Borsa Istanbul Review, 22*(6), 1145–1157.

Kim, M., Lee, D., Son, S., Yang, Y., Lee, H., & Rho, J. (2021). Visibly transparent radiative cooler under direct sunlight. *Advanced Optical Materials, 9*(13), 2002226.

Kou, G., Yüksel, S., & Dinçer, H. (2022). Inventive problem-solving map of innovative carbon emission strategies for solar energy-based transportation investment projects. *Applied Energy, 311*, 118680.

Li, W., Yüksel, S., & Dinçer, H. (2022). Understanding the financial innovation priorities for renewable energy investors via QFD-based picture fuzzy and rough numbers. *Financial Innovation, 8*(1), 1–30.

Li, J., Yüksel, S., Dınçer, H., Mikhaylov, A., & Barykin, S. E. (2022). Bipolar q-ROF hybrid decision making model with golden cut for analyzing the levelized cost of renewable energy alternatives. *IEEE Access, 10*, 42507–42517.

Liang, J., Irfan, M., Ikram, M., & Zimon, D. (2022). Evaluating natural resources volatility in an emerging economy: the influence of solar energy development barriers. *Resources Policy, 78*, 102858.

Martínez, L., Dinçer, H., & Yüksel, S. (2023). A hybrid decision making approach for new service development process of renewable energy investment. *Applied Soft Computing, 133*, 109897.

Mikhaylov, A., Bhatti, I. M., Dinçer, H., & Yüksel, S. (2022). Integrated decision recommendation system using iteration-enhanced collaborative filtering, golden cut bipolar for analyzing the risk-based oil market spillovers. *Computational Economics*, 1–34.

Mukhtarov, S., Yüksel, S., & Dinçer, H. (2022). The impact of financial development on renewable energy consumption: Evidence from Turkey. *Renewable Energy, 187*, 169–176.

Sun, L., Peng, J., Dinçer, H., & Yüksel, S. (2022). Coalition-oriented strategic selection of renewable energy system alternatives using q-ROF DEMATEL with golden cut. *Energy, 256*, 124606.

Xia, R., Zhang, W., Yang, Y., Zhao, J., Liu, Y., & Guo, H. (2021). Transparent wood with phase change heat storage as novel green energy storage composites for building energy conservation. *Journal of Cleaner Production, 296*, 126598.

Xu, X., Yüksel, S., & Dinçer, H. (2022). An integrated decision-making approach with golden cut and bipolar q-ROFSs to renewable energy storage investments. *International Journal of Fuzzy Systems*, 1–14.

Yi, Z., Xu, D., Xu, J., Qian, H., Zhao, D., & Yang, R. (2021). Energy saving analysis of a transparent radiative cooling film for buildings with roof glazing. *Energy and Built Environment, 2*(2), 214–222.

Yuan, G., Xie, F., Dinçer, H., & Yüksel, S. (2021). The theory of inventive problem solving (TRIZ)-based strategic mapping of green nuclear energy investments with spherical fuzzy group decision-making approach. *International Journal of Energy Research, 45*(8), 12284–12300.

Yüksel, S., & Dinçer, H. (2022). Identifying the strategic priorities of nuclear energy investments using hesitant 2-tuple interval-valued Pythagorean fuzzy DEMATEL. *Progress in Nuclear Energy, 145*, 104103.

Yüksel, S., Dinçer, H., Eti, S., & Adalı, Z. (2022). Strategy improvements to minimize the drawbacks of geothermal investments by using spherical fuzzy modelling. *International Journal of Energy Research*. https://doi.org/10.1002/er.7880

Zhang, Y., Zhang, Y., Gong, C., Dinçer, H., & Yüksel, S. (2022). An integrated hesitant 2-tuple Pythagorean fuzzy analysis of QFD-based innovation cost and duration for renewable energy projects. *Energy, 248*, 123561.

Zhi, J., Zhou, M., Zhang, Z., Reiser, O., & Huang, F. (2021). Interstitial boron-doped mesoporous semiconductor oxides for ultratransparent energy storage. *Nature communications, 12*(1), 1–12.

Chapter 10
Analysis of Existing Approaches to Energy Efficiency Management at the Strategic Level

Solomon Eghosa Uhunamure and Tsangyao Chang

Keywords Development · Ecosystem · Economic growth · Energy technologies · Clean energy

10.1 Introduction

Energy analysis is an analytical part of the process of planning energy saving activities and is based on assessing the actual amount of resources consumed, identifying the reasons for deviations from planned values, identifying losses, and determining the potential for reducing energy consumption. This section regulates the procedure for accounting for the most significant objects of resource consumption and the use of this information when forming a balance of energy consumption.

The energy baseline as an important stage of strategic planning of energy consumption is used for comparison with the actual values of energy efficiency indicators in relation to the planned indicators. When compiling the analysis report, the energy baselines established for both significant technological processes for the reporting period and for the calendar year following the reporting period are used (Xu et al., 2022; Bhuiyan et al., 2022; Kou et al., 2022; Ermiş & Güven, 2022). Energy resources that are spent on the technological process and depend on the volume of production will be subject to rationing. Resources that are consumed due to the needs of production support systems and do not have a pronounced dependence on the production process are subject to limitation.

Evaluation of technical measures implemented at the metallurgical enterprise. The main directions of implementation of the strategy for modernization of the

S. E. Uhunamure (✉)
Cape Peninsula University of Technology, Cape Town, South Africa
e-mail: uhunamures@cput.ac.za

T. Chang
Feng Chia University, Taichung City, Taiwan
e-mail: tychang@fcu.edu.tw

H. Dincer, S. Yüksel (eds.), *Economic Development and the Environmental Ecosystem*, Contributions to Economics,
https://doi.org/10.1007/978-3-031-26596-9_10

plant's energy infrastructure facilities in the period from 2017 to 2021 were the introduction of measures in the field of consumption of electric and thermal energy, natural gas and water. The total amount of investment for the implementation of the measures amounted to about 300 million rubles, with an average payback period of 4.5 months.

10.2 Literature Review

An integrated analysis of activities in the period from 2017 to 2020 confirms that the main direction of energy saving is the optimization of technological processes in production. At the same time, investment in energy sector modernization projects is carried out on an irregular basis, and preference is given to projects that have a high degree of development (Nie et al., 2020; Denisova et al., 2019; Nyangarika et al., 2019b; Nyangarika et al., 2019a; Huang et al., 2021a; Huang et al., 2021b; Mikhaylov, 2018; Mikhaylov et al., 2019; Conteh et al., 2021; Mikhaylov, 2022a; Sediqi et al., 2022; Khan et al., 2021; Bhuiyan et al., 2022a; Liu et al., 2021a, 2021b; Daniali et al., 2021; Moiseev et al., 2023; An et al., 2022).

Significant reserves of energy saving are associated with the operation of pipe rolling and electric steelmaking shops. When performing energy analysis, the following areas can be distinguished: electricity and gas consumption in ensuring technological processes for the production of pipe billets and pipes. Also, the steam production site with morally and physically obsolete equipment has a huge potential for energy saving (Mikhaylov et al., 2022c; Mikhaylov, 2021a; Varyash et al., 2020; Zhao et al., 2021; An & Mikhaylov, 2020; Alwaelya et al., 2021; Yumashev & Mikhaylov, 2020; Yumashev et al., 2020; Mutalimov et al., 2021; An & Mikhaylov, 2021).

As recommendations aimed at improving the energy efficiency management system, it is proposed to improve the work of the enterprise in terms of motivating personnel and developing processes for informing and promoting energy conservation at all levels of management. To assess the effectiveness of achieving energy saving indicators, it is necessary to create an internal information system for storing and processing energy consumption data (Dayong et al., 2020; Nyangarika et al., 2018; Danish et al., 2020; Danish et al., 2021; An et al., 2021; Uyeh et al., 2021; Tamashiro et al., 2021; Tamashiro et al., 2023; Shaikh et al., 2021).

Another important step in optimizing the energy efficiency management mechanism is the procedure for distributing responsibility between system participants (An et al., 2019a, 2019b; Mikhaylov & Tarakanov, 2020; An et al., 2020b, 2020a; An et al., 2020c; Moiseev et al., 2020; Moiseev et al., 2021; Gura et al., 2022; Dooyum et al., 2020; Mikhaylov et al., 2020; Mikhaylov, 2020a; Mikhaylov, 2020b; Mikhaylov, 2020c).

10.3 Development of an Algorithm for Making Investment Decisions when Implementation of Energy Saving Projects

Based on the theoretical and practical research conducted in the previous chapters, it can be concluded that due to the increasing competition in the metallurgical industry, the key area that has a huge potential for optimization is improving energy efficiency. Moreover, both technological innovations and organizational changes serve as tools for implementing improvements. The importance of improving energy efficiency for metallurgical enterprises is increasing, which in turn leads to a rethinking of energy sector development strategies (Khan et al., 2022; Dinçer et al., 2022b, 2022d; Badr et al., 2022; Barykin et al., 2022a; Mehta et al., 2022; Kalinina et al., 2022; Shaikh et al., 2022; Mikhaylov et al., 2022; Nyangarika et al., 2022; Mikhaylov et al., 2023; Mikhaylov, 2022b).

The specific nature of energy consumption and features of the power system of a metallurgical enterprise determine some difficulties in choosing one or another approach to improving efficiency (Bhuiyan et al., 2021; Dong et al., 2021, Mikhaylov, 2021b; Barykin et al., 2022b; Liu et al., 2022a, 2022b; Bhuiyan et al., 2022b; Danish et al., 2022a, 2022b; Saqib et al., 2021; Mukhametov et al., 2021, Candila et al., 2021; Mikhaylov & Grilli, 2022; Li et al., 2022a, 2022b, 2022c).

The limiting factor in the development of plant energy is the lack of investment in this area due to the significant cost of projects, which leads to the use of strategies aimed at optimizing consumption at the expense of internal resources. In this case, there is a need to activate the activities of personnel in the direction of rational use through the implementation of motivation mechanisms.

Implementation of a comprehensive and systematic energy efficiency improvement strategy will reduce costs and increase the company's competitiveness in the metallurgical industry.

At the state level, support is provided to enterprises aimed at improving the energy efficiency of production, in order to reduce costs per unit of output, reduce the consumption of traditional fuels and minimize carbon emissions during the operation of energy facilities. The main objective of such measures is to increase the competitiveness of domestic products on the world market and reduce the environmental impact of industrial activities. As part of the regulator's activities, both incentive and administrative measures can be applied to enterprises to encourage them to work in the field of improving the efficiency of using energy resources.

The main approach is to manage the process of using energy resources, which includes setting norms and limits of consumption and monitoring their use, developing an energy efficiency improvement program that determines the strategic direction of energy saving at all plants of the company, and formulating principles for motivating the company's personnel. This approach is fundamental, as it provides an initial statement of the problem of energy saving, and directs management to build a unified system. In conditions of a shortage of financing, due to the unstable financial condition of the industry as a whole, this approach is able to ensure the maintenance of competitiveness of a single entity.

A promising direction for the development of the management system is the introduction of an approach to innovation management, since this area has a significant potential hidden in the human resource. The main indicator of efficiency in this area is the number of implemented improvement projects and innovation proposals aimed at reducing energy consumption. In addition, the creation of project teams capable of solving energy saving issues and implementing projects in the conditions of existing production is no less effective (Fang et al., 2021; Kayacık et al., 2022; Eti et al., 2022; Dinçer et al., 2023).

The development of traditional approaches makes it possible to form a systematic view of energy efficiency management, which is a set of organizational and technical measures, including using elements of training and motivation of personnel.

The driving force behind the transition to system work is the need to move away from the implementation of one-time investment projects in the energy infrastructure and create conditions for a continuous process of development and implementation of organizational and technical projects.

It is obvious that the list of business process managers includes energy conservation management processes, investment projects, financial management areas in the energy sector, as well as mechanisms for stimulating personnel to improve energy efficiency (Eti et al., 2023; Li et al. 2022a, 2022b, 2022c; Haiyun et al., 2021; Yuan et al., 2021). These processes are directly related to the main production processes and form the long-term energy efficiency strategy of the enterprise. Supporting business processes are ensuring the operability of equipment, through repairs to the energy infrastructure, supply and logistics, as well as operational control over production and financial flows and the implementation of approved programs in the field of energy conservation.

Given the previously identified problem of lack of investment in energy infrastructure, there is a need to develop recommendations for making a verified decision regarding the investment object (Carayannis et al., 2022; Li et al. 2022a, 2022b, 2022c; Yüksel et al., 2022; Mikhaylov et al., 2022a). First of all, the basis for making any decision is the initial information. Within the framework of the management system implemented at the enterprise, the source of initial information is internal audits. Based on the results of internal surveys, an analysis and development of measures aimed at improving energy efficiency is carried out. After that, the project database is formed with the division of projects into three categories.

The first group includes projects that are understood by most managers, characterized by relatively low capital investments and a low implementation period with a payback period of less than 1 year.

10.4 Conclusion

The next group includes projects that require significant capital investments, but have a fairly short payback period (2–3 years). As a rule, projects in this category involve technological changes in an entire subdivision or site and in some cases may have insufficient justification due to the lack of the necessary information and intellectual base. Further implementation of these projects requires the involvement of a third-party specialized organization in order to conduct an expert comprehensive survey and develop a feasibility study. The proposed step will minimize project risks in the context of the existing lack of knowledge and experience among managers and will provide the necessary support when making an investment decision in the field of energy conservation (Dong et al., 2022; Dinçer et al. 2022a, 2022b, 2022c; Zhang et al., 2022; Yüksel & Dinçer, 2022).

The third group of projects is considered the most difficult to understand, as it concerns global changes in the energy sector and affects the entire energy system. Projects in this category have a long payback period (5–10 years) and require significant capital investment. In addition, they are often characterized by a complete lack of knowledge and experience in their implementation and subsequent operation. It is for the third group of projects that the best option is to attract an organization that will take over risk assessment, calculation of economic indicators and costs for the implementation and operation of the project being implemented.

After classifying all the projects that were proposed based on the results of the energy audit, the fourth stage follows, at which it is necessary to finally form the entire portfolio of energy saving projects, indicate the essence of each of them and determine the technical and economic indicators of the project: the amount of funding, the expected economic effect, payback periods, etc. (Martínez et al., 2022; Sun et al., 2022; Kafka et al., 2022; Mukhtarov et al., 2022). At this stage, depending on the complexity of the project, the manager decides on whether to.

At the final stage, after deciding on the source of project financing, documentary confirmation is made by including it in the investment program or entering into an agreement with the company and moving to the implementation stage. At the implementation stage, control over the cost of financing and the quality of work performed should be established. An important aspect of the final stage is the creation of a database of best practices for implementing energy-efficient techniques, which can then be replicated to other enterprises of the company and the industry as a whole.

References

Alwaelya, S. A., Yousif, N. B. A., & Mikhaylov, A. (2021). Emotional development in preschoolers and socialization. *Early Child Development and Care, 191*, 16.

An, J., & Mikhaylov, A. (2020). Russian energy projects in South Africa. *Journal of Energy in Southern Africa, 31*(3), 58–64.

An, J., & Mikhaylov, A. (2021). Analysis of energy projects financial efficiency and renewable energy generation in Russia. *Finance: Theory and Practice, 25*(5), 79–91.

An, J., Mikhaylov, A., Dinçer, H., & Yüksel, S. (2022). Economic modelling of electricity generation: Long short-term memory and Q-rung Orthopair fuzzy sets. *Heliyon, 8*, e10759.

An, J., Mikhaylov, A., & Jung, S.-U. (2020b). The strategy of South Korea in the global oil market. *Energies, 13*(10), 2491.

An, J., Mikhaylov, A., & Jung, S.-U. (2021). A linear programming approach for robust network revenue management in the airline industry. *Journal of Air Transport Management, 91*, 101979.

An, J., Mikhaylov, A., & Kim, K. (2020c). Machine learning approach in heterogeneous group of algorithms for transport safety-critical system. *Applied Sciences, 10*(8), 2670.

An, J., Mikhaylov, A., & Moiseev, N. (2019b). Oil price predictors: Machine learning approach. *International Journal of Energy Economics and Policy, 9*(5), 1–6.

An, J., Mikhaylov, A., & Richter, U. H. (2020a). Trade war effects: Evidence from sectors of energy and resources in Africa. *Heliyon, 6*, e05693. https://doi.org/10.1016/j.heliyon.2020.e05693

An, J., Mikhaylov, A., & Sokolinskaya, N. (2019a). Machine learning in economic planning: Ensembles of algorithms. *Journal of Physics: Conference Series, 1353*, 012126.

Badr, A. M. N. A. A., Mohamed, T. I., Osman, N. A. Q., & Mikhaylov, A. (2022). A review of social media website users' interaction paths with governmental accounts during the COVID-19 pandemic. *Informatics, 9*, 50. https://doi.org/10.3390/informatics9030050

Barykin, S. E., Kapustina, I. V., Sergeev, S. M., Daniali, S. M., Kopteva, L. A., Semenova, G. N., Pryadko, I. P., Mikhaylov, A., Baboshkin, P., Datsyuk, P., & Senjyu, T. (2022a). Financial logistics models based on systematic approach improving management solutions. *F1000Research, 11*, –570. https://doi.org/10.12688/f1000research.111252.1

Barykin, S., Mikheev, A., Kiseleva, E., Putikhin, Y., Alekseeva, N., & Mikhaylov, A. (2022b). An empirical analysis of Russian regions' debt sustainability. *Economies, 10*(4), 296.

Bhuiyan, M. A., An, J., Mikhaylov, A., Moiseev, N., & Danish, M. S. S. (2021). Renewable energy deployment and COVID-19 measures for sustainable development. *Sustainability, 13*, 4418.

Bhuiyan, M. A., Dinçer, H., Yüksel, S., Mikhaylov, A., Danish, M. S. S., Pinter, G., Uyeh, D. D., & Stepanova, D. (2022b). Economic indicators and bioenergy supply in developed economies: QROF-DEMATEL and random forest models. *Energy Reports, 8*(2022), 561–570.

Bhuiyan, M. A., Dinçer, H., Yüksel, S., Mikhaylov, A., Danish, M. S. S., Pinter, G., et al. (2022a). Economic indicators and bioenergy supply in developed economies: QROF-DEMATEL and random forest models. *Energy Reports, 8*, 561–570.

Bhuiyan, M. A., Zhang, Q., Khare, V., Mikhaylov, A., Pinter, G., & Huang, X. (2022). Renewable energy consumption and economic growth nexus—A systematic literature review. *Frontiers in Environmental Science., 10*, 878394. https://doi.org/10.3389/fenvs.2022.878394

Candila, V., Maximov, D., Mikhaylov, A., Moiseev, N., Senjyu, T., & Tryndina, N. (2021). On the relationship between oil and exchange rates of oil-exporting and oil-importing countries: From the great recession period to the Covid-19 era. *Energies, 14*, 8065.

Carayannis, E., Kostis, P., Dinçer, H., & Yüksel, S. (2022). Balanced-scorecard-based evaluation of knowledge-oriented competencies of distributed energy investments. *Energies, 15*(21), 8245.

Conteh, F., Takahashi, H., Hemeida, A. M., Krishnan, N., Mikhaylov, A., & Senjyu, T. (2021). Hybrid grid-connected renewable power generation for sustainable electricity supply in Sierra Leone: Case study lungi town. *Sustainability, 13*(18), 1–20.

Daniali, S. M., Barykin, S. E., Kapustina, I. V., Khortabi, F. M., Sergeev, S. M., Kalinina, O. V., Mikhaylov, A., Veynberg, R., Zasova, L., & Senjyu, T. (2021). Predicting volatility index according to technical index and economic indicators on the basis of deep learning algorithm. *Sustainability, 2021*(13), 14011.

Danish, M. S. S., Bhattacharya, A., Stepanova, D., Mikhaylov, A., Grilli, M. L., Khosravy, M., & Senjyu, T. (2020). A systematic review of metal oxide applications for energy and environmental sustainability. *Metals, 10*(12), 1604.

Danish, M. S. S., Senjyu, T., Sabory, N. R., Khosravy, M., Grilli, M. L., Mikhaylov, A., & Majidi, H. (2021). A forefront framework for sustainable aquaponics modeling and design. *Sustainability, 13*, 9313.

Danish, M. S., Senjyu, T. S., Sabory, N. R., & Mikhaylov, A. (2022a). Lessons from COVID-19 conferring environmental re-engineering opportunity. In M. Danish & T. Senjyu (Ed.), *Eco-friendly and agile energy strategies and policy development* (pp. 99–118). IGI Global. https://doi.org/10.4018/978-1-7998-9502-2.ch005.

Danish, M. S., Senjyu, T. S., Sabory, N. R., & Mikhaylov, A. (2022b). Interplay consequences of COVID-19 on global environmental sustainability. In M. Danish, & T. Senjyu (Ed.), *Eco-friendly and agile energy strategies and policy development.* IGI Global. https://doi.org/10.4018/978-1-7998-9502-2.ch003.

Dayong, N., Mikhaylov, A., Bratanovsky, S., Shaikh, Z. A., & Stepanova, D. (2020). Mathematical modeling of the technological processes of catering products production. *Journal of Food Process Engineering, 43*(2), 1–9.

Denisova, V., Mikhaylov, A., & Lopatin, E. (2019). Blockchain infrastructure and growth of global power consumption. *International Journal of Energy Economics and Policy, 9*(4), 22–29.

Dinçer, H., Aksoy, T., Yüksel, S., & Hacioglu, U. (2022a). *Golden cut-oriented q-rung orthopair fuzzy decision-making approach to evaluation of renewable energy alternatives for microgeneration system investments. Mathematical Problems in Engineering*, 2022.

Dinçer, H., Yüksel, S., Çağlayan, Ç., Yavuz, D., & Kararoğlu, D. (2023). Can renewable energy investments be a solution to the energy-sourced high inflation problem?. In *Managing inflation and supply chain disruptions in the global economy* (pp. 220–238). IGI Global.

Dinçer, H., Yüksel, S., & Martínez, L. (2022b). Collaboration enhanced hybrid fuzzy decision-making approach to analyze the renewable energy investment projects. *Energy Reports, 8*, 377–389.

Dinçer, H., Yüksel, S., Mikhaylov, A., Barykin, S. E., Aksoy, T., & Hacioğlu, U. (2022c). Analysis of environmental priorities for green project investments using an integrated q-rung orthopair fuzzy modelling. *IEEE Access, 10.* https://doi.org/10.1109/ACCESS.2022.3174058

Dinçer, H., Yüksel, S., Mikhaylov, A., Pinter, G., & Shaikh, Z. A. (2022d). Analysis of renewable-friendly smart grid technologies for the distributed energy investment projects using a hybrid picture fuzzy rough decision-making approach. *Energy Reports, 8*, 11466–11477. https://doi.org/10.1016/j.egyr.2022.08.275

Dong, B., Ikonnikova, I., Rogulin, R., Sakulyeva, T., & Mikhaylov, A. (2021). Environmentaleconomic approach to optimization of transport communication in megacities. *Journal of Environmental Science and Health, Part A, 56*(6), 660–666.

Dong, W., Zhao, G., Yüksel, S., Dinçer, H., & Ubay, G. G. (2022). A novel hybrid decision making approach for the strategic selection of wind energy projects. *Renewable Energy, 185*, 321–337.

Dooyum, U. D., Mikhaylov, A., & Varyash, I. (2020). Energy security concept in Russia and South Korea. *International Journal of Energy Economics and Policy, 10*(4), 102–107.

Ermiş, A. M., & Güven, M. E. (2022). The role of green energy Investments in Energy Supply Security. In *Circular economy and the energy market* (pp. 67–77). Springer.

Eti, S., Dinçer, H., Gökalp, Y., Yüksel, S., & Kararoğlu, D. (2023). Identifying key issues to handle the inflation problem in the healthcare industry caused by energy prices: An evaluation with decision-making models. *Managing Inflation and Supply Chain Disruptions in the Global Economy*, 162–178.

Eti, S., Dinçer, H., Yüksel, S., & Gökalp, Y. (2022). Analysis of the suitability of the solar panels for hospitals: A new fuzzy decision-making model proposal with the T-spherical TOP-DEMATEL method. *Journal of Intelligent & Fuzzy Systems, Preprint*, 1–13.

Fang, S., Zhou, P., Dinçer, H., & Yüksel, S. (2021). Assessment of safety management system on energy investment risk using house of quality based on hybrid stochastic interval-valued intuitionistic fuzzy decision-making approach. *Safety Science, 141*, 105333.

Gura, D., Mikhaylov, A., Glushkov, S., Zaikov, M., & Shaikh, Z. A. (2022). Model for estimating power dissipation along the interconnect length in single on-chip topology. *Evolutionary Intelligence, 15*, 2369–2373. https://doi.org/10.1007/s12065-020-00407-7

Haiyun, C., Zhixiong, H., Yüksel, S., & Dinçer, H. (2021). Analysis of the innovation strategies for green supply chain management in the energy industry using the QFD-based hybrid interval valued intuitionistic fuzzy decision approach. *Renewable and Sustainable Energy Reviews, 143*, 110844.

Huang, Y., Masrur, H., Shigenobu, R., Hemeida, A. M., Mikhaylov, A., & Senjyu, T. (2021a). A comparative design of a campus microgrid considering a multi-scenario and multi-objective approach. *Energies, 14*, 2853.

Huang, Y., Yona, A., Takahashi, H., Hemeida, A. M., Mandal, P., Mikhaylov, A., Senjyu, T., & Lotfy, M. E. (2021b). Energy management system optimization of drug store operate electric vehicles charging station. *Sustainability, 14*, 1217836.

Kafka, K. I., Dinçer, H., & Yüksel, S. (2022). Impact-relation map of innovative service development regarding the sustainable growth for emerging markets. *Journal of the Knowledge Economy*, 1–24.

Kalinina, O. V., Barykin, S. E., Sergeev, S. M., Semenova, G. N., Fatkullina, A., Mikhaylov, A., & De La Poza, E. (2022). Smart city perspectives in post-pandemic governance: Externalities reduction policy. *F1000Research, 11*, 1032. https://doi.org/10.12688/f1000research.123195.1

Kayacık, M., Dinçer, H., & Yüksel, S. (2022). Using quantum spherical fuzzy decision support system as a novel sustainability index approach for analyzing industries listed in the stock exchange. *Borsa Istanbul Review, 22*(6), 1145–1157.

Khan, A. A., Laghari, A. A., Gadekallu, T. R., Shaikh, Z. A., Javed, A. R., Rashid, M., Estrela, V. V., & Mikhaylov, A. (2022). A drone-based data management and optimization using metaheuristic algorithms and blockchain smart contracts in a secure fog environment. *Computers and Electrical Engineering, 102*, 108234. https://doi.org/10.1016/j.compeleceng.2022.108234

Khan, A. A., Shaikh, Z. A., Baitenova, L., Mutaliyeva, L., Moiseev, N., Mikhaylov, A., Laghari, A. A., Idris, S. A., & Alshazly, H. (2021). QoS-ledger: Smart contracts and metaheuristic for secure quality-of-service and cost-efficient scheduling of medical-data processing. *Electronics, 10*, 3083.

Kou, G., Yüksel, S., & Dinçer, H. (2022). Inventive problem-solving map of innovative carbon emission strategies for solar energy-based transportation investment projects. *Applied Energy, 311*, 118680.

Li, J., Dinçer, H., Yüksel, S., Mikhaylov, A., & Barykin, S. E. (2022a). Bipolar q-ROF hybrid decision making model with golden cut for analyzing the levelized cost of renewable energy alternatives. *IEEE Access, 10*, 35900–35900. https://doi.org/10.1109/ACCESS.2022.3168315

Li, W., Yüksel, S., & Dinçer, H. (2022c). Understanding the financial innovation priorities for renewable energy investors via QFD-based picture fuzzy and rough numbers. *Financial Innovation, 8*(1), 1–30.

Li, J., Yüksel, S., Dınçer, H., Mikhaylov, A., & Barykin, S. E. (2022b). Bipolar q-ROF hybrid decision making model with golden cut for analyzing the levelized cost of renewable energy alternatives. *IEEE Access, 10*, 42507–42517.

Liu, L., Kato, T., Mandal, P., Mikhaylov, A., Hemeida, A. M., & Senjyu, T. (2021a). Multi-area power system load frequency control by using model predictive control by introducing renewable energy sources. *International Conference on Science & Contemporary Technologies (ICSCT), 2021*, 1–6. https://doi.org/10.1109/ICSCT53883.2021.9642521

Liu, L., Kato, T., Mandal, P., Mikhaylov, A., Hemeida, A. M., Takahashi, H., & Tomonobu, S. (2021b). Two cases studies of model predictive control approach for hybrid renewable energy systems. *AIMS Energy, 9*(6), 1241–1259.

Liu, Z.-J., Panfilova, E., Mikhaylov, A., & Kurilova, A. (2022a). COVID-19 crisis impact on the stability between parties in crowdfunding and crowdsourcing. *Wireless Personal Communications, 122*, 915–930.

Liu, Z., Panfilova, E., Mikhaylov, A., & Kurilova, A. (2022b). Assessing stability in the relationship between parties in crowdfunding and crowdsourcing projects during the COVID-19 crisis. *Journal of Global Information Management (JGIM), 30*(4), 1–18. https://doi.org/10.4018/JGIM.297905

Martínez, L., Dinçer, H., & Yüksel, S. (2022). A hybrid decision making approach for new service development process of renewable energy investment. *Applied Soft Computing, 109897.*

Mehta, R., Verghese, J., Mahajan, S., Barykin, S., Bozhuk, S., Kozlova, N., Kapustina, I., Mikhaylov, A., Naumova, E., & Dedyukhina, N. (2022). Consumers' behavior in conversational commerce marketing based on messenger chatbots. *F1000Research, 11*, 647. https://doi.org/10.12688/f1000research.122037.1

Mikhaylov, A. (2018). The yield of the carry trade strategy. *Finance: Theory and Practice, 22*(3), 52–63. https://doi.org/10.26794/2587-5671-2018-22-3-52-63

Mikhaylov, A. (2020a). Cryptocurrency market analysis from the open innovation perspective. *Journal of Open Innovation: Technology, Market, and Complexity, 6*(4), 197.

Mikhaylov, A. (2020b). Geothermal energy development in Iceland. *International Journal of Energy Economics and Policy, 10*(4), 31–35.

Mikhaylov, A. (2020c). Cryptocurrency market development: Hurst method. *Finance: Theory and Practice, 24*(3), 81–91.

Mikhaylov, A. (2021a). Development of Friedrich von Hayek's theory of private money and economic implications for digital currencies. *Terra Economicus, 19*(1).

Mikhaylov, A. (2021b). Lichens as indicators of atmospheric pollution in urban ecosystems. *Israel Journal of Ecology & Evolution, 67*(1–2), 60–68. https://doi.org/10.1163/22244662-bja10016

Mikhaylov, A. (2022a). Efficiency of renewable energy generation in Russia. *Anais da Academia Brasileira de Ciências, 94*(4), e20191226. https://doi.org/10.1590/0001-3765202220191226

Mikhaylov, A. (2022b). Sustainable development and renewable energy: A new view to a global problem. *Energies, 15*, 1397. https://doi.org/10.3390/en15041397

Mikhaylov, A., Bhatti, I. M., Dinçer, H., & Yüksel, S. (2022a). Integrated decision recommendation system using iteration-enhanced collaborative filtering, golden cut bipolar for analyzing the risk-based oil market spillovers. *Computational Economics*, 1–34.

Mikhaylov, A., Bhatti, I. M., Dinçer, H., & Yüksel, S. (2022c). Integrated decision recommendation system using iteration-enhanced collaborative filtering, golden cut bipolar for analyzing the risk-based oil market spillovers. *Computational Economics*. https://doi.org/10.1007/s10614-022-10341-8

Mikhaylov, A., Burakov, D., & Didenko, V. (2019). Relationship between oil price and macroeconomic indicators in Russia. *Finance: Theory and Practice, 23*(2), 105–116. https://doi.org/10.26794/2587-5671-2019-23-2-105-116

Mikhaylov, A., Dinçer, H., & Yüksel, S. (2023). Analysis of financial development and open innovation oriented fintech potential for emerging economies using an integrated decision-making approach of MF-X-DMA and golden cut bipolar q-ROFSs. *Financ Innov, 9*, 10. https://doi.org/10.1186/s40854-022-00234-w

Mikhaylov, A., & Grilli, M. L. (2022). Machine learning methods and sustainable development: Metal oxides and multilayer metal-oxides. *Metals, 12*(4).

Mikhaylov, A., Moiseev, N., Aleshin, K., & Burkhardt, T. (2020). Global climate change and greenhouse effect. *Entrepreneurship and Sustainability Issues, 7*(4), 2897–2913. https://doi.org/10.9770/jesi.2020.7.4(21)

Mikhaylov, A., & Tarakanov, S. (2020). Development of Levenberg-Marquardt theoretical approach for electric network. *Journal of Physics: Conference Series, 1515*, 052006.

Mikhaylov, A., Yumashev, A., & Kolpak, E. (2022). Quality of life, anxiety and depressive disorders in patients with extrasystolic arrhythmia. *Archives of Medical Science, 18*(2), 328–335. https://doi.org/10.5114/aoms.2020.101359

Moiseev, N., Mikhaylov, A., Dinçer, H., & Yüksel, S. (2023). Effects of market capitalization shocks for open innovation models in e-commerce industry: Golden cut QROF MCDM analysis. *Financ Innov, 9*, 32.

Moiseev, N., Mikhaylov, A., Varyash, I., & Saqib, A. (2020). Investigating the relation of GDP per capita and corruption index. *Entrepreneurship and Sustainability Issues, 8*(1), 780–794.

Moiseev, N., Sorokin, A., Zvezdina, N., Mikhaylov, A., Khomyakova, L., & Danish, M. S. S. (2021). Credit risk theoretical model on the base of DCC-GARCH in time-varying parameters framework. *Mathematics, 9*, 2423. https://doi.org/10.3390/math9192423

Mukhametov, A., Bekhorashvili, A., Avdeenko, A., & Mikhaylov, A. (2021). The impact of growing legume plants under conditions of Biologization and soil cultivation on chernozem fertility and productivity of rotation crops. *Legume Research, 44*, 12.

Mukhtarov, S., Yüksel, S., & Dinçer, H. (2022). The impact of financial development on renewable energy consumption: Evidence from Turkey. *Renewable Energy, 187*, 169–176.

Mutalimov, V., Kovaleva, I., Mikhaylov, A., & Stepanova, D. (2021). Assessing regional growth of small business in Russia. Entrepreneurial business and economics review, 9(3), 119–133. 10.15678/EBER.2021.090308.

Nie, D., Panfilova, E., Samusenkov, V., & Mikhaylov, A. (2020). E-learning financing models in Russia for sustainable development. *Sustainability, 12*(11), 4412.

Nyangarika, A., Mikhaylov, A., Muyeen, S. M., Yadykin, V., Mottaeva, A., Pryadko, I., Barykin, S., Fomenko, N., Rykov, G., & Shvandar, K. (2022). Energy stability and decarbonization in developing countries: Random Forest approach for forecasting of crude oil trade flows and macro indicators. *Frontiers in Environmental Science, 10*, 1031343. https://doi.org/10.3389/fenvs.2022.1031343

Nyangarika, A., Mikhaylov, A., & Richter, U. (2019a). Influence oil price towards economic indicators in Russia. *International Journal of Energy Economics and Policy, 9*(1), 123–129.

Nyangarika, A., Mikhaylov, A., & Richter, U. (2019b). Oil price factors: Forecasting on the base of modified auto-regressive integrated moving average model. *International Journal of Energy Economics and Policy, 9*(1), 149–159.

Nyangarika, A., Mikhaylov, A., & Tang, B.-J. (2018). Correlation of oil prices and gross domestic product in oil producing countries. *International Journal of Energy Economics and Policy, 8*(5), 42–48.

Saqib, A., Chan, T.-H., Mikhaylov, A., & Lean, H. H. (2021). Are the responses of sectoral energy imports asymmetric to exchange rate volatilities in Pakistan? Evidence from recent foreign exchange regime. *Frontiers in Energy Research, 9*, 614463. https://doi.org/10.3389/fenrg.2021.614463

Sediqi, M. M., Nakadomari, A., Mikhaylov, A., Krishnan, N., Lotfy, M. E., Yona, A., & Senjyu, T. (2022). Impact of time-of-use demand response program on optimal operation of Afghanistan real power system. *Energies, 15*, 296.

Shaikh, Z. A., Kraikin, A., Mikhaylov, A., & Pinter, G. (2022). Forecasting stock prices of companies producing solar panels using machine learning methods. *Complexity, 2022*, 9186265. https://doi.org/10.1155/2022/9186265

Shaikh, Z. A., Moiseev, N., Mikhaylov, A., & Yüksel, S. (2021). Facile synthesis of copper oxide-cobalt oxide/nitrogen-doped carbon (Cu2O-Co3O4/CN) composite for efficient water splitting. *Applied Sciences., 11*, 9974. https://doi.org/10.3390/app11219974

Sun, L., Peng, J., Dinçer, H., & Yüksel, S. (2022). Coalition-oriented strategic selection of renewable energy system alternatives using q-ROF DEMATEL with golden cut. *Energy, 256*, 124606.

Tamashiro, K., Alharbi, T., Mikhaylov, A., Hemeida, A. M., Krishnan, N., Lotfy, M. E., & Senjyu, T. (2021). Investigation of home energy management with advanced direct load control and optimal scheduling of controllable loads. *Energies, 14*, 7314. https://doi.org/10.3390/en14217314

Tamashiro, K., Omine, E., Krishnan, N., Mikhaylov, A., Hemeida, A. M., & Senjyu, T. (2023). Optimal components capacity based multi-objective optimization and optimal scheduling based MPC-optimization algorithm in smart apartment buildings. *Energy & Buildings, 278*, 112616. https://doi.org/10.1016/j.enbuild.2022.112616

Uyeh, D. D., Asem-Hiablie, S., Park, T., Kim, K.-M., Mikhaylov, A., Woo, S., & Ha, Y. (2021). Could japonica rice be an alternative variety for increased global food security and climate change mitigation? *Food, 10*, 1869. https://doi.org/10.3390/foods10081869

Varyash, I., Mikhaylov, A., Moiseev, N., & Aleshin, K. (2020). Triple bottom line and corporate social responsibility performance indicators for Russian companies. *Entrepreneurship and Sustainability Issues, 8*(1), 313–331.

Xu, X., Yüksel, S., & Dinçer, H. (2022). An integrated decision-making approach with Golden cut and bipolar q-ROFSs to renewable energy storage investments. *International Journal of Fuzzy Systems*, 1–14.

Yuan, G., Xie, F., Dinçer, H., & Yüksel, S. (2021). The theory of inventive problem solving (TRIZ)-based strategic mapping of green nuclear energy investments with spherical fuzzy group decision-making approach. *International Journal of Energy Research, 45*(8), 12284–12300.

Yüksel, S., & Dinçer, H. (2022). Identifying the strategic priorities of nuclear energy investments using hesitant 2-tuple interval-valued Pythagorean fuzzy DEMATEL. *Progress in Nuclear Energy, 145*, 104103.

Yüksel, S., Dinçer, H., Eti, S., & Adalı, Z. (2022). Strategy improvements to minimize the drawbacks of geothermal investments by using spherical fuzzy modelling. *International Journal of Energy Research.*

Yumashev, A., & Mikhaylov, A. (2020). Development of polymer film coatings with high adhesion to steel alloys and high wear resistance. *Polymer Composites, 41*(7), 2875–2880.

Yumashev, A., Ślusarczyk, B., Kondrashev, S., & Mikhaylov, A. (2020). Global indicators of sustainable development: Evaluation of the influence of the human development index on consumption and quality of energy. *Energies, 13*, 2768.

Zhang, Y., Zhang, Y., Gong, C., Dinçer, H., & Yüksel, S. (2022). An integrated hesitant 2-tuple Pythagorean fuzzy analysis of QFD-based innovation cost and duration for renewable energy projects. *Energy, 248*, 123561.

Zhao, Q., Cherkasov, S., Avdeenko, A., Kondratenko, L., & Mikhaylov, A. (2021). Integral estimate of the added value of agricultural crops in the synergetic agriculture on the example of Vicia faba (Vicia faba L.). *Polish Journal of Environmental Studies, 30*(5), 1–9. https://doi.org/10.15244/pjoes/131949

Chapter 11
Sustainability, Corporate Social Responsibility and Renewable Energy: The Key Takeaways

Ayşen Akyüz and Asena Temelli Coşgun

Keywords Renewable energy · Corporate social responsibility · Sustainability

11.1 Introduction

The developments on a global scale, which started with the Industrial Revolution, have put the world into a very complex process. This multi-layered process, which has economic, social, environmental effects and legal reflections, has basically emerged from the mutual relationship between businesses and the environment. The effects of environmental problems, which arise as a result of practices implemented by businesses with purely profit-oriented goals and policies that do not sufficiently consider any parameters other than the economy, have reached international dimensions over time.

While the gigantic development of the industry and the innovations in the field of technology offer endless opportunities for businesses to make a profit, on the other hand, they have created serious dangers on the world and human life. Businesses whose ultimate goal is profit under all circumstances have used natural resources, human and machine power and technology uncontrollably. In the last quarter of the twentieth century, the aim of profit-centered economic growth was fueled by the liberal economic policy adopted by developed and developing countries. With neoliberalism led by Thatcher and Reagan in the 1980s, the borders in front of the circulation of capital became transparent. Neoliberalism, known as modern or late capitalism, has been seen as a solution to transform the vicious circle of capitalism. In the new world order surrounded by neoliberal policies, the borders between the markets have disappeared, thus allowing the circulation of capital in a global market. While neoliberalism brought a new breath to capitalism, it aimed to include the individual and all his actions, natural resources and technology in the market area.

A. Akyüz (✉) · A. T. Coşgun
Faculty of Communication, İstanbul Medipol University, İstanbul, Turkey
e-mail: aakyuz@medipol.edu.tr; acosgun@medipol.edu.tr

H. Dincer, S. Yüksel (eds.), *Economic Development and the Environmental Ecosystem*, Contributions to Economics,
https://doi.org/10.1007/978-3-031-26596-9_11

This was seen as a way of making it possible for businesses to achieve their advanced goals at a time when capitalism was redesigned. As a result of global capital policies, profit has become a concept with an international impact for businesses. Rapid economic growth in the new world order is supported by the policies adopted. While preparing a ground for businesses to have a presence in the international arena and make a profit, on the other hand, global competition requires taking into account many variables for a long-term business life. While the free capital economy suppresses rapid growth, as a result of this, businesses have endangered the nature from which they obtain raw materials in the production process of goods and services. Many reasons such as developing technology, global market, increase in population, change in size of needs have created ecological, social and economic problems for businesses to continue their existence. These reasons have assigned the mission of being a corporate citizen to businesses. To put it more clearly, businesses that use all kinds of resources uncontrollably for a long-term operating life, profit and growth purposes need to act responsibly to compensate for the damage they cause. This situation has made it a necessity for businesses to include sustainability strategies in their management policies in order to fulfill their ecological, economic and social responsibilities.

Sustainability is a policy that requires meeting the needs of the present while respecting the ability of future generations to meet their needs. Corporate sustainability defines a management function in which this policy is integrated into business activities. Accordingly, businesses should not only consider their commercial goals while carrying out all their activities from production to sales, but also include environmental and economic impacts in the plans on the axis of social benefit. Corporate social responsibility, which is one of the elements of corporate sustainability, can be explained as one of the intermediate goals that should be achieved by businesses whose main goal is sustainability. Accordingly, businesses that achieve their living space and life, economic development form and dimension with what they get from the environment and society, have to display a responsible attitude towards the environment and society. To put it more clearly, corporate social responsibility is a management paradigm that adopts giving back what is obtained from the environment to the environment and what is obtained from the society back to the society. The corporate social responsibility understanding of enterprises can exist in a wide range from social aids to be made on behalf of the enterprise to environmental policies.

Ecological problems such as global warming, climate changes and the risk of depletion of natural resources in recent years have placed some responsibilities on businesses in the eyes of society and in the legal arena. Solutions to ecological problems are produced in international initiatives such as the initiatives of the United Nations, the Kyoto Protocol, and the Paris Agreement. Renewable energy is interesting among the solutions offered (Martínez et al., 2022; Sun et al., 2022; Kafka et al., 2022; Mukhtarov et al., 2022). In particular, corporate social responsibility activities of enterprises are starting to gain momentum in this new solution point: renewable energy context (Dong et al., 2022; Dinçer et al., 2022, 2022, 2022; Zhang et al., 2022; Yüksel & Dinçer, 2022).

11.2 Corporate Sustainability

Sustainability is one of the concepts that has been used frequently in the twenty-first century. In its most basic form, sustainability, which means the conscious use of all social, ecological, cultural and human resources, can be defined as a process in which the principle of mutual understanding and respect is adopted (Gladwin et al., 1995). The developments after the industrial revolution, the effects of business policies that do not take the environment into account, have prepared the ground for ecological results that will reach global dimensions in time. With the 1970s, businesses faced social expectations and legal measures regarding the solution of environmental problems they caused (Aktaş, 2017).

The concept of sustainability was first addressed by the United Nations at the conference on "Human and Environment" held in Stockholm in 1972. At the conference, the use of natural resources and the ecological effects of economic growth strategies were evaluated, the protection and improvement of the environment for the future of human life, thus leaving an undisturbed environment for future generations were discussed as an agenda item, and the basis of the sustainability policy was built (Chasek, 2022).

The oil crisis between 1973 and 1978 slowed down the economic growth and put capitalism into a crisis. In the following years, consumer movements started and legal regulations brought obligations to businesses to be sensitive to the environment and society (Aktaş, 2017). In the 1980s, neoliberal policies began to be implemented in developed and developing countries, especially United Kingdom and United States of America, as a solution to save capitalism from the bottleneck it was in. With neoliberalism, national borders in front of the circulation of capital have disappeared. In the market where the state has taken a few steps back, free capital has created a global scale market (Harvey, 2015).

Neoliberal economic policies, which provide businesses with the opportunity to grow rapidly with a global profit, on the other hand, have created multi-scale competition that will necessitate the consideration of many variables. Fueled by the aim of rapid growth and making huge profits, businesses continued to struggle to exist in an international market (Castells, 2008). Businesses aiming to stand out from their competitors have faced the necessity of fulfilling the mission of being a corporate citizen. This situation is shaped by legal regulations as well as being an element of competition.

An important regulation regarding the activities of enterprises is the Brundtland Report prepared by the World Development and Environment Commission in 1987. In this report, the concept of sustainability is considered as a key concept for the healthy continuation of the world order. The Commission defined sustainability as "meeting the needs of the present without compromising the ability of future generations to meet their own needs" (United Nations). Here, sustainability is expressed as a strategy that will not only protect the environment by preventing destruction, but also save humanity from extinction in the long run.

Sustainability is not just a concept that covers the environment. It is a strategy in which economic development and the environment are considered as a whole and the society is involved in every sense. The cornerstone of sustainable development is society. The extraordinary effect of businesses that determines the world order makes the individual passive in the face of all this power. An individual or business alone does not have the power to reverse this order and moreover cannot be held responsible for it. All businesses have to put the environment and society at the base of their economic strategies. This is the foundation of a successful sustainability strategy. In short, there are three basic elements of sustainable development: Environment, economic development and society (VanLoon et al., 2005). According to the Global Reporting Initiative, which prepares standardized sustainability reporting for businesses, the economic dimension of sustainability is related to economic performance, market presence, rapid growth and indirect economic effects in the economic development process. The social dimension is about observing the social balance in all the actions of the enterprise, ensuring the continuity of cultural systems, labor, product responsibility, human rights and people. The environmental dimension is related to maintaining the balance of natural ecology, biodiversity and physical systems, being sensitive to energy, water, waste, compatibility with products and services (Pazienza et al., 2022). The concept of sustainability has become an important element of successful competitive strategies, especially in recent years (Carayannis et al., 2022; Li et al., 2022a, 2022b; Yüksel et al., 2022; Mikhaylov et al., 2022). For hundreds of businesses operating in the same product category in a global market, traditional parameters such as price, quality and promotion are not sufficient to provide competitive advantage. For this reason, businesses fulfill their corporate citizen mission before the society by incorporating sustainability strategies into their corporate governance policies, while catching the advantage of being able to compete in the global market.

Today, only the performance of the enterprises in the production and sale of goods and services is not enough for them to achieve success. Businesses should be in a position that is sensitive to the environment, aware of their responsibilities towards society, sensitive to economic development and making efforts in all these issues. Therefore, the management understanding of businesses whose sole purpose is economic growth and profitability has transformed in the face of the conscious society, more specifically, differentiating consumer expectations (Kör, 2017). The concept of sustainability is in the middle of this transformation. In the traditional management approaches of the enterprises, the environment, energy and natural resources were used in an uncontrolled manner with the aim of economic growth (Eti et al., 2023; Li et al., 2022a, 2022b; Haiyun et al., 2021; Yuan et al., 2021). Communication with the consumer was built with a marketing approach aimed at increasing consumption. With an understanding of corporate sustainability, businesses pay attention to increasing the quality of life, paying attention to the use of low energy and natural resources, and getting maximum efficiency by giving as little damage to the environment as possible. Consumer policy, on the other hand, is designed with a marketing approach aimed at raising awareness in direct proportion to the increasing level of awareness.

There are issues that a business needs to pay attention to in order to successfully implement its sustainability policy. First of all, implementing sustainability requires considering many stakeholders and analyzing various factors. It is a long and complex process. Different areas such as mission and vision, organizational structure, decision-making processes, financial reporting, strategic planning should be integrated and organized under the umbrella of sustainability. In addition, for a successful sustainability practice, it is necessary to manage a healthy communication process inside and outside the enterprise. Implementing sustainability requires fundamental changes in the management approach and activities of the enterprise. All stakeholders should internalize and effectively communicate these changes. (Hoessle, 2013).

Corporate sustainability basically has two characteristics: First, it recommends a new business model. The second requires businesses not only to focus on their current gains but also to invest in the future (Tokgöz & First). Wilson defines corporate sustainability as the new and evolving management function of institutions. Corporate sustainability is a concept that should be taken into account in terms of the growth and maximum profit of a business. Businesses have reached this level of awareness today. According to Wilson, corporate sustainability consists of 4 concepts that businesses and literature are already familiar with (Wilson, 2003): Sustainable Development, Corporate Social Responsibility, Stakeholder Theory and Institutional Accountability Theory. Sustainable development means meeting the need for economic development and growth by balancing environmental protection and social equality. Corporate social responsibility is a concept that emphasizes the social role of an enterprise, which is fed from the moral philosophy. Stakeholder theory emphasizes the necessity of carrying out a correct and healthy relationship with the parties that are affected and affected in a wide range from production to sales process in all activities of enterprises. The purpose of stakeholder theory is to underline the necessity of giving importance to relations with other parties in order to provide a competitive advantage to businesses. Corporate accountability, under the umbrella of sustainability, explains the situation where businesses are held accountable for the environmental, economic and social impacts of business activities and are held accountable when necessary, not only when they are a party to a crime under the law (Wilson, 2003).

11.3 Corporate Social Responsibility

Corporate social responsibility, which is one of the elements of corporate sustainability, has an older history in terms of concept and practice. The first definition of the concept in the literature was made by Bowen in 1953. According to Bowen (1953), corporate social responsibility is "the obligations of businessmen to pursue those policies, to make those decisions, or to follow those lines of action which are desirable in terms of objectives and values of our society". About 20 years after Bowen's work, Davis used the term corporate social responsibility for the first time in his work, defining corporate social responsibility as the responsibilities of businesses beyond their economic interests, legal obligations and technical requirements (Davis, 1973).

Considering the historical development of corporate social responsibility, there was a very limited attempt to define the concept in the 1950s. Since the 1960s, there has been a significant increase in efforts to explain what corporate social responsibility is (Carroll, 1999). The reason for the effort in the 60 s can be explained by some changes in the society in the same years. Worker and consumer rights, ecological regulations, and the emergence of environmentally-friendly production methods have imposed some requirements on businesses in terms of responsibility. Since the 1970s, the concept of corporate social responsibility has gained a global dimension and has turned into a management function that requires businesses to take responsibility in solving problems caused by serious effects on nature and humanity (Türker & Altuntaş Vural, 2016). According to Carroll (1979), corporate social responsibility is the obligation of society to meet the economic, legal, ethical and discretionary expectations that it may demand from businesses at any time. Conceptualizing this definition with a pyramid years later, Carroll divided corporate social responsibility into four categories as economic, legal, ethical and philanthropic. Accordingly, while businesses realize their economic responsibilities for their own development policies, they strive to meet the expectations of the society in legal, ethical and philanthropic categories (Carroll, 1991).

Kotler and Lee points out that corporate social responsibility is an obligation undertaken to improve the well-being of society through discretionary business practices and contributions from corporate resources. Here, the main element that defines the nature of corporate social responsibility is that it is voluntary. To put it more clearly, businesses should implement their activities on a voluntary basis rather than a legal and moral sanction (Kotler & Lee, 2013). A similar definition is made by McWilliams and Siegel (2001). They also define corporate social responsibility activities as actions that should be carried out by considering the social benefit beyond the economic interests and legal obligations of the enterprises.

The purpose of existence of enterprises is naturally to obtain maximum profit in the axis of a long operating life and production consumption cycle. All other purposes are based on realizing this main purpose. There are also definitions that deal with corporate social responsibility from this perspective. Milton Friedman makes the definition of social responsibility under the title of a doctrine that breaks its foundations. According to him, the only social responsibility of businesses is to use all resources and activities to maximize their profits without breaking the rules (Friedman, 1970).

Based on the definitions above, it would not be wrong to say that social responsibility activities are carried out as an obligation or a voluntary requirement for businesses. At this point, it has become a necessity for businesses to take responsibility for their commercial activities, regardless of the intention to be realized. Business activities of businesses create two effects: market and non-market. Although they have incorporated market power and influence into their strategy, non-market impacts such as environmental pollution have traditionally been covered by the community or government. The term social responsibility incorporates these external influences into the management strategies of businesses (Sethi, 1979). To put it more clearly, businesses have to undertake and compensate for the economic, social and environmental effects and even damages of their activities.

Corporate social responsibility is one of the strategies of a successful sustainability policy. The point that brings the two terms closer together is that the activities implemented under the umbrella of corporate social responsibility focus on environmental, social and economic benefits. As stated before, sustainability also refers to a complex process consisting of these three layers. There is a hierarchical relationship between sustainability and corporate social responsibility. Accordingly, corporate social responsibility is an interim application, an interim goal for businesses to realize their sustainability policies (Panapanaan et al., 2003; Wilson, 2003). Businesses that have adopted a corporate sustainability policy also take care to act responsibly about the effects of their activities, along with other parameters. Corporate social responsibility is shaped by the incorporation of practices into management paradigms that will protect the benefit of society and the environment. This can take place in a wide range from regular economic assistance to enterprises to green innovation.

Climate changes, global warming, increase in consumption of energy and natural resources reflect the existence of problems related to the ecological system. The fact that enterprises are held responsible for environmental destruction due to their production activities has created the obligation to act sensitively within sustainable policies (Fang et al., 2021; Kayacık et al., 2022; Eti et al., 2022; Dinçer et al., 2023). Within the scope of sustainable environmental policies, businesses have put issues such as energy efficiency, reduction of hazardous wastes, recycling, and minimizing the use of natural energy resources in their corporate social responsibility practices (Karabulut Temel, 2017).

Following the first step taken with the United Nations Framework Convention on Climate Change, precautionary suggestions and solution efforts regarding global climate policies with the Kyoto Protocol, Copenhagen Agreement and Paris Agreements draw attention. In these efforts, it has been adopted to encourage the use of renewable energy by reducing the use of fossil fuels (Jimenez, 2021). Increasing attention to renewable energy in reducing ecological impacts has caused this sector to start to attract attention in corporate social responsibility initiatives of enterprises.

11.4 Renewable Energy in Sustainability and Corporate Responsibility Context

Although non-renewable energy like oil, coal and natural gas has advantages as having a high energy density, ease of storage, being affordable, and being able to be efficiently converted to the required energy type; reasons such as producing greenhouse gases, causing acid rain, posing a potential threat to human health, causing air/water/soil pollution, being limited and exhaustible resources, reveal the importance of clean energy use. Renewable energy resources do not run out over time, contribute efficiently to the reduction of greenhouse gases, especially CO_2, and any country can meet all its energy needs with renewable energy from the sun, water or wind (Xu et al., 2022; Bhuiyan et al., 2022; Kou et al., 2022; Ermiş & Güven, 2022).

Renewable energy offers climate-safe solutions while simultaneously supporting various socioeconomic benefits as job creation, improved health, and more social inclusion. Since employment is necessary for income generation and consequently for the well-being of both individuals and their families, creation of jobs and retention are crucial indicators of socioeconomic growth. Wage and salary income, particularly from well-paying occupations, enables people to purchase, which result in consistent demand for goods and services, therefore contributing to the health of local and national economies. Thus, the employment metric extends far beyond direct jobs in the renewable energy sector and indirect jobs in the supply chain, to include so-called induced jobs in the broader economy (IRENA, 2017). Renewable energy sources are typically seen to have a significant impact on increasing employment, particularly among the local people where a certain renewable source is located. There are three major phases to adequately illustrate the impact of a power plant life cycle on the quality and quantity of employment, the location and duration of employment, and the indirect development of the "green" economy: (1) technological development, (2) power plant installation/uninstallation, and (3) operation or management and maintenance of technological plants (Maradin, 2021). Another advantage of using renewable energy sources is that it promotes economic development, specifically the development of the energy sector and all linked activities. Renewable energy sources have a substantial multiplier effect on countries whose industries are capable of producing energy machinery and equipment based on technological advancements, particularly in their exports (Granić, 2010; Maradin, 2021). Investment in renewables and energy efficiency, as well as enabling policies such as carbon pricing and the recycling of revenue from decreased income taxes, all contribute to a rise in economic activity. IRENA discovered that reducing global carbon dioxide emissions in accordance with the Paris Agreement will raise GDP in an analysis done under Germany's G20 presidency. However, metrics such as GDP do not represent the whole range of human wellbeing gain. A more comprehensive accounting of benefits includes employment, health, education, reduced greenhouse gas emissions, and changes in material consumption (IRENA, 2017). Renewable energy provides electricity availability in locations where grid extension is either prohibitively expensive or physically impossible. Access provides a variety of socioeconomic advantages, such as increased communications (mobile phone charge), which assist the progress of economic transactions, aids in the development of rural marketplaces, and generates jobs. Improved illumination in homes and schools benefits education and skill development. Furthermore, energy access is critical for enhancing health care (cold storage for medicines, usage of medical equipment that requires electricity), and the use of clean energy instead of highly polluting fuels minimizes indoor air pollution (IRENA, 2012). As indicated in IRENA (2017) report, renewable energy's multifaceted socioeconomic benefits are gaining prominence as a crucial consideration for decision makers. The effects of the energy transition on the economy as a whole - employment, income generation, welfare improvement, and local industrial growth - are becoming obvious. Aside from the environmental and climate benefits of renewable energy deployment, maximizing the social benefits is critical to ensuring a just, timely, and economically efficient transition. An equitable transition disseminates the benefits of renewable energy and increases its adoption in local communities and throughout countries.

Companies are now taking control of their corporate social responsibility efforts in order to better plan their future projects by utilizing a balanced global climate effort, defining ecologically friendly long-term objectives, transparency improvement and encouragement of market-based strategies to minimize costs (Secinaro et al., 2020). As Strielkowski et al. (2022) notes, organizations can show their commitment to social responsibility by supporting and adopting renewable energy. As indicated by the Paris Agreement, several of the world's largest countries are putting in place the costly but necessary plan to generate 100% renewable energy by 2050. Public policies have the potential to play a critical role in fostering a favorable climate for corruption and risk reduction, as well as the growth of sustainable energy development in general. This is owing to the necessity to account for carbon emissions and water purification, which normally occur as the usage of renewable energy increases, as well as the environmental effects of climate change. In latest years, an increasing shift in corporate social responsibility and green energy goals have been observed with corporations such as Google, Facebook, and Microsoft, establishing aggressive targets for sustainability and renewable energy while increasingly placing emphasise on corporate social responsibility targets (Strielkowski et al., 2022).

As Tiep et al. states (2021), in today's global arena, it is critical that resources be used efficiently, and the same is important for energy input. Sustainable energy is defined as energy that is consumed in a negligible proportion to its supply and has manageable side effects, particularly on the environment. A sustainable energy system is one that meets the demands of the present without jeopardizing the needs of future generations. Sustainable energy supply is a primary priority in terms of energy security, energy efficiency, and environmental protection for governments, regions, and the entire world. Sustainable development is a major principle for sustainability that spans four interconnected fields such as ecology, economy, politics, and culture. Sustainable energy development seeks to boost economic development, improve energy security, increase energy access, and minimize climate change. Renewable energy sources include hydroelectricity, solar energy, wind energy, wave energy, geothermal energy, bioenergy, and tidal energy. To that end, encouraging the use of renewable energy and assuring citizens' access to sustainable, reliable, affordable energy help to drive sustainable development (Rajesh & Majid, 2020; Tiep et al., 2021).

Altering the energy structure by increasing the renewable energy resources usage and decreasing the non-renewable energy resources usage is critical for security, the economy, the environment, and society (Tiep et al., 2021). Saad and Talep indicates (2018) that, nonrenewable energy usage has a variety of detrimental effects on the economy, environment, and society. It has been demonstrated that using nonrenewable energy resources will damage not only the environment and public health due to pollutants emitted from the combustion of fossil fuels, but also the economy as a result of air emissions that lead to environmental and health costs at multiple levels such as personal, local, regional, national, and global.

11.5 Conclusion

There is no doubt that a sustainable energy model must be based on renewable technologies. It is clear that renewable energy is inexhaustible, does not contain greenhouse gas emissions, and, by its very nature, will ensure the welfare, progress and development of societies. Renewable energy is obtained from natural resources that are continuously or repeatedly accessible from the natural environment. Since these resources are self-existing and inexhaustible resources, they are included in our lives as clean energy. Investment in the renewable energy sector in a country provides a wide range of socio-economic benefits, for example, it improves regional and rural development, provides job opportunities and moreover contributes to the diversification of energy supply. However, environmental awareness has increased in societies. Individuals care about the ecosystem balance. Many companies consider this sensitivity and transform their production and other processes into environmentally friendly practices. As the world becomes more environmentally conscious, most consumers develop a positive attitude towards companies adopting the green movement. Because they are aware that clean energy is a sustainable way to meet the energy demands without harming the environment.

Well-known businesses in the industry are taking the lead in using renewable energy not only for the environment but also for their own benefits. The world is shifting towards renewable energy sources as one solution to the issue of rising energy consumption and environmental concerns. As a result, alternative energy sources are expected to surpass fossil fuels, even if not in the near future. Individuals around the world want to live more sustainable and it is businesses task to enhance their understanding of the advantages of corporate social responsibility to attain sustainable development goals for wellbeing of both the environment and the society. In order to ensure sustainable development and social welfare, all shareholders must cooperate and coordinate to develop the right energy policies. Countries should acknowledge the importance of corporate social responsibility values for clean energy.

References

Aktaş, H. (2017). *İşletmelerde Sürdürülebilirliğin Sağlanmasında Lider Yöneticilerin Rolü ve Küresel En İyi Uygulama Örnekleri. I. M. Pekdemir içinde, İşletmelerde Sürdürülebilirlik Dinamikleri* (pp. 59–90). Beta Yayınları.

Bhuiyan, M. A., Dinçer, H., Yüksel, S., Mikhaylov, A., Danish, M. S. S., Pinter, G., et al. (2022). Economic indicators and bioenergy supply in developed economies: QROF-DEMATEL and random forest models. *Energy Reports, 8*, 561–570.

Bowen, H. R. (1953). *Social responsibility of the businessman.* Harper & Row.

Carayannis, E., Kostis, P., Dinçer, H., & Yüksel, S. (2022). Balanced-scorecard-based evaluation of knowledge-oriented competencies of distributed energy investments. *Energies, 15*(21), 8245.

Carroll, A. B. (1979). A three-dimensional conceptual model of corporate performance. *Academy of Management Review, 4*(4), 479–505.

Carroll, A. B. (1991). The pyramid of corporate social responsibility: Toward the moral Management of Organizational Stakeholders. *Business Horizons, 34*(4), 39–48.

Carroll, A. B. (1999). Corporate social responsibility evolution of a definitional construct. *Business and Society, 38*(3), 268–295.

Castells, M. (2008). *Enformasyon Çağı: Ekonomi, Toplum ve Kültür Ağ Toplumunun Yükselişi.* (ç. E. Kılıç, Dü.) İstanbul: İstanbul Bilgi Üniversitesi yayınları.

Chasek, P. (2022, June 1). *The legacies of the Stockholm Conference.* International Institute for Sustainable Development. Access October 13, 2022, from https://www.iisd.org/articles/deep-dive/stockholm-conference-legacy.

Davis, K. (1973). The case for and against business assumption of social responsibilities. *The Academy of Management Journal, 16*(2), 312–322.

Dinçer, H., Aksoy, T., Yüksel, S., & Hacioglu, U. (2022). Golden cut-oriented q-rung orthopair fuzzy decision-making approach to evaluation of renewable energy alternatives for microgeneration system investments. *Mathematical Problems in Engineering, 2022*, 2261166.

Dinçer, H., Yüksel, S., Çağlayan, Ç., Yavuz, D., & Kararoğlu, D. (2023). Can renewable energy investments be a solution to the energy-sourced high inflation problem?. In *Managing inflation and supply chain disruptions in the global economy* (pp. 220–238). IGI Global.

Dinçer, H., Yüksel, S., & Martínez, L. (2022). Collaboration enhanced hybrid fuzzy decision-making approach to analyze the renewable energy investment projects. *Energy Reports, 8*, 377–389.

Dinçer, H., Yüksel, S., Mikhaylov, A., Pinter, G., & Shaikh, Z. A. (2022). Analysis of renewable-friendly smart grid technologies for the distributed energy investment projects using a hybrid picture fuzzy rough decision-making approach. *Energy Reports, 8*, 11466–11477.

Dong, W., Zhao, G., Yüksel, S., Dinçer, H., & Ubay, G. G. (2022). A novel hybrid decision making approach for the strategic selection of wind energy projects. *Renewable Energy, 185*, 321–337.

Ermiş, A. M., & Güven, M. E. (2022). The role of green energy Investments in Energy Supply Security. In *Circular economy and the energy market* (pp. 67–77). Springer.

Eti, S., Dinçer, H., Gökalp, Y., Yüksel, S., & Kararoğlu, D. (2023). Identifying key issues to handle the inflation problem in the healthcare industry caused by energy prices: An evaluation with decision-making models. *Managing Inflation and Supply Chain Disruptions in the Global Economy*, 162–178.

Eti, S., Dinçer, H., Yüksel, S., & Gökalp, Y. (2022). Analysis of the suitability of the solar panels for hospitals: A new fuzzy decision-making model proposal with the T-spherical TOP-DEMATEL method. *Journal of Intelligent & Fuzzy Systems, Preprint*, 1–13.

Fang, S., Zhou, P., Dinçer, H., & Yüksel, S. (2021). Assessment of safety management system on energy investment risk using house of quality based on hybrid stochastic interval-valued intuitionistic fuzzy decision-making approach. *Safety Science, 141*, 105333.

Friedman, M. (1970, September 13). The social responsibility of business is to increase its profits. *The New York Times Magazine, 32–33*, 122–124.

Gladwin, T. N., Kennelly, J. J., & Shelomith Krause, T. (1995). Shifting paradigms for sustainable development: Implications for management theory and research. *The Academy of Management Review, 20*(4), 874–907.

Granić, G. (2010). *Kako Promišljati Energetsku Budućnost? [how to rethink energy future?].* Poslovna biblioteka, Energy Institute Hrvoje Pozar.

Haiyun, C., Zhixiong, H., Yüksel, S., & Dinçer, H. (2021). Analysis of the innovation strategies for green supply chain management in the energy industry using the QFD-based hybrid interval valued intuitionistic fuzzy decision approach. *Renewable and Sustainable Energy Reviews, 143*, 110844.

Harvey, D. (2015). *Neoliberalizmin Kısa Tarihi.* (A. Ocak, Dü.). Sel Yayıncılık.

Hoessle, U. (2013). Ten steps towards a sustainable business. *WWS Series, 1*, 1–11.

IRENA. (2012). Renewable energy jobs & access, Abu Dhabi. Access November 11, 2022, from http://www.irena.org/DocumentDownloads/Publications/Renewable_Energy_Jobs_and_Access.pdf.

IRENA. (2017). *Renewable energy benefits: Understanding the socio-economics*. Acess November 11, 2022, from https://www.irena.org/-/media/Files/IRENA/Agency/Publication/2017/Nov/IRENA_Understanding_Socio_Economics_2017.pdf?la=en&hash=C430B7EF772BA0E631190A75F7243B992211F102.

Jimenez, A. (2021, March 22). A brief guide to renewables. United Naitons Climate Change. Access October 10, 2022, from https://unfccc.int/blog/a-brief-guide-to-renewables.

Kafka, K. I., Dinçer, H., & Yüksel, S. (2022). Impact-relation map of innovative service development regarding the sustainable growth for emerging markets. *Journal of the Knowledge Economy*, 1–24.

Karabulut Temel, E. (2017). *Sürdürülebilirlik ve Teknolojik İnovasyon. I. M. Pekdemir içinde, İşletmelerde Sürdürülebilirlik Dinamikleri* (pp. 239–271). Beta Yayınları.

Kayacık, M., Dinçer, H., & Yüksel, S. (2022). Using quantum spherical fuzzy decision support system as a novel sustainability index approach for analyzing industries listed in the stock exchange. *Borsa Istanbul Review, 22*(6), 1145–1157.

Kör, B. (2017). *İşletmelerin Kurumsal Sürdürülebilirlik Stratejileriyle İlgili Düzenlemeler ve Destekler. I. M. Pekdemir içinde, İşletmelerde Sürdürülebilirlik Dinamikleri* (pp. 404–444). Beta Yayınları.

Kotler, P., & Lee, N. (2013). *Kurumsal Sosyal Sorumluluk (Cilt çev. Sibel Kaçamak).* MediaCat Kitapları.

Kou, G., Yüksel, S., & Dinçer, H. (2022). Inventive problem-solving map of innovative carbon emission strategies for solar energy-based transportation investment projects. *Applied Energy, 311*, 118680.

Li, W., Yüksel, S., & Dinçer, H. (2022a). Understanding the financial innovation priorities for renewable energy investors via QFD-based picture fuzzy and rough numbers. *Financial Innovation, 8*(1), 1–30.

Li, J., Yüksel, S., Dınçer, H., Mikhaylov, A., & Barykin, S. E. (2022b). Bipolar q-ROF hybrid decision making model with golden cut for analyzing the levelized cost of renewable energy alternatives. *IEEE Access, 10*, 42507–42517.

Maradin, D. (2021). Advantages and disadvantages of renewable energy sources utilization. *International Journal of Energy Economics and Policy, 11*(3), 176–183.

Martínez, L., Dinçer, H., & Yüksel, S. (2022). A hybrid decision making approach for new service development process of renewable energy investment. *Applied Soft Computing, 133*(3), 109897.

McWilliams, A., & Siegel, D. (2001). Corporate social responsibility: A theory of the firm perspective. *The Academy of Management Review, 26*(1), 117–127.

Mikhaylov, A., Bhatti, I. M., Dinçer, H., & Yüksel, S. (2022). Integrated decision recommendation system using iteration-enhanced collaborative filtering, golden cut bipolar for analyzing the risk-based oil market spillovers. *Computational Economics*, 1–34.

Mukhtarov, S., Yüksel, S., & Dinçer, H. (2022). The impact of financial development on renewable energy consumption: Evidence from Turkey. *Renewable Energy, 187*, 169–176.

Panapanaan, V. M., Linnanen, L., Karvonen, M. M., & Phan, T. V. (2003). Roadmapping corporate social responsibility in Finnish companies. *Journal of Business Ethics, 44*, 133–148.

Pazienza, M., de Jong, M., & Schoenmaker, D. (2022). Clarifying the concept of corporate sustainability and providing convergence for its definition. *MDPI, 14*(13), 7838.

Rajesh, K. J. C., & Majid, M. A. (2020). Renewable energy for sustainable development in India: Current status, future prospects, challenges, employment, and investment opportunities. *Energy, Sustainability and Society, 10*(1), 10.

Saad, W., & Taleb, A. (2018). The causal relationship between renewable energy consumption and economic growth: Evidence from Europe. *Clean Technologies and Environmental Policy, 20*(1), 127–136.

Secinaro, S., Brescia, V., Calandra, D., & Saiti, B. (2020). Impact of climate change mitigation policies on corporate financial performance: Evidence-based on European publicly listed firms. *Corporate Social Responsibility and Environmental Management, 27*(6), 2491–2501.

Sethi, P. (1979). A conceptual framework for environmental analysis of social issues and evaluation of business response patterns. *Academy of Management Review, 4*(1), 63–74.

Strielkowski, W., Tarkhanova, E., Baburina, N., & Streimikis, J. (2022). Corporate social responsibility and the renewable energy development in the Baltic States. *Sustainability, 13*(9860), 1–18.

Sun, L., Peng, J., Dinçer, H., & Yüksel, S. (2022). Coalition-oriented strategic selection of renewable energy system alternatives using q-ROF DEMATEL with golden cut. *Energy, 256*, 124606.

Tiep, L. T., Huan, N. Q., & Hong, T. T. T. (2021). Role of corporate social responsibility in sustainable energy development in emerging economy. *International Journal of Energy Economics and Policy, 11*(2), 172–186.

Türker, D., & Altuntaş Vural, C. (2016). *Kurumsal Sosyal Sorumluluk ve Hayırseverlik. S. Hoştut, & S. D. Van Het Hof içinde, Kurumsal Sosyal Sorumlulukt Güncel Yönelim ve Yaklaşımlar* (pp. 149–171). Nobel Yayıncılık.

VanLoon, G. W., Patil, S. G., & Hugar, L. B. (2005). *Agricultural sustainability: Strategies for assessment.* SAGE Publications.

Wilson, M. (2003). Corporate Sustainability: What is it and where does it come from? *Ivey Business Journal.* Access October 12, 2022, from https://iveybusinessjournal.com/publication/corporate-sustainability-what-is-it-and-where-does-it-come-from/.

Xu, X., Yüksel, S., & Dinçer, H. (2022). An integrated decision-making approach with Golden cut and bipolar q-ROFSs to renewable energy storage investments. *International Journal of Fuzzy Systems*, 1–14.

Yuan, G., Xie, F., Dinçer, H., & Yüksel, S. (2021). The theory of inventive problem solving (TRIZ)-based strategic mapping of green nuclear energy investments with spherical fuzzy group decision-making approach. *International Journal of Energy Research, 45*(8), 12284–12300.

Yüksel, S., & Dinçer, H. (2022). Identifying the strategic priorities of nuclear energy investments using hesitant 2-tuple interval-valued Pythagorean fuzzy DEMATEL. *Progress in Nuclear Energy, 145*, 104103.

Yüksel, S., Dinçer, H., Eti, S., & Adalı, Z. (2022). Strategy improvements to minimize the drawbacks of geothermal investments by using spherical fuzzy modelling. *International Journal of Energy Research.*

Zhang, Y., Zhang, Y., Gong, C., Dinçer, H., & Yüksel, S. (2022). An integrated hesitant 2-tuple Pythagorean fuzzy analysis of QFD-based innovation cost and duration for renewable energy projects. *Energy, 248*, 123561.

Chapter 12
Human Resource Management to Improve the Quality of Energy Efficiency of the Enterprise

Mir Sayed Shah Danish and Emerson Guzzi Zuan Esteves

Keywords Human resources · Renewable energy sources · Technological innovations · Nuclear energy

12.1 Introduction

In addition to organizing training and professional development, the main tasks of forming energy-efficient human resources include creating management teams aimed at motivating employees to save energy, and introducing them to the corporate culture of lean energy consumption.

When studying energy efficiency issues, the term energy-efficient human capital is used, the concept of which includes a set of professional and managerial competencies in the field of energy efficiency management, which makes it possible to increase the competitiveness of an enterprise to the level of the best global usage guidelines.

The implementation of the proposed approach is possible only when forming individual areas of responsibility in the field of energy conservation management, improving the internal culture of energy conservation and involving participants in the process in an open dialogue. Responsibility should be based primarily on indicators of the energy efficiency of human capital. Efficiency assessment should be carried out by managers of energy services using simple and understandable methods, based on publicly available management information material. If necessary, a more detailed analysis is possible by means of narrowly focused surveys, organizing open discussions, and building an organizational profile.

M. S. S. Danish (✉)
University of the Ryukyus, Nishihara, Japan

E. G. Z. Esteves
The State University of Londrina, Londrina, Brazil
e-mail: emerson.esteves@uel.br

H. Dincer, S. Yüksel (eds.), *Economic Development and the Environmental Ecosystem*, Contributions to Economics,
https://doi.org/10.1007/978-3-031-26596-9_12

The existing energy efficiency management strategy at the enterprise, aimed at unlocking the innovative potential of employees and improving the culture of energy consumption, is acceptable (Fang et al., 2021; Kayacık et al., 2022; Eti et al., 2022; Dinçer et al., 2023). However, to improve the chosen direction, it is necessary to provide additional incentives and develop mechanisms to support the energy efficiency management system by implementing the principles of human resource management and creating a favorable internal environment that promotes changes and improves the energy consumption culture.

The human capital planning process is the initial stage of the chosen strategy and includes an analysis of the external environment (studying the labor market, monitoring job seekers 'requests) in order to form the company's personnel policy and then develop a personnel management strategy. The inclusion of the basic principles of energy efficiency in the competence model of job seekers for employment will promote the idea of implementing energy saving principles by means of personnel policy. The list of competencies should include basic knowledge and skills in the field of rational use, starting from every day and everyday actions of employees, ending with professional competencies necessary for the implementation of technical tasks of energy saving (Martínez et al., 2022; Sun et al., 2022; Kafka et al., 2022; Mukhtarov et al., 2022).

12.2 Literature Review

The next process of human capital development is mainly aimed at improving the level of competencies of employees through the organization of professional training. To increase the efficiency of the process, it is necessary to stimulate educational activities by means of investment, motivate staff to learn, and apply modern teaching methods, including using digitalization tools (Denisova et al., 2019; Nyangarika et al., 2019a, 2019b; Huang et al., 2021a; Huang et al., 2021b; Mikhaylov, 2018, 2022a; 2022b; Mikhaylov et al., 2019; Conteh et al., 2021; Sediqi et al., 2022; Khan et al., 2021; Bhuiyan et al., 2022a; Liu et al., 2021a, 2021b; Daniali et al., 2021; Moiseev et al., 2023; An et al., 2022).

The implementation of training programs can be implemented with the participation of internal training units or transferred to specialized organizations, including various universities. A significant potential in the development of the field of study is associated with the creation of cooperation between our own training centers and scientific organizations, since in this case a synergy effect is formed between practical and theoretical knowledge (Bhuiyan et al., 2021; Dong et al., 2021, Mikhaylov, 2021b; Barykin et al., 2022b; Liu et al., 2022a, 2022b; Bhuiyan et al., 2022b; Danish et al., 2022a, 2022b; Saqib et al., 2021; Mukhametov et al., 2021, Candila et al., 2021; Mikhaylov & Grilli, 2022; Li et al. 2022a, 2022b, 2022c).

Training methods should be based on the category of the target audience and the tasks assigned to the training organizers, and can vary from traditional academic lectures to business trainings, practical seminars, as well as using modern training tools—electronic courses, computer modeling (Khan et al., 2022; Dinçer et al., 2022b, 2022d; Badr et al., 2022; Barykin et al., 2022a; Mehta et al., 2022; Kalinina et al., 2022; Shaikh et al., 2022; Mikhaylov et al., 2023; Nyangarika et al., 2022; Mikhaylov et al., 2022).

The scope and content of educational programs should be divided into categories of employees, which will ensure that the necessary knowledge in the field of energy conservation is obtained for a specific target group (Mikhaylov et al., 2022c; Mikhaylov, 2021a; Varyash et al., 2020; Zhao et al., 2021; An & Mikhaylov, 2020; Alwaelya et al., 2021; Yumashev & Mikhaylov, 2020; Yumashev et al., 2020; Mutalimov et al., 2021; An & Mikhaylov, 2021).

For example, non-production staff, which includes office workers, should know the modes of electric lighting, be able to effectively use household and office equipment, and also understand the basic principles of economy (Xu et al., 2022; Bhuiyan et al., 2022; Kou et al., 2022; Ermiş & Güven, 2022). The second category includes workers of production divisions, whose knowledge should include the modes of energy-efficient operation of technological equipment, key performance indicators of the site/division, opportunities and reserves of equipment for saving (Nie et al., 2020; Dayong et al., 2020; Mikhaylov et al., 2018; Nyangarika et al., 2018; Danish et al., 2020; Danish et al., 2021; An et al., 2021; Uyeh et al., 2021; Tamashiro et al., 2021; Tamashiro et al., 2023; Shaikh et al., 2021).

Technical specialists of production units belonging to the third category are required to know energy-efficient design solutions for developing new projects, the principles of forming key energy efficiency indicators, the possibility of using alternative (renewable) energy sources in metallurgy, and, of course, the basic principles of rationing. The latter category includes managers of various levels who deal with issues related to improving the energy efficiency of the departments entrusted to them and the enterprise as a whole (An et al., 2019a, 2019b; Mikhaylov & Tarakanov, 2020; An et al., 2020a, 2020b, 2020c; Moiseev et al., 2020; Moiseev et al., 2021; Gura et al., 2022; Dooyum et al., 2020; Mikhaylov, 2020a; Mikhaylov, 2020b; Mikhaylov, 2020c).

12.3 Human Resource Management to Improve the Quality of Energy Efficiency

The process of preserving human capital is aimed at retaining promising and highly competent employees who are able to show high performance in implementing the chosen strategy, are the driving force behind implementing changes and accumulate positive experience in managing energy efficiency.

It is obvious that in order to encourage and involve employees in energy saving processes, it is necessary to create responsibility centers, and in addition to collective responsibility (teams, sections, workshops), individual responsibility should be formed. In this case, we mean determining the key energy efficiency indicators of an individual employee.

At the level of technical personnel, energy efficiency indicators are interrelated with the specifics of technological processes, so determining the energy saving potential is based on identifying the main processes and sources of costs. The search for these energy consumption objects is based on the available technical documentation and the results of energy surveys. The formation of a list of employees for setting performance indicators should be carried out using the principles of transparency, and the potential for energy saving is tied to the human factor.

At the level of management personnel, the effectiveness of teamwork should be considered. The list of indicators of managerial energy efficiency includes implemented projects to optimize management mechanisms and organizational structures. At the same time, the quality and effectiveness of teamwork is affected by the presence of stable communications between individual performers.

It can be assumed that after the implementation of the proposed key performance indicators, employees will be motivated to improve energy efficiency, and the presence of individual responsibility will encourage them to improve the culture of energy-efficient production.

Another area of energy efficiency management is the introduction of a system for continuously improving the energy consumption culture at a metallurgical enterprise. This tool is based on the principles of implementing a lean production system, but the main losses here are all possible losses of energy resources (technological deviations, transmission losses, irrational use, etc.) (Dong et al., 2022; Dinçer et al., 2022a, 2022b 2022c; Zhang et al., 2022; Yüksel & Dinçer, 2022). The main philosophy of the system is to involve the maximum number of employees in the energy saving process through training in energy efficiency tools, creating teams to implement changes, implementation of these changes on a specific site and subsequent replication in all structural divisions of the enterprise without exception. To increase the level of engagement and maximize the effectiveness of team members, it is necessary to apply measures of material and non-material incentives. The share of the received economic effect from the implemented changes can serve as a source of incentive funds. Of course, it is equally important to inform employees about the number and quality of implemented projects and their significance for the development of energy efficiency of the enterprise.

Building an organization's energy profile. Recommendations for building an improved energy profile of an organization may include a priority analysis of the accumulated energy-efficient human capital as part of staff motivation, or even as part of a separate section of the profile that will consider the effectiveness of training personnel at all levels, progress in developing competencies during mandatory certifications, and experience in promoting and applying energy-efficient technologies (Carayannis et al., 2022; Li et al. 2022a, 2022b, 2022c; Yüksel et al., 2022; Mikhaylov et al., 2022a).

A promising area of implementation of the energy efficiency management process is the formation of energy-efficient human resources as a source of innovative ideas and the main driving force in improving energy efficiency.

The paper reflects the main actions for planning, developing and preserving human resources, which contribute to improving the effectiveness of training processes, as well as motivate employees to use energy-efficient ways of working.

The introduction of key personnel energy efficiency indicators will reflect the effectiveness of the company's investments in personnel training and form professional competencies in the field of energy conservation. The paper offers a set of key indicators, an algorithm for their development and implementation, as well as a range of expected results of implementing these indicators (Eti et al., 2023; Li et al. 2022a, 2022b, 2022c; Haiyun et al., 2021; Yuan et al., 2021).

12.4 Conclusion

The system of continuous improvement of the energy consumption culture proposed for implementation will significantly increase the interest and involve the personnel of the metallurgical enterprise in the process of saving.

The issues of improving energy efficiency and creating an effective management mechanism are typical for all industrial enterprises, especially metallurgical ones, since they are the ones that are distinguished by high rates of energy resource consumption in the global economy. The global energy crisis of the late 70 s of the last century served as an impetus for the creation of a systematic approach to energy conservation issues. The fundamental document that dictates the basic principles of the management system is an international standard that is applicable for most countries and is relevant, including for Russia.

Metallurgical production is rightfully considered one of the most energy—intensive industries, which, according to research conducted by the International Energy Agency, has an energy saving potential of about 35–40%. The most promising ones in terms of reducing consumption are electric steelmaking shops, whose share in the total balance of the enterprise reaches 30%.

Based on the results of the theoretical study, three approaches to the implementation of the energy efficiency management process at the enterprise are identified: technocratic, systemic and innovative. All these approaches have a certain set of advantages and are based on the use of production and technical resources and the intellectual potential of employees. These tools form the basis of planning, consumption, and performance monitoring management processes.

References

Alwaelya, S. A., Yousif, N. B. A., & Mikhaylov, A. (2021). Emotional development in preschoolers and socialization. *Early Child Development and Care, 191*, 16.

An, J., & Mikhaylov, A. (2020). Russian energy projects in South Africa. *Journal of Energy in Southern Africa, 31*(3), 58–64.

An, J., & Mikhaylov, A. (2021). Analysis of energy projects financial efficiency and renewable energy generation in Russia. *Finance: Theory and Practice, 25*(5), 79–91.

An, J., Mikhaylov, A., Dinçer, H., & Yüksel, S. (2022). Economic modelling of electricity generation: Long short-term memory and Q-rung Orthopair fuzzy sets. *Heliyon, 8*, e10759.

An, J., Mikhaylov, A., & Jung, S.-U. (2020b). The strategy of South Korea in the global oil market. *Energies, 13*(10), 2491.

An, J., Mikhaylov, A., & Jung, S.-U. (2021). A linear programming approach for robust network revenue management in the airline industry. *Journal of Air Transport Management, 91*, 101979.

An, J., Mikhaylov, A., & Kim, K. (2020c). Machine learning approach in heterogeneous group of algorithms for transport safety-critical system. *Applied Sciences, 10*(8), 2670.

An, J., Mikhaylov, A., & Moiseev, N. (2019b). Oil price predictors: Machine learning approach. *International Journal of Energy Economics and Policy, 9*(5), 1–6.

An, J., Mikhaylov, A., & Richter, U. H. (2020a). Trade war effects: Evidence from sectors of energy and resources in Africa. *Heliyon, 6*, e05693. https://doi.org/10.1016/j.heliyon.2020.e05693

An, J., Mikhaylov, A., & Sokolinskaya, N. (2019a). Machine learning in economic planning: Ensembles of algorithms. *Journal of Physics: Conference Series, 1353*, 012126.

Badr, A. M. N. A. A., Mohamed, T. I., Osman, N. A. Q., & Mikhaylov, A. (2022). A review of social media website users' interaction paths with governmental accounts during the COVID-19 pandemic. *Informatics, 9*, 50. https://doi.org/10.3390/informatics9030050

Barykin, S. E., Kapustina, I. V., Sergeev, S. M., Daniali, S. M., Kopteva, L. A., Semenova, G. N., Pryadko, I. P., Mikhaylov, A., Baboshkin, P., Datsyuk, P., & Senjyu, T. (2022a). Financial logistics models based on systematic approach improving management solutions. *F1000Research, 11*, 570. https://doi.org/10.12688/f1000research.111252.1

Barykin, S., Mikheev, A., Kiseleva, E., Putikhin, Y., Alekseeva, N., & Mikhaylov, A. (2022b). An empirical analysis of Russian regions' debt sustainability. *Economies, 10*(4), 296.

Bhuiyan, M. A., An, J., Mikhaylov, A., Moiseev, N., & Danish, M. S. S. (2021). Renewable energy deployment and COVID-19 measures for sustainable development. *Sustainability, 13*, 4418.

Bhuiyan, M. A., Dinçer, H., Yüksel, S., Mikhaylov, A., Danish, M. S. S., Pinter, G., et al. (2022a). Economic indicators and bioenergy supply in developed economies: QROF-DEMATEL and random forest models. *Energy Reports, 8*, 561–570.

Bhuiyan, M. A., Dinçer, H., Yüksel, S., Mikhaylov, A., Danish, M. S. S., Pinter, G., Uyeh, D. D., & Stepanova, D. (2022b). Economic indicators and bioenergy supply in developed economies: QROF-DEMATEL and random forest models. *Energy Reports, 8*(2022), 561–570.

Bhuiyan, M. A., Zhang, Q., Khare, V., Mikhaylov, A., Pinter, G., & Huang, X. (2022). Renewable energy consumption and economic growth nexus—A systematic literature review. *Frontiers in Environmental Science., 10*, 878394. https://doi.org/10.3389/fenvs.2022.878394

Candila, V., Maximov, D., Mikhaylov, A., Moiseev, N., Senjyu, T., & Tryndina, N. (2021). On the relationship between oil and exchange rates of oil-exporting and oil-importing countries: From the great recession period to the Covid-19 era. *Energies, 14*, 8065.

Carayannis, E., Kostis, P., Dinçer, H., & Yüksel, S. (2022). Balanced-scorecard-based evaluation of knowledge-oriented competencies of distributed energy investments. *Energies, 15*(21), 8245.

Conteh, F., Takahashi, H., Hemeida, A. M., Krishnan, N., Mikhaylov, A., & Senjyu, T. (2021). Hybrid grid-connected renewable power generation for sustainable electricity supply in Sierra Leone: Case study lungi town. *Sustainability, 13*(18), 1–20.

Daniali, S. M., Barykin, S. E., Kapustina, I. V., Khortabi, F. M., Sergeev, S. M., Kalinina, O. V., Mikhaylov, A., Veynberg, R., Zasova, L., & Senjyu, T. (2021). Predicting volatility index according to technical index and economic indicators on the basis of deep learning algorithm. *Sustainability, 2021*(13), 14011.

Danish, M. S. S., Bhattacharya, A., Stepanova, D., Mikhaylov, A., Grilli, M. L., Khosravy, M., & Senjyu, T. (2020). A systematic review of metal oxide applications for energy and environmental sustainability. *Metals, 10*(12), 1604.

Danish, M. S. S., Senjyu, T., Sabory, N. R., Khosravy, M., Grilli, M. L., Mikhaylov, A., & Majidi, H. (2021). A forefront framework for sustainable aquaponics modeling and design. *Sustainability, 13*, 9313.

Danish, M. S., Senjyu, T. S., Sabory, N. R., & Mikhaylov, A. (2022a). Lessons from COVID-19 conferring environmental re-engineering opportunity. In M. Danish & T. Senjyu (Eds.), *Eco-friendly and agile energy strategies and policy development* (pp. 99–118). IGI Global. https://doi.org/10.4018/978-1-7998-9502-2.ch005

Danish, M. S., Senjyu, T. S., Sabory, N. R., & Mikhaylov, A. (2022b). Interplay consequences of COVID-19 on global environmental sustainability. In M. Danish & T. Senjyu (Eds.), *Eco-friendly and agile energy strategies and policy development*. IGI Global. https://doi.org/10.4018/978-1-7998-9502-2.ch003

Dayong, N., Mikhaylov, A., Bratanovsky, S., Shaikh, Z. A., & Stepanova, D. (2020). Mathematical modeling of the technological processes of catering products production. *Journal of Food Process Engineering, 43*(2), 1–9.

Denisova, V., Mikhaylov, A., & Lopatin, E. (2019). Blockchain infrastructure and growth of global power consumption. *International Journal of Energy Economics and Policy, 9*(4), 22–29.

Dinçer, H., Aksoy, T., Yüksel, S., & Hacioglu, U. (2022a). Golden cut-oriented q-rung orthopair fuzzy decision-making approach to evaluation of renewable energy alternatives for microgeneration system investments. *Mathematical Problems in Engineering, 2022*, 2261166.

Dinçer, H., Yüksel, S., Çağlayan, Ç., Yavuz, D., & Kararoğlu, D. (2023). Can renewable energy investments be a solution to the energy-sourced high inflation problem?. In *Managing inflation and supply chain disruptions in the global economy* (pp. 220–238). IGI Global.

Dinçer, H., Yüksel, S., & Martínez, L. (2022b). Collaboration enhanced hybrid fuzzy decision-making approach to analyze the renewable energy investment projects. *Energy Reports, 8*, 377–389.

Dinçer, H., Yüksel, S., Mikhaylov, A., Barykin, S. E., Aksoy, T., & Hacioğlu, U. (2022c). Analysis of environmental priorities for green project investments using an integrated q-rung orthopair fuzzy modelling. *IEEE Access, 10*. https://doi.org/10.1109/ACCESS.2022.3174058

Dinçer, H., Yüksel, S., Mikhaylov, A., Pinter, G., & Shaikh, Z. A. (2022d). Analysis of renewable-friendly smart grid technologies for the distributed energy investment projects using a hybrid picture fuzzy rough decision-making approach. *Energy Reports, 8*, 11466–11477. https://doi.org/10.1016/j.egyr.2022.08.275

Dong, B., Ikonnikova, I., Rogulin, R., Sakulyeva, T., & Mikhaylov, A. (2021). Environmentaleconomic approach to optimization of transport communication in megacities. *Journal of Environmental Science and Health, Part A, 56*(6), 660–666.

Dong, W., Zhao, G., Yüksel, S., Dinçer, H., & Ubay, G. G. (2022). A novel hybrid decision making approach for the strategic selection of wind energy projects. *Renewable Energy, 185*, 321–337.

Dooyum, U. D., Mikhaylov, A., & Varyash, I. (2020). Energy security concept in Russia and South Korea. *International Journal of Energy Economics and Policy, 10*(4), 102–107.

Ermiş, A. M., & Güven, M. E. (2022). The role of green energy Investments in Energy Supply Security. In *Circular economy and the energy market* (pp. 67–77). Springer, .

Eti, S., Dinçer, H., Gökalp, Y., Yüksel, S., & Kararoğlu, D. (2023). Identifying key issues to handle the inflation problem in the healthcare industry caused by energy prices: An evaluation with decision-making models. *Managing Inflation and Supply Chain Disruptions in the Global Economy*, 162–178.

Eti, S., Dinçer, H., Yüksel, S., & Gökalp, Y. (2022). Analysis of the suitability of the solar panels for hospitals: A new fuzzy decision-making model proposal with the T-spherical TOP-DEMATEL method. *Journal of Intelligent & Fuzzy Systems, Preprint*, 1–13.

Fang, S., Zhou, P., Dinçer, H., & Yüksel, S. (2021). Assessment of safety management system on energy investment risk using house of quality based on hybrid stochastic interval-valued intuitionistic fuzzy decision-making approach. *Safety Science, 141*, 105333.

Gura, D., Mikhaylov, A., Glushkov, S., Zaikov, M., & Shaikh, Z. A. (2022). Model for estimating power dissipation along the interconnect length in single on-chip topology. *Evolutionary Intelligence, 15*, 2369–2373. https://doi.org/10.1007/s12065-020-00407-7

Haiyun, C., Zhixiong, H., Yüksel, S., & Dinçer, H. (2021). Analysis of the innovation strategies for green supply chain management in the energy industry using the QFD-based hybrid interval valued intuitionistic fuzzy decision approach. *Renewable and Sustainable Energy Reviews, 143*, 110844.

Huang, Y., Masrur, H., Shigenobu, R., Hemeida, A. M., Mikhaylov, A., & Senjyu, T. (2021a). A comparative design of a campus microgrid considering a multi-scenario and multi-objective approach. *Energies, 14*, 2853.

Huang, Y., Yona, A., Takahashi, H., Hemeida, A. M., Mandal, P., Mikhaylov, A., Senjyu, T., & Lotfy, M. E. (2021b). Energy management system optimization of drug store operate electric vehicles charging station. *Sustainability, 14*, 1217836.

Kafka, K. I., Dinçer, H., & Yüksel, S. (2022). Impact-relation map of innovative service development regarding the sustainable growth for emerging markets. *Journal of the Knowledge Economy*, 1–24.

Kalinina, O. V., Barykin, S. E., Sergeev, S. M., Semenova, G. N., Fatkullina, A., Mikhaylov, A., & De La Poza, E. (2022). Smart city perspectives in post-pandemic governance: Externalities reduction policy. *F1000Research, 11*, 1032. https://doi.org/10.12688/f1000research.123195.1

Kayacık, M., Dinçer, H., & Yüksel, S. (2022). Using quantum spherical fuzzy decision support system as a novel sustainability index approach for analyzing industries listed in the stock exchange. *Borsa Istanbul Review, 22*(6), 1145–1157.

Khan, A. A., Laghari, A. A., Gadekallu, T. R., Shaikh, Z. A., Javed, A. R., Rashid, M., Estrela, V. V., & Mikhaylov, A. (2022). A drone-based data management and optimization using metaheuristic algorithms and blockchain smart contracts in a secure fog environment. *Computers and Electrical Engineering, 102*, 108234. https://doi.org/10.1016/j.compeleceng.2022.108234

Khan, A. A., Shaikh, Z. A., Baitenova, L., Mutaliyeva, L., Moiseev, N., Mikhaylov, A., Laghari, A. A., Idris, S. A., & Alshazly, H. (2021). QoS-ledger: Smart contracts and metaheuristic for secure quality-of-service and cost-efficient scheduling of medical-data processing. *Electronics, 10*, 3083.

Kou, G., Yüksel, S., & Dinçer, H. (2022). Inventive problem-solving map of innovative carbon emission strategies for solar energy-based transportation investment projects. *Applied Energy, 311*, 118680.

Li, J., Dinçer, H., Yüksel, S., Mikhaylov, A., & Barykin, S. E. (2022a). Bipolar q-ROF hybrid decision making model with golden cut for analyzing the levelized cost of renewable energy alternatives. *IEEE Access, 10*, 35900–35900. https://doi.org/10.1109/ACCESS.2022.3168315

Li, W., Yüksel, S., & Dinçer, H. (2022c). Understanding the financial innovation priorities for renewable energy investors via QFD-based picture fuzzy and rough numbers. *Financial Innovation, 8*(1), 1–30.

Li, J., Yüksel, S., Dınçer, H., Mikhaylov, A., & Barykin, S. E. (2022b). Bipolar q-ROF hybrid decision making model with golden cut for analyzing the levelized cost of renewable energy alternatives. *IEEE Access, 10*, 42507–42517.

Liu, L., Kato, T., Mandal, P., Mikhaylov, A., Hemeida, A. M., & Senjyu, T. (2021a). Multi-area power system load frequency control by using model predictive control by introducing renewable energy sources. In *2021 International Conference on Science & Contemporary Technologies (ICSCT)*, pp. 1–6. https://doi.org/10.1109/ICSCT53883.2021.9642521.

Liu, L., Kato, T., Mandal, P., Mikhaylov, A., Hemeida, A. M., Takahashi, H., & Tomonobu, S. (2021b). Two cases studies of model predictive control approach for hybrid renewable energy systems. *AIMS Energy, 9*(6), 1241–1259.

Liu, Z.-J., Panfilova, E., Mikhaylov, A., & Kurilova, A. (2022a). COVID-19 crisis impact on the stability between parties in crowdfunding and crowdsourcing. *Wireless Personal Communications, 122*, 915–930.

Liu, Z., Panfilova, E., Mikhaylov, A., & Kurilova, A. (2022b). Assessing stability in the relationship between parties in crowdfunding and crowdsourcing projects during the COVID-19 crisis. *Journal of Global Information Management (JGIM), 30*(4), 1–18. https://doi.org/10.4018/JGIM.297905

Martínez, L., Dinçer, H., & Yüksel, S. (2022). A hybrid decision making approach for new service development process of renewable energy investment. *Applied Soft Computing, 133*, 109897.

Mehta, R., Verghese, J., Mahajan, S., Barykin, S., Bozhuk, S., Kozlova, N., Kapustina, I., Mikhaylov, A., Naumova, E., & Dedyukhina, N. (2022). Consumers' behavior in conversational commerce marketing based on messenger chatbots. *F1000Research, 11*, 647. https://doi.org/10.12688/f1000research.122037.1

Mikhaylov, A. (2018). The yield of the carry trade strategy. *Finance: Theory and Practice, 22*(3), 52–63. https://doi.org/10.26794/2587-5671-2018-22-3-52-63

Mikhaylov, A. (2020a). Cryptocurrency market analysis from the open innovation perspective. *Journal of Open Innovation: Technology, Market, and Complexity, 6*(4), 197.

Mikhaylov, A. (2020b). Geothermal energy development in Iceland. *International Journal of Energy Economics and Policy, 10*(4), 31–35.

Mikhaylov, A. (2020c). Cryptocurrency market development: Hurst method. *Finance: Theory and Practice, 24*(3), 81–91.

Mikhaylov, A. (2021a). Development of Friedrich von Hayek's theory of private money and economic implications for digital currencies. *Terra Economicus, 19*(1), 53–62.

Mikhaylov, A. (2021b). Lichens as indicators of atmospheric pollution in urban ecosystems. *Israel Journal of Ecology & Evolution, 67*(1–2), 60–68. https://doi.org/10.1163/22244662-bja10016

Mikhaylov, A. (2022a). Efficiency of renewable energy generation in Russia. *Anais da Academia Brasileira de Ciências, 94*(4), e20191226. https://doi.org/10.1590/0001-3765202220191226

Mikhaylov, A. (2022b). Sustainable development and renewable energy: A new view to a global problem. *Energies, 15*, 1397. https://doi.org/10.3390/en15041397

Mikhaylov, A., Bhatti, I. M., Dinçer, H., & Yüksel, S. (2022a). Integrated decision recommendation system using iteration-enhanced collaborative filtering, golden cut bipolar for analyzing the risk-based oil market spillovers. *Computational Economics*, 1–34.

Mikhaylov, A., Bhatti, I. M., Dinçer, H., & Yüksel, S. (2022c). Integrated decision recommendation system using iteration-enhanced collaborative filtering, golden cut bipolar for analyzing the risk-based oil market spillovers. *Computational Economics*. https://doi.org/10.1007/s10614-022-10341-8

Mikhaylov, A., Burakov, D., & Didenko, V. (2019). Relationship between oil price and macroeconomic indicators in Russia. *Finance: Theory and Practice, 23*(2), 105–116. https://doi.org/10.26794/2587-5671-2019-23-2-105-116

Mikhaylov, A., Dinçer, H., & Yüksel, S. (2023). Analysis of financial development and open innovation oriented fintech potential for emerging economies using an integrated decision-making approach of MF-X-DMA and golden cut bipolar q-ROFSs. *Financ Innov, 9*, 10. https://doi.org/10.1186/s40854-022-00234-w

Mikhaylov, A., & Grilli, M. L. (2022). Machine learning methods and sustainable development: Metal oxides and multilayer metal-oxides. *Metals, 12*(4), 17–33.

Mikhaylov, A., Sokolinskaya, N., & Nyangarika, A. (2018). Optimal carry trade strategy based on currencies of energy and developed economies. *Journal of Reviews on Global Economics, 7*, 582–592.

Mikhaylov, A., & Tarakanov, S. (2020). Development of Levenberg-Marquardt theoretical approach for electric network. *Journal of Physics: Conference Series, 1515*, 052006.

Mikhaylov, A., Yumashev, A., & Kolpak, E. (2022). Quality of life, anxiety and depressive disorders in patients with extrasystolic arrhythmia. *Archives of Medical Science, 18*(2). https://doi.org/10.5114/aoms.2020.101359

Moiseev, N., Mikhaylov, A., Dinçer, H., & Yüksel, S. (2023). Effects of market capitalization shocks for open innovation models in e-commerce industry: Golden cut QROF MCDM analysis. *Financ Innov, 9*, 32.

Moiseev, N., Mikhaylov, A., Varyash, I., & Saqib, A. (2020). Investigating the relation of GDP per capita and corruption index. *Entrepreneurship and Sustainability Issues, 8*(1), 780–794.

Moiseev, N., Sorokin, A., Zvezdina, N., Mikhaylov, A., Khomyakova, L., & Danish, M. S. S. (2021). Credit risk theoretical model on the base of DCC-GARCH in time-varying parameters framework. *Mathematics, 9*, 2423. https://doi.org/10.3390/math9192423

Mukhametov, A., Bekhorashvili, A., Avdeenko, A., & Mikhaylov, A. (2021). The impact of growing legume plants under conditions of Biologization and soil cultivation on chernozem fertility and productivity of rotation crops. *Legume Research, 44*, 12.

Mukhtarov, S., Yüksel, S., & Dinçer, H. (2022). The impact of financial development on renewable energy consumption: Evidence from Turkey. *Renewable Energy, 187*, 169–176.

Mutalimov, V., Kovaleva, I., Mikhaylov, A., & Stepanova, D. (2021). Assessing regional growth of small business in Russia. *Entrepreneurial Business and Economics Review, 9*(3), 119–133. https://doi.org/10.15678/EBER.2021.090308

Nie, D., Panfilova, E., Samusenkov, V., & Mikhaylov, A. (2020). E-learning financing models in Russia for sustainable development. *Sustainability, 12*(11), 4412.

Nyangarika, A., Mikhaylov, A., Muyeen, S. M., Yadykin, V., Mottaeva, A., Pryadko, I., Barykin, S., Fomenko, N., Rykov, G., & Shvandar, K. (2022). Energy stability and decarbonization in developing countries: Random Forest approach for forecasting of crude oil trade flows and macro indicators. *Frontiers in Environmental Science, 10*, 1031343. https://doi.org/10.3389/fenvs.2022.1031343

Nyangarika, A., Mikhaylov, A., & Richter, U. (2019a). Influence oil price towards economic indicators in Russia. *International Journal of Energy Economics and Policy, 9*(1), 123–129.

Nyangarika, A., Mikhaylov, A., & Richter, U. (2019b). Oil price factors: Forecasting on the base of modified auto-regressive integrated moving average model. *International Journal of Energy Economics and Policy, 9*(1), 149–159.

Nyangarika, A., Mikhaylov, A., & Tang, B.-J. (2018). Correlation of oil prices and gross domestic product in oil producing countries. *International Journal of Energy Economics and Policy, 8*(5), 42–48.

Saqib, A., Chan, T.-H., Mikhaylov, A., & Lean, H. H. (2021). Are the responses of sectoral energy imports asymmetric to exchange rate volatilities in Pakistan? Evidence from recent foreign exchange regime. *Frontiers in Energy Research, 9*, 614463. https://doi.org/10.3389/fenrg.2021.614463

Sediqi, M. M., Nakadomari, A., Mikhaylov, A., Krishnan, N., Lotfy, M. E., Yona, A., & Senjyu, T. (2022). Impact of time-of-use demand response program on optimal operation of Afghanistan real power system. *Energies, 15*, 296.

Shaikh, Z. A., Kraikin, A., Mikhaylov, A., & Pinter, G. (2022). Forecasting stock prices of companies producing solar panels using machine learning methods. *Complexity, 2022*, 9186265. https://doi.org/10.1155/2022/9186265

Shaikh, Z. A., Moiseev, N., Mikhaylov, A., & Yüksel, S. (2021). Facile synthesis of copper oxide-cobalt oxide/nitrogen-doped carbon (Cu2O-Co3O4/CN) composite for efficient water splitting. *Applied Sciences., 11*, 9974. https://doi.org/10.3390/app11219974

Sun, L., Peng, J., Dinçer, H., & Yüksel, S. (2022). Coalition-oriented strategic selection of renewable energy system alternatives using q-ROF DEMATEL with golden cut. *Energy, 256*, 124606.

Tamashiro, K., Alharbi, T., Mikhaylov, A., Hemeida, A. M., Krishnan, N., Lotfy, M. E., & Senjyu, T. (2021). Investigation of home energy management with advanced direct load control and optimal scheduling of controllable loads. *Energies, 14*, 7314. https://doi.org/10.3390/en14217314

Tamashiro, K., Omine, E., Krishnan, N., Mikhaylov, A., Hemeida, A. M., & Senjyu, T. (2023). Optimal components capacity based multi-objective optimization and optimal scheduling based MPC-optimization algorithm in smart apartment buildings. *Energy & Buildings, 278*, 112616. https://doi.org/10.1016/j.enbuild.2022.112616

Uyeh, D. D., Asem-Hiablie, S., Park, T., Kim, K.-M., Mikhaylov, A., Woo, S., & Ha, Y. (2021). Could japonica rice be an alternative variety for increased global food security and climate change mitigation? *Food, 10*, 1869. https://doi.org/10.3390/foods10081869

Varyash, I., Mikhaylov, A., Moiseev, N., & Aleshin, K. (2020). Triple bottom line and corporate social responsibility performance indicators for Russian companies. *Entrepreneurship and Sustainability Issues, 8*(1), 313–331.

Xu, X., Yüksel, S., & Dinçer, H. (2022). An integrated decision-making approach with Golden cut and bipolar q-ROFSs to renewable energy storage investments. *International Journal of Fuzzy Systems*, 1–14.

Yuan, G., Xie, F., Dinçer, H., & Yüksel, S. (2021). The theory of inventive problem solving (TRIZ)-based strategic mapping of green nuclear energy investments with spherical fuzzy group decision-making approach. *International Journal of Energy Research, 45*(8), 12284–12300.

Yüksel, S., & Dinçer, H. (2022). Identifying the strategic priorities of nuclear energy investments using hesitant 2-tuple interval-valued Pythagorean fuzzy DEMATEL. *Progress in Nuclear Energy, 145*, 104103.

Yüksel, S., Dinçer, H., Eti, S., & Adalı, Z. (2022). Strategy improvements to minimize the drawbacks of geothermal investments by using spherical fuzzy modelling. *International Journal of Energy Research.*

Yumashev, A., & Mikhaylov, A. (2020). Development of polymer film coatings with high adhesion to steel alloys and high wear resistance. *Polymer Composites, 41*(7), 2875–2880.

Yumashev, A., Ślusarczyk, B., Kondrashev, S., & Mikhaylov, A. (2020). Global indicators of sustainable development: Evaluation of the influence of the human development index on consumption and quality of energy. *Energies, 13*, 2768.

Zhang, Y., Zhang, Y., Gong, C., Dinçer, H., & Yüksel, S. (2022). An integrated hesitant 2-tuple Pythagorean fuzzy analysis of QFD-based innovation cost and duration for renewable energy projects. *Energy, 248*, 123561.

Zhao, Q., Cherkasov, S., Avdeenko, A., Kondratenko, L., & Mikhaylov, A. (2021). Integral estimate of the added value of agricultural crops in the synergetic agriculture on the example of Vicia faba (Vicia faba L.). *Polish Journal of Environmental Studies, 30*(5), 1–9. https://doi.org/10.15244/pjoes/131949

Chapter 13
Wind Power Plant as a City Skyline and City Energy Center: The Case of Çatalca

Adem Bağış Alçiçek

Keywords Wind power plant · Energy · City skyline · Çatalca

13.1 Introduction

The concept of sustainability was used for the first time in the "World Nature Charter" adopted by the United Nations General Assembly on October 29, 1982. What is emphasized with sustainability is the use and depletion of environmental resources. In this process, the necessity of transferring natural resources to future years was emphasized. In order to leave a renewable nature and sustainable energy resources to the new generation, it is necessary to understand sustainability well. However, it is important to inject it into local, national and global policies (Aksu Çam, 2014).

As the use of wind energy increases, greenhouse gas emissions will decrease. There is such a trend. However, in order for this trend to continue to increase, countries with strong economies with large industries should have a leading role (Barthelmie & Pryor, 2021).

The wind energy sector has major expansion targets until 2030 (Davy et al., 2018). Urban design, local energy planning, climatic change and bioethics have been the concepts that have been expressed and gained importance in the last 40 years (Ekin Erkan, 2014).

Energy supply and generating energy has always been an important issue from past to present. Basic energy sources have diversified as time passes and technology develops. In this diversity, it has been effective for people to discover energy potentials that they could not solve and use before. Looking at the last century, it is seen that nuclear energy sources have been added to the older energy sources (Baş et al., 2022).

A. B. Alçiçek (✉)
Vocational School of Social Sciences, İstanbul Medipol University, İstanbul, Türkiye
e-mail: abalcicek@medipol.edu.tr

H. Dincer, S. Yüksel (eds.), *Economic Development and the Environmental Ecosystem*, Contributions to Economics,
https://doi.org/10.1007/978-3-031-26596-9_13

The energy demand in the world has increased over the years. Estimates regarding the depletion time frame of energy reserves; according to the estimates for 2015, it is foreseen as 40 years for oil, 65 years for natural gas and 200 years for coal. Wind energy, on the other hand, is used quite unlimitedly compared to other sources. Energy seems to be an increasingly important element for countries. The developments in industry and technology are the reason for this. Depending on these, as the level of urbanization increases, the need for energy increases by diversifying. Türkiye has a great energy demand due to its economic and social structure. This energy demand tends to increase. Considering the countries with growing energy demand in the first 10-year period since 2000, Türkiye has been one of the countries with the highest increase in energy demand, being the third after China and India. In the ongoing process, it is natural to focus on alternative energy sources in order to reduce foreign dependency in energy demand. In this context, wind energy has become one of the areas that Türkiye focuses on and focuses on in order to increase its energy potential (Bencuya İpekçioğlu & Vardar, 2017).

13.2 Wind Power Plants

The basis of the formation of wind, which is the main element of wind energy, on Earth is based on the Sun. Wind energy is a type of energy that is indirectly dependent on the Sun. The formation of the wind is based on the temperature formed on Earth in this framework. Temperature is related to sunlight. Basically, wind movement occurs when there is a different temperature in one place and a different temperature in another. This movement is popularly known as wind blowing. Essentially, the structure carried by the air causes the wind movement. In a unit volume of air with a low temperature, the number of molecules and atoms is high. Atoms in low-temperature air have low energy. Atoms also move slowly. When the temperature of the air with a high temperature or the temperature of the air with a low temperature rises, the atoms in the air begin to move faster. The number of atoms per unit volume of air will be lower. The energy of atoms in hot air rises. This is basically why warm air is lighter than cold air. This is also why cold air is heavier than warm air. Light air or air with a high temperature tends to rise and a low pressure area is formed. The situation is different in heavy air or low temperature air. In a place where there is cold air, molecules exhibit an acceleration towards the earth due to weight. In this case, a high pressure area is formed with the air collapsing down. Wind, on the other hand, is basically the reflection of the movement of the high pressure air wave towards the low pressure air wave. Basically, there is displacement of air. This change is called wind. Although wind energy is thought of very differently, it is essentially a type of solar energy. It is a natural energy. Even if it is caused by the sun, there is no restriction such as being and being used only in the daytime period. It has an increasing value in the energy market (Tong, 2010).

In a study conducted in 2005, the world's wind energy potential was approximated based on various data and preliminary studies. In this research, it is claimed that if the potential of all winds to be converted into energy is revealed, a point that will reach up to 5 times the entire energy demand in the world. However, it is argued that only 1 in 5 of the said potential will reach 7 times the electricity demand in the world (Archer & Jacobson, 2005).

The construction of wind turbines used in wind power plants is only the visible side of the business for the place where it is installed. However, the design and creation of wind turbines, which form the basis of wind power plants, is a stage that should not be ignored. Models are being made for related wind turbines. Simulations are used to measure the success of the models before they are established. There are also aerodynamic models among the models made. The aerodynamic system and the mechanical system are modeled and planned in separate stages. Apart from these, the systems that actuate the generator, the main control system, the step system related to the operation of the mechanical steps, the sub-systems of the mechanical system and the protective systems of the whole system are located inside the wind power plant. Wind power plants, which seem quite simple in silhouette, have a very complex structure. The integrated data of all systems are used as a support for simulations to produce results that are very close to reality (Knudsen & Nielsen, 2012).

Wind farm establishments tend to increase gradually. Horizontal axis wind turbine is the most common type. However, there are also vertical axis wind turbines. It is possible to state that these are divided into two subgroups as Darrieus turbine and H-rotor. The calculation of the blade area of the turbines differs according to the turbine types. The number of wings and the swept area are common data. Blade area and the strength of the blade surface are very important. Robustness should not be overlooked to use more potential. This can lead to danger and a higher cost of possible damage (Eriksson et al., 2008).

Electricity is produced by wind power plants. This situation reveals the fact that wind energy is an important field for the electricity industry. Electricity production is an issue that is at the forefront of the world in terms of developing technology, increasing industrialization and increasing population. From the perspective of the electricity market, the importance of the situation will be seen. Wind-based energy is evaluated in the context of renewable energy. Wind energy is both a renewable energy and a safe type of energy (Foley et al., 2012).

13.3 City Skyline

The silhouette of the city has direct links with the images that the city creates in people's minds. Since the city silhouette consisting of the words "sky" and "line" was used to describe cities with skyscrapers in the first place, the etymological adventure of the concept is related to cities with rising buildings. However, it is clear that the city skyline is not just a concept used for skyscraper cities. "Silhouette" is a necessity for city depictions since the Middle Ages. In this context, it can mean three different things. City views, landmarks and city representations (Şevkin & Gül, 2017).

Important cities in the world see the task of conveying a certain message, sometimes consciously and sometimes unconsciously. These messages are realized with the silhouettes of the cities. Various images send the recipients images of what the city symbolizes. The city's buildings, intertwined with the city's skyline, form the silhouette of the city. While nature comes to the fore in daylight, when the sun goes down, a completely different silhouette can be formed with a certain amount of lighting and shadows. But basically the silhouette of a city; sky, natural landforms, forests, rivers, seas and plants can reveal. However, man-made residences, facilities and other types of structures can also reveal material for the city silhouettes that are engraved in the minds (Karimimoshaver et al., 2021).

Reducing greenhouse gas emissions and carbon footprint is very important for cities. It is important that local and central governments work in coordination and raise awareness for the climate policies to be created within this framework. Of course, each individual should not hesitate to fulfill his/her duty as a stakeholder in this issue. If we associate the city skyline with greenhouse gas and carbon emissions, we need to consider industrialization criteria. A city that does not prefer or prefers less environmental energies will take on a silhouette surrounded by smoke and harmful gases. This situation reveals the danger of a dystopian city painting. Environmental energy policies regarding these are of great importance (Dascher, 2014).

13.4 Çatalca Urban Texture and Characteristics of the City

The urban texture of Çatalca can be defined as a wide area with botanical diversity, together with the breadth of its rural areas. This botanical diversity is a richness. On the other hand, as a result of the researches on this botanical diversity, it has been determined that the plants that are the subject of richness have different local names (Ecevit Genç & Özhatay, 2004).

Geographically, flood plains formed due to the rivers feeding Büyükçekmece Lake are seen around the villages of Bahşayiş and Ahmediye. On the other hand, there are artificial levees built in order to prevent the damage of agricultural lands with the flooding of the lake. There are also various irrigation channels. However, there are drainage channels built to ensure correct water drainage. Urbanization is limited in areas with high flood hazard. In this framework, it is possible to observe a micro scale of the urbanization policy at this point (Tuna & Sarıkaya, 2014).

An important part of the urban texture of Çatalca can be expressed as İnceğiz. The village of İnceğiz and the very old caves with limestone content that you will encounter right at the end of the village are the historical and cultural richness of Çatalca. Right next to the İnceğiz Caves, İnceğiz Stream is located. In this framework, while there are human-induced shapings in the cave, there are different natural geographical shapes formed as a result of long-term natural events around the cave and stream (Tuna & Sarıkaya, 2014).

Istanbul is located in the Çatalca-Kocaeli Section of the Marmara Region. It is located on a transition zone between Black Sea and Mediterranean climates. Istanbul is under the maritime influence of the Marmara Sea from the south and the Black Sea from the north. On the other hand, Anatolia and the Balkans are under the influence of continentality. The climate of Istanbul can show different micro features from each other. Both polar air masses and tropical air masses are effective on the climate of Istanbul. Effective tropical air masses have different sub-types originating from the Azores, the Great Sahara, the Red Sea Arabian Peninsula and the Persian Gulf. It is known that the effective polar air masses originate from the Icelandic low pressure area. It is possible to talk about two important wind types in Istanbul. The first is the wind blowing from the northeast and called "northern". The other is the wind blowing from the southwest direction and called "lodos". Northwest wind blows from northeast to southwest, causing cold weather and occasional storms. When the northerly wind blows with the "star" blowing from the north, it is very cold and has a stormy intensity in places, while it has a cooling effect against the summer heat, especially in summer. Lodos, on the other hand, is a wind blowing from the southwest to the northeast, causing sweltering heat in the summer and abundant precipitation in the winter (Biricik, 2013).

13.5 Çatalca City History and Traces of Past Residents

Çatalca is located in the region called Thrace in Antiquity. İnceğiz Caves, located in Çatalca, show that there are very old human settlements in the relevant area. İnceğiz Caves are an open-air museum today. In Çatalca, there are the remains of an ancient Greek colony called Ergiske. It is thought that the Çatalca region was called Metris since the Hellenistic period. In the Byzantine Period, the name of the relevant region is referred to as Metris. The region was known as Hanica before passing under Ottoman rule. Hanica is thought to be etymologically Greek. According to Evliya Çelebi, Hanica is the name of a princess and a castle built by her father, who was also a king, was named after Hanica. There is a legend that even the redbud flowers, which are symbolized by Çatalca and whose festivals are held, change color due to the tears that Hanica sheds out of the sadness of the person she loves. Apart from the myth, the redbud tree has been symbolized by Çatalca for centuries. Redbud festivals are of great importance for Çatalca from past to present. The word hanica is not etymologically related, but has a relation with the judas tree plant in relation to its connection in the myth. Evliya Çelebi reports that the region called Hanica (Haniçe) is also called Çatalca because it is located at the foot of Çatal (Fork) Mountain. However, there is also a claim that the name Çatalca was given because of the similarity to the fork shape. Çatalca has been a strategic defense line throughout history and the Anastasius Walls are an important historical monument in this context (Gürçay, 2019a).

The geo-strategic importance of the Çatalca region and the defense lines built in the region throughout history have caused the region to have a rich heritage in terms of defense lines. The defense lines of Çatalca reach the historical bridge in Büyükçekmece, which was built during the period of Mimar Sinan. There is a defensive line along the eastern shore of Büyükçekmece Lake. The defense line in question extends from Büyükçekmece to Terkos Lake. In this context; It is possible to talk about a defensive line passing through the regions that are old villages such as Yazlık, Çanakça, Kestanelik, Örcünlü, Nakkaş, Bahşayiş and Karaağaç, which are now called neighborhoods (Efeoğlu & Eyüpgiller, 2021).

Due to its geographical location, Çatalca has been a place open to social, commercial and cultural interaction for many years. Muslim Turks who migrated due to the population exchange in the Republican period settled mainly in Yeniköy District, Elbasan District and Kaleiçi District. These neighborhoods are referred to as pre-exchange Christian neighborhoods. Çatalca is recorded as the "Sixth Area", where people who migrated from Greece to Turkey through population exchange settled. In similar field determinations, the occupations and populations of the immigrants were taken into consideration. In the same period, it is stated that 14,000 Greek population migrated from Çatalca to Greece in the same way, depending on the population exchange. The fact that some of the immigrants who migrated to Çatalca preferred to settle in rural areas despite their planned settlement in different cities is related to their farmer origin. It is possible to say that this situation had a small effect on agricultural activities in the early periods. As an example, it is known that 450 immigrants, who were planned to be sent to Samsun, expressed their demands to settle in Çatalca against the public authority. In this context, the social structure in Çatalca after the population exchange; Local people of Anatolian origin (Gacal), patriots migrating from Greece, and immigrants migrating from Bulgaria were shaped in a basic triple structure. Today, although the concept of immigrant is used as a broader concept throughout Turkey, it is used to describe immigrants of Bulgarian origin in the example of Çatalca. Apart from the aforementioned basic tripartite structure, it is possible to talk about social groups consisting of fewer immigrants. It is possible to express these as Albanian, Bosnian, Caucasian, Pomak, Tatar and Rumanian. In the final analysis, it would not be wrong to define both the geo-strategic position of the region and some historical and political events as factors in the origins of the multicultural social structure of Çatalca (Gürçay, 2019b).

Considering the boundaries of Çatalca District, the aforementioned district is located on the northern side of the Marmara Sea. The district is located in the southwest of the Black Sea. Çerkezköy and Saray Districts, which are affiliated to Tekirdağ Province, are located in the west of the district. Büyükçekmece and Silivri Districts of Istanbul Province are located in the south and southwest. In the east of Çatalca district, Arnavutköy District of Istanbul Province is located. On the other hand, it would be correct to state that a part of Terkos Lake is located within the boundaries of Çatalca District. Çatalca is the largest district of Istanbul in terms of surface area. Although Çatalca District is the district with the largest surface area of Istanbul, with the establishment of Arnavutköy District, some villages of Çatalca were included in Arnavutköy. Even this situation did not change the feature of Çatalca being the biggest district of Istanbul. In 2012, some villages from

Büyükçekmece and Arnavutköy were included in the borders of Çatalca. In the following process, it is useful to remind that all the villages within the metropolitan municipality have passed to the status of neighborhood (Garipağaoğlu & Duman, 2018).

13.6 Wind Power Plants Changing Çatalca's Skyline

In the wind measurements made for Çatalca in 2008, 2009 and 2010; Within the framework of the wind energy potential, accurate results have been obtained regarding the establishment of power plants at 30 meters, 60 meters and 80 meters heights. In the context of generating electricity from wind energy, according to the simulation created as a result of Çatalca wind data, heights of 30 meters, 60 meters and 80 meters seem to be efficient in terms of energy potential. In the measurements made, the lowest speed value average was found in June and the highest speed value average was in October (Wadi et al., 2019).

There are also earlier studies on wind energy potential measurement in Turkey. In the early 2000s, when the importance of renewable energy was realized, studies in this context increased. A study published in 2006 shed light on the country's energy potential from 1998 to 2002. In addition, evaluations were made together with the measurements regarding the wind energy potential of İzmir (Özerdem et al., 2006).

The construction of Hacıbey Wind Power Plant in Çatalca, which is the largest district of Istanbul in Türkiye, started in 2020. The power plant consists of 18 units, or in other words, 18 turbines. Hacıbey Wind Power Plant, which is the second wind power plant after Çatalca Wind Power Plant in Çatalca District, has a 1/5000 scale master development plan and 1/1000 scale implementation zoning plan within the framework of the letter of the Ministry of Environment and Urbanization dated 13.11.2020. has received the necessary approvals. The abbreviation used as "RES" is an abbreviation used in Turkish with the initials of the words Wind (Rüzgar), Energy (Enerjisi) and Power Plant (Santrali). The related project is referred to as the Hacıbey WPP Project (Hacıbey RES Projesi) in various sources. The date of 18.01.2012 is taken into account as the start date of the project. In this context, the first target of the said project is to show production activity for 49 years. These 49 years are calculated from 2012. Hacıbey Wind Power Plant was given a generation license by the Energy Market Regulatory Board with the decision dated 18.01.2012 within the scope of the Electricity Market Law numbered 4628 and other relevant legislation. The aforementioned master zoning plan and implementation zoning plan are related to the turbine installation and the environmental arrangement of the power plant. The aforementioned master zoning plan and implementation zoning plan have been approved by the Presidential Decree No. 1 on 13.11.2020 in accordance with the Zoning Law No. 3194. The aforementioned zoning plans have been suspended both on the bulletin board of the Provincial Directorate of Environment and Urbanization and on the official website for 1 month as of 16.11.2020 in accordance with the legislation (Article 8 of the Zoning

Law No. 3194). The abbreviations "Hacıbey 1000" and "Hacıbey 5000" are used for the plans in question (Hacıbey Wind Power Plant Zoning Plans, Ministry of Environment, Urbanization and Climate Change, 2022; Hacıbey Wind Power Plant Project Information, Kıvanç Energy Group, 2022).

Çatalca Wind Power Plant is located in Çatalca, the largest district of Istanbul. The wind power plant in question welcomes those who approach the district center of this large district as a silhouette of the city and a piece of urban fabric. As of September 2022, it is the country's 160th and Istanbul's sixth largest power plant. In terms of wind power plants classification, it draws attention as the 22nd largest wind power plant in the country. The wind power plant, which operates with an installed power of 93 MWe, is expected to reach 10 MWe when it reaches full capacity. There are 30 Vestas wind turbines in the mentioned wind power plant. The phases of the power plant's progress appear to be from 60 MWe to 76.5 MWe, from 76.5 MWe to 93 MWe, and finally from 93 MWe to 100 MWe. Çatalca Wind Power Plant has the capacity to meet the daily electricity needs of 60,476 people with its average generation capacity. It is possible to deal with the mentioned electricity usage areas in various fields in the form of being used in housing, industry, street and street lighting and public institutions. Considering the ratio of the said electricity generation capacity to meet the needs in terms of population, it is possible to say that only Çatalca Wind Power Plant has the capacity to meet the demand of approximately 80 percent of the district's population, considering that the Çatalca District had a population of 72,966 in 2018 according to official data. (Çatalca Wind Power Plant Atlas, Energy Atlas, 2022; Istanbul Population Data, Istanbul Governorship, 2022).

The installed power of Çatalca Wind Power Plant is 100 MW ($20 \times 3.0 + 10 \times 3.3$). Annual energy production is calculated as 285 million kWh. The start date of the power plant project was August 2007. Thanks to the use of wind energy, the amount of carbon dioxide that will not be released into the atmosphere is calculated as 240,000 tons per year. It is stated that 570 new trees have been planted as a replacement for the trees cut down due to the power plant installation (Çatalca Wind Power Plant Project Information, Sanko Holding, 2022). Çatalca Wind Power Plant consists of 30 turbines. Çatalca WPP is included in the 2019 Atlas, but Hacıbey WPP was included in the equation later. However, the power plants in Çatalca are not limited to these two. (Turkish Wind Power Plant Atlas, Turkish Wind Energy Association, 2019).

Apart from Çatalca Wind Power Plant and Hacıbey Wind Power Plant, there are İstanbul Wind Power Plant, Aydos Wind Power Plant, Yamaçtepe (2) Wind Power Plant, Küptepe Wind Power Plant and Çataltepe Wind Power Plant in Çatalca District. Istanbul Wind Power Plant is the third largest power plant in Istanbul with an installed capacity of 200 MWe, and it is the fourth largest wind power plant in Turkey. Established in 2021, the Istanbul Wind Power Plant was criticized by environmentalists during its construction on the grounds that it would harm the environment. Environmentalists opposed the project because it is located in the Çilingoz Nature Park and Wildlife Development Area. When we compare it with Çatalca Wind Power Plant, which was established in 2008 and grew gradually, it is possible to say that Istanbul Wind Power Plant took over the title of Çatalca's largest wind power plant. Yamaçtepe (2) Wind Power Plant, which became operational in 2019, ranks third in the ranking of the largest wind power plants in Çatalca, ahead of Hacıbey Wind Power Plant established in 2020. Aydos Wind Power Plant, established in 2021, ranks fifth among the operating wind power plants. Çataltepe Wind Power Plant established in 2016 and Küptepe Wind Power Plant established in 2020 share the sixth place as wind power plants with the same power capacity (Wind Energy Map, Energy Atlas, 2022; Turkish Wind Power Plant Atlas, Turkish Wind Energy Association, 2019).

13.7 Conclusion

There are 7 active wind power plants in Çatalca. 2 wind power plants are under construction. On the other hand, one company received a license for the construction of a wind power plant, and another company received an associate license for the construction of a wind power plant. In this context, it seems highly probable that the number of wind power plants in Çatalca will reach 11 in the near future. When the 7 operating wind power plants are classified in terms of their installed power; Istanbul Wind Power Plant 200 MWe, Çatalca Wind Power Plant 100 MWe, Yamaçtepe (2) Wind Power Plant 30 MWe, Hacıbey Wind Power Plant 16 MWe, Aydos Wind Power Plant 14 MWe, Çataltepe Wind Power Plant 10 MWe, Kültepe Wind Power Plant 10 It has an installed capacity of MWe (Wind Energy Map, Energy Atlas, 2022; Turkish Wind Power Plant Atlas, Turkish Wind Energy Association, 2022).

Natural and artificial structures can form a city's silhouette in a mixed form. While the early period structures of the city are a collection of symbols and images, urban transformation can change the situation. New buildings and facilities built in a city can add color to the city skyline and even change the city skyline from start to finish. Wind power plants symbolize environmental and clean energy. However, it also has an image of electricity needs and industrial cities that depend on electricity. In the example of Çatalca, wind power plants, which are increasing day by day, both add a new shape to the city skyline and meet the increasing electrical energy needs of the region. Until wind energy gained such importance, Çatalca had a unique urban texture. On the other hand, it is a special example with its high wind energy potential and its natural nature in the periphery of the metropolitan city. The historical and sociological background of the district is directly related to what kind of urbanization process it has gone through. In the final analysis, the wind power plants, which have the function of energy center, have changed the city silhouette in Çatalca, but have added a different atmosphere to the district. Despite the fact that wind energy is in the environmental energy class, the increasing trend of the said power plant has the possibility of harming the natural environment. There is a danger of damaging vegetation and wildlife during the installation and operation of wind power plants. In this context, it is critical to take measures in national and local policies in the establishment and operation of wind power plants in a way that will cause the least damage to nature.

References

Aksu Çam, Ç. (2014). Uluslararası Metinlerde "Çevre". In *Şehir Kavramlarının Yolculuğu* (pp. 242–279). İdeal Kültür Yayıncılık.

Archer, C. L., & Jacobson, M. Z. (2005). Evaluation of global wind power. *Journal of Geophysical Research: Atmospheres, 110*(D12), 1–20.

Barthelmie, R. J., & Pryor, S. C. (2021). Climate change mitigation potential of wind energy. Climate, 9(9), 136, 1–22.

Baş, H., Eti, S., & Ersin, İ. (2022). Importance of renewable energy investments for qualified workforce. In *Multidimensional strategic outlook on global competitive energy economics and finance*. Emerald Publishing Limited., , (pp.141–152).

Bencuya İpekçioğlu, R. G., & Vardar, A. (2017). Türkiye 2017 Yılı Güncel Rüzgâr Enerjisi Görünümü. *Uludağ Üniversitesi Ziraat Fakültesi Dergisi, 31*(2), 177–181.

Biricik, A. S. (2013). İstanbul Şehri ve Su. *Marmara Coğrafya Dergisi, 1*(2), 11–32.

Çatalca Wind Power Plant Atlas, Energy Atlas. (2022). Accessed September 27, 2022, from https://www.enerjiatlasi.com/ruzgar/catalca-ruzgar-santrali.html.

Çatalca Wind Power Plant Project Information, Sanko Holding. (2022). Accessed September 27, 2022, from https://www.sanko.com.tr/tr/sektorel-enerji-catalca-ruzgar-santrali.aspx.

Dascher, K. (2014). City silhouette, world climate. *World Climate (January 20, 2014)*, 1–28.

Davy, R., Gnatiuk, N., Pettersson, L., & Bobylev, L. (2018). Climate change impacts on wind energy potential in the European domain with a focus on the Black Sea. *Renewable and Sustainable Energy Reviews, 81*, 1652–1659.

Ecevit Genç, G., & Özhatay, N. (2004). An ethnobotanical study from European part of Istanbul (Çatalca) in Turkey (I). *Journal of Faculty of Pharmacy of Istanbul University, 37*, 67–74.

Efeoğlu, M., & Eyüpgiller, K. K. (2021). Çatalca Bölgesi Savunma Yapıları Üzerine Bir Değerlendirme. *Sanat Tarihi Dergisi, 30*(1), 391–433.

Ekin Erkan, N. (2014). Şehircilik Kavram Kümesinin Evrimi. In *Şehir Kavramlarının Yolculuğu* (pp. 280–299). İdeal Kültür Yayıncılık.

Eriksson, S., Bernhoff, H., & Leijon, M. (2008). Evaluation of different turbine concepts for wind power. *Renewable and Sustainable Energy Reviews, 12*(5), 1419–1434.

Foley, A. M., Leahy, P. G., Marvuglia, A., & McKeogh, E. J. (2012). Current methods and advances in forecasting of wind power generation. *Renewable Energy, 37*(1), 1–8.

Garipağaoğlu, N., & Duman, E. (2018). Çatalca İlçesi'nin Arazi Kullanımında Meydana Gelen Değişimler(1987–2016). *Marmara Coğrafya Dergisi, 37*, 219–232.

Gürçay, S. (2019a). Evliya Çelebi Seyahatnamesi'nde Çatalca. *Uluslararası Halkbilimi Araştırmaları Dergisi, 2*(3), 135–145.

Gürçay, S. (2019b). Lozan Mübadelesi'nin etkileri: Çatalca örneği. *RumeliDE Dil ve Edebiyat Araştırmaları Dergisi, 15*, 274–284.

Hacıbey Wind Power Plant Project Information, Kıvanç Energy Group. (2022). Accessed November 14, 2022, from https://www.kivancenerji.com.tr/hacibeyres.html.

Hacıbey Wind Power Plant Zoning Plans, Ministry of Environment, Urbanization and Climate Change. (2022). Accessed October 26, 2022, from https://istanbul.csb.gov.tr/istanbul-ili-catalca-ilcesi-hacibey-ruzgar-enerjisi-santrali-1-5000-olcekli-nazim-imar-plani-ve-1-1000-olcekli-uygulama-imar-plani-duyuru-411193.

Istanbul Population Data, Istanbul Governorship. (2022). Accessed November 24, 2022, from http://www.istanbul.gov.tr/nufus-bakimindan-turkiyenin-en-buyuk-kenti-istanbul.

Karimimoshaver, M., Parsamanesh, M., Aram, F., & Mosavi, A. (2021). The impact of the city skyline on pleasantness; state of the art and a case study. Heliyon, 7(5), e07009, 1–9.

Knudsen H., & Nielsen J. N. (2012). Dynamic modelling of wind turbines for power system studies. In *Wind power in power systems*. John Wiley & Sons. Limited., , (pp.523–554).

Özerdem, B., Özer, S., & Tosun, M. (2006). Feasibility study of wind farms: A case study for Izmir, Turkey. *Journal of Wind Engineering and Industrial Aerodynamics, 94*, 725–743.

Şevkin, E., & Gül, M. (2017). İstanbul Silüetindeki Değişim. *tasarım+ kuram dergisi, 13*(23), 1–14.

Tong, W. (2010). Fundamentals of wind energy. In *Wind power generation and wind turbine design*. WIT Press., , (pp.3–48).

Tuna, F., & Sarıkaya, M. (2014). Coğrafya Eğitiminde Fiziki Coğrafya Öğretimi İçin Bir Rota Önerisi: Çatalca Yarımadası Batısı, İstanbul. *Marmara Coğrafya Dergisi, 30*, 45–68.

Turkish Wind Power Plant Atlas, Turkish Wind Energy Association. (2019). Accessed November 14, 2022, from https://tureb.com.tr/eng/lib/uploads/a894074504a33b99.pdf.

Wadi, M., Kekezoglu, B., Baysal, M., Tur, M. R., & Shobole, A. (2019). Feasibility study of wind energy potential in Turkey: Case study of Catalca district in Istanbul. In *2019 2nd International Conference on Smart Grid and Renewable Energy (SGRE)*. IEEE, (pp. 1–6).

Wind Energy Map, Energy Atlas. (2022). Accessed November 27, 2022, from https://www.enerjiatlasi.com/ruzgar-enerjisi-haritasi/istanbul.

Chapter 14
Evolution of Pension System Financial Models for Sustainable Economic Growth

Mikhail Dorofeev and Kanato Tamashiro

Keywords Social policy · Economic inequality · Government debt · Finance · Pension system · Taxes · Globalization · ESG

14.1 Introduction

The pension system is the most important element of social protection for the older population. Their main task is to accumulate financial resources from mandatory, earnings-related and voluntary contribution into funds, for providing retirement incomes to meet a minimum standard of living in old age. The remoteness of the time of retirement makes any pension system susceptible to the uncertainties and risks associated with long-term technological, demographic, and economic cycles. To manage these risks, governments use special budgetary rules and automatic financial stabilizers built into the mechanism of pension systems. These stabilizers periodically carry out necessary parametric changes in the size of obligations to the older population to prevent pension schemes from becoming increasingly unsustainable. Fine-tuning of the financial mechanism of pension systems traditionally takes place through the adoption of legislative measures of raising the retirement age, introducing various budget rules, changing the requirements for the length of working experience, indexation of pension, etc. Such measures help to solve existing problems in the short term, but in the long term there is a gradual accumulation of problems and risks that sooner or later will have to be solved (Dorofeev, 2022; Jain & Ranjan, 2020; Tridico & Meloni, 2018).

M. Dorofeev (✉)
Financial University under the Government of the Russian Federation, Moscow, Russia
e-mail: mldorofeev@fa.ru

K. Tamashiro
University of the Ryukyus, Okinawa, Japan
e-mail: k218483@eve.u-ryukyu.ac.jp

H. Dincer, S. Yüksel (eds.), *Economic Development and the Environmental Ecosystem*, Contributions to Economics,
https://doi.org/10.1007/978-3-031-26596-9_14

The purpose of this study is to analyze the evolutionary vector of development of financial and investment models of pension provision for Sustainable Economic Growth.

14.2 Fundamental Principles of Formation of Financial and Investment Models of Pension Provision

The pension system is the largest component in the social security systems of the most countries in terms of its contribution to the GDP (Chybalski, 2015). It protects older population against poverty and mitigates the negative effects of changes in the level of market income of workers after reaching the retirement age. Tt is also closely related economically to the labor market, the level of income in a country and the financial mechanism income distribution and redistribution in the economy. This relationship is determined by the design of pension provision financial model in a particular country (Čaić et al., 2019; Hammond & O'Brien, 2021; Hu et al., 2021; Matthews et al., 2021; Valdez, 2022; Wang et al., 2022).

There are three typical designs for pension system financial models, which differ according to the criterion of the organization of pension plans: (1) pension plans depending on the average retirement-income provision and target level of pensions, (2) pension plans depending on the contributions and pension provision related to earnings and (3) mixed (hybrid) financial models (OECD, 2021).

The first type of the pension system financial model operates on the conditional-accumulative principles of financing. It operates based on solidary redistribution of income between employees and pensioners and is used to finance basic pension rights. Basic pensions can take two different forms: (1) residence-based benefit or (2) a benefit that is only available to those who contributed during their career. The calculation and assignment of pensions depends on the age, gender, profession, working conditions and other parameters of country's social security system. The effectiveness of the first type pension system financial model depends on the demographic load factor. With the growing number of pensioners, this model usually becomes less effective and requires special reforms to remain sustainable or needs increasing of labor productivity. The growth in labor productivity theoretically should lead for a temporary increase in wages and in the volume of contributions, which can be used to finance pension plans formed before the moment of salary increase (An et al., 2022; Bhuiyan, Zhang, et al., 2022b; Conteh et al., 2021; Daniali et al., 2021; Huang, Masrur, et al., 2021a; Huang, Yona, et al., 2021b; Khan et al., 2021; Liu, Kato, Mandal, Mikhaylov, Hemeida, & Senjyu, 2021a; Liu, Kato, Mandal, Mikhaylov, Hemeida, Takahashi, & Tomonobu, 2021b; Mikhaylov, 2022a; Moiseev et al., 2023; Sediqi et al., 2022).

The second type financial model of pension system is more flexible than the first one and fundamentally differs from it. This financial model is built on earnings-related principles of funding, where pension benefits proportionally depend on the size of the employee's market income and his or her contributions into personal pension capital. This type of pension system financial model sometimes is improved via public co-financing programs, which encourage more workers to increase their personal voluntary pension savings. This type of financial model is also called a funded pension system or a funded pension plan. Financing is provided through the accumulation of the contributions on the special individual saving accounts and investing these financial resources into bonds and stocks on a long-term basis (Barykin, Mikheev, et al., 2022b; Bhuiyan, Dinçer, et al., 2022a; Candila et al., 2021; Danish, Senjyu, et al., 2022a, 2022b; Dong et al., 2021; Li, Yüksel, Dınçer, Mikhaylov, & Barykin, 2022b; Liu et al., 2022a, 2022b; Mikhaylov, 2015, 2021b, 2022b; Mikhaylov & Grilli, 2022; Mukhametov et al., 2021; Saqib et al., 2021).

Mixed (hybrid) design of pension plan is the third type financial model of pension system. It is based on various combinations of redistributive and accumulative pension plans and can include up to three tiers of pension provision and several different public and private components of pension: basic, minimum, targeted, public, private, mandatory, voluntary etc. This financial model is more sustainable than the others and meets interests of a wider range of population.

Combating poverty of older population is one of one of the most important socio-economic development goals from the list of United Nations SDG. An efficient welfare state with appropriate system of social security is able to succeed in solving the problem of extreme poverty of older population. The development of the methodology for assessing the quality and the improvement of the efficiency of the public social security system is very relevant. The definition of minimum, fair, sufficient and preferred level of pension provision also cause a number of discussions, including in the context of studies of income inequality among pensioners (Badr et al., 2022; Barykin, Kapustina, et al., 2022a; Dinçer, Aksoy, Yüksel, & Hacioglu, 2022a; Dinçer, Yüksel, & Martínez, 2022b; Kalinina et al., 2022; Khan et al., 2022; Mehta et al., 2022; Mikhaylov, Bhatti, et al., 2022a; Mikhaylov et al., 2023; Nyangarika et al., 2022; Shaikh et al., 2022).

A fair level of pension provision should be directly related to the efforts of the pensioner which were made to form pension rights during the career of contribution. It can consist of two components: first tier (basic and mandatory earnings-related pension provision) and second tier (voluntary earnings-related pension provision). The funded component is an important addition to the social security system, guaranteeing its fairness in accordance with the voluntary funded contribution of each worker to his personal pension capital (Mikhaylov, 2021a; Mikhaylov, Yumashev, & Kolpak, 2022b; Mutalimov et al., 2021; Varyash et al., 2020; Zhao et al., 2021).

The theoretical level of sufficient level of pension provision cannot be less than the minimum pension. Combating with the poverty of older population is very efficient through the practice of paying a basic and targeted residence-based retirement-income provision in first tier component of pension system financial model. This practice can guarantee a minimum sufficient level of retirement-income for pensioners (Danish et al., 2021; Dayong et al., 2020; Mikhaylov et al., 2019; Shaikh et al., 2021; Tamashiro et al., 2021, 2023; Uyeh et al., 2021).

The preferred level of pension can be determined on the basis of sociological surveys. Obviously, the results of surveys will depend on the category of respondents, the average wage and standard of living in the region of their residence.

14.3 Evolution of Financial Models of Pension Provision

The fact of first practical implementation of the public pension system in 1889 is attributed to German Chancellor Otto von Bismarck (Byrkjeflot et al., 2022; Valdez, 2022). According to his ideas the government should guarantee the minimum level of social provision, the employer is responsible for appropriate replacement rate of wages for retired employees and employee also makes his personal contributions into pension system.

The main factors of evolution of any pension system are the following: (1) the level of poverty, (2) life expectancy, (3) the share of wages in the economy (in % of GDP), (4) gender and age structure of the population, (5) unemployment rate, etc.

Share of wages in the economy (in % of GDP) is steadily declining, and the number of contributors to pension system is decreasing as well. These tendencies occur due to changes in the gender and age structure of the population and an increase in average life expectancy. Improvement of the quality and accessibility of the health care system and the rise in the average standard of living gradually change parameters of almost all pension system financial models. The current problem of population aging is a significant challenge for social security system, because it has a significant impact on the average standard of living of the population, the labor market and the structure of employment and also increases the population's needs for various types of medical services, increasing the costs of health provision in public budgets (An, Mikhaylov, & Jung, 2020a; An, Mikhaylov, & Kim, 2020b; Dooyum et al., 2020; Gura et al., 2022; Mikhaylov, 2020; Mikhaylov et al., 2020; Mikhaylov & Tarakanov, 2020; Moiseev et al., 2020, 2021).

The evolutionary vector of pension systems financial model development in most countries in the first quarter of the twenty-first century shifts to gradual reduction of the number of countries with the first type of financial model (redistributive) of the pension system and transition to the third type (hybrid). Chronic public budget deficits and a rapid rise of public debt increase the probability of cutting the volume of governmental social obligations in the part of the existing imbalance between the social contributions and budgetary expenditures (Karaev et al., 2022). Most likely that in the long-term the government will be able to guarantee only a minimum, basic or targeted level of pension provision to combat poverty and unemployment. Thus, the average and high level of pension provision will increasingly be financed and limited by the employer's funds and voluntary savings funds of employee.

14.4 Current Challenges for the Sustainability of Financial Models of Pension Provision and Ways to Solve Them

The future design of pension system financial models will develop under the influence of three groups of risks to social security systems: natural socio-economic challenges, problems in the development of international trade and corresponding financial risks. The first group of threats includes (1) deep structural changes in the labor market associated with the exponential development of the industrial revolution and the acceleration of technological progress; (2) population ageing. The second group of threats includes (3) deglobalization, trade wars and economic sanctions, the inability of governments of the world's leading countries to find common ground and cooperate for sustainable development, (4) changing priorities in goal setting of the corporate sector, and (5) a new trend towards regionalization of the global economy. The third group of threats includes (6) unprecedented growth of inflation and nominal interest rates against the background of rising global debt; (7) chronic budget deficits in developed countries and the "habit of living in debt" developed over several decades in accordance with the practical implementation of theories of neoclassical synthesis and modern monetary theory of economic growth and budgetary policy; (8) institutional and financial imbalances of social security systems. Together, these threats make the first and the second types of pension system financial models more vulnerable, while the third one becomes more flexible, sustainable and therefore more preferred for future development.

The Industrial Revolution 4.0 has a significant impact on the trajectory of business development and technological value chains (Martinelli et al., 2021). The main driver of business development in the twentieth century was the desire to maximize profits and increase the capitalization of equity. To do this, management needed to increase the company's competitiveness through more intensive development and implementation of new technologies, as well as continue the cost reductions, including the policies of labor costs optimization (Eti et al., 2023; Haiyun et al., 2021; Li, Yüksel, & Dinçer, 2022a; Yuan et al., 2021). The final phases of globalization of the world economy at the beginning of the twenty-first century and the rapid growth of new technologies have made it possible to transform many companies from local businesses into global corporations with a huge capitalization and a wide geography of production chains (Singh et al., 2022). These processes have fundamentally changed the requirements for the qualification of the labor force. Since the great recession of 2008, the global economy has seen a surge in automation, reducing low-skilled jobs and replacing them with robots and software algorithms.

The exponential acceleration of technological progress and a noticeable reduction in the life cycle of working professions, along with the lengthening of life expectancy, have created new social risks of changing a type of job profession several times during working career (Dinçer et al., 2023; Eti et al., 2022; Fang et al., 2021; Kayacık et al., 2022). At the same time, the obvious trend towards an increase in the number of self-employed and a reduction in full-time employees among employers poses a significant threat to the underfunding of the social security systems in many countries. A number of studies show that this trend can negatively affect the dynamics of socio-economic inequality (Dorofeev, 2022; Tridico & Meloni, 2018). The public finance system is forced to respond to these threats by finding additional sources of funding for special education and requalification programs, as well as developing special tax regimes for new types of employment, such as self-employed workers (Jain & Ranjan, 2020).

The aging of the population in developed countries, associated with a slowdown in the birth rate and an increase in life expectancy, has created obvious and constantly increasing risks for the social security systems. An increase in the demographic burden on the economy is the reason for worsening of the third group of problems due to the corresponding budget and debt risks. The growth of life expectancy and the raising of the retirement age are changing the effectiveness of social risk coverage of pension systems. Future generations have to work longer during their life and make more contributions into pension system but instead of that they are offered social guarantees, covering a smaller part of their life, because the length of survival period remains approximately the same due to the effect of automatic adjustment mechanisms of modern pension system financial models.

One of the possible responses to the first group of threats is the use of digital technologies and the robotization of the social security and education system (Pedersen et al., 2018). This helps more people to adapt to the rapid structural changes in the labor market. The development of robotics and digital technologies in the field of social security and social finance is also a strong response to the first group of challenges (Čaić et al., 2019).

The second group of threats is connected with the processes of deglobalization, accompanied by a significant increase in the number of mutual sanctions and obstacles to the smooth operation of global value chains. These processes increase vulnerability of welfare state in all countries and negatively affect sustainable growth of the world economy (Hu et al., 2021). Significant escalation of sanctions in 2022 led to an economic crisis in the world economy, caused an unprecedented increase in commodity prices and a decrease in real incomes of the older population (Dinçer, Yüksel, Mikhaylov, Barykin, et al., 2022c; Dinçer, Yüksel, Mikhaylov, Pinter, & Shaikh, 2022d, 2022e; Dong et al., 2022; Yüksel & Dinçer, 2022; Zhang et al., 2022). A sharp increase in nominal interest rates and volatility in financial markets increases the risks of destabilization of financial and investment models of the second type. The trend towards regionalization of the global economy creates risks of a decrease in productivity and profitability of the corporate sector. In turn, this could make the inflation problem long-term and create additional uncertainty for social security systems in the context of possible future reforms of global currency system (Wang et al., 2022).

To overcome the second group of threats, governments of different countries will have to make special efforts to stop trade and currency wars and instead of that move to healthy market competition and international cooperation in building an efficient and sustainable welfare state (Kafka et al., 2022; Martínez et al., 2022; Mukhtarov et al., 2022; Sun et al., 2022). To do this, it is highly likely that the global economy will have to go through a significant cyclical crisis of international relations with the change of global leader.

The third group of threats is caused by financial risks arising from the first two ones. Chronic budget deficits over several decades in the countries with high income per capita shifted net public wealth into negative territory. The increased obligations of social security systems and the declining internal sources of their financing create significant financial imbalances in the social security systems of many countries. Global debt problem creates enormous risks for social security systems of all types in countries with high level of public leverage and low level of international reserves during the period of high volatility and uncertainty and the rise of nominal interest rates (Pekhterev et al., 2019).

Solutions for the third group of threats should be fiscal consolidation measures, normalization of debt policies and serious rethinking of the possible consequences of implementing the financial risks described above. The important task for governments for the period structural transformation of pension and financial systems and the return of the global economy to cooperation and sustainable growth trajectory will be to preserve the real value of pension savings. (Popkova et al., 2021).

14.5 Conclusion

Pension provision is an important component of the social security system. An effective pension system solves many problems, ranging from combating poverty of older people to providing appropriate retirement-income provision. There are three main types of financial models of pension systems. The evolution of pension systems since the creation of the first pilot project in Germany has come a long way and today, it is seeking new effective mechanisms for stabilizing and adapting to cyclical fluctuations in the global economy.

The paper identified three groups of threats facing modern financial models of pension systems. The first group of threats includes (1) deep structural changes in the labor market associated with the exponential development of the industrial revolution and the acceleration of technological progress; (2) population ageing. The second group of threats includes (3) deglobalization, trade wars and economic sanctions, the inability of governments of the world's leading countries to find common ground and cooperate (Bhuiyan, Dinçer, et al., 2022a; Ermiş & Güven, 2022; Kou et al., 2022; Xu et al., 2022), (4) changing goal setting in the corporate sector, and (5) a new trend towards regionalization of the global economy. The third group of threats includes (6) unprecedented growth of inflation and interest rates against the background of the colossal debt problem of the global economy; (7) chronic budget deficits in developed countries and the "habit of living in debt" developed over several decades in accordance with the practical implementation of theories of neoclassical synthesis and modern monetary theory of economic growth and budgetary policy; (8) institutional and financial imbalances of social security systems. Together, these threats pose significant risks to the financial stability of the first and second types, as well as make the more stable third type of financial models of pension systems more vulnerable and less effective.

Conceptual directions for minimizing these threats are proposed. The first group of threats can be overcome by taking reasonable advantages of technological progress for creation new technological solutions for social welfare of the future. Moving in this direction requires special attention in terms of managing technological and socio-economic inequality, which can become higher in the context of increasing restrictions on international trade and escalating sanctions rhetoric of countries with high income and developed economy. The second group of threats should be addressed through efforts of smoothing out the consequences of long-term economic cycles and transforming the format of the international trade and the global financial systems basing on ESG principles. The third group of threats should be addressed by reviewing the financial and debt policies of countries with excessive leverage and budget deficits, since the prospects for maintaining high inflation rates and rising nominal interest rates pose unacceptable risks to the sustainability of existing financial models of pension systems (Carayannis et al., 2022; Li, Yüksel, & Dinçer, 2022a; Mikhaylov, Bhatti, et al., 2022a; Yüksel et al., 2022).

Funding The publication is based on the results of budgetary-supported research according to the state task carried out by the Financial University under the Government of the Russian Federation, Moscow, Russia.

References

An, J., Mikhaylov, A., Dinçer, H., & Yüksel, S. (2022). Economic modelling of electricity generation: Long short-term memory and Q-rung orthopair fuzzy sets. *Heliyon, 8*, e10759.

An, J., Mikhaylov, A., & Jung, S.-U. (2020a). The strategy of South Korea in the global oil market. *Energies, 13*(10), 2491.

An, J., Mikhaylov, A., & Kim, K. (2020b). Machine learning approach in heterogeneous group of algorithms for transport safety-critical system. *Applied Sciences, 10*(8), 2670.

Badr, A. M. N. A. A., Mohamed, T. I., Osman, N. A. Q., & Mikhaylov, A. (2022). A review of social media website users' interaction paths with governmental accounts during the COVID-19 pandemic. *Informatics, 9*, 50. https://doi.org/10.3390/informatics9030050

Barykin, S. E., Kapustina, I. V., Sergeev, S. M., Daniali, S. M., Kopteva, L. A., Semenova, G. N., Pryadko, I. P., Mikhaylov, A., Baboshkin, P., Datsyuk, P., & Senjyu, T. (2022a). Financial logistics models based on systematic approach improving management solutions. *F1000Research, 11*, 570. https://doi.org/10.12688/f1000research.111252.1

Barykin, S., Mikheev, A., Kiseleva, E., Putikhin, Y., Alekseeva, N., & Mikhaylov, A. (2022b). An empirical analysis of russian regions' debt sustainability. *Economies, 10*(4), 296.

Bhuiyan, M. A., Dinçer, H., Yüksel, S., Mikhaylov, A., Danish, M. S. S., Pinter, G., Uyeh, D. D., & Stepanova, D. (2022a). Economic indicators and bioenergy supply in developed economies: QROF-DEMATEL and random forest models. *Energy Reports, 8*, 561–570.

Bhuiyan, M. A., Zhang, Q., Khare, V., Mikhaylov, A., Pinter, G., & Huang, X. (2022b). Renewable energy consumption and economic growth nexus—A systematic literature review. *Frontiers in Environmental Science., 10*, 878394. https://doi.org/10.3389/fenvs.2022.878394

Byrkjeflot, H., Mjøset, L., Mordhorst, M., & Petersen, K. (2022). The making and circulation of Nordic models, ideas and images. In *Nordic studies in a global context*. Boston University. https://doi.org/10.4324/9781003156925-13.

Čaić, M., Mahr, D., & Oderkerken-Schröder, G. (2019). Value of social robots in services: Social cognition perspective. *Journal of Services Marketing, 33*(4), 463–478. https://doi.org/10.1108/jsm-02-2018-0080

Candila, V., Maximov, D., Mikhaylov, A., Moiseev, N., Senjyu, T., & Tryndina, N. (2021). On the relationship between oil and exchange rates of oil-exporting and oil-importing countries: From the great recession period to the Covid-19 era. *Energies, 14*, 8065.

Carayannis, E., Kostis, P., Dinçer, H., & Yüksel, S. (2022). Balanced-scorecard-based evaluation of knowledge-oriented competencies of distributed energy investments. *Energies, 15*(21), 8245.

Chybalski, F. (2015). The multidimensional efficiency of pension system: Definition and measurement in cross-country studies. *Social Indicators Research, 128*(1), 15–34. https://doi.org/10.1007/s11205-015-1017-3

Conteh, F., Takahashi, H., Hemeida, A. M., Krishnan, N., Mikhaylov, A., & Senjyu, T. (2021). Hybrid grid-connected renewable power generation for sustainable electricity supply in Sierra Leone: Case study Lungi Town. *Sustainability, 13*(18), 11435.

Daniali, S. M., Barykin, S. E., Kapustina, I. V., Khortabi, F. M., Sergeev, S. M., Kalinina, O. V., Mikhaylov, A., Veynberg, R., Zasova, L., & Senjyu, T. (2021). Predicting volatility index according to technical index and economic indicators on the basis of deep learning algorithm. *Sustainability, 2021*(13), 14011.

Danish, M. S. S., Senjyu, T., Sabory, N. R., Khosravy, M., Grilli, M. L., Mikhaylov, A., & Majidi, H. (2021). A forefront framework for sustainable aquaponics modeling and design. *Sustainability, 13*, 9313.

Danish, M. S., Senjyu, T. S., Sabory, N. R., & Mikhaylov, A. (2022a). Lessons from COVID-19 conferring environmental re-engineering opportunity. In M. Danish & T. Senjyu (Eds.), *Eco-friendly and agile energy strategies and policy development* (pp. 99–118). IGI Global. https://doi.org/10.4018/978-1-7998-9502-2.ch005

Danish, M. S., Senjyu, T. S., Sabory, N. R., & Mikhaylov, A. (2022b). Interplay consequences of COVID-19 on global environmental sustainability. In M. Danish & T. Senjyu (Eds.), *Eco-friendly and agile energy strategies and policy development*. IGI Global. https://doi.org/10.4018/978-1-7998-9502-2.ch003

Dayong, N., Mikhaylov, A., Bratanovsky, S., Shaikh, Z. A., & Stepanova, D. (2020). Mathematical modeling of the technological processes of catering products production. *Journal of Food Process Engineering, 43*(2), 1–9.

Dinçer, H., Aksoy, T., Yüksel, S., & Hacioglu, U. (2022a). Golden cut-oriented q-rung orthopair fuzzy decision-making approach to evaluation of renewable energy alternatives for microgeneration system investments. *Mathematical Problems in Engineering, 2022*, 2261166.

Dinçer, H., Yüksel, S., Çağlayan, Ç., Yavuz, D., & Kararoğlu, D. (2023). Can renewable energy investments be a solution to the energy-sourced high inflation problem? In *Managing inflation and supply chain disruptions in the global economy* (pp. 220–238). IGI Global.

Dinçer, H., Yüksel, S., & Martínez, L. (2022b). Collaboration enhanced hybrid fuzzy decision-making approach to analyze the renewable energy investment projects. *Energy Reports, 8*, 377–389.

Dinçer, H., Yüksel, S., Mikhaylov, A., Barykin, S. E., Aksoy, T., & Hacioğlu, U. (2022c). Analysis of environmental priorities for green project investments using an integrated q-rung orthopair fuzzy modelling. *IEEE Access, 10*, 50996. https://doi.org/10.1109/ACCESS.2022.3174058

Dinçer, H., Yüksel, S., Mikhaylov, A., Pinter, G., & Shaikh, Z. A. (2022d). Analysis of renewable-friendly smart grid technologies for the distributed energy investment projects using a hybrid picture fuzzy rough decision-making approach. *Energy Reports, 8*, 11466–11477. https://doi.org/10.1016/j.egyr.2022.08.275

Dinçer, H., Yüksel, S., Mikhaylov, A., Pinter, G., & Shaikh, Z. A. (2022e). Analysis of renewable-friendly smart grid technologies for the distributed energy investment projects using a hybrid picture fuzzy rough decision-making approach. *Energy Reports, 8*, 11466–11477.

Dong, B., Ikonnikova, I., Rogulin, R., Sakulyeva, T., & Mikhaylov, A. (2021). Environmentaleconomic approach to optimization of transport communication in megacities. *Journal of Environmental Science and Health, Part A, 56*(6), 660–666.

Dong, W., Zhao, G., Yüksel, S., Dinçer, H., & Ubay, G. G. (2022). A novel hybrid decision making approach for the strategic selection of wind energy projects. *Renewable Energy, 185*, 321–337.

Dooyum, U. D., Mikhaylov, A., & Varyash, I. (2020). Energy security concept in Russia and South Korea. *International Journal of Energy Economics and Policy, 10*(4), 102–107.

Dorofeev, M. L. (2022). Interrelations between income inequality and sustainable economic growth: Contradictions of empirical research and new results. *Economies, 10*(2), 44. https://doi.org/10.3390/economies10020044

Ermiş, A. M., & Güven, M. E. (2022). The role of green energy investments in energy supply security. In *Circular economy and the energy market* (pp. 67–77). Springer.

Eti, S., Dinçer, H., Gökalp, Y., Yüksel, S., & Kararoğlu, D. (2023). Identifying key issues to handle the inflation problem in the healthcare industry caused by energy prices: An evaluation with decision-making models. *Managing Inflation and Supply Chain Disruptions in the Global Economy*, 162–178.

Eti, S., Dinçer, H., Yüksel, S., & Gökalp, Y. (2022). Analysis of the suitability of the solar panels for hospitals: A new fuzzy decision-making model proposal with the T-spherical TOP-DEMATEL method. *Journal of Intelligent and Fuzzy Systems, Preprint*, 1–13.

Fang, S., Zhou, P., Dinçer, H., & Yüksel, S. (2021). Assessment of safety management system on energy investment risk using house of quality based on hybrid stochastic interval-valued intuitionistic fuzzy decision-making approach. *Safety Science, 141*, 105333.

Gura, D., Mikhaylov, A., Glushkov, S., Zaikov, M., & Shaikh, Z. A. (2022). Model for estimating power dissipation along the interconnect length in single on-chip topology. *Evolutionary Intelligence, 15*, 2369–2373. https://doi.org/10.1007/s12065-020-00407-7

Haiyun, C., Zhixiong, H., Yüksel, S., & Dinçer, H. (2021). Analysis of the innovation strategies for green supply chain management in the energy industry using the QFD-based hybrid interval valued intuitionistic fuzzy decision approach. *Renewable and Sustainable Energy Reviews, 143*, 110844.

Hammond, P. B., & O'Brien, A. (2021, September 28). Pensions and ESG: An institutional and historical perspective. Wharton Pension Research Council Working Paper No. 2021–19, Available at SSRN: https://ssrn.com/abstract=3936028 or https://doi.org/10.2139/ssrn.3936028

Hu, X., He, L., & Cui, Q. (2021). How do international conflicts impact China's energy security and economic growth? A case study of the US economic sanctions on Iran. *Sustainability, 13*, 6903. https://doi.org/10.3390/su13126903

Huang, Y., Masrur, H., Shigenobu, R., Hemeida, A. M., Mikhaylov, A., & Senjyu, T. (2021a). A comparative design of a campus microgrid considering a multi-scenario and multi-objective approach. *Energies, 14*, 2853.

Huang, Y., Yona, A., Takahashi, H., Hemeida, A. M., Mandal, P., Mikhaylov, A., Senjyu, T., & Lotfy, M. E. (2021b). Energy management system optimization of drug store operate electric vehicles charging station. *Sustainability, 14*, 1217836.

Jain, A., & Ranjan, S. (2020). Implications of emerging technologies on the future of work. *IIMB Management Review, 32*(4), 448. https://doi.org/10.1016/j.iimb.2020.11.004

Kafka, K. I., Dinçer, H., & Yüksel, S. (2022). Impact-relation map of innovative service development regarding the sustainable growth for emerging markets. *Journal of the Knowledge Economy*, 1–24.

Kalinina, O. V., Barykin, S. E., Sergeev, S. M., Semenova, G. N., Fatkullina, A., Mikhaylov, A., & De La Poza, E. (2022). Smart city perspectives in post-pandemic governance: Externalities reduction policy. *F1000Research, 11*, 1032. https://doi.org/10.12688/f1000research.123195.1

Karaev, A., Gorlova, O., Ponkratov, V., Sedova, M., Shmigol, N., & Vasyunina, M. (2022). A comparative analysis of the choice of mother wavelet functions affecting the accuracy of forecasts of daily balances in the treasury single account. *Economies, 10*, 213. https://doi.org/10.3390/economies10090213

Kayacık, M., Dinçer, H., & Yüksel, S. (2022). Using quantum spherical fuzzy decision support system as a novel sustainability index approach for analyzing industries listed in the stock exchange. *Borsa Istanbul Review, 22*(6), 1145–1157.

Khan, A. A., Laghari, A. A., Gadekallu, T. R., Shaikh, Z. A., Javed, A. R., Rashid, M., Estrela, V. V., & Mikhaylov, A. (2022). A drone-based data management and optimization using metaheuristic algorithms and blockchain smart contracts in a secure fog environment. *Computers and Electrical Engineering, 102*, 108234. https://doi.org/10.1016/j.compeleceng.2022.108234

Khan, A. A., Shaikh, Z. A., Baitenova, L., Mutaliyeva, L., Moiseev, N., Mikhaylov, A., Laghari, A. A., Idris, S. A., & Alshazly, H. (2021). QoS-ledger: Smart contracts and metaheuristic for secure quality-of-service and cost-efficient scheduling of medical-data processing. *Electronics, 10*, 3083.

Kou, G., Yüksel, S., & Dinçer, H. (2022). Inventive problem-solving map of innovative carbon emission strategies for solar energy-based transportation investment projects. *Applied Energy, 311*, 118680.

Li, W., Yüksel, S., & Dinçer, H. (2022a). Understanding the financial innovation priorities for renewable energy investors via QFD-based picture fuzzy and rough numbers. *Financial Innovation, 8*(1), 1–30.

Li, J., Yüksel, S., Dınçer, H., Mikhaylov, A., & Barykin, S. E. (2022b). Bipolar q-ROF hybrid decision making model with golden cut for analyzing the levelized cost of renewable energy alternatives. *IEEE Access, 10*, 42507–42517.

Liu, L., Kato, T., Mandal, P., Mikhaylov, A., Hemeida, A. M., & Senjyu, T. (2021a). Multi-area power system load frequency control by using model predictive control by introducing renewable energy sources. *International Conference on Science & Contemporary Technologies (ICSCT), 2021*, 1–6. https://doi.org/10.1109/ICSCT53883.2021.9642521

Liu, L., Kato, T., Mandal, P., Mikhaylov, A., Hemeida, A. M., Takahashi, H., & Tomonobu, S. (2021b). Two cases studies of model predictive control approach for hybrid renewable energy systems. *AIMS Energy, 9*(6), 1241–1259.

Liu, Z.-J., Panfilova, E., Mikhaylov, A., & Kurilova, A. (2022a). COVID-19 crisis impact on the stability between parties in crowdfunding and crowdsourcing. *Wireless Personal Communications, 122*, 915–930.

Liu, Z., Panfilova, E., Mikhaylov, A., & Kurilova, A. (2022b). Assessing stability in the relationship between parties in crowdfunding and crowdsourcing projects during the COVID-19 crisis. *Journal of Global Information Management (JGIM), 30*(4), 1–18. https://doi.org/10.4018/JGIM.297905

Martinelli, A., Mina, A., & Moggi, M. (2021). The enabling technologies of industry 4.0: Examining the seeds of the fourth industrial revolution. *Industrial and Corporate Change, 30*(1), 161–188. https://doi.org/10.1093/icc/dtaa060

Martínez, L., Dinçer, H., & Yüksel, S. (2022). A hybrid decision making approach for new service development process of renewable energy investment. *Applied Soft Computing, 133*, 109897.

Matthews, B., See, Z. S., & Day, J. (2021). Crisis and extended realities: Remote presence in the time of COVID-19. *Media International Australia, 178*(1), 198–209. https://doi.org/10.1177/1329878X20967165

Mehta, R., Verghese, J., Mahajan, S., Barykin, S., Bozhuk, S., Kozlova, N., Kapustina, I., Mikhaylov, A., Naumova, E., & Dedyukhina, N. (2022). Consumers' behavior in conversational commerce marketing based on messenger chatbots. *F1000Research, 11*(647), 647. https://doi.org/10.12688/f1000research.122037.1

Mikhaylov, A. (2015). Russian oil and gas budget revenues in 2015: Estimation and risk. *Financial Journal, 2015*(2), 52–59.

Mikhaylov, A. (2020). Cryptocurrency market development: Hurst method. *Finance: Theory and Practice, 24*(3), 81–91.

Mikhaylov, A. (2021a). Development of Friedrich von Hayek's theory of private money and economic implications for digital currencies. *Terra Economicus, 19*(1), 53.

Mikhaylov, A. (2021b). Lichens as indicators of atmospheric pollution in urban ecosystems. *Israel Journal of Ecology and Evolution, 67*(1–2), 60–68. https://doi.org/10.1163/22244662-bja10016

Mikhaylov, A. (2022a). Efficiency of renewable energy generation in Russia. *Anais da Academia Brasileira de Ciências, 94*(4), e20191226. https://doi.org/10.1590/0001-3765202220191226

Mikhaylov, A. (2022b). Sustainable development and renewable energy: A new view to a global problem. *Energies, 15*, 1397. https://doi.org/10.3390/en15041397

Mikhaylov, A., Bhatti, I. M., Dinçer, H., & Yüksel, S. (2022a). Integrated decision recommendation system using iteration-enhanced collaborative filtering, golden cut bipolar for analyzing the risk-based oil market spillovers. *Computational Economics*, 1–34. https://doi.org/10.1007/s10614-022-10341-8

Mikhaylov, A., Burakov, D., & Didenko, V. (2019). Relationship between oil price and macroeconomic indicators in Russia. *Finance: Theory and Practice, 23*(2), 105–116. https://doi.org/10.26794/2587-5671-2019-23-2-105-116

Mikhaylov, A., Dinçer, H., & Yüksel, S. (2023). Analysis of financial development and open innovation oriented fintech potential for emerging economies using an integrated decision-making approach of MF-X-DMA and golden cut bipolar q-ROFSs. *Financial Innovation, 9*, 10. https://doi.org/10.1186/s40854-022-00234-w

Mikhaylov, A., & Grilli, M. L. (2022). Machine learning methods and sustainable development: Metal oxides and multilayer metal-oxides. *Metals, 12*(4), 836.

Mikhaylov, A., Moiseev, N., Aleshin, K., & Burkhardt, T. (2020). Global climate change and greenhouse effect. *Entrepreneurship and Sustainability Issues, 7*(4), 2897–2913. https://doi.org/10.9770/jesi.2020.7.4(21)

Mikhaylov, A., & Tarakanov, S. (2020). Development of Levenberg-Marquardt theoretical approach for electric network. *Journal of Physics: Conference Series, 1515*, 052006.

Mikhaylov, A., Yumashev, A., & Kolpak, E. (2022b). Quality of life, anxiety and depressive disorders in patients with extrasystolic arrhythmia. *Archives of Medical Science, 18*(2), 328. https://doi.org/10.5114/aoms.2020.101359

Moiseev, N., Mikhaylov, A., Dinçer, H., & Yüksel, S. (2023). Effects of market capitalization shocks for open innovation models in e-commerce industry: Golden cut QROF MCDM analysis. *Financial Innovation, 9*, 32.

Moiseev, N., Mikhaylov, A., Varyash, I., & Saqib, A. (2020). Investigating the relation of GDP per capita and corruption index. *Entrepreneurship and Sustainability Issues, 8*(1), 780–794.

Moiseev, N., Sorokin, A., Zvezdina, N., Mikhaylov, A., Khomyakova, L., & Danish, M. S. S. (2021). Credit risk theoretical model on the base of DCC-GARCH in time-varying parameters framework. *Mathematics, 9*, 2423. https://doi.org/10.3390/math9192423

Mukhametov, A., Bekhorashvili, A., Avdeenko, A., & Mikhaylov, A. (2021). The impact of growing legume plants under conditions of Biologization and Soil Cultivation on Chernozem fertility and productivity of rotation crops. *Legume Research, 44*, 12.

Mukhtarov, S., Yüksel, S., & Dinçer, H. (2022). The impact of financial development on renewable energy consumption: Evidence from Turkey. *Renewable Energy, 187*, 169–176.

Mutalimov, V., Kovaleva, I., Mikhaylov, A., & Stepanova, D. (2021). Assessing regional growth of small business in Russia. *Entrepreneurial Business and Economics Review, 9*(3), 119–133. https://doi.org/10.15678/EBER.2021.090308

Nyangarika, A., Mikhaylov, A., Muyeen, S. M., Yadykin, V., Mottaeva, A., Pryadko, I., Barykin, S., Fomenko, N., Rykov, G., & Shvandar, K. (2022). Energy stability and decarbonization in developing countries: Random Forest approach for forecasting of crude oil trade flows and macro indicators. *Frontiers in Environmental Science, 10*, 565454.

OECD. (2021). *Pensions at a glance 2021: OECD and G20 indicators*. OECD Publishing. https://doi.org/10.1787/ca401ebd-en

Pedersen, I., Reid, S., & Aspevig, K. (2018). Developing social robots for aging populations: A literature review of recent academic sources. *Sociology Compass, 12*(6), e12585. https://doi.org/10.1111/soc4.12585

Pekhterev, A., Domaschenko, D., & Guseva, I. (2019). Modelling of trends in the volume and structure of accumulated credit indebtedness in the banking system. *Computer Research and Modeling, 11*(5), 965–978. https://doi.org/10.20537/2076-7633-2019-11-5-965-978

Popkova, E., Bernardi, P., Tyurina, Y., & Sergi, B. (2021). A theory of digital technology advancement to address the grand challenges of sustainable development. *Technology in Society, 68*, 101831. https://doi.org/10.1016/j.techsoc.2021.101831

Saqib, A., Chan, T.-H., Mikhaylov, A., & Lean, H. H. (2021). Are the responses of sectoral energy imports asymmetric to exchange rate volatilities in Pakistan? Evidence from recent foreign exchange regime. *Frontiers in Energy Research, 9*, 614463. https://doi.org/10.3389/fenrg.2021.614463

Sediqi, M. M., Nakadomari, A., Mikhaylov, A., Krishnan, N., Lotfy, M. E., Yona, A., & Senjyu, T. (2022). Impact of time-of-use demand response program on optimal operation of Afghanistan real power system. *Energies, 15*, 296.

Shaikh, Z. A., Kraikin, A., Mikhaylov, A., & Pinter, G. (2022). Forecasting stock prices of companies producing solar panels using machine learning methods. *Complexity, 2022*, 9186265. https://doi.org/10.1155/2022/9186265

Shaikh, Z. A., Moiseev, N., Mikhaylov, A., & Yüksel, S. (2021). Facile synthesis of copper oxide-cobalt oxide/nitrogen-doped carbon (Cu2O-Co3O4/CN) composite for efficient water splitting. *Applied Sciences, 11*, 9974. https://doi.org/10.3390/app11219974

Singh, A., Jha, S., Srivastava, D. K., & Somarajan, A. (2022). Future of work: A systematic literature review and evolution of themes. *Foresight, 24*(1), 99–125. https://doi.org/10.1108/FS-09-2020-0093

Sun, L., Peng, J., Dinçer, H., & Yüksel, S. (2022). Coalition-oriented strategic selection of renewable energy system alternatives using q-ROF DEMATEL with golden cut. *Energy, 256*, 124606.

Tamashiro, K., Alharbi, T., Mikhaylov, A., Hemeida, A. M., Krishnan, N., Lotfy, M. E., & Senjyu, T. (2021). Investigation of home energy management with advanced direct load control and optimal scheduling of controllable loads. *Energies, 14*, 7314. https://doi.org/10.3390/en14217314

Tamashiro, K., Omine, E., Krishnan, N., Mikhaylov, A., Hemeida, A. M., & Senjyu, T. (2023). Optimal components capacity based multi-objective optimization and optimal scheduling based MPC-optimization algorithm in smart apartment buildings. *Energy and Buildings, 278*, 112616. https://doi.org/10.1016/j.enbuild.2022.112616

Tridico, P., & Meloni, W. P. (2018). Economic growth, welfare models and inequality in the context of globalisation. *The Economic and Labour Relations Review, 29*, 118–139.

Uyeh, D. D., Asem-Hiablie, S., Park, T., Kim, K.-M., Mikhaylov, A., Woo, S., & Ha, Y. (2021). Could Japonica rice be an alternative variety for increased global food security and climate change mitigation? *Food, 10*, 1869. https://doi.org/10.3390/foods10081869

Valdez, J. (2022). Social protection, capitalist production: The Bismarckian welfare state in the German political economy, 1880–2015. By Philip Manow. Oxford: Oxford University Press, 2020. 192p. New York: Routledge, 2021. 274p, $160.00 cloth. *Perspectives on Politics, 20*(1), 345–346. https://doi.org/10.1017/S153759272100342X

Varyash, I., Mikhaylov, A., Moiseev, N., & Aleshin, K. (2020). Triple bottom line and corporate social responsibility performance indicators for Russian companies. *Entrepreneurship and Sustainability Issues, 8*(1), 313–331.

Wang, X., Di, D., & Liu, R. (2022). The evolving international monetary system: Will dollar hegemony outlive the digital revolution? In P. B. Rana & X. Ji (Eds.), *From centralised to decentralising global economic architecture*. Palgrave Macmillan. https://doi.org/10.1007/978-981-19-2041-7_6

Xu, X., Yüksel, S., & Dinçer, H. (2022). An integrated decision-making approach with golden cut and bipolar q-ROFSs to renewable energy storage investments. *International Journal of Fuzzy Systems*, 1–14. https://doi.org/10.1007/s40815-022-01372-2

Yuan, G., Xie, F., Dinçer, H., & Yüksel, S. (2021). The theory of inventive problem solving (TRIZ)-based strategic mapping of green nuclear energy investments with spherical fuzzy group decision-making approach. *International Journal of Energy Research, 45*(8), 12284–12300.

Yüksel, S., & Dinçer, H. (2022). Identifying the strategic priorities of nuclear energy investments using hesitant 2-tuple interval-valued Pythagorean fuzzy DEMATEL. *Progress in Nuclear Energy, 145*, 104103.

Yüksel, S., Dinçer, H., Eti, S., & Adalı, Z. (2022). Strategy improvements to minimize the drawbacks of geothermal investments by using spherical fuzzy modelling. *International Journal of Energy Research*. https://doi.org/10.1002/er.7880

Zhang, Y., Zhang, Y., Gong, C., Dinçer, H., & Yüksel, S. (2022). An integrated hesitant 2-tuple Pythagorean fuzzy analysis of QFD-based innovation cost and duration for renewable energy projects. *Energy, 248*, 123561.

Zhao, Q., Cherkasov, S., Avdeenko, A., Kondratenko, L., & Mikhaylov, A. (2021). Integral estimate of the added value of agricultural crops in the synergetic agriculture on the example of Vicia faba (Vicia faba L.). *Polish Journal of Environmental Studies, 30*(5), 1–9. https://doi.org/10.15244/pjoes/131949

Chapter 15
Determining Effective Human Resources Strategies for Renewable Energy Companies

Oya Alhan

Keywords Renewable energy · Energy companies · Human resources · Human resources strategies

15.1 Introduction

Energy is an important element for national economies. States and international organizations compete with each other to obtain energy resources (oil, natural gas, coal, …). Energy is the infrastructure of industrialization and an indispensable element of daily life. Therefore, the need for energy has a very important place on the national and international agenda. Due to the exhaustion of energy resources, the existence of foreign dependency and environmental effects; today, producing safe, sufficient, cheap, and clean energy for countries is among the main problems of economic and social life. The need for energy is constantly increasing in countries that are growing rapidly with their industry, economy and population. For this reason, it is of great importance to use the produced energy with high efficiency and to evaluate the potential of alternative and renewable energy sources as well as existing energy sources. Energy, which is necessary for meeting the needs of people and maintaining the development in a healthy way; it is especially used in sectors such as industry, housing and transportation. However, energy; In addition to its indispensable benefits in our lives, it also causes environmental pollution largely during production and consumption (Ermiş & Güven, 2022).

The efficient use of energy helps to restore the greenhouse gas balance in the atmosphere by reducing the amount of greenhouse gases that occur in production and consumption. Doing more work with the same amount or less greenhouse gas emissions is possible with the efficient use of energy. Reducing energy consumption with highly efficient equipment helps companies achieve their sustainability goals. Efficient use of energy resources helps to reducing costs. We can say that greenhouse

O. Alhan (✉)
The School of Business, İstanbul Medipol University, Istanbul, Turkey

H. Dincer, S. Yüksel (eds.), *Economic Development and the Environmental Ecosystem*, Contributions to Economics,
https://doi.org/10.1007/978-3-031-26596-9_15

gases released into the atmosphere during energy production and consumption play an important role in the growth of the carbon footprint and the deterioration of the living ecosystem. Energy efficiency, which is linked to the continuity of goals such as economic growth and social development, is an important factor in reducing greenhouse gas emissions. Efficient use of energy in the world; It is important because of its contribution to natural balances. It is important that the performance of energy companies is good nationally and clean energy (Kou et al., 2022). For energy companies to be successful, effective human resources are needed. Since renewable energy projects involve complex engineering processes, qualified and competent employees are needed in these projects. This chapter will focus on these issues.

15.2 Human Resources Strategies

Human Resources Management is defined as the process of recruiting, training, developing, motivating and evaluating a sufficient number of qualified employees to perform the activities necessary for the company to achieve its goals. HRM functions can be listed as follows, human resources planning, recruitment management, training and development, performance management, wages and benefits management, career management, industrial relations and motivation.

Human resources planning is to provide the workforce to work in the company in a certain order in terms of quality and quantity. In addition, HRP can be defined as an action to predict how many and what qualifications of employee will be needed, and to what extent this demand is likely to be met. Human resources planning refers to all the studies to determine the number of employees that will be needed in the future, on the basis of units and job titles.

Objectives of Human Resource Planning

- The most efficient use of existing human resources,
- Maintaining the number of employees with appropriate skills, expertise and qualifications,
- Forecasting future staffing needs,
- Adapting to rapidly changing conditions,
- Anticipating potential advantages and shortcomings of employees

Recruitment management is one of the most critical processes to be defined after the HR planning function. Because the success of an organization largely depends on the qualifications of its employees. The purpose of the recruitment management is to try to determine whether the person(s) who can perform the job properly are at a sufficient level in terms of knowledge, skills and abilities.

The recruitment process includes a series of special studies that begin with the identification of the need for employee and end with the acceptance of the selected person into the organization.

The recruitment process is extremely important in terms of not only making an impact in the relevant period, but also maintaining the company's existence and improving itself in the long run. For this reason, a systematic evaluation should be made by considering the talents, skills, attitudes and interests of the candidates.

Today, more than one system is used as a recruitment method. Developing information systems have a timesaving function at this stage. In addition, it is beneficial to use psycho-technical tests such as mental and physical ability tests, knowledge and skill accumulation tests, and personality inventory in this process. In addition to these, although it is very classical, there are important advantages of meeting the candidate directly in the selection process.

Finally, indicators such as the width of the candidate pools prepared for the relevant positions, the number of candidates suitable for the job applications for the open positions, the interview/recruitment rate, the recruitment period, the recruitment cost, the probationary performance results and the duration of employment are the elements that show the effectiveness of recruitment management.

Following the completion of the recruitment process, orientation regarding the task undertaken is required. During the orientation process, both physical space adaptation or introduction to the company employee should be done and the training curriculum for the job to be done should be explained to the new employee/ employees. This is the first step of in-house training.

No matter what technique is used in the process of finding and selecting human resources, it is very difficult to find an employee who is fully compatible with the job. This difficulty arises from the difficulty of recognizing people and identifying their characteristics rather than the inadequacy of the selection method. The best way to overcome the deficiencies brought by this difficulty is education. In addition, even if a completely healthy choice is made, the continuous change and development seen in the economic, social and technological fields forces both businesses and employees to renew themselves in terms of adapting to these, that is, to training. If suitable for employees if the necessary knowledge and skills are not gained through training programs, this situation to the enterprise, production error rate, increase in unit costs and so on. Things will return with unprocessed data.

Human resources training is the educational actions that increase the knowledge, manners and skills that aim to provide positive changes in thinking, rational decision-making, behavior and attitude, habits and understanding of the employees so that they can perform their duties in the organization more effectively and successfully.

For businesses, training is the most important of the activities to increase the productivity and performance of employees. However, some businesses today ignore it. Although training is defined as a "change process", the main purpose of the trainings are to ensure that the desired change in employee behavior. Within the framework of this purpose, it is tried to provide the employees with the necessary knowledge, skills and attitudes through training in order to be more productive.

Development is the whole of the activities designed to increase the performance during the period from the entry of the employee to the organization. No business can operate efficiently if its employees do not have an effort to improve themselves.

In this respect, hiring the best and raising them on the job after starting the job with training and development is the prerequisite for realizing efficiency.

Performance is a concept that is frequently used in the field of human resources management, but its limits and content are not sufficiently explained. Different definitions of the concept of performance mentioned by different authors are given below;

Performance is the amount of goods or services produced in a certain unit of time and is expressed in the literature as a result of the interaction between the concepts of "efficiency", "efficiency", "output" according to its function, as well as the individual's ability and motivation (Torrinton & Hall, 1995).

Performance is the good, service or idea that is put forward to fulfill the task and achieve the purpose, in a way that meets the predetermined criteria within the framework of the task (Pugh, 1991).

Performance evaluation has attracted the attention of researchers working in the field of human resource management, organizational behavior and industrial/organizational psychology for many years. Performance appraisals are an important part of organizational life because they assist many functions/purposes, including resolving performance problems, setting goals, enforcing rewards and disciplinary sanctions, and firing (Holbrook Jr, 2002). According to academicians and managers, performance evaluation is the most important component of an effective human resource management strategy as well as one of the basic elements that enable organizational management to reach its goals.

Performance evaluation methods, which have a significant impact on businesses, have become even more important with the increasing competitive environment and structural changes in the business world.

Performance evaluation, which is one of the most complex and controversial issues of human resources management, has great importance for employees and organizations.

It can be said that performance evaluation serves two main purposes. First, it provides managers with information that forms the basis for promotions, pay increases, and other management decisions. The second purpose of performance evaluation is to provide information about the extent to which employees approach the predetermined standards for them as a result of performance analysis. This gives feedback to the management about what needs to be done to continue this if the targets have been achieved, depending on the performance level reached by the employees at the end of the period, if not, the reasons for it and what kind of training and development program will be implemented.

Wage management is one of the core HR functions, but also one of the most controversial. Although the wage is referred to as the price of the labor of the personnel, it is a means of subsistence for the personnel that makes the wage valuable.

If wage management is not based on equal work and equal sharing, corporate belonging and HR policies remain sluggish. Because all kinds of payments, bonuses or incentives received by the personnel for fulfilling their duties in the company affect both their performance and job satisfaction. Compensation management is therefore the most complex and sensitive HR function along with performance management. Businesses apply quite different wage systems according to the HR policies they follow and their own structural characteristics. Apart from these factors, if technical grouping is used, wage systems are classified according to seniority, performance, skills, teamwork, sales volume and incentives. In addition, indirect rewards such as reward systems, social rewards and individual responsibility, horizontal or vertical promotion are other wage-like factors that affect employee motivation. However, this monetary.

Inappropriate rewards cannot have a positive effect as much as fair and acceptable wage management.

Wage management has a dynamic structure like performance management. For this reason, it is necessary to restructure the wage system in some periods. If the company loses its competitiveness in its sector, if low wages or high wages and financial aids offered by competitors are effective in leaving the job, and if qualified personnel cannot be recruited due to low wages, the company needs to restructure its wage management.

Otherwise, wage systems that tend to become chronic in a negative sense will render all HR functions ineffective in achieving corporate goals. There will be a significant downward trend in personnel relations and job motivation as well as deviations from companyal targets. The increase in personalized applications, the increase in the reward-promotion relationship.

Disproportions, non-transparent wage management, staff complaining about wages among themselves and making comparisons are examples of these motivation losses.

Career is a person's progress in a professional field throughout his/her working life and gaining experience and skills in this way. Career management is the process of aligning these goals with the corporate goals while trying to reach the individual goal of the person. Thanks to the efforts to be made in this direction, the individual reaches his individual career plans, while the company creates targets, plans and strategies to meet the HR needs and puts them into effect. What is important at this stage is that both parties mutually share their common expectations and that these expectations are checked at regular intervals.

Career management is often used as a motivation tool by business management in order to enable personnel to identify their career goals by being aware of promotion opportunities and options. In fact, an effective career management includes the organization of training programs suitable for the career goals of the personnel. Corporate trainings, vocational technical trainings, language trainings and trainings based on managerial competencies, especially before the exams for promotion, are complementary elements of career management.

When career management is considered as a process, it is important to determine the career field of the personnel, to draw the career path for each job position, to appoint career coaches or consultants and to control and develop individual plans. These factors vary according to the scale of the company and the sector. When this process is organized as an action plan, it gains meaning and gets rid of personal effort and the unilateral initiative of the senior management.

For these reasons, management has an effect that can be measured less as a process compared to performance management and wage management but can create corporate awareness and increase individual performance if applied on site.

Although the protection function in business life covers industrial relations, industrial relations and protection are two separate concepts. Industrial relations show themselves when making a service contract with the personnel. Determining the rights and obligations subject to the contract, working conditions, wages, working hours, leaves, holidays and other issues fall within the scope of industrial relations. These regulations are made by means of labor laws, relevant legal regulations, directives issued by the parties in the workplace and internal regulations. Other components that affect industrial relations include political and economic structure, unions, and legal controls.

The aim of HRM is to increase productivity and quality through the effective use of human resources. Protection, occupational safety and employee health, physical protection, social protection, legal protection, right to organize, job security, etc. includes topics. Two of the most important of these are occupational safety and employee health. Occupational safety aims to prevent unsafe behaviors of employees and/or occupational accidents that may be caused by an unsafe environment. The purpose of employee health is not to harm the health of the employees due to the work they do. In short, the purpose of the protection function is to protect the physical and mental assets of the employees in the workplace environment.

The contribution of the personnel to the company is based on three elements; body, mind and heart power. Motivation is directly related to the effective use of the power of the heart. By means of this factor, companies that are active especially in the service sector make a difference to their competitors in terms of efficiency and quality. Motivation is defined as determination and management of behaviors. Motivation refers to a person's enthusiasm and determination to perform a certain action, with the strength he gets from some internal and external factors. Studies on this subject focus on the forces and motives that move people in business life, the qualities of the factors that push or attract employees to certain behaviors, and how these qualities can be improved. Thanks to motivation techniques and practices, the company and staff gain indirect and direct positive results. Thus, the personnel acquired their virtues in a certain period; knowledge and experience gained from previous jobs; competencies such as problem solving and analytical approach; personality traits such as honesty, dedication, loyalty; uses its social capital effectively. In return for these actions, financial returns such as wages, premiums and incentives from the company; social security service depending on the company's policies and future potential; company's belonging to a group; opportunity to participate in informal group memberships; obtaining respect and status based on the company's image level; education and.

Depending on the opportunities for promotion, individual development opportunities are obtained. Among the benefits to be provided by practices aimed at increasing motivation, corporate commitment/low employee turnover, low recruitment cost, high performance, job satisfaction/employee satisfaction, company image/attractiveness, productivity increase, idea development, more use of employee potential, attracting qualified candidates can be listed.

15.3 Effective Human Resources Strategy in Renewable Energy Companies

Technological developments, industrialization and the increase in the world population increase the demand for energy rapidly. Energy, which is the basic input in production, is a necessary element for increasing the welfare level of societies and is used in almost every field of daily life. In short, energy, which is defined as the ability to do work, can be found in different types such as mechanical (potential and kinetic), heat, electrical, chemical and nuclear, can be transformed from one type to another with appropriate methods and can be classified in different ways (Bhuiyan et al., 2022).

Energy sources; divided into two according to their use and convertibility. According to their use, they are divided into exhaustible (non-renewable) energy sources and inexhaustible (renewable) energy sources. It can be classified as primary and secondary energy sources according to its convertible feature (Xu et al., 2022).

The type of energy that has not been interfered with from the outside and thus has not undergone any change is called primary energy. In general, the main sources are; coal, oil, natural gas, solar, wind, hydraulic, nuclear, biomass and wave (Dinçer et al., 2023). Secondary energy is the type of energy that occurs when the primary energy source is changed by an outside intervention, thus transforming into a different energy type. Exhaustible energy resources refer to energy resources that have a certain reserve level and are predicted to be depleted in the future. These are mainly divided into parameters as coal, natural gas and oil under the heading of fossil origin. Inexhaustible energy source, on the other hand, means renewable energy obtained by natural means, which is open to permanent use and has a long future (Eti et al., 2022). The main types are classified as wind, hydraulic, solar, hydrogen, biomass, geothermal, wave. In addition, since inexhaustible energy resources can be obtained by natural means, there is no need for special production or purchase from foreign countries. However, since renewable energy has the potential to reduce carbon emissions in order not to harm nature, investments in these energy sources are increasing day by day around the world.

The use of renewable energy in the world's electricity production is very important in terms of not harming nature and producing inexhaustible energy with its own natural methods. It is important because it does not harm the environment and provides benefits. The sustainable feature of renewable energies is another factor that increases its importance (Kayacık et al., 2022). Renewable energies affect natural ecology less than fossil energy technologies, as they do not leave polluting waste to the environment. This energy will always exist, since its source is not depleted.

A clean energy source means low or zero carbon and greenhouse emissions. While fossil fuels cause global warming, they emit large amounts of greenhouse gases and carbon dioxide, which are largely responsible for climate change and deterioration of air quality. Fossil fuels contribute to the emission of sulfur into the atmosphere, which causes acid rain. Acid rains can damage buildings (Fang et al., 2021). Solar and wind power are considered environmentally friendly as they do not emit zero toxic gases into the environment. The use of renewable energy significantly reduces the dependence on fossil fuels as an energy source, thus reducing air pollution.

Being a renewable resource, it means that it does not run out for a lifetime and they are not likely to run out (sustainable energy source). Energy sources such as fossil fuels (oil, gas and coal) are considered limited resources and are likely to run out in the future. Renewable energy can significantly reduce developing countries' reliance on fossil fuels. Strong winds, heat from below the earth, sunlight and moving water guarantee a large and stable energy supply to a country for many years.

Renewable energy is a reliable source of energy. Fossil fuel use has risen sharply in the previous few decades. Our over-reliance on these fossil fuels has put our security at risk. Fossil fuels are prone to trade disputes, political instability, rising energy prices and unnecessary wars. These variables affect much more than a nation's energy policies. They can significantly drain a county's economy (Yuan et al., 2021). While many argue that solar and wind power are unreliable, a solid infrastructure puts this argument to rest. If solar and wind power plants are distributed over a large geographic area, there may be little disruption to electricity production because weather disruptions in one place cannot be the same in other places (Haiyun et al., 2021).

Renewable energy makes a real economic contribution to the region because it is a cheaper alternative to most traditional energy sources (Li, Yüksel, & Dinçer, 2022b). Since the inception of renewable energy, new and stable jobs have been added to most world economies. For example, many jobs have already been created in Germany and the UK thanks to their relentless efforts to develop and promote forms of renewable energy. Experts think they will employ thousands of people with ongoing campaigns to adopt renewable energy.

Renewable energy has stabilized global energy prices. Switching to renewable energy sources means stabilizing energy prices around the world. This is because the cost of renewable energy depends on the initial cost of installing renewable energy technologies versus fossil fuels, which increases and decreases due to current inflation and resource availability. Because after the power plant is established, our source is the sun, wind, etc. are unlimited resources. All governments have to do is cover the initial costs (Eti et al., 2023).

In summary, the positive aspects of clean and renewable energy sources can be listed as follow;

- Being clean
- Reducing air pollution
- Reducing water pollution
- Reducing the greenhouse effect
- Reducing nuclear pollution
- Reduction of soil erosion and protection of flora and fauna
- Being renewable (inexhaustible)
- Being local
- Being economical
- Low external (social) costs
- Low fuel costs
- Low security costs
- Low operating costs
- Low cost of disposal of waste
- Low end-of-life dismantling costs
- Having more job fields (employment opportunities)
- Ensuring the country's independence in the energy sector
- Supporting internal and external peace
- Contemporary (contemporary)
- Respecting the rights of present and future generations
- Being ecological
- Supporting social and economic development
- Breaking up fuel monopolies
- Reducing the proliferation risk of nuclear (nuclear) weapons (Carayannis et al., 2022; Li, Yüksel, Dınçer, Mikhaylov, & Barykin, 2022a; Mikhaylov et al., 2022; Yüksel et al., 2022).

As in all sectors, human resources strategies are vital importance in companies operating in the energy sector. Without an effective human resources policy, it is impossible to talk about the success of energy companies.

In the energy sector where dynamics are changing rapidly, energy investments are increasing and many new players are entering, the need for human resources should be met especially by candidates who graduated from engineering, technical high schools and technical high schools. However, considering the dynamism of the sector, new human resources should be trained by experienced experts and supported by vocational and technical training. However, it is very important that the analytical aspect of the human resource to be recruited is strong (Dinçer et al., 2022a, 2022b, 2022c; Dong et al., 2022; Yüksel & Dinçer, 2022; Zhang et al., 2022).

In addition, renewable energy consultancy, renewable energy engineering, wind energy expertise, wind energy technician, carbon sales expertise, environmental and energy law expertise, organic agriculture engineering, ecological tourism consultancy, thermal insulation expertise, environmental engineering, ecological building design, waste water expertise such as "green collar workers" are seen as professions that attract attention and will be demanded in the future.

15.4 Conclusion

Some countries in the world are very rich in renewable energy sources. However, the utilization potential of these resources cannot be evaluated to the extent required. The cycle of continuity of nature and ecological system will continue by minimizing the damage to nature with the use of renewable energy. While leaving a cleaner natural environment and world to the future, individuals and societies will lead a more prosperous life. In order to achieve all these, the economic goals of the state, individuals, businesses and nature (Kafka et al., 2022; Martínez et al., 2022; Mukhtarov et al., 2022; Sun et al., 2022).

They need to act with a total consciousness and ideal. In this direction, a synergistic approach needs to be implemented. Especially renewable energy companies need to determine an effective human resources strategy for themselves. There are some issues that these companies should pay attention to in their recruitment processes. However, it is important for them to cooperate with universities and vocational high schools for new positions.

It should not be forgotten that the feature that businesses will provide the greatest competitive advantage is human resources.

References

Bhuiyan, M. A., Dinçer, H., Yüksel, S., Mikhaylov, A., Danish, M. S. S., Pinter, G., Uyeh, D. D., & Stepanova, D. (2022). Economic indicators and bioenergy supply in developed economies: QROF-DEMATEL and random forest models. *Energy Reports, 8*, 561–570.

Carayannis, E., Kostis, P., Dinçer, H., & Yüksel, S. (2022). Balanced-scorecard-based evaluation of knowledge-oriented competencies of distributed energy investments. *Energies, 15*(21), 8245.

Dinçer, H., Aksoy, T., Yüksel, S., & Hacioglu, U. (2022a). Golden cut-oriented q-rung orthopair fuzzy decision-making approach to evaluation of renewable energy alternatives for microgeneration system investments. *Mathematical Problems in Engineering, 2022*, 2261166.

Dinçer, H., Yüksel, S., & Martínez, L. (2022b). Collaboration enhanced hybrid fuzzy decision-making approach to analyze the renewable energy investment projects. *Energy Reports, 8*, 377–389.

Dinçer, H., Yüksel, S., Mikhaylov, A., Pinter, G., & Shaikh, Z. A. (2022c). Analysis of renewable-friendly smart grid technologies for the distributed energy investment projects using a hybrid picture fuzzy rough decision-making approach. *Energy Reports, 8*, 11466–11477.

Dinçer, H., Yüksel, S., Çağlayan, Ç., Yavuz, D., & Kararoğlu, D. (2023). Can renewable energy investments be a solution to the energy-sourced high inflation problem?. In *Managing inflation and supply chain disruptions in the global economy* (pp. 220–238). IGI Global.

Dong, W., Zhao, G., Yüksel, S., Dinçer, H., & Ubay, G. G. (2022). A novel hybrid decision making approach for the strategic selection of wind energy projects. *Renewable Energy, 185*, 321–337.

Ermiş, A. M., & Güven, M. E. (2022). The role of green energy investments in energy supply security. In *Circular economy and the energy market* (pp. 67–77). Springer.

Eti, S., Dinçer, H., Yüksel, S., & Gökalp, Y. (2022). Analysis of the suitability of the solar panels for hospitals: A new fuzzy decision-making model proposal with the T-spherical TOP-DEMATEL method. *Journal of Intelligent and Fuzzy Systems, Preprint*, 1–13.

Eti, S., Dinçer, H., Gökalp, Y., Yüksel, S., & Kararoğlu, D. (2023). Identifying key issues to handle the inflation problem in the healthcare industry caused by energy prices: An evaluation with decision-making models. *Managing Inflation and Supply Chain Disruptions in the Global Economy*, 162–178.

Fang, S., Zhou, P., Dinçer, H., & Yüksel, S. (2021). Assessment of safety management system on energy investment risk using house of quality based on hybrid stochastic interval-valued intuitionistic fuzzy decision-making approach. *Safety Science, 141*, 105333.

Haiyun, C., Zhixiong, H., Yüksel, S., & Dinçer, H. (2021). Analysis of the innovation strategies for green supply chain management in the energy industry using the QFD-based hybrid interval valued intuitionistic fuzzy decision approach. *Renewable and Sustainable Energy Reviews, 143*, 110844.

Holbrook, R. L., Jr. (2002). Contact points and flash points: Conceptualizing the use of justice mechanisms in the performance appraisal interview. *Human Resource Management Review, 12*(1), 101–123.

Kafka, K. I., Dinçer, H., & Yüksel, S. (2022). Impact-relation map of innovative service development regarding the sustainable growth for emerging markets. *Journal of the Knowledge Economy*, 1–24.

Kayacık, M., Dinçer, H., & Yüksel, S. (2022). Using quantum spherical fuzzy decision support system as a novel sustainability index approach for analyzing industries listed in the stock exchange. *Borsa Istanbul Review, 22*(6), 1145–1157.

Kou, G., Yüksel, S., & Dinçer, H. (2022). Inventive problem-solving map of innovative carbon emission strategies for solar energy-based transportation investment projects. *Applied Energy, 311*, 118680.

Li, J., Yüksel, S., Dınçer, H., Mikhaylov, A., & Barykin, S. E. (2022a). Bipolar q-ROF hybrid decision making model with golden cut for analyzing the levelized cost of renewable energy alternatives. *IEEE Access, 10*, 42507–42517.

Li, W., Yüksel, S., & Dinçer, H. (2022b). Understanding the financial innovation priorities for renewable energy investors via QFD-based picture fuzzy and rough numbers. *Financial Innovation, 8*(1), 1–30.

Martínez, L., Dinçer, H., & Yüksel, S. (2022). A hybrid decision making approach for new service development process of renewable energy investment. *Applied Soft Computing, 133*, 109897.

Mikhaylov, A., Bhatti, I. M., Dinçer, H., & Yüksel, S. (2022). Integrated decision recommendation system using iteration-enhanced collaborative filtering, golden cut bipolar for analyzing the risk-based oil market spillovers. *Computational Economics*, 1–34.

Mukhtarov, S., Yüksel, S., & Dinçer, H. (2022). The impact of financial development on renewable energy consumption: Evidence from Turkey. *Renewable Energy, 187*, 169–176.

Pugh, D. (1991). *Organizational behaviour*. Prentice Hall Interneational (UK) Ltd..

Sun, L., Peng, J., Dinçer, H., & Yüksel, S. (2022). Coalition-oriented strategic selection of renewable energy system alternatives using q-ROF DEMATEL with golden cut. *Energy, 256*, 124606.

Torrinton, D., & Hall, L. (1995). *Personnel management: HRM in action*. Prentice Hall.

Xu, X., Yüksel, S., & Dinçer, H. (2022). An integrated decision-making approach with golden cut and bipolar q-ROFSs to renewable energy storage investments. *International Journal of Fuzzy Systems*, 1–14.

Yuan, G., Xie, F., Dinçer, H., & Yüksel, S. (2021). The theory of inventive problem solving (TRIZ)-based strategic mapping of green nuclear energy investments with spherical fuzzy group decision-making approach. *International Journal of Energy Research, 45*(8), 12284–12300.

Yüksel, S., & Dinçer, H. (2022). Identifying the strategic priorities of nuclear energy investments using hesitant 2-tuple interval-valued Pythagorean fuzzy DEMATEL. *Progress in Nuclear Energy, 145*, 104103.

Yüksel, S., Dinçer, H., Eti, S., & Adalı, Z. (2022). Strategy improvements to minimize the drawbacks of geothermal investments by using spherical fuzzy modelling. *International Journal of Energy Research, 145*, 104103.

Zhang, Y., Zhang, Y., Gong, C., Dinçer, H., & Yüksel, S. (2022). An integrated hesitant 2-tuple Pythagorean fuzzy analysis of QFD-based innovation cost and duration for renewable energy projects. *Energy, 248*, 123561.

Chapter 16
Impact of Green Human Resources Management on Job Satisfaction

Elif Baykal, Ayşe Öykü Yılmaz, and Seray Kayra Koktekin

Keywords Green human resources management · Sustainability · Job satisfaction · Green management practices

16.1 Introduction

Problems such as the wrong and excessive use of limited resources, ever increasing occurrence of unwanted natural events, increasing global warming, as well as climate change, created greater sensitiveness regarding sustainability. Sustainability has been an important issue for everyone and now companies pay great attention to this issue. Businesses are a part of society and cannot be considered separately from environmental problems. In the studies conducted for sustainability, it has been understood that human resources management has an important role in the adoption of a sustainability culture in a company. In order to protect the world and the ecological system, green practices have emerged that will support environmental and sustainable development. One of the prominent approaches for green practices to contribute to sustainability is green human resources management. The word "green" is used in this period to describe almost all environmental problems and practices in almost every sense. The term Green Human Resources Management (GHRM) is used for the Human Resources Management (HRM), one of the most important departments of the companies, to give importance to environmental practices, to identify environmental problems and to produce solutions and contribute to them (Öselmiş, 2020). In order for the company to be successful in environmental sustainability practices, human resources practices must be applied correctly (Kedikli & Uslu, 2017: 69). Green human resources management adopts environmentally friendly human resources policies to support sustainability by reducing the

E. Baykal (✉) · A. Ö. Yılmaz · S. K. Koktekin
The School of Business, İstanbul Medipol University, İstanbul, Turkey
e-mail: elifbaykal@medipol.edu.tr; oyku.yilmaz@std.medipol.edu.tr; kayra.koktekin@std.medipol.edu.tr

H. Dincer, S. Yüksel (eds.), *Economic Development and the Environmental Ecosystem*, Contributions to Economics,
https://doi.org/10.1007/978-3-031-26596-9_16

negative effects of companies that cause environmental pollution (Shaikh, 2010; Uddin, 2015). GHRM is an environmentally friendly strategy and is a method applied in companies to disseminate successive sustainable practices that will increase employee morale, motivation and satisfaction.

16.2 Green Human Resource Management

Green-collar employees and green-collar jobs have started to gain great importance in human resources, with the increasing interest and importance in the environment and sustainability. With the restructuring that started with the importance of this idea, in this period when a great change was experienced, countries, organizations and people also started to change. In the field of human resources management, the "human" that initiated the change has also started green thinking, green transformation and as a result, green human resources management practices. Green Human Resources is a business function that supports creating green projects that can embrace and evaluate the green culture in a company (Aksu & Doğan, 2021). The term GHRM defined by Douglas Renwick as the relationship between human resource management and environmental management and took its place in the literature for the first time in this way.

Green human resources are also a part of corporate social responsibility. In the first studies on green human resources, it was evaluated in the context of sustainability and human resources and evaluated at maximum and minimum level. Green human resource management can be defined as the workforce skills, motivation and contribution to the economic and environmental sustainability of an organization and practices related to this issue (Renwick et al., 2013). At the same time, green human resources management means "an action that promotes green initiatives to increase employee awareness and commitment on environmental sustainability issues". During the recruitment process and selection of candidates, it determines environmentally friendly methods on issues to be determined by human resources management such as training and development, salary, rewards, employee participation, organizing and managing manpower. With the ever-changing environment, companies must develop and implement environmental methods in order to gain a sustainable advantage. However, in order to be successful, the most suitable methods for businesses should be selected. Businesses which do not have human resources management that adopt environmentally friendly actions as a philosophy of life and act accordingly will not be able to have environmentally friendly practices (Öselmiş, 2020). Green human resources management creates a sustainable environment-friendly and advantageous thanks to its employees (Renwick et al., 2008; Deshwal, 2015). Of course, it is necessary to ensure the continuity of green projects by developing projects that include employees who have a good command of these issues and can be productive (Ceyhan & Ada, 2015: 121).

Green human resources management means supporting every employee in sustainable practices and increasing their awareness of sustainability. Green human resources management aims to increase the human resources strategies of companies to use resources more effectively and efficiently (Rezaei-Moghaddam, 2016). In green human resources management, company managers play an important role in making their companies more socially and environmentally sensitive by adopting the concept of corporate social responsibility in all human resources.

Demonstrated the importance of green human resources management to create a green culture by developing human resources management strategies to motivate the sustainable use of the resources that companies have and by determining the strategies that will increase the sensitivity and commitment of employees to the environment. It is also defined as a combination of human resources practices such as recruitment, training, performance appraisal and remuneration that support the achievement of an enterprise's environmental management goals (Teixeira et al., 2012).

Defines green human resources management by using human resources management practices in order to promote the sustainable use of resources that will reinforce the cause of environmental sustainability in general. It covers human resources initiatives to advocate for sustainable practices and increase employee awareness and commitment to sustainability issues. GHMR motivates and empowers employees whose green performance is rewarded and encourages employee engagement by creating an eco-friendly climate (Ansari et al., 2021).

Green human resource management is actually part of a broader corporate social responsibility policy including the implementation of HR policies to promote sustainable use of company resources and support ecology. The aim of green human resources management is to make company employees aware of how their behavior affects the environment by developing ecological sensitivity (Bombiak & Marciniuk-Kluska, 2018). Suggest that GHRM supports specific human resources policies and practices based on three main sustainability topics: environmental, social and economic balance.

Renwick (2013) has categorized the environmental management elements of the human resources perspective. First, green human resource management is about recruiting, selecting, training and developing green talent. In this process, recruitment and employee selection, which are the two important functions of human resources, and training and development functions come to the fore. Second, green human resource management motivates green employees by evaluating and rewarding their green performance. Third is the recognition of green opportunities. You can implement many known employee engagement practices on environmental management. However, in order to offer suggestions in terms of environmental management, it is recommended to create a supportive climate and get the support of the union in order to encourage employees, empower employees, and increase employee engagement.

Rezaei-Moghaddam (2016) divided the formation and aims of green human resources management into three parts in a study they conducted. The first of these purposes is the development of green strategies and practices, the second is the creation and adoption of green thinking and corporate culture, and the third is the establishment of performance evaluation and rewarding and motivation systems in accordance with the green strategies and practices created.

In his study, Mathapati (2013) stated that various human resources practices such as recruitment and selection, performance evaluation, wages and benefits and training in green human resources management are designed to create a workforce that accepts, adopts and supports green management in the organization. The most important goal here is to create the most appropriate human capital to gain competitive advantage with the sustainability of green products or increased eco-efficiency. For this reason, green human resources management can increase the economic performance of companies that have adopted environmental sustainability policies by taking a step forward in the market and providing competitive advantage. Green human resource management can be a useful practice for achieving companies' overall human resource management goals, such as increasing employee motivation and retaining the most valuable employees.

16.3 Transformation of Human Resources Functions into Green Human Resources Functions

Human resources management, providing the management of manpower, which is the most important asset of an organization, constitutes the most important function of management. While implementing green practices, HRM systems, policies and practices will help create a green structure with the participation of all employees (Gjika & Koli, 2019). Adaptation or replacement of human resource management functions to green human resource management is a final for GHRM to ensure that a company complies with green practices and that employees have the correct green performance. Actually, all HRM functions can be made green. Supporting this view Razab et al. (2015) revealed that the environmental awareness of companies is shaped around human resources practices together with company employees and classified these functions under four headings as recruitment and selection, training and development, performance management system, and remuneration and rewarding.

16.4 Job Satisfaction

Vroom (1964) defined job satisfaction as the attitudes and behaviors of the employees towards the duties they undertake in the companies they work for, and also defines the negative behaviors of the employees as job dissatisfaction. Job satisfaction is expressed as the pleasure that the employee feels for the content of the job he is in charge of, and job dissatisfaction as negative feelings about the job conditions or the environment at work (Herzberg, 1965). Defined it as "positive emotions that occur during an individual's evaluation of his/her work or experiences".

Job satisfaction is expressed as all of the feelings and thoughts that a person has in the working environment (Saravani & Abbasi, 2013: 474). It has been accepted that individuals who have positive thoughts about the company or environment they work for are more motivated and productive in their work (Chahal et al., 2013).

Employees' job satisfaction has been the subject of many researches not only in social sciences but also in the field of health. Many people continue their work lovingly and willingly, considering that it is important for their life. On the other hand, the rest of the people see their work life as a necessity and continue to work reluctantly and unhappy (Ali & Anwar, 2021). Job satisfaction shows how much people love their job and do it willingly. Knowing the level of job satisfaction is important for many reasons, and the results of job satisfaction studies affect both employees and the organization. It is believed that for a company to be successful, it will happen when employees are more motivated and feel connected to the company environment and the job provides them with a high level of satisfaction (Paais & Pattiruhu, 2020).

When the literature is examined, it is understood that there are two differences that affect job satisfaction. The first of these is the individual factors that affect job satisfaction. Individual factors were examined under three main headings: gender, age and education level. The second factor affecting job satisfaction is organizational factors. Organizational factors were also examined, including the nature of the job, working conditions, salary and promotion opportunities.

The individual factors affecting job satisfaction are mostly the characteristics of the employees individually. Employees interact with their colleagues in the company. For this reason, while examining the individual factors of job satisfaction, their possible mental and psychological effects are examined.

Studies have shown that women's job satisfaction is more affected by their gender. For example, Dumas and Stanko (2017) argued in their research that women attach more importance to family responsibilities than men and therefore cannot allocate the necessary time for their business life. It has been seen that job satisfaction is affected more by many reasons such as women and different factors than men (Lee et al., 2020). The inequalities between men and women that occur due to such social problems experienced today can cause a change in the feelings of employees about job satisfaction.

Age factor is also one of the individual factors affecting job satisfaction. As people get older, the experience, experience and level of life they gain from life progress (Karakulle, 2020). When the literature is examined, it has been determined that older employees have higher job satisfaction levels than younger employees. Kooij et al. (2011) have shown that for older employees, success and success at work are becoming increasingly important. It is thought that older workers may occupy higher positions in the workplace. It has been observed in studies that older employees who are more senior have higher job satisfaction. Kim and Kang (2017) showed that older employees have longer careers than younger employees, have strong career identities, and show more commitment to their jobs. It can be said that age has an effect on job satisfaction due to the fact that older employees have more experience and experience, while their adaptation to the company and the job is high, while younger employees have less promotion opportunities, lack of experience and high expectations from the organization.

The level of education of individuals also has a significant effect on job satisfaction. It is thought that the employees of the different departments of the companies should have a good education for different levels of expertise and knowledge. It was determined that the employees with a high level of education achieved less job satisfaction (Demir, 2007; Toker, 2007; Öztürk & Güzelsoydan, 2001), in some studies it has been revealed that the higher the education level, the higher the job satisfaction. it is seen that the satisfaction of the people increases (Çolak Alsat, 2016; Baştemur, 2006; Karakulle, 2020). Employees with a high level of education have high expectations from their employers, resulting in lower job satisfaction. There is a linear relationship between companies' meeting these expectations and job satisfaction.

Organizational factors are those that cannot be interfered with by the employees themselves. Administrative, technical and social activities implemented by the organization have an impact on job satisfaction (Karakulle, 2020). When the quality of the job is high, many factors such as encouraging employees to learn new information that will improve themselves, being able to reveal their competencies and competencies, enabling them to take responsibility for their work and produce solutions cause the employee to achieve job satisfaction.

One of the most important factors in increasing the satisfaction of the employees with the work they have done is the wage or salary they get at the end of a job (Özaydın & Özdemir, 2014). Wage is the price provided and paid by the organization as a result of the mental and physical work of the employees in a certain labor and time period (Karakulle, 2020). Going beyond the standards in terms of salary determination for employees and considering merit also creates a positive structure in terms of job satisfaction (Özmen, 2021).

The fact that company employees have employees with high job satisfaction leads to the desired results by many organizations, such as less absenteeism, decrease in personnel turnover rate, increase in quality and productivity, decrease in workforce losses, and increase in organizational commitment (Karakulle, 2020).

16.5 Green Recruitment and Selection

Green recruitment and selection are another function that is among the green human resources management practices that have attracted a lot of attention recently. If a successful green recruitment and selection process is carried out, the following functions can be implemented more easily. The green recruitment process is one of the functions that ensure the continuity of environmental protection and sustainability. The reason for this is that the employees who are recruited or elected to the company know the importance the company attaches to environmental protection and sustainability and apply to the company accordingly. People working in companies that adopt green management should also adopt and support green management.

In order for the green recruitment process to be a green process, the steps to be taken in this process must contribute to sustainability and environmentalism. For example, technology can be used in the recruitment process, thus reducing the company's carbon footprint. Following methods such as online interviews, using e-mails in applications and working online will take important steps such as cost advantage of the company and reduction of environmental waste materials. Green recruitment can be implemented through the integration of sustainability and environmental protection with the business (Acar, 2022).

Recruitment and selection begin with the selection of employees who have a command of green knowledge, environmentalism and sustainability when choosing personnel. When making this choice, companies should choose personnel who are willing to environmentalism and have a command of environmental culture. Employees who apply to companies with green management apply to companies with environmental awareness and high environmental image and reputation. The company has the potential to be actively and properly green, potentially attracting high-level employees as an elite green employer (Renwick et al., 2013). For these reasons, companies should continue this process as a whole when they recruit and select. In other words, company employees should accept the green culture of the company as one of their values, they prefer companies that have similarities between their own values and the values of their institutions (Öselmiş, 2020).

Acar (2022) examined the recruitment and selection process, which is one of the important functions of green human resources management, under three headings, namely green criteria. The first of these is the green awareness of the applicants. He suggest that the first important criterion is having people who have personal characteristics such as green consciousness, conscience and harmony in reaching environmental goals. The second green criterion is the green employer brand and is formed by the company's GHRM practices. This criterion refers to environmental management image and reputation. In other words, having a green image for businesses is an effective method for revealing the potential of green-minded employees and attracting them to the company. The last criterion is the evaluation and selection of employees according to green criteria. While recruiting personnel to the company, they may state that they should have environmental awareness in their job descriptions and in the features that employees should have. In the interviews, they can choose candidates with higher performance by asking questions that those who need to have environmental awareness can know.

Green recruitment can be defined as the process of hiring new competencies who know the concepts of sustainable living, environmentalism and environmental protection, green management and sustainable environment. In green recruitment and selection, company employees are selected based on their ability to understand concepts such as recycling, sustainability, and environmental protection that make the company a greener environment (Deepika & Karpagam, 2016).

There are some advantages and disadvantages that companies gain when hiring or selecting green workers. In his research, Çekirdekoğlu (2019) explained the advantages and disadvantages of adoption of GHRM. According to Çekirdekoğlu, one of the advantages of green recruitment of companies is the decrease in the cost of intermediation, the second, the decrease in paper and transaction costs and the increase in the performance of the interviews with the online interviews. Among the disadvantages, more people applying to interviews online, and more work falling on the human resources staff to evaluate these applications can be counted.

Employees hired with green recruitment are enthusiastic and passionate about their job, willing to be employees of an environmentally friendly and green company. Thanks to the participation of green-minded employees in the company, organizations' sustainability processes and green recruitment and selection for recycling, environmental protection and a cleaner world support the continuity of these issues.

16.6 Green Education and Development

Green education and development, which is one of the functions of green human resources management, is a process that motivates employees to gain more knowledge on issues such as sustainability, environmental skills and green management. Green development practices, on the other hand, is the process by which employees build on their previous education and improve themselves more on these issues (Lok & Chin, 2019). According to green education and development are the factors that are harmful to the environment of company employees. They defined the process of developing ideas on how to eliminate them and protecting the environment, and the development of appropriate knowledge, behavior and skills as the main purpose of the function. Company motivating their employees to take environmental initiatives tends to use green training and development they have an environment (Turan & Sundu, 2021). The green training and development function provides training and development for company employees on issues such as protecting the environment, protecting natural resources, and raising awareness within the company, while helping employees to solve environmental problems (Zoogah, 2011). Thanks to this green training and development of the employees, they get used to the green culture of the company more quickly and enable them to adapt.

It is very important for green human resources management that companies provide green training to their employees and raise their awareness on this issue. With the trainings held after that, company employees have green attitudes and environmentalist behaviors. Yavuz (2020) defined the green education and development function as a continuous training process on sustainability and environmental issues in order to achieve the environmental management goals of companies.

This process causes employees to develop more knowledge, skills and attitudes about green management and environmental management.

The main goal of green education is to develop the attitude of protecting natural resources, recycling and protecting the environment (Öselmiş, 2020). Acar (2022) mentioned in his study that green education and development by companies have two purposes. He mentioned that the first of these purposes is to teach employees about the green targets set by the company, and the second goal is to raise awareness of employees about environmentalism and sustainability.

At the end of the green training, it should be evaluated whether this training is beneficial or not. In this context, company managers should measure the changes in the behavior and attitudes of employees about environmental protection. Employees should know if they want to work in the management of a green company and they should make sure that they fully understand the concept of green management.

16.7 Green Compensation and Reward Management

Company employees are rewarded or remunerated for their performance throughout their employment, using the method of reward and remuneration. The wage management is a way of appreciating the efforts of the employees (Ahmad, 2015). Wage and reward management can be defined as the giving of money or gifts given by managers to motivate them in response to the development and performance of individuals working in companies. This method is the most important method among HR applications that makes the employee and the institution more connected to each other (Acar, 2022). One of the important purposes of the remuneration and rewarding method is to motivate the employees by developing them to specialize even more. In this case, their companies have some gains, for example, by giving such rewards and extra wages to the employee, to retain successful employees and to increase the employee's loyalty to the institution.

Green reward and remuneration method is seen as an important system for companies to be more environmentally friendly and to create a green organizational culture (Yavuz, 2020). The green rewards and remuneration that companies start to implement play an important role in ensuring that employees comply with green practices, improve themselves in this regard, and increase environmental awareness (Ahmad, 2015; Mandago, 2018; Tang et al., 2018). Thanks to green wage management, the green behaviors of the employees can be rewarded with financial support, encouraging employees to participate in environmental initiatives and environmental programs by encouraging them.

Renwick et al. (2013) argued that companies can realize the following practices together with the green wage and reward method: Additional rewards can be given to employees who fulfill or contribute to the realization of the company's environmental goals, develop an intangible environmental management reward system (paid leave, vacation) or return. Awards that support transformation and sustainability can be given. In his research, mentioned that green awards motivate employees more and are busier with their work, increase their loyalty to the company, and contribute more to increasing the reputation of the institution they work for. While rewarding employees with green awards helps to support environmental performance, it also encourages the continuity of environmental programs determined by companies and increases employee motivation (Al-romeedy, 2019).

16.8 Conclusion

In this study, on the contrary to our expectations Green recruitment and selection has come about to be unrelated with job satisfaction of employees. This indicates that adopting environmentally friendly practices during recruitment does not make much sense for candidates after they are hired, and it also shows that hiring environmentally friendly candidates does not create a situation related to job satisfaction for these environmentally friendly candidates. In other words, they may not be aware that they are being hired because it is environmentally friendly or that this factor is effective in their employment. It was also meaningful to expect that Green Training and Education effect job satisfaction of individuals. Thanks to environmentally friendly trainings and programs that increase environmental sensitivity, employees realize how sensitive their organizations are, thus increasing their satisfaction with their organizations. Moreover, in this study, we also revealed positive effect of Green Performance Management on job satisfaction. Employees, whose job designs and performance measurements are shaped to contribute to the environmentally friendly activities of the organization, will be rewarded and honored for their environmentally friendly contributions, and their job satisfaction will be positively affected.

The green thinking of the employees in a company plays a major role in achieving the company's green goals. Green-minded individuals always want to protect the environment and their companies to take part in such projects. When companies move from normal human resources management to green human resources management, they provide various information to their employees. Employees' adoption of company goals enables them to gain a great advantage in the competition between companies. GHRM enables individual organizations to adapt to green management more quickly. Argued in their research that sustainable environmental benefits can be achieved by implementing GHRM practices that include training and development, teamwork of employees, and a clear mindset to embrace the green concept. The fact that green employees feel responsible for the environment and encourage their colleagues to act environmentally friendly supports green management (Cheng et al., 2022). It is stated that green human resources management (GHRM) (Renwick et al., 2013), which is the human resources management that adopts environmentalism, facilitates the work life of employees, which affects their commitment to their companies, their psychological state such as psychological green climate and pro-environmental psychological capital (Cheng et al., 2022). Green human resource management improves employees' organizational-based self-esteem and increases their belief in themselves (Cheng et al., 2022) increasing their motivation and job satisfaction.

In the literature review based on the green human resources practices that form the basis of the research, there were not many studies measuring the effect of green human resources management on job satisfaction. Human resources practices, which are the basis of green human resources management practices, are based on. In the literature review, examined the effect of HRM practices on job satisfaction in public banks in Ethiopia. As a result of this study, he said that there is a positive relationship between human resources practices such as recruitment and selection, training and development, performance evaluation, wages and rewards and job satisfaction. Nawangsari and Sutawidjaya (2018) stated in their study that training & development, compensation & reward and performance evaluation have a direct and positive result on job satisfaction. Mira et al. (2019), in the study in which human resource management practices measure the job satisfaction and employee performance of employees, it has been seen that training and development, rewarding, recruitment and selection have a direct positive effect on employee job satisfaction and performance. In another research, it has been predicted that HRM applications will increase organizational trust and job satisfaction, and with this, the business will be more successful. As a result of the necessary analyzes, this hypothesis was supported and it was concluded that HRM practices had a positive effect on job satisfaction (Yılmaz & Karahan, 2011). In the research conducted to measure the effect of wage and training practices on job satisfaction in human resources management, it was concluded that the training given to company employees increased their job satisfaction. In the same study, it was understood that the increase in wages and rewards that employees receive in return for their efforts positively affects their job satisfaction (Yılmaz, 2018). In Pinzone et al.'s (2019) study conducted in the health sector in Italy, the effects of pro-environmental behaviors caused by green education on job satisfaction were investigated. As a result of the research, it was concluded that green education directly affects the job satisfaction of employees positively. Our study is parallel with the findings of the above mentioned studies in the point that it confirmed GHRM practices on job satisfaction. This study is unique in the point that it is the first study revealing this relationship in Turkish context.

References

Acar, Ö. G. D. S. (2022). *Örgütlerde Yeşil İnsan Kaynaklari Yönetiminin Önemi.*

Ahmad, S. (2015). Green human resource management: Policies and practices. *Cogent Business & Management, 2*(1), 1–13.

Aksu, B. Ç., & Doğan, A. (2021). Çevresel Sürdürülebilirlik ve İnsan Kaynakları Yönetimi Fonksiyonlarının Yeşil İKY Bağlamında Değerlendirilmesi. *Aksaray Üniversitesi İktisadi ve İdari Bilimler Fakültesi Dergisi, 13*(3), 137–148.

Ali, B. J., & Anwar, G. (2021). An empirical study of employees' motivation and its influence job satisfaction. *International Journal of Engineering, Business and Management, 5*(2), 21–30.

Al-Romeedy, B. S. (2019). Green human resource management in Egyptian travel agencies: Constraints of implementation and requirements for success. *Journal of Human Resources in Hospıtalıty & Tourısm, 18*(4), 529–548.

Ansari, N. Y., Farrukh, M., & Raza, A. (2021). Green human resource management and employees pro-environmental behaviours: Examining the underlying mechanism. *Corporate Social Responsibility and Environmental Management, 28*(1), 229–238.

Baştemur, Y. (2006). *İş Tatmini İle Yaşam Tatmini Arasındaki İlişkiler: Kayseri Emniyet Müdürlüğü'nde Bir Araştırma*. Erciyes Üniversitesi Sosyal Bilimler Enstitüsü, Yüksek Lisans Tezi.

Bombiak, E., & Marciniuk-Kluska, A. (2018). Green human resource management as a tool for the sustainable development of enterprises: Polish young company experience. *Sustainability, 10*(6), 1739.

Çekirdekoğlu, Y. (2019). *Yeşil insan kaynakları yönetimi uygulamalarının kurumsal sosyal sorumluluktaki rolü*. Master dissertation, Yıldız Teknik Üniversitesi, SBE, İşletme Ana Bilim Dalı, İnsan Kaynakları Yönetimi Programı, İstanbul.

Ceyhan, S., & Ada, S. (2015). İşletme Fonksiyonları Açısından Çevreye Duyarlı İşletmecilik. *Uluslararası Yönetim İktisat ve İşletme Dergisi, 1*(26), 115–137.

Chahal, A., Chahal, S., Chowdhary, B., & Chahal, J. (2013). Job satisfaction among bank employees: An analysis of the contributing variables towards job satisfaction. *International Journal of Scientific & Technology Research, 2*(8), 11–20.

Cheng, Y., Liu, H., Yuan, Y., Zhang, Z., & Zhao, J. (2022). What makes employees green advocates? Exploring the effects of green human resource management. *International Journal of Environmental Research and Public Health, 19*(3), 1807.

Çolak Alsat, O. (2016). *Çalışan Motivasyonunu Etkileyen Faktörlerin İş Tatminine Etkisinin Belirlenmesine Yönelik Bir Uygulama*. Selçuk Üniversitesi Sosyal Bilimler Enstitüsü, Yayımlanmamış Doktora Tezi.

Deepika, R., & Karpagam, V. (2016). A study on green HRM practices in an organisation. *International Journal of Applied Research, 2*(8), 426–429.

Demir, N. (2007). *Örgüt Kültürü ve İş Tatmini*. Türkmen Kitabevi.

Deshwal, P. (2015). Green HRM: An organizational strategy of greening people. *International Journal of Applied Research, 1*(13), 176–181.

Dumas, T. L., & Stanko, T. L. (2017). Married with children: How family role identification shapes leadership behaviors at work. *Personnel Psychology, 70*, 597–633.

Girma, S. (2016). The relationship between leadership style, job satisfaction and culture of the organization. *International Journal of Applied Research, 2*(4), 35–45.

Gjika, I., & Koli, Z. (2019). Policies and practices of green human resource management. *Journal of International Cooperation and Development, 2*(2), 60–60.

Herzberg, F. (1965). The motivation to work among Finnish supervisors. *Personnel Psychology, 18*(4), 393–402.

Karakulle, İ. (2020). *İŞ MEMNUNİYETİ VE KARİYER TATMİNİ: BANKA ÇALIŞANLARI ÜZERİNE BİR UYGULAMA*. Ulusal Tez Merkezi.

Kedikli, E., & Uslu, Y. D. (2017). Sürdürülebilirlik Kapsamında Yeşil İnsan Kaynakları Yönetimine Genel Bir Bakış. *Third Sector Social Economic Review, 52*(3), 66–81.

Keser, A. (2019). *Çalışma Yaşamında Motivasyon*. Umuttepe Yayınları.

Kim, N., & Kang, S. W. (2017). Older and more engaged: The mediating role of age-linked resources on work engagement. *Human Resource Management, 56*(5), 731–746.

Kooij, D. T., De Lange, A. H., Jansen, P. G., Kanfer, R., & Dikkers, J. S. (2011). Age and work-related motives: Results of a meta-analysis. *Journal of Organizational Behavior, 32*(2), 197–225.

Lee, H. W., Robertson, P. J., & Kim, K. (2020). Determinants of job satisfaction among US federal employees: An investigation of racial and gender differences. *Public Personnel Management, 49*(3), 336–366.

Lok, S. Y. P., & Chin, T. L. (2019). Linking green HRM practices and employee sustainability engagement. *Global Business and Management Research: An International Journal, 11*(2), 151–156.

Mandago, R. J. (2018). Influence of green reward and compensation practice on environmental sustainability in selected service based state corporations in Kenya. *European Journal of Business and Strategic Management, 3*(6), 1–12.

Mathapati, C. M. (2013). Green HRM: A strategic facet. *Tactful Management Research Journal, 2*(2), 1–6.

Mira, M., Choong, Y., & Thim, C. (2019). The effect of HRM practices and employees' job satisfaction on employee performance. *Management Science Letters, 9*(6), 771–786.

Nawangsari, L. C., & Sutawidjaya, A. H. (2018, December). The impact of human resources practices affecting organization citizenship behaviour with mediating job satisfaction in university. In *3rd annual international seminar on transformative education and educational leadership (AISTEEL 2018)* (Vol. 200, pp. 291–297). Atlantis Press.

Öselmiş, M. (2020). *Yeşil İnsan Kaynaklari Yönetimi Uygulamalari; Literatür Taramasi Ve Bir Ölçek Uyarlama Çalişmasi.* Master's thesis, Aydin Adnan Menderes Üniversitesi Sosyal Bilimler Enstitüsü.

Özaydın, M. M., & Özdemir, Ö. (2014). Çalışanların Bireysel Özelliklerinin İş Tatmini Üzerindeki Etkileri: Bir Kamu Bankası Örneği. *İşletme Araştırmaları Dergisi, 6*(1), 251–281.

Özmen, B. (2021). *İş Memnuniyeti Ve Kariyer Tatmini: Banka Çalışanları Üzerine Bir Uygulama*, Van, Ulusal Tez Merkezi.

Öztürk, A., & Güzelsoydan, Y. S. (2001). Büyük Mağazalarda Çalışan Personelin İş Doyumu Üzerine Çukurova Bölgesinde Bir Araştırma. *Erzurum: Atatürk Üniversitesi İktisadi ve idari Bilimler Dergisi, 15*(1–2), 334.

Paais, M., & Pattiruhu, J. R. (2020). Effect of motivation, leadership, and organizational culture on satisfaction and employee performance. *The Journal of Asian Finance, Economics, and Business, 7*(8), 577–588.

Pinzone, M., Guerci, M., Lettieri, E., & Huisingh, D. (2019). Effects of 'green' training on pro-environmental behaviors and job satisfaction: Evidence from the Italian healthcare sector. *Journal of Cleaner Production, 226*, 221–232.

Razab, M. F., Udin, Z. M., & Osman, W. N. (2015). Understanding the role of GHRM towards environmental performance. *Journal of Global Business and Social Entrepreneurship (GBSE), 1*(2), 118–125.

Renwick, D., Redman, T., & Maguire, S. (2008). Green HRM: A review, process model, and research agenda. *University of Sheffield Management School Discussion Paper, 1*, 1–46.

Renwick, D., Redman, T., & ve Maguire S. (2013). Green human resource management: A review and research agenda. *International Journal of Management Reviews, 15*, 1–14.

Rezaei-Moghaddam, K. (2016). Green management of human resources in organizations: An approach to the sustainable environmental management. *Journal of Agricultural Technology, 12*(3), 509–522.

Saravani, S. R., & Abbasi, B. (2013). Investigating the influence of job rotation on performance by considering skill variation and job satisfaction of bank employees. *Tehnicki Vjesnik, 20*(3), 473–478.

Shaikh, M. W. (2010). Green HRM, a requirement of 21st century. *National Monthly Refereed Journal of Research in Commerce & Management, 1*(10).

Tang, G., Chen, Y., Jiang, Y., Paillé, P., & Jia, J. (2018). Green human resource management practices: Scale development and validity. *Asia Pacific Journal of Human Resources, 56*(1), 31–55.

Teixeira, A. A., Jabbour, C. J., & Jabbour, A. B. (2012). Relationship between green management and environmental training in companies located in Brazil: A theoretical framework and case studies. *International Journal of Production Economics, 140*, 318–329.

Toker, B. (2007). Demografik Değişkenlerin İş Tatminine Etkileri, İzmir'deki Beş ve Dört Yıldızlı Otellere Yönelik Bir Uygulama. *Doğuş Üniversitesi Dergisi, 8*(1), 92–107.

Turan, İ., & Sundu, M. (2021). Yeşil insan kaynakları yönetimi ölçeği'ni Türkçeye uyarlama çalışması. *Elektronik Sosyal Bilimler Dergisi, 20*(78), 731–744.

Uddin, M. M. (2015). Green HRM: Goal attainment through environmental sustainability. *The Journal of Nepalese Business Studies*, (9).

Vroom, V. H. (1964). *Work and motivation*. Wiley.

Yavuz, N. (2020). Yeşil insan kaynakları yönetimi ve yeşil iş yetkinliklerinin içerik analizi yöntemi ile değerlendirilmesi. *İşletme Araştırmaları Dergisi, 12*(3), 2669–2681.

Yılmaz, R. (2018). *İnsan Kaynakları Yönetiminde Ücret Ve Eğitim Uygulamalarının Çalışanların İş Tatmini Üzerine Etkisi Ve Bir Araştırma*. Ulusal Tez Merkezi.

Yılmaz, H., & Karahan, A. (2011). İnsan kaynakları yönetimi uygulamalarının örgütsel güven ve iş tatmini üzerindeki etkilerinin araştırılması: Afyonkarahisar'da bir araştırma. *ISGUC The Journal of Industrial Relations and Human Resources, 13*(3), 95–118.

Zoogah, D. B. (2011). The dynamics of green HRM behaviors: A cognitive social information processing approach. *German Journal of Human Resource Management, 25*(2), 117–139.

Chapter 17
Defining Reverse and Green Supplier Selection Criteria with a Strategic Management Approach

Gonca Reyhan Akkartal and Filiz Mızrak

Keywords Reverse logistics · Supply chain management · Strategic management

17.1 Introduction

With the emergence of the industrial revolution in the 1800s, the industrialization process showed a great increase. This development and change process has brought many important problems, and the environmental problems that have emerged over time and the depletion of natural resources have forced businesses and managers to consider environmental factors while determining their management styles. The preference for environmentally friendly products has made supply chains environmentally sensitive. Environmental inputs such as reducing the use of natural resources, using environmentally friendly raw materials, eliminating the resulting wastes without harming the environment, attaching importance to remanufacturing and recycling processes, and making the best network design in logistics activities have revealed the concept of green supply chain (Rodrigue et al., 2017).

Green supply chain management is generally defined as planning, organizing, executing, and controlling the activities of supply chain members who act in accordance with environmental standards or care about their environmental performance. The green supplier selection approach, on the other hand, envisages monitoring suppliers that develop environmentally friendly product and service strategies, relying on environmental performance, and cooperating only with green suppliers that meet environmental standards. In this respect, companies require to improve some strategies to select suppliers which attach importance to reverse and green activities (Wang et al., 2020).

Green supplier selection is a strategy that improves the performance of the supply chain. Choosing the right supplier and ensuring its sustainability helps reduce costs

G. R. Akkartal (✉) · F. Mızrak
The School of Business, İstanbul Medipol University, İstanbul, Turkey
e-mail: gonca.akkartal@medipol.edu.tr; fmizrak@medipol.edu.tr

H. Dincer, S. Yüksel (eds.), *Economic Development and the Environmental Ecosystem*, Contributions to Economics,
https://doi.org/10.1007/978-3-031-26596-9_17

and remain competitive by meeting the expectations of stakeholders in the supply chain efficiently. Another aim here is to increase ecological efficiency, increase market share and financial capacity by minimizing environmental negative effects. For the environmental benefit, remanufacturing preserves raw materials and energy for the future and reduces carbon emissions (Fang et al., 2021; Kayacık et al., 2022; Eti et al., 2022; Dinçer et al., 2023). From the economic and social point of view, remanufacturing create jobs, reduces cost, and increase the company's reputation (Sarkar & Bhuniya, 2022).

In addition to the green management approach, the contribution of reverse logistics to recycling is important in terms of environmental sustainability. Reverse logistics is the reorganization of supply chain activities to use, recycle, replace, reuse, or dispose of resources effectively. As a result of ensuring efficiency in reverse logistics application, customer satisfaction is achieved by increasing the trust of customers in businesses. The purchasing costs of the business decrease and its profitability increases. Producers gain economic advantage as reverse logistics will reduce the costs of obtaining new products by reprocessing the surplus stock products that are idle and cannot be sold, making them usable and presenting them to the market (De Oliveira et al., 2021).

In this context, the purpose of this study is to reveal the criteria that should be considered when choosing reverse and green suppliers by benefiting from the current literature and to shed light on the strategies that companies should develop when choosing suppliers. In the first part of the study after the introduction, detailed definition of green and reverse logistics activities has been made. Furthermore, the criteria set has been formed benefiting from the current literature and in the conclusion part, this criteria set has been summarized to guide the companies which aim to select suppliers paying attention to environment.

17.2 Conceptual Framework

Climate change, reduction of biodiversity, pollution of air, water, soil and resource scarcity are among the most important environmental problems of the twenty-first century. In order to overcome ecological problems, it is necessary to develop environmental awareness in all behaviors from the individual level to the business and government level. Although environmental awareness has increased at all levels of society in recent years, the perception in the business world has been against the environment in the relationship between the environment and profitability. However, with the increasing concerns about pollution in the 1960s, business managers realized that it was necessary to pay more attention to the natural environment as an externality of production. Paying attention to these environmental issues is seen as an opportunity in the growth and development of businesses as it enables to differentiate the business in the mind of the consumer or to innovate in completely new ways (Agyabeng-Mensah et al., 2020).

As globalization increasingly integrates countries and societies, the environment has been exposed to negative externalities that threaten the supply of natural resources. Increasing awareness of environmental issues that threaten economic sustainability has made the public more sensitive to purchasing behavior and consumption activities. Realizing that they have a negative impact on the environment, consumers have become worried about their daily habits. Consumers believe in the importance of green sensitivity for future generations to lead a better and healthier life and shape their purchasing behavior with this perspective (Li et al., 2021).

Increasing pressures with globalization have prompted businesses to improve their environmental performance. For this reason, businesses have become concerned for the environment for the last 20 years. The increase in environmental concern has become an increasingly part of the general corporate culture, and this has caused businesses to reconsider their strategies. Pressures for environmental protection are not only caused by legal obligations, but also consumers put pressure on businesses. In response to this pressure, the green logistics approach emerged in the 1990s, which went beyond the standard logistics understanding and brought a new perspective to logistics, delivering products and services to consumers in an efficient, effective, and fast manner with the perspective of environmental protection. Green logistics management plays an important role in addressing environmental concerns, as environmental impacts occur at all stages of a product's life cycle (Wang et al., 2018).

Green logistics aims to create sustainable business value by balancing economic and environmental efficiency. In other words, it means integrating environmental thinking throughout the entire life cycle of the product. Benefits of a business from green logistics is expressed as a reduction in carbon dioxide emissions, significant cost savings, increasing supply chain optimization, and increased operating performance. Green logistics management, which is a new trend in logistics management, also emphasizes long-term interests that reflect the green image of institutions and carry multi-faceted concerns for the environment. From this point of view, businesses have tried to develop their strategies in this direction by switching from a human-centered understanding to environment-centered understanding, with the thought that the negative effects of their activities on the environment will decrease (Yingfei et al., 2022).

In the performance measurements of enterprises, environmental effects have been started to be evaluated along with financial performance. The increasing importance of corporate social responsibility has led businesses to leave their negative environmental impacts to positive ones. In addition to these, the regulations implemented on a global scale also force businesses to act in line with their sustainability goals. With these developments, within the scope of reviewing the processes in the enterprises, the logistics activities have been designed in a way that will ensure the recycling of waste materials (Cricelli et al., 2021).

When the definitions in the literature are examined, it is seen that the common aspects are the regulation of the flow of used products to the original manufacturer. The emergence of reverse logistics has an important place in terms of sending products and materials back to production through recycling. Turning many used products into a new product by processing is extremely important in terms of sustainability. Reverse logistics enables businesses to work more effectively by reprocessing waste. Businesses using reverse logistics applications in sectors where competition is high increase their profit margins thanks to the low-cost advantage. To protect the environment, great attention has been paid to re-evaluation, or in other words, recycling and waste management in recent years, and serious measures have been taken in this regard. In this way, the wastes were eliminated, and the way was opened for the processing and reuse of the wastes (Govindan & Gholizadeh, 2021).

As a result of ensuring efficiency in reverse logistics application, customer satisfaction is achieved by increasing the trust of customers in businesses. The purchasing costs of the business decrease and its profitability increases. Producers gain economic advantage as reverse logistics will reduce the costs of obtaining new products by reprocessing the surplus stock products that are idle and cannot be sold, making them usable and presenting them to the market. With the establishment of recycling enterprises, glass, plastic, paper, etc. collected from the consumer by reintroducing the products to the economy, a resource is created to produce raw materials and a strong production ring is created. Reverse logistics is not limited to these products, but is used in sectors where automotive, chemistry, medicine, steel, electronic goods are produced (Garai & Sarkar, 2022).

The way businesses work, the rapid technological changes experienced, and the new marketing and consumption understanding formed by the effect of globalizing markets have changed. As such, it has become difficult for businesses to survive, and it has become necessary for all actors in the flow from suppliers to end customers to act jointly. This requirement has led to the emergence of the supply chain structure. Therefore, businesses that can produce output with the least cost under competitive conditions and that can also provide this output in a quality and time that meet the expectations of the customers gain an important competitive advantage (Jauhar et al., 2021).

Recovery and reuse of products reduces negative impacts on the environment, mainly by reducing waste disposal, use of raw materials, emissions such as transportation and distribution. In addition, businesses can gain value from end-of-life products by reusing components, recycling materials, or recovering energy through disposal (Martínez et al., 2022; Sun et al., 2022a, b; Kafka et al., 2022; Mukhtarov et al., 2022). Finally, reverse logistics applications can reduce customer risk and increase customer value when purchasing a product. However, the success of reverse logistics implementation requires coordination of the forward and reverse flows of both material and information. The reverse flow of products entering the supply chain affects the dynamics of supply chain members' inventories. This affects the dynamics of ordering to suppliers and thus the performance of the entire supply chain in terms of increased order and inventory variance (Fu et al., 2021).

Economic Reasons: Businesses that want to increase their profitability can achieve this by reducing their use of new raw materials through reverse logistics activities. While adding value to the products with recycling, they can provide customer satisfaction with a return or service guarantee. The protection of the market is ensured by regulating customer-supplier relations with applicable laws (Xu et al., 2021).

Marketing Reasons: Businesses that use the concept of green and reverse logistics together try to create a conscious society in terms of recycling of product packaging, product consumption and collection of product deposits with environmental and social responsibility campaigns. Today, businesses that evaluate the returned products, pay back the cost of the defective product to the customer, develop a good collateral policy and provide a good after-sales service have begun to dominate the markets more (Yang, 2022).

Legal Reasons: Laws protecting consumer rights oblige businesses to take back defective products and collect objectionable products. In addition, these costs are undertaken by the enterprises themselves. With the sanctions brought by green laws, businesses are compelled to reduce the environmental impact of packaging and waste. While businesses accept the return of their used products, they also perform reverse logistics activities to protect the information about the special components of the product and the intellectual property rights of the product (Roudbari et al., 2021).

Reverse and green purchasing benefits businesses in many ways. It is possible to classify these benefits under four main headings: financial benefits, managerial benefits, environmental benefits, and social benefits (Konys, 2019).

Green purchasing can benefit all organizations. It reduces costs and increases productivity by enabling more efficient management of inputs, outputs, and materials. By reducing total expenses, it increases profitability and improves equity. Organizations that want to exist in the future must carefully manage their financial performance and purchasing decisions. The financial benefits would be much greater if they could add a product lifecycle approach to their total cost ownership process (Qu et al., 2020).

Since the materials and processes to be used to produce green products require less resource use, it will be ensured that the use of materials and resources is reduced. Considering the product life cycle, the cost reduction will not only be limited to the use of materials and resources, but also the costs of waste disposal and environmental, occupational health and safety will be reduced. With the green purchasing preference, both the amount of material to be used during production and the use of energy and water to be used for production will decrease (Xu et al., 2022; Bhuiyan et al., 2022; Kou et al., 2022; Ermiş & Güven, 2022). With the purchase of environmentally friendly materials and production tools, material costs, energy consumption and waste costs will be reduced (Haeri & Rezaei, 2019).

By purchasing green materials, a business can greatly reduce its waste costs. In a process that will involve suppliers, the manufacturer can work to reduce packaging waste, thus reducing both costs and waste. Green products generally last longer, and because their lifespan is longer, waste disposal costs are also reduced in this perspective. In addition, green products reduce costs as they use resources more efficiently while performing their functions (Gao et al., 2020).

Since there will be no need for special teams and equipment for the use and storage of environmentally friendly products, a manufacturer who purchases environmentally friendly materials will also reduce occupational health and safety costs. Green purchasing also reduces operating, maintenance, and replacement costs. With the efficient use of energy, it is possible to achieve significant cost improvements. The green materials and process purchases of businesses also enable some costs to improve in the long run (Eti et al., 2023; Li et al., 2022a, b; Haiyun et al., 2021; Yuan et al., 2021). Storage and disposal costs can be reduced by purchasing green materials. Since special precautions will not be required during the storage and use of environmentally friendly products, it will not bring additional occupational health and safety costs (Rouyendegh et al., 2020).

Green purchasing is an important indicator for an organization's stakeholders. It demonstrates the firm's commitment to the results of its activities and the importance it attaches to occupational health and safety issues. Sensitivity on these issues will have a positive impact on the public and will facilitate compliance with the legal regulations of the state. Thanks to public and government support, the company will be able to strengthen its image and gain financial benefits from this situation (Abdullah et al., 2019).

Reverse and green purchasing activities help a business improve its management systems and processes. It guides all processes, from how to integrate policies into business processes, to how to spread this awareness among their employees. Businesses define their goals and values and share them with the public. Green purchasing activities play an important role in realizing these goals and values that they have determined. Recently, many businesses revealed their social, ethical, and environmental values, corporate social responsibility principles they have determined and share this with all their stakeholders. As a result of harmonizing the defined values and goals with business processes, stakeholder support will increase, and the trust of customers and the public will be gained (Ecer, 2020).

Businesses always want to reduce their business risks. The green purchasing approach provides advantages to businesses in this sense. Evaluating environmental, social, and ethical dimensions in business processes will be beneficial in terms of reducing risks. Proactive approaches in management help reduce risks. Manufacturers also want to manage the risks that may arise from their suppliers. The environmental impacts of the materials and services to be purchased can be brought under control with the green purchasing policies and procedures that will be established to serve this purpose (Chen et al., 2019).

Green purchasing has many environmental benefits. With the effective use of resources, it is possible to protect natural resources that are approaching to depletion rapidly. Green products and services cause less pollution and as a result are beneficial in reducing emissions that cause global warming. It is possible to reduce the waste generated because of the production and use of the product, with improvements to be made in the production processes. Moreover, reducing waste in this way will not only be beneficial for the environment, but also less energy and materials will be used for the disposal of reduced waste (Wei et al., 2021).

When deciding on the materials to be used in the design phase of the products, the option of using recycled materials should also be taken into consideration. Likewise, in the design process, care should be taken to ensure that the product is recyclable or reusable after completing its life. Considering all these suggestions, it will be possible to reduce waste by purchasing materials and technologies (Yazdani et al., 2019).

Equivalent purchasing has a direct impact on reducing resource use as it supports the purchase of recycled and reusable materials. Especially in the decision to purchase paper and plastic products, choosing recyclable and reusable materials will provide both environmental and economic benefits. The choice of manufacturers to purchase more environmentally friendly materials has a direct impact on the amount of greenhouse gas emissions that will be released during production. It is possible to reduce greenhouse gas emissions by purchasing more environmentally friendly materials (Tirkolaee et al., 2021).

Green products benefit all players in the supply chain, from the manufacturer to the supplier, from the customer to the public. It supports the protection of the environment and human health, ensures the occupational health and safety of the employees, and provides a competitive advantage for the manufacturer (Duan et al., 2019).

Supplier selection is to choose the most optimal one among more than one criterion for companies. In this way, it will provide many advantages for the company, especially in terms of finance. In addition, with the increasing importance of environmental issues in recent years, supplier selection with green and reverse applications is also gaining importance. Among the most important reasons for this are the benefits it provides to the environment and human health. Moreover, companies that want to have a competitive advantage in global economies have begun to care more about supplier selection (Zhang & Cui, 2019).

Today, not only consumers but also governments have begun to worry about environmental sustainability. The most important indicator of this is the symposiums and congresses implemented by the states on this issue. However, to prevent environmental pollution, protect natural resources and ensure environmental sustainability, supply chain processes need to be started from the very beginning. In this respect, choosing a green supplier means working with companies that have all these features (Ma et al., 2020).

The increase in consumers' awareness of environmental sustainability has led to the need for a more circular supply chain structure. In addition, the need for green supplier selection has increased because of fines paid by companies due to environmental issues. Furthermore, the environmental management approach, which includes many logistics activities such as green purchasing, production, and green marketing, brings the obligation to work with a green supplier from the beginning of the process (Deshmukh & Sunnapwar, 2019).

There are many companies in the world that can be shown as an example of green practices. One of the most important of these is undoubtedly Walmart. In 1989, Walmart took some green practice decisions to address the growing environmental concerns of consumers. In those years, the company succeeded in convincing its suppliers to provide environmentally soluble, that is, recyclable products. Along with all these, the company started to sell nearly 300 green products at green spots. In addition, the company began to display these products (Maamoun, 2020).

Supplier selection begins with the identification of needs. The need is usually determined by the manufacturers' R&D departments. After this stage, the task of the buyers is to identify potential sources of supply and to communicate with them. In the selection to be made among the supplier candidates who can meet the necessary conditions for the material sought, methods such as bargaining or tender can be used (Konys, 2019).

The flow in the process of determining the supplier is as follows (Konys, 2019).

- Determination of needs
- Determination of selection criteria
- Tender
- Evaluation
- Vote
- Performance evaluation

The process in green supplier selection works similarly, but the most important change is seen in the determination of selection criteria and performance evaluation steps. The supplier selection criteria in traditional purchasing can be listed as follows (Haeri & Rezaei, 2019).

- Unit price
- Ability to meet demands on time
- Meeting the quality expectation
- Honest communication
- Industrial knowledge and experience
- Flexibility, speed of response to sudden demands
- Financial situation
- Compliance with ethical standards
- References
- Size of the supplier
- Cultural harmony between the manufacturer and the supplier

The effect of increasing environmental awareness on the supplier selection and evaluation processes of manufacturers has been inevitable. Especially in the last 20 years, it is seen that there are many research and publications on environmental approaches. Many new environmental criteria have been added to the traditional supplier selection criteria and green purchasing/green supplier selection issues have been studied by many researchers and scientists. After the latest literature review, below criteria have been found to be among the most important ones of the reverse and green supplier selection criteria (Masoomi et al., 2022).

- Adding environmentally friendly supply chain activities to business policies,
- Preparing strategic management plans,
- Proving that they act with environmental concerns by preparing sustainability reports,
- Revise the organizational structures with a green perspective,

- Having ISO 9001 Quality Management System and ISO 14001 Environmental Management System,
- Minimizing the carbon footprint by developing environmentally friendly operations,
- Using environmentally friendly fuel vehicles (LPG, CNG, etc.),
- Using systems with low greenhouse gas emissions in transportation and distribution systems,
- Reducing carbon emissions by using intermodal transportation systems,
- Adding electric vehicles with zero carbon emission during transportation to the fleet,
- Reducing energy consumption in warehouses with automatic separation systems (Dong et al., 2022; Dinçer et al., 2022a–c; Zhang et al., 2022; Yüksel & Dinçer, 2022),
- Instantly measuring the electricity in the company with automatic meter reading systems and taking measures for saving,
- Keeping the packaging material used during product packaging as little as possible,
- Paying attention to the high recyclability rate in the selection of packaging materials,
- Recycling the product with environmentally friendly methods,
- Ensuring that waste motor oils are collected and disposed of without harming the environment,
- Reducing the noise pollution in the production and distribution stages,
- Raising awareness of the personnel and customers working within the company about environmental sensitivities.

Many businesses consider factors such as green product, pollution control and green packaging in supplier evaluation. A business that practices green purchasing can integrate environmental standards into purchasing policies, which are necessary for supplier selection, evaluation, and development of relations with suppliers. Environmental cooperation with suppliers, commitment of top management and consumer pressure positively affect the green purchasing of the enterprise. To develop high quality and environmentally friendly products, businesses work closely with their suppliers to recognize risks early and share risks with suppliers, thus achieving cost savings (Huang et al., 2022).

Cost, which is one of the most important criteria in the supplier selection process, is not the only factor to be considered. Green sourcing is environmental purchasing that consists of activities that include reuse, reduction, and recycling of materials in the purchasing processes. Green sourcing, which refers to purchasing products with recycled ingredients, is a start-up strategy with proven success. When faced with a competitive choice, materials that have less adverse effects on human health and the environment should be chosen. When comparing the choices, many factors such as means of distribution, whether the resources used are renewable or not, the cleanliness of the production processes, the energy used in production, the amount and type of resources are taken into consideration (Carayannis et al., 2022; Li et al., 2022a, b; Yüksel et al., 2022; Mikhaylov et al., 2022; Verma et al., 2022).

17.3 Conclusion

Establishing sustainable relations with the right suppliers has become more important than ever in today's world where there is intense competition among manufacturers. In this direction, manufacturers had to consider many criteria in supplier selection. These criteria can vary depending on the working areas of the manufacturers, the characteristics of the product they produce, the production conditions, the legal regulations in the location where they produce, the legal regulations in the sales locations, brand images and many other parameters (Asgharnezhad & Darestani, 2022).

Green purchasing requires mastering the raw material of a product, where it comes from, who produced it, and how the final product will be disposed of. To reduce the environmental impact of a product, it is possible to make improvements such as reducing resources used in production, designing environmentally friendly production processes, replacing packaging materials and transportation methods with more environmentally friendly ones, and reuse (Wang et al., 2022).

One of the most important points in the supplier selection problem is to determine the appropriate supplier selection criteria for the problem. The first step in the traditional supplier selection process is to determine the need and the working criteria according to this need. Suppliers that meet these criteria are included in the tender under equal conditions and the appropriate supplier is selected because of the evaluation. The main criteria considered in selecting the appropriate supplier are unit price, meeting demands on time, meeting quality expectations, honest communication, industrial knowledge and experience, flexibility, speed of response to sudden demands, financial situation, compliance with ethical standards, references, size of the supplier and cultural harmony between the manufacturer and the supplier. Necessary conditions for green supplier selection include some environmental conditions as well as the criteria listed above.

In this study, green purchasing and green supplier selection issues are examined in detail and green supplier selection criteria are proposed by making use of many articles written on these issues. The most important of these criteria can be summarized as follows.

- Waste management
- Certification
- Reverse logistics
- Compliance with legal regulations
- Environmental management programs

The most important result of the study is that purchasing decisions are no longer only focused on unit price, and that the green perceptions and competencies of the suppliers are also effective in the purchasing decision. This result shows parallelism with previous studies. Even when choosing a green supplier, costs are still important in the selection decision, but environmental factors also have a significant impact on the decision.

References

Abdullah, L., Chan, W., & Afshari, A. (2019). Application of PROMETHEE method for green supplier selection: A comparative result based on preference functions. *Journal of Industrial Engineering International, 15*(2), 271–285.

Agyabeng-Mensah, Y., Afum, E., & Ahenkorah, E. (2020). Exploring financial performance and green logistics management practices: Examining the mediating influences of market, environmental and social performances. *Journal of Cleaner Production, 258*, 120613.

Asgharnezhad, A., & Darestani, S. A. (2022). A green supplier selection framework in polyethylene industry. *Management Research Review*.

Bhuiyan, M. A., Dinçer, H., Yüksel, S., Mikhaylov, A., Danish, M. S. S., Pinter, G., et al. (2022). Economic indicators and bioenergy supply in developed economies: QROF-DEMATEL and random forest models. *Energy Reports, 8*, 561–570.

Carayannis, E., Kostis, P., Dinçer, H., & Yüksel, S. (2022). Balanced-scorecard-based evaluation of knowledge-oriented competencies of distributed energy investments. *Energies, 15*(21), 8245.

Chen, K. S., Wang, C. H., & Tan, K. H. (2019). Developing a fuzzy green supplier selection model using six sigma quality indices. *International Journal of Production Economics, 212*, 1–7.

Cricelli, L., Greco, M., & Grimaldi, M. (2021). An investigation on the effect of inter-organizational collaboration on reverse logistics. *International Journal of Production Economics, 240*, 108216.

De Oliveira, U. R., Neto, L. A., Abreu, P. A. F., & Fernandes, V. A. (2021). Risk management applied to the reverse logistics of solid waste. *Journal of Cleaner Production, 296*, 126517.

Deshmukh, S., & Sunnapwar, V. (2019). Fuzzy analytic hierarchy process (FAHP) for green supplier selection in Indian industries. In *Proceedings of international conference on intelligent manufacturing and automation* (pp. 679–687). Springer.

Dinçer, H., Yüksel, S., & Martínez, L. (2022a). Collaboration enhanced hybrid fuzzy decision-making approach to analyze the renewable energy investment projects. *Energy Reports, 8*, 377–389.

Dinçer, H., Aksoy, T., Yüksel, S., & Hacioglu, U. (2022b). Golden cut-oriented q-rung orthopair fuzzy decision-making approach to evaluation of renewable energy alternatives for microgeneration system investments. *Mathematical Problems in Engineering*.

Dinçer, H., Yüksel, S., Mikhaylov, A., Pinter, G., & Shaikh, Z. A. (2022c). Analysis of renewable-friendly smart grid technologies for the distributed energy investment projects using a hybrid picture fuzzy rough decision-making approach. *Energy Reports, 8*, 11466–11477.

Dinçer, H., Yüksel, S., Çağlayan, Ç., Yavuz, D., & Kararoğlu, D. (2023). Can renewable energy investments be a solution to the energy-sourced high inflation problem? In *Managing inflation and supply chain disruptions in the global economy* (pp. 220–238). IGI Global.

Dong, W., Zhao, G., Yüksel, S., Dinçer, H., & Ubay, G. G. (2022). A novel hybrid decision making approach for the strategic selection of wind energy projects. *Renewable Energy, 185*, 321–337.

Duan, C. Y., Liu, H. C., Zhang, L. J., & Shi, H. (2019). An extended alternative queuing method with linguistic Z-numbers and its application for green supplier selection and order allocation. *International Journal of Fuzzy Systems, 21*(8), 2510–2523.

Ecer, F. (2020). Multi-criteria decision making for green supplier selection using interval type-2 fuzzy AHP: A case study of a home appliance manufacturer. *Operational Research*, 1–35.

Ermiş, A. M., & Güven, M. E. (2022). The role of green energy investments in energy supply security. In *Circular economy and the energy market* (pp. 67–77). Springer.

Eti, S., Dinçer, H., Yüksel, S., & Gökalp, Y. (2022). Analysis of the suitability of the solar panels for hospitals: A new fuzzy decision-making model proposal with the T-spherical TOP-DEMATEL method. *Journal of Intelligent Fuzzy Systems*, (Preprint), 1–13.

Eti, S., Dinçer, H., Gökalp, Y., Yüksel, S., & Kararoğlu, D. (2023). Identifying key issues to handle the inflation problem in the healthcare industry caused by energy prices: An evaluation with decision-making models. In *Managing inflation and supply chain disruptions in the global economy* (pp. 162–178).

Fang, S., Zhou, P., Dinçer, H., & Yüksel, S. (2021). Assessment of safety management system on energy investment risk using house of quality based on hybrid stochastic interval-valued intuitionistic fuzzy decision-making approach. *Safety Science, 141*, 105333.

Fu, R., Qiang, Q. P., Ke, K., & Huang, Z. (2021). Closed-loop supply chain network with interaction of forward and reverse logistics. *Sustainable Production and Consumption, 27*, 737–752.

Gao, H., Ju, Y., Gonzalez, E. D. S., & Zhang, W. (2020). Green supplier selection in electronics manufacturing: An approach based on consensus decision making. *Journal of Cleaner Production, 245*, 118781.

Garai, A., & Sarkar, B. (2022). Economically independent reverse logistics of customer-centric closed-loop supply chain for herbal medicines and biofuel. *Journal of Cleaner Production, 334*, 129977.

Govindan, K., & Gholizadeh, H. (2021). Robust network design for sustainable-resilient reverse logistics network using big data: A case study of end-of-life vehicles. *Transportation Research Part E: Logistics and Transportation Review, 149*, 102279.

Haeri, S. A. S., & Rezaei, J. (2019). A grey-based green supplier selection model for uncertain environments. *Journal of Cleaner Production, 221*, 768–784.

Haiyun, C., Zhixiong, H., Yüksel, S., & Dinçer, H. (2021). Analysis of the innovation strategies for green supply chain management in the energy industry using the QFD-based hybrid interval valued intuitionistic fuzzy decision approach. *Renewable and Sustainable Energy Reviews, 143*, 110844.

Huang, J., Jiang, N., Chen, J., Balezentis, T., & Streimikiene, D. (2022). Multi-criteria group decision-making method for green supplier selection based on distributed interval variables. *Economic Research-Ekonomska Istraživanja, 35*(1), 746–761.

Jauhar, S. K., Amin, S. H., & Zolfagharinia, H. (2021). A proposed method for third-party reverse logistics partner selection and order allocation in the cellphone industry. *Computers & Industrial Engineering, 162*, 107719.

Kafka, K. I., Dinçer, H., & Yüksel, S. (2022). Impact-relation map of innovative service development regarding the sustainable growth for emerging markets. *Journal of the Knowledge Economy*, 1–24.

Kayacık, M., Dinçer, H., & Yüksel, S. (2022). Using quantum spherical fuzzy decision support system as a novel sustainability index approach for analyzing industries listed in the stock exchange. *Borsa Istanbul Review, 22*(6), 1145–1157.

Konys, A. (2019). Green supplier selection criteria: From a literature review to a comprehensive knowledge base. *Sustainability, 11*(15), 4208.

Kou, G., Yüksel, S., & Dinçer, H. (2022). Inventive problem-solving map of innovative carbon emission strategies for solar energy-based transportation investment projects. *Applied Energy, 311*, 118680.

Li, X., Sohail, S., Majeed, M. T., & Ahmad, W. (2021). Green logistics, economic growth, and environmental quality: Evidence from one belt and road initiative economies. *Environmental Science and Pollution Research, 28*(24), 30664–30674.

Li, W., Yüksel, S., & Dinçer, H. (2022a). Understanding the financial innovation priorities for renewable energy investors via QFD-based picture fuzzy and rough numbers. *Financial Innovation, 8*(1), 1–30.

Li, J., Yüksel, S., Dınçer, H., Mikhaylov, A., & Barykin, S. E. (2022b). Bipolar q-ROF hybrid decision making model with golden cut for analyzing the levelized cost of renewable energy alternatives. *IEEE Access, 10*, 42507–42517.

Ma, W., Lei, W., & Sun, B. (2020). Three-way group decisions under hesitant fuzzy linguistic environment for green supplier selection. *Kybernetes*.

Maamoun, A. (2020). Shades of green: Amazon, Walmart, and retail sustainability. In *SAGE business cases*. SAGE Publications: SAGE Business Cases Originals.

Martínez, L., Dinçer, H., & Yüksel, S. (2022). A hybrid decision making approach for new service development process of renewable energy investment. *Applied Soft Computing*, 109897.

Masoomi, B., Sahebi, I. G., Fathi, M., Yıldırım, F., & Ghorbani, S. (2022). Strategic supplier selection for renewable energy supply chain under green capabilities (fuzzy BWM-WASPAS-COPRAS approach). *Energy Strategy Reviews, 40*, 100815.

Mikhaylov, A., Bhatti, I. M., Dinçer, H., & Yüksel, S. (2022). Integrated decision recommendation system using iteration-enhanced collaborative filtering, golden cut bipolar for analyzing the risk-based oil market spillovers. *Computational Economics*, 1–34.

Mukhtarov, S., Yüksel, S., & Dinçer, H. (2022). The impact of financial development on renewable energy consumption: Evidence from Turkey. *Renewable Energy, 187*, 169–176.

Qu, G., Zhang, Z., Qu, W., & Xu, Z. (2020). Green supplier selection based on green practices evaluated using fuzzy approaches of TOPSIS and ELECTRE with a case study in a Chinese internet company. *International Journal of Environmental Research and Public Health, 17*(9), 3268.

Rodrigue, J. P., Slack, B., & Comtois, C. (2017). Green logistics. In *Handbook of logistics and supply-chain management*. Emerald Group Publishing.

Roudbari, E. S., Ghomi, S. F., & Sajadieh, M. S. (2021). Reverse logistics network design for product reuse, remanufacturing, recycling and refurbishing under uncertainty. *Journal of Manufacturing Systems, 60*, 473–486.

Rouyendegh, B. D., Yildizbasi, A., & Üstünyer, P. (2020). Intuitionistic fuzzy TOPSIS method for green supplier selection problem. *Soft Computing, 24*(3), 2215–2228.

Sarkar, B., & Bhuniya, S. (2022). A sustainable flexible manufacturing–remanufacturing model with improved service and green investment under variable demand. *Expert Systems with Applications, 202*, 117154.

Sun, L., Peng, J., Dinçer, H., & Yüksel, S. (2022a). Coalition-oriented strategic selection of renewable energy system alternatives using q-ROF DEMATEL with golden cut. *Energy, 256*, 124606.

Sun, X., Yu, H., & Solvang, W. D. (2022b). Towards the smart and sustainable transformation of Reverse Logistics 4.0: A conceptualization and research agenda. *Environmental Science and Pollution Research*, 1–19.

Tirkolaee, E. B., Dashtian, Z., Weber, G. W., Tomaskova, H., Soltani, M., & Mousavi, N. S. (2021). An integrated decision-making approach for green supplier selection in an agri-food supply chain: Threshold of robustness worthiness. *Mathematics, 9*(11), 1304.

Verma, M., Prem, P. R., Ren, P., Liao, H., & Xu, Z. (2022). Green supplier selection with a multiple criteria decision-making method based on thermodynamic features. *Environment, Development and Sustainability*, 1–33.

Wang, D. F., Dong, Q. L., Peng, Z. M., Khan, S. A. R., & Tarasov, A. (2018). The green logistics impact on international trade: Evidence from developed and developing countries. *Sustainability, 10*(7), 2235.

Wang, Y., Peng, S., Zhou, X., Mahmoudi, M., & Zhen, L. (2020). Green logistics location-routing problem with eco-packages. *Transportation Research Part E: Logistics and Transportation Review, 143*, 102118.

Wang, X., Wang, H., Xu, Z., & Ren, Z. (2022). Green supplier selection based on probabilistic dual hesitant fuzzy sets: A process integrating best worst method and superiority and inferiority ranking. *Applied Intelligence, 52*(7), 8279–8301.

Wei, G., Wei, C., & Guo, Y. (2021). EDAS method for probabilistic linguistic multiple attribute group decision making and their application to green supplier selection. *Soft Computing, 25*(14), 9045–9053.
Xu, Z., Elomri, A., Liu, W., Liu, H., & Li, M. (2021). Robust global reverse logistics network redesign for high-grade plastic wastes recycling. *Waste Management, 134*, 251–262.
Xu, X., Yüksel, S., & Dinçer, H. (2022). An integrated decision-making approach with golden cut and bipolar q-ROFSs to renewable energy storage investments. *International Journal of Fuzzy Systems*, 1–14.
Yang, J. (2022). Reverse logistics. In *From zero waste to material closed loop* (pp. 175–183). Springer.
Yazdani, M., Chatterjee, P., Pamucar, D., & Abad, M. D. (2019). A risk-based integrated decision-making model for green supplier selection: A case study of a construction company in Spain. *Kybernetes*.
Yingfei, Y., Mengze, Z., Zeyu, L., Ki-Hyung, B., Avotra, A. A. R. N., & Nawaz, A. (2022). Green logistics performance and infrastructure on service trade and environment-measuring firm's performance and service quality. *Journal of King Saud University-Science, 34*(1), 101683.
Yuan, G., Xie, F., Dinçer, H., & Yüksel, S. (2021). The theory of inventive problem solving (TRIZ)-based strategic mapping of green nuclear energy investments with spherical fuzzy group decision-making approach. *International Journal of Energy Research, 45*(8), 12284–12300.
Yüksel, S., & Dinçer, H. (2022). Identifying the strategic priorities of nuclear energy investments using hesitant 2-tuple interval-valued Pythagorean fuzzy DEMATEL. *Progress in Nuclear Energy, 145*, 104103.
Yüksel, S., Dinçer, H., Eti, S., & Adalı, Z. (2022). Strategy improvements to minimize the drawbacks of geothermal investments by using spherical fuzzy modelling. *International Journal of Energy Research*.
Zhang, H., & Cui, Y. (2019). A model combining a Bayesian network with a modified genetic algorithm for green supplier selection. *Simulation, 95*(12), 1165–1183.
Zhang, Y., Zhang, Y., Gong, C., Dinçer, H., & Yüksel, S. (2022). An integrated hesitant 2-tuple Pythagorean fuzzy analysis of QFD-based innovation cost and duration for renewable energy projects. *Energy, 248*, 123561.

Chapter 18
The Contribution of Sustainable Energy Policies to the Economic Improvements of the Countries

Muhammed Emrullah Güven and Ahmet Murat Ermiş

Keywords Sustainable energy policies · Sustainability · Energy economics · Energy investments

18.1 Introduction

The concept of sustainability is increasingly present in our daily lives. Although it has a history as old as human history, its consideration within a institutional framework is a relatively new approach. We can roughly define sustainability as meeting our needs without compromising the rights of future generations. Institutionally, sustainability was first addressed in the context of development. Development is among the priorities of all societies. Improving living standards and increasing levels of prosperity are among the top goals of societies. However, the problems arising from development have led to the evolution of development thinking and the discussion of sustainability (Martínez et al., 2022). In this context, the concept of sustainable development has entered our lives. Sustainable development has also given rise to the concept of sustainable energy. When we examine the Sustainable Development Goals declared by the United Nations, the importance of sustainable energy stands out.

In these days when the importance of the concept of sustainability is increasing, efforts to transition from a fossil fuel-based economic model to a sustainable energy-based economy are continuing rapidly. The trend towards renewable and green energy sources is increasing day by day. In order for sustainability to fully enter our lives, energy demand and supply must also be sustainable. In particular, energy needs should be met using environmentally friendly technologies. Renewable energy sources are prominent in this regard. Energy can be obtained from renewable energy sources without damaging the environment (Sun et al.,

M. E. Güven (✉) · A. M. Ermiş
The School of Business, İstanbul Medipol University, İstanbul, Turkey
e-mail: meguven@medipol.edu.tr; mermis@medipol.edu.tr

H. Dincer, S. Yüksel (eds.), *Economic Development and the Environmental Ecosystem*, Contributions to Economics,
https://doi.org/10.1007/978-3-031-26596-9_18

2022). Renewable energy sources do not have to deal with the problem of limited resources. They are sustainable sources because they are renewable. In order for the transition from fossil fuels to renewable energy sources to be realized, appropriate policies need to be implemented. Sustainable energy policies should be sufficient to achieve the desired transformation.

Sustainable energy policies are the collection of policies that have been determined to make sustainable energy applicable. Policy makers can be political institutions or civil society organizations. In order to create a social consensus and roadmap, sometimes even households can determine and implement policies on their own. The involvement of all sections of society in determining policies is due to the fact that energy is used intensively in our daily lives. Parties that use energy in every aspect of life can be opinion leaders in terms of the problems encountered and better practices (Kafka et al., 2022). When these opinions are combined with the knowledge and skills of experts, they turn into successful policies. Ensuring the participation of social actors in the creation of sustainable energy policies will increase the success of these policies.

Although the process of creating policy may seem simple, it is actually quite complex and requires careful thought and consideration. The determination of appropriate policies can be achieved through a thorough evaluation of all societal layers and a clear understanding of the current situation. Each society faces certain constraints when creating its policies, due to both geographical and economic reasons (Mukhtarov et al., 2022). In order to achieve policy goals, objectives and constraints must be optimized and combined at the most suitable point. When all these factors are taken into consideration, it becomes clear that policy-making is not an easy process. The selection of appropriate tools for sustainable energy policies is a sensitive issue. Any wrong choice can lead to serious problems.

18.2 The Objectives of Sustainable Energy Policy

Every state needs energy to develop and raise its level of prosperity. Energy is the foundation of industrial production. Without energy, factories cannot produce. The breakdown of production systems can trigger many problems, from declining national income to unemployment and social distress. In addition to these factors, energy has a deep potential to affect daily life. The rapid and intense increase in demand for energy has been facilitated by developments in the field of information technology (Dong et al., 2022). At this point, it is impossible to manage daily life without energy. In order to raise or maintain the level of prosperity, it is necessary to meet the energy needs. The ability to constantly meet energy needs is of vital importance to states. It has a significant impact on both economic and social factors. This situation has made it necessary for every state to develop its own energy policy. Sustainable energy is a state policy that is implemented by all states. When developing policies in such a sensitive and important area as energy, one of the first steps to be taken is to outline the policy objectives in order to achieve the desired results. If the objectives are not adequately defined, there may be deficiencies in the selection and use of policy tools. Policy tools can only be effectively evaluated in the context of objectives.

The aim of sustainable energy policy is to meet energy needs in a way that respects future generations and does not create negative externalities, as with all sustainability elements. Energy is one of the main factors that cause negative externalities. The idea of negative externalities is to avoid damaging the environment. The damage caused by fossil fuels to nature is a serious problem (Dinçer et al., 2022a–c). It causes greenhouse gas formation. The climate crisis and carbon constraints that we face today are mainly caused by the burning of fossil fuels. In order to prevent or minimize these negative effects, renewable energy sources must be used. Renewable energy sources do not cause negative externalities. In this way, the goal of sustainable energy policy is to meet the energy needs of the present without compromising the ability of future generations to meet their own needs. The use of renewable energy sources is an important step in achieving this goal. The selection of appropriate policy tools for achieving the goals of sustainable energy policy is a crucial issue. The wrong choice can cause serious problems.

In addition to the general objectives of sustainable energy policies, there are specific objectives. Every policy has specific objectives in addition to its general objectives. This is also the case for sustainable energy policies. Policies can vary depending on the situation of the society in which they are implemented (Zhang et al., 2022). All societies aim to achieve the highest level of their interests. It is inevitable that there will be specific objectives in such an important and sensitive area as energy for societies. In the face of the transformation happening in the world, every nation must both adapt and maximize its own benefit. Although similar policies may appear to be applied, in reality, each state designs and uses its policy toolset according to its own situation. Providing clean energy, smooth access to energy, energy efficiency, healthy functioning of the energy market, and energy security are the objectives of sustainable energy policies.

18.3 Providing Clean Energy

At the top of the objectives of sustainable energy policies is the provision of clean energy. Clean energy, also known as green energy, is the name given to all energies that meet our energy needs without harming nature. Renewable energy sources are also clean energy sources. When fossil fuels are burned, they release energy and carbon dioxide gas into the environment (Yüksel & Dinçer, 2022). Carbon emissions are one of the important parameters that cause climate change. Renewable energy sources do not produce carbon emissions. For this reason, providing clean energy is an important objective of sustainable energy policies. The use of renewable energy sources is an important step in achieving this objective. The choice of appropriate policy tools for this purpose is crucial. Wrong choices can cause serious problems.

Climate change refers to the changes in natural events. Climate crisis is used to refer to the negative changes in natural events. Both climate change and climate crisis are undesirable. Changes in the current system have always led to difficult processes. The increase in uncertainty also increases risk. Experts show that climate change will lead to climate crisis, that is, its effects will be quite negative. The studies show the irreversible problems caused by global warming and carbon emissions from all angles (Carayannis et al., 2022).

Global warming refers to the increase in the temperature of our planet. Fossil fuels cause the formation of greenhouse gases when burned. Greenhouse gases are essential for separating harmful radiation from beneficial radiation in the atmosphere. Naturally occurring greenhouse gases contribute to the balance of the earth and support the sustainability of life. However, the unnatural increase in greenhouse gases disrupts the balance (Li et al., 2022a, b). The disrupted balance turns the greenhouse effect, which should provide a more suitable environment for living beings, into negative effects. The increase of gases such as carbon in the atmosphere is an undesirable situation. In order to maintain the breath and heat balance of our world, greenhouse gases should be kept at a level that does not disrupt the natural balance.

The energy we get from fossil fuels causes global warming. Fossil fuels, which release greenhouse gases into the atmosphere when burned, pose a threat to the earth and humanity. Greenhouse gases contain high levels of carbon. The increase of carbon in the atmosphere means that the earth will become even warmer (Yüksel et al., 2022). The increase in global temperature causes changes in climate, such as rain no longer falling in places that used to rain. As a result of the increase in temperature, glaciers are melting and the water level is rising. The melting of glaciers means the disruption of the world order. The rise in water level and temperature affects both land and sea creatures. The increase in temperature puts many species at the brink of extinction. If action is not taken, the diversity of life will decrease rapidly and the current order will evolve into a difficult path that is impossible to predict (Mikhaylov et al., 2022).

In the context of global warming and climate change, the energy we use is very important. Choosing nature-friendly and green energy sources is a must for the future of our world. Care must be taken to prevent the loss of biodiversity and damage to the ecosystem. Renewable energy sources are also green and nature-friendly energy sources. They are among the sustainable energy sources. When formulating a sustainable energy policy, energy sources that do not harm the environment, cause climate change, or emit gases that heat the planet should be preferred (Eti et al., 2023). When formulating policies, it is essential to focus on clean energy sources.

18.4 Ensuring Uninterrupted Access to Energy

Energy is vital in today's world. All sectors are integrated with energy processes. A well-designed energy system has a great impact on all sectors and services, from the pharmaceutical industry to the chemical industry, from education to health. If there is no energy, many sectors will be negatively affected and unable to function. In this sense, access to energy is very important. Energy should be provided wherever it is needed and should ensure the smooth functioning of life (Li et al., 2022a, b). In addition to economic sectors, energy is also an indispensable element for our individual lives. The ability to meet basic needs is parallel to access to energy.

To achieve sustainable development, the eradication of energy deficiency is necessary. Equal distribution of energy will support equal development and fair income distribution. Equal human development is also related to access to energy. The education that took place online instead of face-to-face during the Covid-19 period is one of the best examples. Unfortunately, education, which is essential for human development, could not be implemented in places where there was no electricity or internet (Haiyun et al., 2021). These and similar situations show us how important access to energy is. As a requirement of equal citizenship, the state should provide equal opportunities to everyone. Access to energy can be accepted as one of the fundamental human rights.

Energy access is also a technical issue. Steps must be taken to ensure the accessibility of energy. This can be achieved in two ways. The first is to identify centers in need of energy and make sustainable energy investments according to the structure of the area (Yuan et al., 2021). The energy investment referred to here is the availability of the appropriate energy source. For example, if the region has a high wind energy potential, investments in wind energy should be made. The second is the distribution of energy from a specific area to other areas thanks to advancements in energy storage technology and transportation. The energy needs can be met in this way. Energy access can be achieved by sending stored energy to the required areas through certain channels.

When determining sustainable energy policies, ensuring the smooth access to energy is one of the goals of energy policies. As a result of its meaning, energy access is an indispensable and irreplaceable element of policies. Policy makers must organize an energy network that meets the needs of all segments of society and living in any position, and ensure the functioning of the process. It is also the responsibility of policy makers to make the necessary infrastructure investments and support research projects that will enable technological development. Ensuring the smooth access to energy is also one of the goals of sustainable development in terms of improving the quality of life and raising the living standards of future generations (Fang et al., 2021). Ensuring the access to energy is not only necessary for the sustainability of development, but also for the realization of human rights.

18.5 Energy Efficiency

We feel more and more that we need to change our approaches and attitudes towards energy every day. It is a well-known fact that if we continue with our current patterns of energy production and consumption, we will face serious problems. Focusing on energy efficiency will cause our production and consumption patterns to change (Kayacık et al., 2022). Sustainable energy policies should be implemented to increase energy efficiency. One of the goals of sustainable energy policies is to increase energy efficiency. As a result of increased energy efficiency, waste is prevented and economic benefits are increased. In addition, increasing energy efficiency reduces the negative impact on the environment to a minimum. In today's world where the effects of climate change are increasing, energy efficiency is a very sensitive issue.

Efficiency is the process of maximizing output by optimizing the relationship between the factors used to achieve the desired output. In this context, energy efficiency can be defined as reducing energy consumption without reducing the quality or quantity of energy supply. It can also be expressed as preventing energy waste by using energy more carefully. There are many definitions in the literature (Eti et al., 2022). It is the process of maximizing the benefits obtained from a unit of energy. These processes are carried out to increase the productivity of energy. It is not to reduce the amount of energy or to obtain the same output with less quality energy. Increasing energy efficiency does not necessarily mean decreasing social welfare or economic development. It means increasing the marginal benefit of energy resources through various methods. When we think about how important energy is, it is clear how important energy efficiency is.

Energy waste is the most important obstacle to energy efficiency. The most important step in increasing energy efficiency is to prevent energy waste. Energy conservation can also be possible by preventing energy waste. Unnecessary energy consumption should be avoided, and only the necessary amount of energy should be used when needed. Every sector and group in society, from the industrial sector to households, should be sensitive to energy conservation. Although it is possible to prevent energy waste to a certain extent by creating a legal infrastructure, the basic approach is to increase the level of awareness to implement energy conservation. The consciousness that each energy lost to energy waste is a value stolen from our national wealth and the future lives of our generations should be established (Dinçer et al., 2023). Education should be provided on how energy conservation can be implemented. Policies should be created in this direction.

Another way to increase energy efficiency is to determine energy efficiency standards. Energy efficiency standards for conventional energy sources should be determined, as well as for renewable energy sources. If the energy performance of products is regulated by energy efficiency standards, effective energy use will be achieved. If the standards are supported by legal regulations, it will be possible to increase energy efficiency and promote technological development (Xu et al., 2022). Research and development activities and technological investments will increase.

Energy efficiency standards should regulate energy performance gradually and regulate sanctions accordingly. The functioning of the monitoring mechanism is necessary for the implementation of the standards. The construction of the institutional structure will have a positive impact on increasing energy efficiency.

Some of the energy efficiency standards can be mandatory, while others can be voluntary. The basic goals can be determined politically, and mandatory applications and conditions can be determined. The separation of standards into mandatory and voluntary will increase the effectiveness of policies. If standards are only determined to be mandatory, a level that is optimal for everyone to implement will be preferred. However, if voluntary standards are determined and special advantages are offered to those who reach those standards, the policy goal can be pulled from the optimal level to the maximum level (Bhuiyan et al., 2022). Tax exemptions and financing facilities to be applied will provide opportunities to increase the orientation towards energy efficiency. Standards may also vary according to the renewable energy source. Efficiency approaches for the characteristics of the used source may vary. Energy efficiency standards can be created based on the source, taking into account the characteristics of the energy source.

18.6 The Healthy Functioning of the Energy Market

The healthy functioning of the energy market is another of the goals of energy policies. The sources used in energy production must be constantly supplied. There must be facilities that can supply enough energy for sufficient energy production. For this, it is important that the market has functioned and a supply-demand balance has been formed. The quality and efficiency of energy production must be increased by making the necessary investments. A market with a large number of energy suppliers and demanders must be created in order to introduce low-cost and environmentally friendly energies to the market. It must be financially strong, stable and transparent in structure (Kou et al., 2022).

The clear definition of the areas of activity and rights and responsibilities of the actors in the energy market will ensure the healthy functioning of the market. The performance of the market should be monitored and performance standards should be established and followed. Regulations and regulations should be updated and regulated accordingly. The transmission, storage and infrastructure requirements of energy should be organized according to the market situation. Market supervision processes are also essential elements of a healthy market, like other processes. Necessary institutions should be established to enable market supervision and regulation. Particular attention should be paid to the regulations on the sustainable energy market.

For the energy market to be healthy, it is necessary to organize it properly by taking into account market failures. In normal conditions, the market must be free of entry and exit barriers in order to be efficient. However, there are barriers to entry and exit in the sustainable energy market. In general, having a license is often required to enter the market. Regardless of the sustainable energy tool, a license is generally required to enter the market. Similarly, it is not easy to exit the market. The main reason for the barriers to entry and exit is the strategic importance of the energy market. There is also asymmetric information. Companies that want to enter or enter the market do not have as much information as players in the market. The energy market is not a perfectly competitive market.

Another failure of the energy market is externalities on the network. Each user can affect other users. The positive or negative nature of externalities on the network varies depending on the use of energy and their impacts. An individual who burns fossil fuels for heating creates a negative externality by polluting the air with fossil fuels. This is a negative externality on the network. Investments made for energy access positively affect many people. The resulting positive effect creates a positive externality on the network.

Considering the unique dynamics of the energy market mentioned above, it is clear that increasing the efficiency of the market is necessary for the success of sustainable energy policies. When the healthy functioning of the market is combined with the sustainability perspective, it becomes one of the objectives of policy makers. When developing sustainable energy policies, policies must be developed to support and ensure the healthy functioning of the market.

18.7 Energy Security

One of the goals of sustainable energy policies is to ensure energy security. In today's world where energy is so important for societies, ensuring energy security is very valuable. Ensuring energy security will allow current processes to continue without interruption. Ensuring energy security with sustainable energy sources is easier than with conventional energy sources. Policy makers must act responsibly on the strategically important issue of energy security. Steps must be taken in the direction of ensuring energy security when policies are determined.

The use of sustainable energy sources has advantages in terms of energy security. One of the most important risks for countries that need energy is the possibility of not being able to obtain the energy they need. Countries with a difference between energy demand and supply must import from outside to close this gap. Renewable energy sources can offer solutions for increasing existing capacity. It provides the opportunity to develop solutions quickly without harming the environment.

Another problem for countries with an energy deficit is that they become dependent on the countries they import energy from. Countries with an energy surplus sometimes use this as soft power, sometimes as hard power. During the last energy crisis we had the opportunity to observe clearly how this situation could have consequences. Many energy-dependent countries had to face very difficult conditions. A country that exports energy may not always use energy as a power. Even if the exporting country does not use energy as a weapon, there will always be psychological pressure on the importing country. Sustainable energy sources obtain energy from local sources. Energy is obtained by using the most appropriate energy source for the region. In this way, sustainable energy use reduces energy dependence and will ensure progress in this direction. Having the country meet its own energy needs will eliminate the problem of energy dependence.

Another dimension of energy security is economic factors. Countries that need energy have to bear some economic costs in order to import energy. The need for foreign exchange arises because energy payments are made in dollars. This can cause a deficit in the current account and cause problems for the country's economy. Dollars must be obtained to meet energy needs. Any disruptions in energy supply will also have economic impacts. The operation of all sectors depends on the availability of energy. Any problems that arise will directly affect production. Disruptions in production will affect national income, economic growth, and the labor market. The economic effects of any difficulties in energy security can be very deep.

18.8 Tools of Sustainable Energy Policy

The most important tool used to implement sustainable energy policies is the guidelines and goals set by policy makers. Inclusive, transparent, and continuous legal regulations are crucial for increasing the importance of sustainable energy in our lives. Legal frameworks must be designed to be comprehensive, understandable, and implementable. The legislation and regulations to be established must be prepared in parallel with the objectives of sustainable energy policies (Ermiş & Güven, 2022). The market must function efficiently and respond to problems with a solution-oriented approach.

Network services must be designed to meet the needs of producers and consumers. Priorities and investment choices in network services must be transparent. To achieve this, necessary legal regulations must be made. Both producers and consumers must be considered on their own scale. There may be some differences in regulations for small, medium and large-scale producer companies and regulations for small-scale companies. Similarly, household energy consumption expenses should be different from industrial energy consumption expenses. Tariffs should be flexible. Legal infrastructures should be regulated taking into account these possibilities and requirements. Self-consumption and self-production plans should be allowed, but a suitable area should be created without allowing it to disrupt the market.

Sustainable energy legislation can be created from scratch, but it may also need to be updated from time to time due to changing conditions. Especially since technological changes have significantly affected and transformed the game system, it is inevitable to review legal regulations. Changes made should not create additional costs for market actors. Legal regulations must be made to create the confidence of investors. Investors should be able to invest easily.

Feed-In Tariff is one of the policy tools used to promote the use of renewable energy sources. It means that energy producers are guaranteed to sell their energy at a fixed amount above the market price. A certain amount above the market price is paid to producers for the energy they provide to the grid. It generally gives effective results in areas where producers are hesitant to enter the market and there are economic barriers. Because sustainable energy is still in its development phase, it may not be as economic as conventional energy sources in some cases within the network. Investment in sustainable energy sources is necessary, which increases costs. The tariff guarantee policy tool is aimed at achieving the desired results by overcoming economic concerns.

Tariff guarantee is also a policy tool used to achieve strategic objectives. It can be used to guide the market and increase technological investments as part of an energy strategy. Long-term contracts and price guarantees provide investors with the opportunity to invest. The contracts are generally for more than 10 years. The price is determined in proportion to the costs incurred and capital used in production. Different prices are determined according to the technology used, the region, and the location of the energy source. It is a vital policy tool for sustainable energy investments around the world. When we look at countries that make intensive investments in the field of sustainable energy, we see that they actively use the tariff guarantee policy tool. The tariff guarantee tool provides successful results with appropriate strategies without disturbing the market order.

Financial incentives are used as a tool in sustainable energy policies. The aim is to solve the financial difficulties of investors who want to invest in sustainable energy sources. In addition, the aim is to direct investments to this area with the incentives given. Financial incentives vary according to the size of the investment. Large-scale investment incentives aim to increase the energy capacity. In general, it is an incentive given to projects that will raise the technological level. Regional incentives aim to increase the country's access to energy and ensure that no region remains without access to energy. In addition, the most suitable energy source is planned to be selected according to geographical features. Another dimension is the strategic dimension. Incentives are given to areas or regions that are prioritized according to long-term strategic plans within the scope of national policies.

Generally, flexible loans, cheap financing, grants, tax breaks and exemptions are used in financial incentives. The aim of using flexible loans is to provide payment convenience. In particular, cash flows from new investments may not be regular. Flexibility in payment amounts and dates is an important incentive for investors. Flexible loans provide payment convenience and cheap financing opportunities are also offered within the scope of financial incentives. Financial costs are significantly reduced with a special interest rate. In some projects, grant support is also provided. Financial support provided is non-repayable. Grant support is provided especially in strategic priority areas. Tax breaks and exemptions are also financial incentives that help reduce investment costs.

18.9 Conclusion

Currently, we are going through a process of redesigning the world order and the economic system. In this period of restructuring, policies are being designed to provide long-term gains, rather than focusing on the present state of the country. The concept of sustainability, which has become the key word for transformation, brings both opportunities and challenges in every field. Every state is trying to position itself in the new order and maximize its gains. At this point, policies become very important. Long-term and comprehensive policies will enable countries to develop and gain competitive advantage. Policy makers must accurately determine strategic goals and carry out micro actions within the scope of those goals, designing them on a macro level. Only in this way can the desired goals be achieved. Policies should be created through the blending of participation in a broad framework and different perspectives. The weight of the concept of sustainability in policies should be increased. In other words, policies should be increased. Previous approaches and evaluation criteria should be changed, and political processes should be activated. The sub-elements of political approaches should be determined, and their content should be designed accordingly.

The concept of sustainability has begun to become the key to our energy system, as it has entered all areas of our lives. Meeting the energy needs without damaging the environment and without experiencing resource shortages is only possible with sustainable energy sources. The use of fossil fuels is being reduced and replaced with sustainable energy sources due to the damage they cause. The process that is targeted to be completed will be completed in a very short time in essence. Developing countries are also seriously considering the opportunities in line with the intense investments of developed countries. Many steps need to be taken in this context. Feasibility studies on sustainable energy sources should be carried out. The most suitable energy source should be created and used in the most suitable places. The aim is to increase resource efficiency to the highest levels. The benefit of sustainable energy is also important for all sections of the community. In the later stages of sustainable energy, it will not only meet our energy needs but will also play a role in meeting our basic needs. Electric vehicles are the most basic example of this. Electric vehicles will also change many sub-manufacturing items and businesses that provide complementary products such as petrol stations will have to change. An important transformation will also take place in the economic context. Sectoral transformations will bring new professions and updating of the education system. To summarize, the sustainable energy revolution means a social transformation.

References

Bhuiyan, M. A., Dinçer, H., Yüksel, S., Mikhaylov, A., Danish, M. S. S., Pinter, G., et al. (2022). Economic indicators and bioenergy supply in developed economies: QROF-DEMATEL and random forest models. *Energy Reports, 8*, 561–570.

Carayannis, E., Kostis, P., Dinçer, H., & Yüksel, S. (2022). Balanced-scorecard-based evaluation of knowledge-oriented competencies of distributed energy investments. *Energies, 15*(21), 8245.

Dinçer, H., Yüksel, S., & Martínez, L. (2022a). Collaboration enhanced hybrid fuzzy decision-making approach to analyze the renewable energy investment projects. *Energy Reports, 8*, 377–389.

Dinçer, H., Aksoy, T., Yüksel, S., & Hacioglu, U. (2022b). Golden cut-oriented q-rung orthopair fuzzy decision-making approach to evaluation of renewable energy alternatives for microgeneration system investments. *Mathematical Problems in Engineering*.

Dinçer, H., Yüksel, S., Mikhaylov, A., Pinter, G., & Shaikh, Z. A. (2022c). Analysis of renewable-friendly smart grid technologies for the distributed energy investment projects using a hybrid picture fuzzy rough decision-making approach. *Energy Reports, 8*, 11466–11477.

Dinçer, H., Yüksel, S., Çağlayan, Ç., Yavuz, D., & Kararoğlu, D. (2023). Can renewable energy investments be a solution to the energy-sourced high inflation problem? In *Managing inflation and supply chain disruptions in the global economy* (pp. 220–238). IGI Global.

Dong, W., Zhao, G., Yüksel, S., Dinçer, H., & Ubay, G. G. (2022). A novel hybrid decision making approach for the strategic selection of wind energy projects. *Renewable Energy, 185*, 321–337.

Ermiş, A. M., & Güven, M. E. (2022). The role of green energy investments in energy supply security. In *Circular economy and the energy market* (pp. 67–77). Springer.

Eti, S., Dinçer, H., Yüksel, S., & Gökalp, Y. (2022). Analysis of the suitability of the solar panels for hospitals: A new fuzzy decision-making model proposal with the T-spherical TOP-DEMATEL method. *Journal of Intelligent Fuzzy Systems*, (Preprint), 1–13.

Eti, S., Dinçer, H., Gökalp, Y., Yüksel, S., & Kararoğlu, D. (2023). Identifying key issues to handle the inflation problem in the healthcare industry caused by energy prices: An evaluation with decision-making models. In *Managing inflation and supply chain disruptions in the global economy* (pp. 162–178).

Fang, S., Zhou, P., Dinçer, H., & Yüksel, S. (2021). Assessment of safety management system on energy investment risk using house of quality based on hybrid stochastic interval-valued intuitionistic fuzzy decision-making approach. *Safety Science, 141*, 105333.

Haiyun, C., Zhixiong, H., Yüksel, S., & Dinçer, H. (2021). Analysis of the innovation strategies for green supply chain management in the energy industry using the QFD-based hybrid interval valued intuitionistic fuzzy decision approach. *Renewable and Sustainable Energy Reviews, 143*, 110844.

Kafka, K. I., Dinçer, H., & Yüksel, S. (2022). Impact-relation map of innovative service development regarding the sustainable growth for emerging markets. *Journal of the Knowledge Economy*, 1–24.

Kayacık, M., Dinçer, H., & Yüksel, S. (2022). Using quantum spherical fuzzy decision support system as a novel sustainability index approach for analyzing industries listed in the stock exchange. *Borsa Istanbul Review, 22*(6), 1145–1157.

Kou, G., Yüksel, S., & Dinçer, H. (2022). Inventive problem-solving map of innovative carbon emission strategies for solar energy-based transportation investment projects. *Applied Energy, 311*, 118680.

Li, W., Yüksel, S., & Dinçer, H. (2022a). Understanding the financial innovation priorities for renewable energy investors via QFD-based picture fuzzy and rough numbers. *Financial Innovation, 8*(1), 1–30.

Li, J., Yüksel, S., Dınçer, H., Mikhaylov, A., & Barykin, S. E. (2022b). Bipolar q-ROF hybrid decision making model with golden cut for analyzing the levelized cost of renewable energy alternatives. *IEEE Access, 10*, 42507–42517.

Martínez, L., Dinçer, H., & Yüksel, S. (2022). A hybrid decision making approach for new service development process of renewable energy investment. *Applied Soft Computing*, 109897.

Mikhaylov, A., Bhatti, I. M., Dinçer, H., & Yüksel, S. (2022). Integrated decision recommendation system using iteration-enhanced collaborative filtering, golden cut bipolar for analyzing the risk-based oil market spillovers. *Computational Economics*, 1–34.

Mukhtarov, S., Yüksel, S., & Dinçer, H. (2022). The impact of financial development on renewable energy consumption: Evidence from Turkey. *Renewable Energy, 187*, 169–176.

Sun, L., Peng, J., Dinçer, H., & Yüksel, S. (2022). Coalition-oriented strategic selection of renewable energy system alternatives using q-ROF DEMATEL with golden cut. *Energy, 256*, 124606.

Xu, X., Yüksel, S., & Dinçer, H. (2022). An integrated decision-making approach with golden cut and bipolar q-ROFSs to renewable energy storage investments. *International Journal of Fuzzy Systems*, 1–14.

Yuan, G., Xie, F., Dinçer, H., & Yüksel, S. (2021). The theory of inventive problem solving (TRIZ)-based strategic mapping of green nuclear energy investments with spherical fuzzy group decision-making approach. *International Journal of Energy Research, 45*(8), 12284–12300.

Yüksel, S., & Dinçer, H. (2022). Identifying the strategic priorities of nuclear energy investments using hesitant 2-tuple interval-valued Pythagorean fuzzy DEMATEL. *Progress in Nuclear Energy, 145*, 104103.

Yüksel, S., Dinçer, H., Eti, S., & Adalı, Z. (2022). Strategy improvements to minimize the drawbacks of geothermal investments by using spherical fuzzy modelling. *International Journal of Energy Research.*

Zhang, Y., Zhang, Y., Gong, C., Dinçer, H., & Yüksel, S. (2022). An integrated hesitant 2-tuple Pythagorean fuzzy analysis of QFD-based innovation cost and duration for renewable energy projects. *Energy, 248*, 123561.

Chapter 19
Post-Epidemic National and Institutional Energy Strategies

Mehmet Ali Alhan

Keywords Energy · Strategy · Pandemic · Management

19.1 Introduction

It is difficult to predict the specific strategies that energy companies will adopt after the pandemic, as the trajectory of the industry will depend on a range of factors, including economic conditions, energy demand, technological advancements, and government policies. But That being said, it is likely that energy companies will continue to focus on meeting the energy needs of their customers while also working to reduce their environmental impact. Some possible strategies that energy companies may consider include: Diversifying their energy mix: Many energy companies are looking to diversify their energy mix by increasing their reliance on renewable energy sources such as solar, wind, and hydroelectric power. This can help to reduce their carbon footprint and increase their resilience to fluctuations in fossil fuel prices. Investing in advanced technologies: Energy companies can invest in advanced technologies such as advanced nuclear power and/or electric vehicles to reduce their environmental impact and meet the changing energy needs of their customers. However, in this case, investors should focus on many different factors at the same time in order not to lose (Wang et al., 2019). Collaborating with other stakeholders: Energy companies may seek to collaborate with governments, regulators, and other stakeholders to develop and implement policies that support the transition to a low-carbon economy. Focusing on customer service: In the post-pandemic world, energy companies may prioritize customer service and offer flexible billing options, online services, and other support to meet the changing needs of their customers. Ultimately, the strategies that energy companies adopt after the pandemic will depend on a range of factors and will likely evolve over time as the industry continues to change.

M. A. Alhan (✉)
The School of Business, İstanbul Medipol University, İstanbul, Turkey

H. Dincer, S. Yüksel (eds.), *Economic Development and the Environmental Ecosystem*, Contributions to Economics,
https://doi.org/10.1007/978-3-031-26596-9_19

Expanding into new markets: Energy companies may look to expand into new markets, either domestically or internationally, in order to diversify their customer base and revenue streams. Promoting energy efficiency: Energy companies may promote energy efficiency to their customers by offering energy-saving products and services, as well as providing education and resources to help customers reduce their energy consumption. Developing new business models: Energy companies may look to develop new business models that take advantage of emerging technologies and changing customer preferences. But the decision to abandon fossil fuels for renewable energies depends on a number of variables, including the strategy of the country of origin. In other words, oil companies founded in countries whose energy strategy is more focused on fossil fuels are less prone to transformation (Dong et al., 2022; Dinçer et al., 2022a–c; Zhang et al., 2022; Yüksel & Dinçer, 2022). For example, some companies may offer on-demand energy services or subscription-based energy plans. Fostering innovation: Energy companies may invest in research and development to foster innovation and stay ahead of industry trends. This could involve partnering with universities or startups, or establishing in-house research and development teams.

Managing regulatory compliance: Energy companies will likely continue to face regulatory requirements and will need to develop strategies to manage compliance and minimize risk. This may involve working with governments and regulatory bodies to understand and meet evolving requirements. Maintaining financial stability: Energy companies will need to focus on maintaining financial stability in order to weather market fluctuations and continue to invest in the business. This may involve diversifying revenue streams, managing debt, and maximizing operational efficiency. However, whether the energy-politics-centered bloc has a function to prevent conflicts of interest in international relations and whether the energy pursued in crisis regions, which has the potential to pose a problem even in democratic and liberal systems, is a public power, serious analyzes and evaluations in this direction have been made in the academic literature made mandatory (Alhan, 2021).

19.2 Post-Pandemic Strategies and Policies of Global Energy Powers

Tensions over the repositioning of the world's leading oil and gas producers, the oil pricing process, and medium-term production processes are expected to increase. Especially with regard to long-term global energy demand, significant changes may occur in energy policies in the environment of uncertainty after the COVID-19 epidemic and the Russia-Ukraine war. The COVID-19 pandemic has had a significant impact on the global energy sector, with demand for energy falling due to lockdowns and economic downturns. In response, many countries have implemented a range of strategies and policies to support their energy industries and ensure energy security. Here are a few examples of post-pandemic strategies and policies that have been implemented by some of the world's major energy powers: The United States: In response to the pandemic, the U.S. government has implemented a range of measures to support the energy sector. This includes extending deadlines for oil and gas lease auctions, providing financial assistance to small businesses in the energy sector, and issuing waivers for the transportation of energy products. The U.S. has also continued to promote the development of renewable energy sources, such as wind and solar power.

China: China is the world's largest energy consumer and has implemented a range of measures to support its energy sector during the pandemic. This includes providing financial assistance to energy companies, expanding investment in renewable energy sources, and implementing policies to improve energy efficiency.

Russia: Russia is a major energy producer and has implemented a range of measures to support its energy sector during the pandemic. This includes providing financial assistance to energy companies, including oil and gas producers, and promoting the development of new energy technologies.

Saudi Arabia: Saudi Arabia is a major oil producer and has implemented a range of measures to support its energy sector during the pandemic. This includes providing financial assistance to energy companies, including oil and gas producers, and promoting the development of new energy technologies. It is important to note that the specific strategies and policies implemented by individual countries will vary depending on their unique energy needs and resources. Here are a few more examples of post-pandemic strategies and policies implemented by some global energy powers.

India: India is the world's third-largest energy consumer and has implemented a range of measures to support its energy sector during the pandemic. India has taken great strides in the energy sector in recent years and has gained an important place in the global energy field (Gribkova & Milshina, 2022). The "Energy transition to nurture India's growth path" roadmap emphasizes that the energy sector should be growth centered, industry friendly and environmentally conscious (Gribkova & Milshina, 2022). However, uncertainty about the strength of the recovery is likely to complicate commitments to these countries' goals of reducing coal consumption and accelerating measures to increase the use of low-carbon energy sources (Xu et al., 2020). This includes providing financial assistance to energy companies, expanding investment in renewable energy sources, and implementing policies to improve energy efficiency. According to Aggarwal et al. (2020), in addition to the tax increase, the Indian government has planned a support program to reduce the needs for the coal industry in 2020. The government announced actions to relax and improve existing environmental protection measures. Many of these measures are immeasurable, but investment commitments were around \$6 billion. This demonstrates the desire of the Indian authorities to place "self-sufficiency" as the core value of their energy policies. Germany: Germany has a strong focus on renewable energy and has implemented a range of measures to support its energy sector during the pandemic. This includes providing financial assistance to energy companies, expanding investment in renewable energy sources, and implementing policies to improve energy efficiency.

Brazil: Brazil is a major energy producer and has implemented a range of measures to support its energy sector during the pandemic. This includes providing financial assistance to energy companies, including oil and gas producers, and promoting the development of new energy technologies. Canada: Canada is a major energy producer and has implemented a range of measures to support its energy sector during the pandemic. This includes providing financial assistance to energy companies, including oil and gas producers, and promoting the development of renewable energy sources, such as wind and solar power. It is worth noting that the COVID-19 pandemic has also led to increased interest in and investment in renewable energy sources, as countries look to diversify their energy mix and reduce their reliance on fossil fuels. Many countries have also implemented policies to improve energy efficiency and reduce greenhouse gas emissions, as part of their efforts to address climate change. Expanding into new markets: Energy companies may look to expand into new markets, either domestically or internationally, in order to diversify their customer base and revenue streams.

Although it is claimed that the possibility of progress in renewable energy will increase due to the revival of the Chinese economy, natural gas is likely to play a strategic role in Chinese energy policy in the medium term. In addition, the repercussions of the COVID-19 outbreak are expected to increase energy use in China. Therefore, if this crisis cannot be resolved, it will be certain that coal energy does not actually have an economic benefit (Du et al., 2020). Promoting energy efficiency: Energy companies may promote energy efficiency to their customers by offering energy-saving products and services, as well as providing education and resources to help customers reduce their energy consumption. Developing new business models: Energy companies may look to develop new business models that take advantage of emerging technologies and changing customer preferences. For example, some companies may offer on-demand energy services or subscription-based energy plans. Fostering innovation: Energy companies may invest in research and development to foster innovation and stay ahead of industry trends. This could involve partnering with universities or startups, or establishing in-house research and development teams. Managing regulatory compliance: Energy companies will likely continue to face regulatory requirements and will need to develop strategies to manage compliance and minimize risk. This may involve working with governments and regulatory bodies to understand and meet evolving requirements. Maintaining financial stability: Energy companies will need to focus on maintaining financial stability in order to weather market fluctuations and continue to invest in the business. This may involve diversifying revenue streams, managing debt, and maximizing operational efficiency. It is difficult to predict the specific strategies that energy companies will adopt after the pandemic, as the trajectory of the industry will depend on a range of factors, including economic conditions, energy demand, technological advancements, and government policies. That being said, it is likely that energy companies will continue to focus on meeting the energy needs of their customers while also working to reduce their environmental impact.

Some possible strategies that energy companies may consider include: Diversifying their energy mix: Many energy companies are looking to diversify their energy mix by increasing their reliance on renewable energy sources such as solar, wind, and hydroelectric power. This can help to reduce their carbon footprint and increase their resilience to fluctuations in fossil fuel prices. Therefore, if this crisis cannot be resolved, it will be certain that coal energy does not actually have an economic benefit (Du et al., 2020). Collaborating with other stakeholders: Energy companies may seek to collaborate with governments, regulators, and other stakeholders to develop and implement policies that support the transition to a low-carbon economy. Focusing on customer service: In the post-pandemic world, energy companies may prioritize customer service and offer flexible billing options, online services, and other support to meet the changing needs of their customers. Ultimately, the strategies that energy companies adopt after the pandemic will depend on a range of factors and will likely evolve over time as the industry continues to change.

In Russia, where Energy Resources (Oil and natural gas) are of great economic importance, it will strategically remain at the center of the energy issue. As mentioned before, Russia, as a regional and global power, has attempts to prevent the formation of new producers and their development in the sector. In order to meet the demand in Russia's European market (especially with the post-war embargoes), it takes steps against the growth of market shares of all competitors, especially the USA, and keeps production and price under control.

Besides war and embargoes, Russia faces a major challenge: the vast majority of its approximately 1800 active production sites have reached maturity. Of this number, 20 plants (the largest) account for about a third of Russian energy production. These factors mean that Russia's energy strategy converges:

1. Maintaining its status as Europe's main gas supplier while improving exports to China,
2. In order to prevent economic contraction in case of war, to increase production volumes to obtain foreign currency in the fight against the crisis and to solve embargo problems.

One of the biggest energy-related difficulties in Russia's post-pandemic and Ukrainian war is the refinery issue. Currently, energy supply in Russia is far above the demand. This has a negative impact on global competition.

The excess production in Russian refineries, which started in 2019, rose to the ceiling point after the pandemic and during the war period. With the decrease in consumption caused by the epidemic, the gap between the refining capacity in the country and the consumption of petroleum products has widened. The war between Russia and Ukraine and the embargo imposed by the EU triggered the crisis, resulting in a situation that would ultimately increase operating costs.

- *Post-crisis, China could achieve an increase in coal-fired electricity generation and industrial capacity. The geopolitical situation and increased supply chain and disruption risks may cause China to focus on energy security strategies. China's rich coal reserves may increase the trend towards fossil fuels as an effective alternative to sustaining energy supply. After COVID-19, China's investments in renewable energy sources have decreased.*

In the new world order, the United States is the new owner of the position of the major oil and gas producer in the global energy market. After the embargoes against Russia, it became an oil supplier. In the coming years, this situation is expected to be predominantly oil and natural gas exporter.

After the pandemic, Noble Energy, Concho Resources and WPX Energy acquired large US-based energy companies such as Chevron, and small-scale companies such as ConocoPhillips and Devon Energy, respectively.

After Trump's defeat in the presidential election, given the importance they place on America's economic recovery, it seems unlikely that Democrats will withdraw their support for the oil and shale industries to which they are closely tied.

European Union countries, the post-pandemic Russia-Ukraine war, dependence on oil imports, and policy makers have taken action to plan the transition from oil to renewable energy. However, these policies also seem to be a sign of the decline of Europe's power in oil geopolitics. Of course, this situation creates an emergency situation in order to focus the energy policy of EU countries on the increasing use of renewable energies and to determine their strategies in this direction. The low oil reserves in the European continent, the number of energy production companies and the dependence on the supply of the energy producing country are gradually weakening the position of the European Union.

European Union countries more determined than other parts of the world to improve the use of renewable energies. From a global governance perspective, it plays an important role in energy transition forums, strengthening its leadership position in energy transition geopolitics (Martínez et al., 2022; Sun et al., 2022; Kafka et al., 2022; Mukhtarov et al., 2022).

In this context, the epidemic offers an opportunity to intensify the "European Green Deal." It proposes a €750 billion package for economic recovery within the framework of a long-term budget of €1100 billion (2021–2027), launched in December 2019. A quarter of this long-term budget is devoted to the energy transition, which aims to make Europe carbon neutral by 2050. This situation has gained a strategic dimension in terms of the recovery of the economy in the post-pandemic period and the post-Russian-Ukrainian war period.

In general, especially during the epidemic, national strategies are associated with country interests, dependencies/autonomy and how COVID-19 affects them. Currently, the energy transition appears to be subject to these elements, although important (Carayannis et al., 2022; Li et al., 2022a, b; Yüksel et al., 2022; Mikhaylov et al., 2022).

19.3 Evolving Strategies of Global Oil Companies

Although the leaders promised in their statements that they would continue to invest in renewable energies during the pandemic crisis, the main fears of the major oil production companies were short-term financial risks, and they have taken budget cuts especially in the name of oil production. This situation brought with it difficulties in meeting the increase in demand in the medium term together with the Russia-Ukraine war. However, many large oil production companies hold and even plan to implement their existing project plans to reduce carbon intensity.

Europe's four major power generation companies (BP, Total, ENI and Shell) have announced their future strategies aimed at zero greenhouse gas (GHG) emissions. To build the world's largest geological carbon sequestration project, Total, Equinor and Shell have announced plans to build a landfill in the Troll bed in the Norwegian North Sea. But of course, it is very difficult to predict which projects will be restricted even though large companies restrict their capital expenditures and support renewable energy investment plans during the pandemic-effective crisis phase.

However, the strategies of energy companies in the face of the crisis are directly related to the energy demand balance of the market, the timing of this situation and the government decisions and policies implemented to support the energy transition (Eti et al., 2023; Li et al., 2022a, b; Haiyun et al., 2021; Yuan et al., 2021). Looking at the recent actions of large companies, it is clear that they do not share a common vision of the future. Strategic moves planned for the future include being prepared for the crisis and increasing the diversity of activities for different scenarios, energy efficiency and devaluation of assets.

Generally, companies adjust their investments by reducing their production and optimizing their upstream and downstream assets. In this sense, a possible relative increase in renewable energy is related to a decrease in exploration and production (E&P) projects rather than decreases in other sectors of activity (Fang et al., 2021; Kayacık et al., 2022; Eti et al., 2022; Dinçer et al., 2023).

While the UK-based BP energy company plans to accelerate the transition to renewable energy, it is currently implementing two of the four main strategies are related to the fossil fuel industry:

1. Increasing energy efficiency in oil and gas resources,
2. Strengthening the refining stage and post-processing of the final product,
3. Increasing efficiency with new low-carbon projects,
4. Increasing the importance given to digitalization and accelerating the process.

Clearly, BP's priority during the pandemic is to move away from low-profit vehicles and increase the profitability of its E&P (Exploration and Production) phases. This shows that BP has turned to the production of oil and its derivatives in the US market in response to the reduced demand due to the epidemic and the high cost of producing oil and shale gas. However, BP said in a statement that it has no intention of balancing European production with refining yet. It continues its investments in the renewable energy segment in Asia and Oceania.

The company announced plans to radically change its strategic plan and operating procedures to meet environmental regulation demands for a low-carbon economy, driven by the pandemic. The company said in a statement that this result was driven by "the great uncertainty of the macroeconomic situation" in the context of the epidemic.

In terms of energy supply, Shell company, under the effect of the pandemic, reduced the utilization rate of its refineries by 81% to 60–70% in the second half of 2020, and reduced its oil processing volumes to 3–4 million barrels per day. During the epidemic, which affected more than 3 billion consumers, which is about 40% of the world population, there was a serious decrease in demand with the curfew. As a result of all the events, the Norwegian company Equinor announced in March that its production in regions other than its own national territory had slowed down. "All Equinor drilling and well completion activities in US gas-focused shale assets have been suspended to reduce costs and subsequently build volume," the company said in its statement. Besides project costs and time issues, another factor that the company describes as savings is the location of its investments. In this case, the first priority is the continuity of domestic investments, which takes precedence over foreign investments.

US energy company ExxonMobil initially excluded any revisions to its spending plans for this year (Correia, 2021). After the COVID-19 epidemic, it had to take precautions in the backward market conditions. The company's board of directors said it will "continue to evaluate the longer-term production impacts as well as the effects of lower demand on production levels in 2020" and may opt for additional reductions if needed.

In its response, Chevron company announced a new action plan at the end of March, depending on market conditions and to deal with the crisis caused by the pandemic. In the press release, the company announced that it is planning a new package of measures to support its past performance, along with reducing its capital expenditures.

19.4 Conclusion

The article explains how oil and gas can continue to play a vital role in the energy sector in the medium term. The progress made by countries with large energy resources (Brazil and Canada's oil production, Qatar and Australia's liquid natural gas production) and the rise in the energy demand of the People's Republic of China provide these countries with opportunities to evaluate their energy potential.

The fact that COVID-19 has created deep uncertainties about the future has led many energy giant countries and companies to be careful in their attempts to avoid radical changes in their production structure in the short and medium term. When we look at the measures taken, we observe that states, with exceptions, are trying to protect their industries and reduce their dependence on energy imports, even though it is observed that they increase the use of alternative sources despite more fossil fuels. Companies, on the other hand, generally concentrate on the oil and gas segment, focusing on projects with higher profitability and trying to reduce investments in low-profit assets. It is expected that the new reserve exploration expenditures in Europe's leading energy companies will decrease in the short term due to the decrease in oil and gas production, renewable energy projects will be protected and the share of these financial resources in the portfolio will increase. In this respect, it shows that oil and natural gas is an important instrument in the global energy sector. Of course, this does not mean that no investment has been made in favor of the energy transition. It is observed that many countries invest more and more in clean energy resources in response to their energy needs, especially with the energy crisis that emerged as a result of the sanctions imposed by the European Union during and after the Russia-Ukraine war. The subject of this study is to clarify the importance of the individual energy transition and to provide information about the implementation process. Simultaneously, it makes several strategic proposals for replacing clean energy sources with fossil fuels. However, most of these estimates fail to take into account all the elements and actors involved in this process.

For some, the war in Ukraine is profitable. Energy companies are among the lucky companies that make high profits thanks to the increase in oil and gas prices. Shell, Europe's largest oil company, announced a profit of 11.5 billion dollars last quarter. Its first quarter profit was "only" $9.1 billion; but even this result was considered a record profit. In this way, Shell increased its profit fivefold compared to the same period of the previous year. French energy group Total Energies and Spanish group Repsol also posted significantly higher profits (Peña-Ramos et al., 2021). The first managed to increase its profit in the first half to $9.8 billion, a record level and nearly triple the profit in the first half of 2021. Repsol doubled its profits to 2.5 billion euros (Ghirelli et al., 2021). Finally, the British oil company BP also presented quarterly figures and announced that it had significantly increased its profits. In the second quarter, it tripled its profit compared to the same period of the previous year and announced it as 8.5 billion (Christophers, 2022). These gains are not based on performance and innovation, but solely on rising market prices, and BP is expected to post similarly high profits in the coming quarter. "Continuously" high prices are expected due to the ongoing "outage" of supplies from Russia and decreasing stocks.

The economic importance of the deployment of renewable energies in the foreseeable future, the proliferation of renewable energies will require additional costs compared to the currently prevailing costs of conventional energy supply. However, in the medium term, renewable energy sources (in a suitable combination with the efficiency strategy) may appear to be the most economically advantageous solution to the strategic energy supply problem. They represent energy technologies that can be substantially reduced through continuous technological advances (mobilization also requires sufficient start-up capital) and modernization and expansion of the plant. We urgently need a clean energy system based solely on the efficient use of renewable energy sources, designed to save us from climate disaster, protect the environment and ensure sustainable development. We need an energy system that does not make our cities uninhabitable, does not increase the radioactive burden of future generations, and does not lead to the proliferation of nuclear weapons, in other words, a global energy revolution (Xu et al., 2022; Bhuiyan et al., 2022; Kou et al., 2022; Ermiş & Güven, 2022).

References

Aggarwal, P., Viswamohanan, A., Narayanaswamy, D., & Sharma, S. (2020). *Unpacking India's electricity subsidies: Reporting, transparency and efficacy.*

Alhan, M. A. (2021). On the axis of the East Mediterranean energy resources: A comparative emotion analysis of the news headlines in Turkey, Europe and the USA. *Istanbul Commerce University Journal of Social Sciences, 20*(42), 1438–1466.

Bhuiyan, M. A., Dinçer, H., Yüksel, S., Mikhaylov, A., Danish, M. S. S., Pinter, G., et al. (2022). Economic indicators and bioenergy supply in developed economies: QROF-DEMATEL and random forest models. *Energy Reports, 8*, 561–570.

Carayannis, E., Kostis, P., Dinçer, H., & Yüksel, S. (2022). Balanced-scorecard-based evaluation of knowledge-oriented competencies of distributed energy investments. *Energies, 15*(21), 8245.

Christophers, B. (2022). Fossilized capital: Price and profit in the energy transition. *New Politics Economy, 27*(1), 146–159.

Correia, A. M. F. C. (2021). *Equities research-ExxonMobil Corporation.* Doctoral dissertation, Institute Superior de Economia e Gestao.

Dinçer, H., Yüksel, S., & Martínez, L. (2022a). Collaboration enhanced hybrid fuzzy decision-making approach to analyze the renewable energy investment projects. *Energy Reports, 8*, 377–389.

Dinçer, H., Aksoy, T., Yüksel, S., & Hacioglu, U. (2022b). Golden cut-oriented q-rung orthopair fuzzy decision-making approach to evaluation of renewable energy alternatives for microgeneration system investments. *Mathematical Problems in Engineering.*

Dinçer, H., Yüksel, S., Mikhaylov, A., Pinter, G., & Shaikh, Z. A. (2022c). Analysis of renewable-friendly smart grid technologies for the distributed energy investment projects using a hybrid picture fuzzy rough decision-making approach. *Energy Reports, 8*, 11466–11477.

Dinçer, H., Yüksel, S., Çağlayan, Ç., Yavuz, D., & Kararoğlu, D. (2023). Can renewable energy investments be a solution to the energy-sourced high inflation problem? In *Managing inflation and supply chain disruptions in the global economy* (pp. 220–238). IGI Global.

Dong, W., Zhao, G., Yüksel, S., Dinçer, H., & Ubay, G. G. (2022). A novel hybrid decision making approach for the strategic selection of wind energy projects. *Renewable Energy, 185*, 321–337.

Du, L., Dinçer, H., Ersin, İ., & Yüksel, S. (2020). IT2 fuzzy-based multidimensional evaluation of coal energy for sustainability economic development. *Energies, 13*(10), 2453.

Ermiş, A. M., & Güven, M. E. (2022). The role of green energy investments in energy supply security. In *Circular economy and the energy market* (pp. 67–77). Springer.

Eti, S., Dinçer, H., Yüksel, S., & Gökalp, Y. (2022). Analysis of the suitability of the solar panels for hospitals: A new fuzzy decision-making model proposal with the T-spherical TOP-DEMATEL method. *Journal of Intelligent Fuzzy Systems*, (Preprint), 1–13.

Eti, S., Dinçer, H., Gökalp, Y., Yüksel, S., & Kararoğlu, D. (2023). Identifying key issues to handle the inflation problem in the healthcare industry caused by energy prices: An evaluation with decision-making models. In *Managing inflation and supply chain disruptions in the global economy* (pp. 162–178).

Fang, S., Zhou, P., Dinçer, H., & Yüksel, S. (2021). Assessment of safety management system on energy investment risk using house of quality based on hybrid stochastic interval-valued intuitionistic fuzzy decision-making approach. *Safety Science, 141*, 105333.

Ghirelli, C., Pérez, J. J., & Urtasun, A. (2021). The spillover effects of economics policy uncertainty in Latin America on the Spanish economy. *Latin American Journal of Central Banking, 2*(2), 100029.

Gribkova, D., & Milshina, Y. (2022). Energy transition as a response to energy challenges in post-pandemic reality. *Energies, 15*(3), 812.

Haiyun, C., Zhixiong, H., Yüksel, S., & Dinçer, H. (2021). Analysis of the innovation strategies for green supply chain management in the energy industry using the QFD-based hybrid interval valued intuitionistic fuzzy decision approach. *Renewable and Sustainable Energy Reviews, 143*, 110844.

Kafka, K. I., Dinçer, H., & Yüksel, S. (2022). Impact-relation map of innovative service development regarding the sustainable growth for emerging markets. *Journal of the Knowledge Economy*, 1–24.

Kayacık, M., Dinçer, H., & Yüksel, S. (2022). Using quantum spherical fuzzy decision support system as a novel sustainability index approach for analyzing industries listed in the stock exchange. *Borsa Istanbul Review, 22*(6), 1145–1157.

Kou, G., Yüksel, S., & Dinçer, H. (2022). Inventive problem-solving map of innovative carbon emission strategies for solar energy-based transportation investment projects. *Applied Energy, 311*, 118680.

Li, W., Yüksel, S., & Dinçer, H. (2022a). Understanding the financial innovation priorities for renewable energy investors via QFD-based picture fuzzy and rough numbers. *Financial Innovation, 8*(1), 1–30.

Li, J., Yüksel, S., Dınçer, H., Mikhaylov, A., & Barykin, S. E. (2022b). Bipolar q-ROF hybrid decision making model with golden cut for analyzing the levelized cost of renewable energy alternatives. *IEEE Access, 10*, 42507–42517.

Martínez, L., Dinçer, H., & Yüksel, S. (2022). A hybrid decision making approach for new service development process of renewable energy investment. *Applied Soft Computing*, 109897.

Mikhaylov, A., Bhatti, I. M., Dinçer, H., & Yüksel, S. (2022). Integrated decision recommendation system using iteration-enhanced collaborative filtering, golden cut bipolar for analyzing the risk-based oil market spillovers. *Computational Economics*, 1–34.

Mukhtarov, S., Yüksel, S., & Dinçer, H. (2022). The impact of financial development on renewable energy consumption: Evidence from Turkey. *Renewable Energy, 187*, 169–176.

Peña-Ramos, J. A., Del Pino-García, M., & Sánchez-Bayón, A. (2021). The Spanish energy transition into the EU green deal: Alignments and paradoxes. *Energies, 14*(9), 2535.

Sun, L., Peng, J., Dinçer, H., & Yüksel, S. (2022). Coalition-oriented strategic selection of renewable energy system alternatives using q-ROF DEMATEL with golden cut. *Energy, 256*, 124606.

Wang, S., Li, W., Dincer, H., & Yuksel, S. (2019). Recognitive approach to the energy policies and investments in renewable energy resources via the fuzzy hybrid models. *Energies, 12*(23), 4536.

Xu, M., Kelly, S., & Obayashi, Y. (2020). China drives global oil demand recovery out of coronavirus collapse. *Reuters*.

Xu, X., Yüksel, S., & Dinçer, H. (2022). An integrated decision-making approach with golden cut and bipolar q-ROFSs to renewable energy storage investments. *International Journal of Fuzzy Systems*, 1–14.

Yuan, G., Xie, F., Dinçer, H., & Yüksel, S. (2021). The theory of inventive problem solving (TRIZ)-based strategic mapping of green nuclear energy investments with spherical fuzzy group decision-making approach. *International Journal of Energy Research, 45*(8), 12284–12300.

Yüksel, S., & Dinçer, H. (2022). Identifying the strategic priorities of nuclear energy investments using hesitant 2-tuple interval-valued Pythagorean fuzzy DEMATEL. *Progress in Nuclear Energy, 145*, 104103.

Yüksel, S., Dinçer, H., Eti, S., & Adalı, Z. (2022). Strategy improvements to minimize the drawbacks of geothermal investments by using spherical fuzzy modelling. *International Journal of Energy Research*.

Zhang, Y., Zhang, Y., Gong, C., Dinçer, H., & Yüksel, S. (2022). An integrated hesitant 2-tuple Pythagorean fuzzy analysis of QFD-based innovation cost and duration for renewable energy projects. *Energy, 248*, 123561.

The manufacturer's authorised representative in the EU is Springer Nature Customer Service Centre GmbH, Europaplatz 3, 69115 Heidelberg, Germany. If you have any concerns regarding our products, please contact ProductSafety@springernature.com

Printed and bound by CPI Group (UK) Ltd, Croydon, CR0 4YY
01/10/2026
02225894-0020